The Best of Pickering

Sam Pickering
THE BEST OF PICKERING

UNIVERSITY OF MICHIGAN PRESS   ANN ARBOR

Copyright © by Sam Pickering 2004
All rights reserved
Published in the United States of America by
The University of Michigan Press
Manufactured in the United States of America
☹ Printed on acid-free paper

2007   2006   2005   2004   4   3   2   1

*A CIP catalog record for this book is available
from the British Library.*

Library of Congress Cataloging-in-Publication Data

Pickering, Samuel F., 1941–
    [Selections. 2004]
    The best of Pickering / Sam Pickering.
       p.   cm.
    ISBN 0-472-11378-X (cloth : alk. paper)
  AC8 .P6725   2004
  081—dc22   2003019069

Foreword by Jay Parini

SAM PICKERING COUNTS among the handful of contemporary writers who practice, with aplomb, the art of the essay. This genre is, in many ways, our most native accomplishment, and Pickering's work stands firmly in the line of essayists from Thoreau and Emerson through Mark Twain, E. B. White, Robert Benchley, John McPhee, Scott Russell Sanders, Barry Lopez, and others. But he remains sui generis, a writer difficult to define, but one who deserves a wide readership. This generous selection of his best essays puts him before readers in such a way that his virtues will become obvious. He is, in the fullest sense, an American classic.

The word *essay*, of course, derives from a French term: *essai*. It represents, in its root sense, an "attempt," an exploration, a form of verbal wandering. It is, by its nature, a form of autobiography, as the wandering eye becomes a wandering "I." The genre has its roots in the essays of Montaigne, the sixteenth-century French essayist who might well be considered the original ancestor of Pickering himself: the learned man who lets his mind range freely over deeply human topics, such as the nature of nature or the nature of human relations. He is, at once, bookish and common, a reader who refers to literature and ideas in a casual way while describing the world before him with an easy familiarity.

Pickering, who grew up in Tennessee and was educated at the University of the South (as well as Princeton and Cambridge) is a southerner to the core, and his core values are those one associates with that group of southern writers who are called the Fugitives. That is, Pickering is fiercely traditional, almost radically so, and his work reflects this bias. Like Robert Penn Warren and John Crowe Ransom—two of the original Fugitives—he admires the countryside, taking immense pleasure in the natural world; he is instinctively against industrialization and its discontents. The whole project of literary modernism, with its emphasis on Freud, on dislocation, on obliquity, goes against his grain. Pickering also has something in common with Wendell Berry, the Kentucky regionalist (another master of the essay), although Pickering does not himself, like Berry, practice the agrarian life.

Though a perpetual southerner in his persona, Pickering left the Deep South for the East at a youngish age, taking his Ph.D. in English literature from Princeton University. He also spent time at Cambridge University, in England (where he took a second bachelor's degree in 1965). His first teaching job was at Dartmouth College, in New Hampshire, where he began his writing career as an essayist. From Dartmouth, in 1978, he moved to the University of Connecticut, where he has remained, publishing eleven books of essays to date (2002), one book-length autobiographical volume, and three books of literary scholarship. In addition to this primary work, Pickering has been a prolific book reviewer, writing countless review-essays for the *Sewanee Review*, the *Virginia Quarterly*, and other periodicals.

In the essay format, which he has perfected, Pickering adopts the persona of the congenial, wise, bemused southern gentleman who is perpetually astonished by what he discovers in his peregrinations. He is the bright amateur, at home in the world of books and children, academics and the natural world. Indeed, in the more recent essays, the natural world comes to play an increasingly important part in his life as he wanders the woods of Connecticut or Nova Scotia or the Antipodes.

A typical Pickering essay begins with a peculiar, eye-catching sentence: "Pod Malone was the worst stutterer in Smith County, Tennessee" or "Reading occasionally influences life." One can expect almost anything to follow from such an observation as the writer's mind roves. Pickering has a kind of wildness in him that is reflected in the forms the essays take. As the narrative proceeds, way always leads on to way, and the reader knows that one will never get back to the original starting point. But one does not regret this lack of traditional unity; Pickering is the quintessential essayist-as-wanderer, and it would be churlish to expect a neat package, a return ticket to the point of embarkation.

The twenty-four essays in this selected volume begin with his amusing exploration of celebrity, which fell upon him when a film, *Dead Poets Society*, appeared, and it became known that the central character, played by Robin Williams, was modeled on Pickering. The essays then wander through the life and preoccupations of Pickering in five sections, with essays that explore such things as the perils and delights of raising children, a decision not to run for Congress, academic life, book touring, travels abroad in Syria, England, and elsewhere, and the natural world. There are amusing and witty anecdotes on virtually every page of Pickering: he is a man who treasures good humor and delights in the absurd.

Although the content of each essay varies widely, the form is relatively constant: something strikes the narrator, the well-crafted persona; beginning with personal observation, the speaker (often literally) takes a walk through the world, collecting anecdotes, waltzing with ideas, piecing things together, making sense of a senseless world. The tone is always lighthearted, often extremely funny, although dark undertones can be heard if one listens closely. In the end, one feels one knows Sam Pickering, although even this is part of the fiction itself, the "familiar" part of the familiar essay. More importantly, one learns something about the world itself as reading translates into knowledge, as delight passes into wisdom. These are the gifts awaiting the reader of this ample, affecting work.

Contents

Introduction

WHEN EDWARD, MY YOUNGER SON, was in high school, dinners were silent. One cold night his junior year, he said a single word, "Grapefruit," this in response to the six-word question, "What do you want for dessert?" After Edward left the table, Vicki and I subjected his silence to paragraphs steamy with crisp verbs and tart nouns. In the sixteenth century Montaigne said that essays depicted "passing." That's true, but familiar essays also freeze event. For the familiar essayist moments matter more than decades. Small things like Edward's silence become the stuff of thought and sentences. For twenty-five years I have described the doings of life and family. My pages wind through Connecticut, Tennessee, Nova Scotia, and occasionally over the hills and far away. No matter how my words twist, life goes straight. Children are born one day; the next they go to college. Parents die, and houses are sold. Like Jack-in-the-boxes, memories clatter through the mind in the morning; by afternoon they are buried in the attic. My hair has thinned, and my waist has thickened. When bouncing girls giggle, they no longer giggle for me. Some days Time seems an ocean; other days, a creek, something I skipped across unconsciously. Yet, no matter the fallings from me, no matter the chances missed, I've enjoyed life.

I'm a sentimentalist. I believe that touching up days with pink and yellow, and even blue, enables people to endure the dark. I'm too old for great expectations, but I hope these essays will brighten an hour and make readers pause and amble through their minds into moments green and smiling, be those moments past or future. That aside, however, several constants frame the essays. Montaigne was right: change is inevitable. In December the Cup of Sun, a local café, closed. Three mornings a week for twelve years, Ellen, Roger, and I met in "the Cup," drank coffee, ate muffins, and chatted, friendship and age freeing us to roam comfortably over the antics of the world and its people. On the window sill in front of me lies a snapshot taken the day the Cup closed. Edges of the picture curl upward; lint collects in the middle, and by year's end I will drop the snapshot into a waste can. Across the picture itself stretches a dark table with a brown Formica top. Pushed against the table are two metal chairs, their seats green vinyl. Atop the table stand two paper coffee cups, one blue, the other white. Both cups are empty; to the right of the cups are plastic salt and pepper shakers, the former white, the latter black. "Too stark for memory," Vicki said when she saw the snapshot. "Who knows?" I said.

Not quite so stark are classroom matters. For thirty-five years I have taught English. I'm a good teacher. Occasionally students learn something about life, if not necessarily about subjects described in catalogues. Students are various and invariably turn assignments into matters for essays. "I don't want you to think I'm just another talentless grademonger," a boy wrote last week asking me to reconsider a mark I gave him. "I'm actually an upperclassman trying to repent for past sins. It's just that my attempts at overachievement are pathetic. I've been crying myself to sleep this past weekend because of this test." I told the boy to forget the grade and plan his next paper. "Shut the spillway," I advised, "and read a good mystery." "Any title by P. D. James," I suggested. Shortly after talking to the boy, I began to weep, the tears provoked by laughter, not despondency. For a class on nature writing, another boy described lying on a rock in the middle of mountain pool. The boy was on the university swimming team. "Startled I shot up," he wrote, "a splash having plunked the water directly below me, nerves wound tight or so my mother likes to tell me after she jumps out from behind closet doors. I rolled around to my stomach and peered head first into the pool. My assumptions were correct when I noticed echoing rings in the water's surface. These could only have been produced by a force strong enough to break apart the hydrogen glue that holds all water together. Sure enough, the culprit appeared in the form of a small tree frog situated near the pool's surface. He must have dove from the swinging branch above and I wondered what type of dive he had chosen? Had it been a difficult dive with a double twist or back flip? Was it a half-gainer and was it performed with the grace and elegance of a turtle or a swan?" "A belly flop," Vicki said after I read the description aloud.

Decades in the classroom have made me supple. I enjoy papers that resemble grammatical and imaginative cannonballs. I resisted embellishing the dive with stinging commentary and gave the boy a *C*, simply noting that the acrobatic reptile was probably a bullfrog. On March 15, I received an email from Dan, another student. During my last three lectures, Dan studied "glasses-related activity," in layman's terms, the number of times I put on and took off my glasses. On Wednesday the eighth, I first touched my glasses at 10:04. I last touched them 42 minutes later at 10:46. During that time I removed my glasses nineteen times and replaced them nineteen times, a total of thirty-eight "glasses-related movements," the average minutes for a cycle of removal and replacement being 2.21. Two days later on the 10th, I touched my glasses first at 10:03 and last at 10:45. During class I removed then replaced my glasses thirty-two times for a total of sixty-four glasses-related movements, the average time for a cycle being 1.31 minutes and the average time between any sort of movement being .655 minutes or 39.3 seconds. On the thirteenth I first touched my glasses at 10:01 and last touched them at 10:46, the number of "touches" amounting to forty-eight. This worked out to .94 minutes or 56.25 seconds per touch. "A significant statistic," Dan noted, "is that the movements are more rapid in the first part of class. For example on the 10th, you had nineteen removals and replacements in the first fourteen minutes, but in the next twenty-eight minutes, you had only thirteen." "What does all this mean?" Eliza asked. "It means Dan gets an *A*," I said. "But," Eliza said, "you teach Short Story, and these numbers have nothing to do with the course." "Exactly, the work is extra credit. Dan earned an *A*," I said, adding, "by the by, I call the course Teensy Tales, not Short Story."

My essays describe ordinary life. Four times a year I donate blood. After a blood-letting in January, I fainted, a half-eaten tuna fish sandwich in my right hand. Never before had I collapsed after giving blood. "Your blood pressure was high," a nurse explained, "and it sank so fast you fainted." "You should see a doctor." "Maybe," I said and got no further. A girl in a blue sweater stood, staggered, and collapsed, dropping a cup of orange juice onto the floor. "Holy God," exclaimed a woman waiting to be stuck. "Everyone is fainting. I can't stand this," she said, hopping off a pallet, "I'm going home." Even at home I cannot escape high blood pressure and the vapors, if not fainting. Like Dan I am fond of mathematics. This fall all three of my children will be in college, fees and tuitions, I calculated yesterday afternoon, amounting to 223% of my take-home pay, a fact that first made me laugh then retire to the bedroom with *Death of an Addict*, a Hamish Macbeth mystery written by M. C. Beaton.

Routine determines the meanderings of my sentences, usually keeping grammar and thought simple. Every morning near the end of breakfast, Penny, a small Jack Russell, places her right front paw on my right foot. "Time for Elevator," Vicki says. I hoist Penny to my shoulder and turning sideways carry her to the sink, so she can look out the kitchen window and see squirrels under the bird feeders in the back yard. For two years twenty minutes after lifting Penny, Elevator became Mule. During her freshman and sophomore years, Eliza walked to high school, strolling through the woods behind our house and along Bolton Road. Before leaving home she crammed lunch and a library of books into a backpack. She then filled two carryalls, one with the rest of her books, the other with athletic gear: shoes, socks, and running tops and bottoms. At five minutes after seven, I set Penny on the floor and became Mule, shouldering the carryalls and accompanying Eliza to school. The walks brightened mornings, and no matter the weather, I insisted on carrying Eliza's bags.

During the past two years my pace has slowed while Eliza's has sped up, both physically and intellectually. I no longer walk her to school. Still, we talk a great deal, the conversations, I am afraid, smacking more of classroom absurdity than they should. Last fall we discussed ethnicity. When I said Pickerings were ethnic, Eliza said aggressively, "Well, then, what are our tribal dances?" "The foxtrot, and if we are feeling particularly gay," I said, "a restrained jitterbug." On Eliza's asking if a smidgen of ethnicity aside from Englishness ever enlivened a Pickering, I said, "Certainly not—if you mean ancestors from ersatz tribes like the French or the Norwegian. On the other hand, your mother sprang from a rail or two beneath me on the social fence, and she may be burdened with an unbecoming gene." "Your maternal grandmother was from Nebraska," I continued, "and the dark possibility exists that she was descended from sodbusters, that is, Germans, Czechs, or Hungarians, in brief some clan not to be mentioned in public." My answer did not please Eliza, and after pausing for a moment, she asked, "What are people like us noted for?" "Exploitation and guilt," I said. "We are splendid at exploiting the unfortunate, so much so that we forever feel guilty. In fact guilt makes us happy and is the highest pleasure in our lives, much more satisfying than sexual intercourse." "Oh, Lord," Vicki moaned. "I'm so tired of living in a cartoon."

Vicki lives in a mock colonial house in Storrs, Connecticut, not a comic strip. Still, a quarter century of writing short declarative sentences has affected my personality. Putting periods where they should not be thus shutting down thought before complexity obtrudes has made me cranky and opinionated. Three Marches ago, Francis left Princeton and returned to Storrs in order to attend a friend's funeral. Because Francis was in Connecticut, he couldn't apply for his next dormitory room in person, as regulations demanded. Francis faxed an application to the housing office at the university then telephoned and explained that a funeral prevented his appearing. The man in charge of housing instructed Francis to report to the office the following Monday and submit proof that he had attended a funeral. I wrote the man, saying I assumed my letter would be sufficient proof. "Only the mad," I declared, "fill their pockets with souvenirs at funerals. If you wish to discuss angel makers, defunct corpses, wooden kimonos, dirt naps, or matters generally necrophilic, contact me at the telephone number engraved at the bottom of this letter."

The letter sufficed. Francis did not have to imitate Thanatos and appear at the housing office bearing a page snipped from the Book of the Dead. With matters domestic, both quick and basketed, I am effective. No concern of mine, however, has ever influenced the great world. Once or twice I have popped into view, my nose, alas, red and bulbous, my remarks clownish. "Don't worry," my friend Josh said last year; "truths make slow progress with mankind, however obvious they may appear to other fellows." Late in February, the telephone rang while I was napping. A reporter for the *Financial Times* wanted to know what I thought about the president. No good comes of talking when sleepy. I should have asked the reporter to state his questions then hang up and call back thirty minutes later. By then brightness would have tripped from my tongue. Unfortunately, I was too weary for circumspection, and I staggered through a signature of broken sentences. The only consolation, I thought later, was that none of my friends would see the remarks. I was wrong. In chatting with the reporter, I said, "George W. Bush ought to be spanked." One morning a week later, Jay Parini received a telephone call from England. On the line was one of London's literary lights and a homosexual bon vivant. "Is the Pickering quoted in today's *Financial Times* your friend in Connecticut?" the man asked. On Jay's saying yes, the man said, "You can tell him from me that he has titillated the entire Empire." After an Internet magazine chose my statement as quote of the day, I prepared an answer for people liable to criticize the indelicacy of my recommendation. "I'll not be caught in pajamas again," I told Vicki. "Because of the overwhelming favorable reaction to the interview in the *Financial Times*, I am unable to respond personally to your letter," I wrote. "But nevertheless I want to thank you for your support. Rest assured that I will continue to sing with that great chorus of Americans whose voices will forever rise like hymnals even in the rocket's red glare." Here I should have stopped. Alas, essayists can resist anything except an empty page. "In letters many of you mentioned the rumor beating about Washington that the president occasionally fancies a little spanky-poo. Why else, several of you asked, would he have married a librarian? For my part I cannot confirm or deny the statement. Still, I think our fine nation and our finer people would be better served if such rumors were wrapped in winding sheets and consigned to Cement City."

Words interest me more than politics, and soon I abandoned the present and the presidential for Carthage, Tennessee. Carthage is a real town, once home to three generations of Pickerings. My great- grandfather settled in Carthage after the Civil War. He became postmaster and late in life ran against Cordell Hull for a seat in the House of Representatives. In my essays, however, Carthage is a fictional place. Whenever matters bother me, I visit Carthage. Doings there perk me up, even though I haunt cemeteries. Funerals blossom in spring, March being, as the surgeon-general recently put it, the only month during which a person can catch two colds in a single day. Just after the *Financial Times* published the interview, Sefus Pettiwee's wife Didelphis died. After the funeral Sefus walked from the Mountain Graveyard back to his house on South Street. Turlow Gutheridge accompanied him and on reaching the front stoop of the house, asked Sefus how he was doing. "Well," Sefus responded, "it's mighty thoughtful of you to ask, and I want you to know that this little stroll has made me feel considerably better." "That's just fine," Turlow said, attempting to clothe Sefus's bare words with becoming platitude, "you won't find Didelphis's equal in this world." "I don't know as I can," Sefus said, climbing the stoop and leaning over the railing, "but with our Heavenly Father's righteous guidance, I'll do my best to root up an adequate replacement." In Tennessee I eschewed the *Financial Times* and read the *Carthage Courier*. "Wanted," a notice read the day I arrived, "A gardener by a Christian Family. Must be young and vigorous and savingly acquainted with the Lord Jesus Christ. It would also be nice if he knew something about plumbing and potatoes. Reply to Box 3. Amen." Carthage buzzes with religious activity, most honeyed, if not sanctified. The first Sunday of my visit, Malachi Ramus, the most ignorant Ramus of them all and First Brother at the Church of the Chastening Rod, railed against Episcopalians, saying they baptized lies and confirmed frauds. At St. George's in Nashville, Malachi claimed, Father Hyacinth gave little girls Bibles with mirrors pasted inside the front covers. "So they can fix their hair before they eat lunch at the Belle Meade Country Club," he said.

Although Republicans once urged me to run for Congress, the ludicrous class attracts me more than the political, though, of course, the two often merge. Moreover, I don't squander many paragraphs dissecting fashionable cultural doings. Home is where the wholesome is. Unlike me my friend Josh delights in flailing the contemporary, a practice that soils. Recently Josh has watched "reality television," programs which flaunt propriety like *The Bachelorette* and *Married by America*. Last week Josh burst into my office in the English department, saying that he had written to the Fox Network proposing a new show entitled *Quickie*. The first episode, he recounted, would occur in fall during the height of leaf season. Two senior citizens would meet at the bus station in Hartford. There they would board a Greyhound and travel together to New Fane, Vermont, where they would picnic under a sugar maple, after which they would misbehave inside a red barn. Starring in the second episode would be two young adults, one decorated with dreadlocks. United Airlines would fly the couple in separate planes to Nepal where they would meet then participate in the Yak Butter Festival, at the end of which they would retire to their private luxury yurt. "Josh," I said, "there's a problem. Yurts are Mongolian not Nepalese." "No matter," he responded, "Americans are more ignorant than squirrels and wouldn't know a yurt from an ice cream cone."

Occasionally I think myself responsible for ignorance. Before I wrote essays, I spent hours ferreting out truths which I cast before students and readers. Indeed, remnants of that research and devotion to high seriousness spot my early essays. Habit makes the man, but age makes a life. I remain bookish, and I still ferret about. Now, though, the things I discover matter only to me. After Christmas I checked John Muir's *A Thousand-Mile Walk to the Gulf* out of the university library, the Riverside edition published in 1916. Inside the cover appeared the inscription, "For Mrs. Acheson with hope that this too is not a duplicate. As a nature lover you will like this man's love of trees. See pages 2–26, 163–7, 187." I studied the pages. The first bundle described Kentucky oaks; the second, agaves in Cuba, and the third forests blooming across Panama. Sharing Mrs. Acheson's woody enthusiasm lifted my spirits. That night at home I continued my research, perusing Alibris Books on the Internet. Several of my books were for sale, two inscribed. For $38 from Cat Purr Books a bibliophile could purchase *Living to Prowl*, "To Bill" written on the title page, each word of the inscription costing nineteen dollars. Priced at $19.98 by Fred's First and containing a seven-word inscription—"For Christine, I hope you enjoy this"—*May Days* seemed the better bargain, the price of a single word amounting to only $2.85.

Although odd folks wander my essays, few people aside from family and friends from Carthage appear in more than one essay. In spring wacky individuals pop out of hibernation. Three years ago I met a man in the meadow below the university sheep barn. The man was in his forties and had a thick beard. Beside him stood an aged Irish setter. While the man smoked a cigarette, we talked about birds. "I've lived in all the towns around here," he said, "and I've seen a lot of birds." After every three or four words, the man paused and looking up studied the sky. "When I go for a walk, I carry binoculars," he said. "That's why I see so many birds." "Birds aren't the reason I bring binoculars," the man continued. "I carry them to be sure that planes aren't army planes." "Oh," I said. Almost everyday something startles me. Near the end of March as I stood in the yard, a sharp-shinned hawk dashed past and knocked a mourning dove out of the air. The dove splashed across the ground, its wings paddling grass, the hawk straddling its back, tramping and ripping out gouts of feathers. As the hawk stripped the dove, five crows landed nearby, calls racketing around them. One crow spread his beak into scissors and raked leaves in front of the hawk. The hawk fanned its tail, raised the feathers around its neck into a ruff, and pulled its body into a muscular coil. On the crow's teasing forward, the hawk floundered toward him, dragging the dove. Immediately the other crows scrambled behind the hawk and in hopes of spading up nubs of meat, dug through feathers the hawk had torn from the dove. For forty minutes the crows tantalized the hawk, drawing him this way and that like picadors infuriating a bull. When the hawk tore the intestine from the dove's carcass, a crow lured the hawk into carelessness. Immediately another crow darted forward and jerked the intestine away. Despite the hullabaloo the hawk fed well, periodically raising its tail and spitting excrement. In the sunlight the red circles around the bird's eyes glowed like wine, and feathers along his flanks blossomed into sprays of yellow, white, and gray.

In hopes of knowing place and thus my place I spend many pages roaming ridge and field. Walking makes unhappiness and the fears that accompany happiness bearable. Yesterday a muskrat glided across Unnamed Pond. In scrub below the pond hares had gnawed bark off spindles of autumn olive. Catkins curled like fingers around willow, the upper surfaces breaking into yellow hangnails. Near a cold stream a pickerel frog stamped itself flat and metallic under a rock, and a northern two-lined salamander dozed in a half-moon of water. Wood frogs clattered in spring pools below the sheep barn. In the beaver pond, peepers belled, individual songs frail, but the chorus heavy and plated. A phoebe perched on a red maple. Around the pond cattails burst into stuffing. A meadow mouse hid under a board, and between two stones scales flaked off the skin of a ring-necked snake. At dusk robins called from trees around the pond, their songs shrill and fluttering. Woodcocks buzzed, and wind played across the wings of Canada geese, strumming them like taut rubber bands. "Did you have a good walk?" Vicki asked at dinner. "Yes," I said, "walks are always good."

Part One: Dead Poets Stuff

Celebrity

TWENTY YEARS AGO MY FATHER attended the Swan Ball, a dance held to benefit Cheekwood, a center for the arts in Nashville, Tennessee. Arriving shortly before Father, a newspaper reporter and an accompanying photographer settled into place at the foot of the long spiral staircase near the entrance to Cheekwood. "When anyone important appears, I'll tell you," the reporter told the photographer just as Father started down the stairs. "I took my time on the steps, and the girl looked at me," Father said later, "but the camera didn't click." Rarely has a Pickering been thought newsworthy, and although I have written hard for fifteen years, few cameras have pointed my way. What attention I have received has usually been inaccurate or embarrassing, lending itself more toward notoriety than importance. Last fall I spoke at a potluck supper sponsored by the Friends of the Mansfield Library. The crowd was large, well over a hundred people, brought out in part, I am afraid, by a flyer announcing that the speaker was the author of children's books and a religious novel. When my mother died two years ago, her obituary stated that she was a native of Hanover Courthouse, Virginia, the daughter of the late Mr. and Mrs. John L. Ratcliffe, the wife of Samuel F. Pickering, and then, horror of horrors, "the mother of the noted essayist Samuel F. Pickering, Jr. of Storrs, Connecticut." My God, I thought, what will people think? I imagined old friends at breakfast tables flipping through their papers and stopping to read Mother's obituary. "Jesus, Varina, look at this," I could hear Jeffrey saying; "Sam's trying to sell books on his mother's grave." "Huh, that doesn't surprise me," Varina would answer, taking the paper away to read it; "he always was a scoundrel. He may have fooled you and those friends of yours for a long time, but he never fooled me."

In February I received a letter addressed to "Samuel Pickering, Jr. WRITER," *writer* being printed in red and circled by two black lines as thick and gloomy as mourning bands. Inside the letter was a note reading, "God loves you very much. You are precious to Him" and then a tract entitled "A Rock Through The Window." "Your heavenly Father," the tract stated, "wants to deal with you as His beloved child, not as a guilty delinquent." I had spent a quiet, and in this world what passes for the same thing, a moral winter, indeed a quiet last decade and so I paid little attention to the tract. Still, the sender might have known me better than I knew myself. In April I traveled to a conference in Arkansas to discuss "Parents and Children in Southern Autobiography." The conference was solemn, and the talks and audience thoughtful, at least they were until I spoke. As I climbed the stairs toward the stage, a noisemaker began wailing, the sound rising shrill then snapping off in a cackle of laughter. For late morning the audience seemed oddly alert, and I wondered why until I reached the lectern. Spread open on the lectern was a *Playboy* magazine, the centerfold pink and creamy and looking like a mound of overly ripe cantaloupes. For a moment I paused, taste buds pricking delinquently; but then buckling appetite about with thought, I closed the magazine and began lecturing. In truth I did not pause long, for at forty-seven I was not the trencherman I once was, the boy who long years ago ate seventeen ears of corn at one sitting. Indeed since marrying Vicki I have bought groceries at Shop Rite, avoiding natural food stores and in matters personal preferring the institutional and the packaged to the organically grown.

Recently attention paid to my writing has changed slightly, becoming at times almost serious. In an article a writer mentioned my "aristocratic impulse." "Too bad," Vicki said when I read her the phrase, "too bad it's only an impulse." In March the wife of the president of the University of Connecticut interviewed me for a newsletter published by the regional arts council. At the middle school one Saturday morning we met in her new silver Subaru station wagon, and she taped our conversation while our children practiced soccer on a nearby field. Last winter Bill Berry, an old friend, wrote an essay recalling his days in the graduate college at Princeton. He sent me an early draft in which I often appeared as aggressive and frivolous, once eating a lunch of flowers in order to startle the stuffy and the boring. Still, Bill also recalled that I often ate with "a severely afflicted friend who had great difficulty eating and speaking." He said I befriended those less fortunate than myself and while my friend struggled to speak I "focused on his face and understood the words that most did not watch form." Until I read Bill's draft I had forgotten those meals but I was glad he brought them back, for what seemed insignificant twenty years ago now struck me as important. At eight, Francis my older boy is ashamed of me. Indeed I sometimes think he despises me. Perhaps someday, I thought, he will read Bill's article and decide that maybe, just maybe, his father wasn't so bad. Alas, Bill's editor made him cut the article, and when the essay appeared, the lunch of flowers remained, its stems coarse and silly, while the meals with my friend had been mowed and had fallen away to be lost in the mulch of time.

Family stories matter to me. I want my children to have a sense of their history. I hope they will be able to think beyond self and see themselves as part of a community, not simply of a present but of the past and of a future. If they recognize the influences of the past, perhaps they will see ties in the present and realize that they have responsibilities for the future. And so for me, the most important attention my writing has evoked has been private, not public, appearing in letters, not magazines. On the jacket of my second collection of essays was a sketch of my father's home in Carthage, Tennessee. While browsing through a bookstore in Nashville, a woman from Carthage saw the jacket and recognized the house. She bought the book and later wrote me about my grandmother "Miss Frances" and recounted the history of the house: that Miss Frances sold it to the McDuffees in 1950 and that in 1976 they sold it to the Gammons who moved it off Main Street down the hill toward the river, after which they built a grocery store on the site. In that second collection of essays I mentioned attending Ransom School in Nashville. When a neighbor on Eastwood read that, she sent me a copy of the Ransom School song, noting that we were fellow alumni. The song is innocent and optimistic. "There is no school like John B. Ransom School," the song bounced along to the tune of the "Washington and Lee Swing."

We do our lessons 'cording to the rules.
We can read and write and cipher, too.
And we do just what our teachers tell us to.
We have a Mothers' Club that's hard to beat.
They gave us sidewalks so we keep dry feet.
They gave us flower beds and shade trees, too.
Shade trees, too—Ransom sch-ool.

Among the essays in the book was a sketch of Father, and after reading it a woman who worked for the Travelers Insurance Company in Nashville wrote me. She wanted, she explained, to tell me "how he appeared to the clerical workers." She never met him outdoors, she recounted, when "he didn't remove his hat." The staff benefited from his "gentlemanly instincts," she recalled, saying, "One of the first things I ever heard about him was that he would never say anything improper to a lady or allow anyone else to," noting that "this was mighty valuable protection in the days before corporations had sexual harassment policies. He was all the protection we needed, and if you had a problem, you went to him. Some of the managers were afraid to make waves, but he wasn't." This past June I received a letter from the press which was publishing my next book. "Here," it read, "is another marketing questionnaire that we'd like to have you fill out for *Stiff Life*." Unfortunately Father's gentlemanly instincts have run shallow in me, becoming at best only impulses, and I wrote back that although I was flattered I had not lost the reputation of my vigorous younger days, the title of my book was more detumescent, *Still*, not *Stiff Life*. Although I did not recognize it at the time, the letter was a harbinger of raucous days of attention and celebrity. In April I received a letter from Tom Schulman, a former student of mine at Montgomery Bell Academy in Nashville. I myself attended MBA, and before going to graduate school and just after leaving Cambridge, I returned and taught English there for a year. I was twenty-four and Tommy was fifteen, a sophomore. The students were bright and generous, and I had a marvelous time, but the year like the meals with my friend at Princeton had dropped out of thought until Tommy's letter reminded me of it. He had written, he said, a screenplay "inspired in part by your teaching" and he urged me to go to the film, saying I would enjoy seeing "how what you taught affected at least one of your students." The name of the movie was *Dead Poets Society*, probably a zombie film I guessed at the time, appropriate enough, I thought, for the teaching profession in which being one of the walking dead was often more an asset than handicap. Still, I was proud of Tommy. I liked him enormously at MBA, and happy that he was doing well, I wrote and told him so. When he replied that being my student "had a profound effect" on his life and that I "reached out with an approving smile and an unconcealed joy that inspired self-confidence and happiness," I was touched, so much so that I kept the letters, not for myself but for Francis in hopes, of course, that someday he would see them and think better of me.

The end of the semester rush of papers and examinations began, and I soon forgot about the movie. The second week in June, however, Bill Weaver, my closest boyhood friend, telephoned from Nashville, saying there was a rumor going around that I was the model for John Keating, a character, he explained, in a movie about a prep school and played by a comic actor named Robin Williams. Years ago, I told Bill, I taught Tommy Schulman, the screenwriter, at MBA, but, I stressed, the film could not contain much of me. "Well," Bill answered, "I'm going to the movie tonight, and I'll let you know." Late that night Bill telephoned. "It's you," he said, "all your mannerisms, and I have called the paper." The next day a reporter from the *Nashville Tennessean* telephoned and interviewed me. I repeated to him what I told Bill: that whatever there was of me in the Keating character had to be small, and he assured me he would dig about thoroughly before writing a story. Several days passed, and then on June 22, a half-page article appeared in the *Tennessean*. Headlined "Robin Williams, meet Dr. Sam Pickering, Jr.," the article had pictures of Tommy and me in the upper right corner, and then down in the lower left, taken from the MBA yearbook for 1966, a picture of me sitting cross-legged on my desk, reading and declaiming. That morning the telephone began ringing, mostly friends from Nashville wanting to discuss the movie. Because my children had chicken pox when the movie showed in Willimantic, I hadn't seen it, so I took the occasion to renew acquaintances and ask about family doings. One man said he was soon leaving with his children for a vacation on the dude ranch where Hemingway wrote *A Farewell to Arms;* another's older daughter was working on Cape Cod while the younger went to sailing camp in North Carolina and his son studied language in France. That night a cousin called, and when she said, "I can't tell you how proud I am," I suddenly realized that matters were out of my control. This past spring three literary agents wrote, asking to represent me. Knowing that I often described my children, one sent a picture of his daughter, a smiling brown-eyed little girl wearing a blue dress and eating a chocolate bar, actually a Hershey bar with almonds or so it appeared when I examined the picture under a hand lens. Although I am sweet on Hersheys and children, I declined the agents' offers to represent me, explaining that I valued controlling my affairs more than I did money.

Now caught up in the popularity of *Dead Poets Society*, I was losing control. Moreover I started doubting my teaching. Tommy was not the only student to write last year. On my desk was a postcard from Portugal. "Played a little in a Metro Station in Lisbon with a couple of Rastafarians," George wrote, explaining that he planned to work his way across Europe as a street musician. "Now," he continued, "I'm sharing a room in the home of a sweet old Portuguese couple with an insane German girl. The day we got here after renting the room she says that maybe it's not good that we sleep in the same bed and the next day on the beach she is lying there next to me, completely naked!" What sort of effect, I asked myself, had I had upon George. Whatever it was, it smacked more of lecterns in Arkansas than it did of profundity.

The following day I received only one call from Nashville, an invitation to attend the MBA spaghetti supper. Both the Willimantic and Hartford papers, however, obtained copies of the article in the *Tennessean* and interviewed me over the telephone. I wasn't home when the reporter from the Hartford paper first called, so she talked to Vicki. Whom had we told about the movie, she asked. On Vicki's saying, "No one. Sam had nothing to do with the movie," the reporter paused then asked, "What is it like being married to an eccentric?" "Eccentric?" Vicki responded. "Sam's not eccentric. He's normal, very normal, so normal in fact that he's abnormally normal." That, I am afraid, ended the conversation. The following day, though, articles about the movie and me appeared in both the *Willimantic Chronicle* and the *Hartford Courant*. In the English department late that afternoon a colleague greeted me, saying, "You are certainly becoming notorious. I went to the podiatrist today to have my ingrowing toenails chopped out, and when I told the receptionist I taught at the University of Connecticut, she asked, 'Do you know Sam Pickering?'" I smiled; no longer did I have the leisure to think my way into doubt or embarrassment. On the twenty-eighth Vicki and I and the children were leaving Storrs for our farm in Nova Scotia. Little chores clogged my hours, and I didn't have time for celebrity. The chimney on the house was collapsing inward, and that morning Mr. Brown examined it and estimated the cost of repairs. Mr. Brown was a fine mason, but he wasn't young, and when he talked to me, his false teeth slipped. Pushing them back up into the roof of his mouth, he explained, "I forgot to put the cement in this morning." "Oh, Lord," I thought, "suppose he forgets to put the mortar between the bricks when he rebuilds the chimney." At lunch Vicki informed me that only one key to the house was left. For most people getting keys is easy. Our house, though, was once owned by the university and the locks on the doors take keys, the blanks of which are sold only to the state. To obtain new keys necessitates obtaining a work order, and work orders are issued only for state buildings, not private houses. "I'm sorry. I don't know how you can get new keys without replacing all the locks on your doors," a sympathetic woman told me. "I leave for Nova Scotia the day after tomorrow," I said; "I can't replace the locks." Four hours and six telephone calls later, I had nine keys, too many for Vicki's liking but just the right number I think.

That night while I was gathering things to be packed, a reporter from the Associated Press called. Saying he had read the piece in the *Courant*, he asked to interview me. I explained I was leaving for Nova Scotia in two days but said that if he could be at my house at two the next afternoon, I would fit him in between getting a haircut and mowing the grass. He arrived on time, and we spent a genial hour and a half talking first about teaching, then about writing, and finally our children. Just after he left, his photographer appeared, and for thirty minutes I posed around the yard: on the front stoop, leaning against a hickory tree, and finally on a rock near the children's swing set where mosquitoes dropped on me like leaves in the fall, big mosquitoes with black and white, candy-cane-striped legs.

The next morning we left for Portland and the ferry to Yarmouth. Although the drive was only two hundred miles, the trip took six hours. We stopped to let the children run about, and I drove slowly, never faster than fifty miles an hour. Last summer I did not pass a single vehicle, and this year I passed only two: a rusty Pontiac creeping along the shoulder of the road, its exhaust system dragging on the ground and then near South Portland a pickup truck towing a wagon carrying a yellow race car with the number forty-seven painted on it in blue. Because I drive in an eddy, letting traffic sweep around me, the trip was almost easy, and I spent time thinking over the interviews which I gave and the articles which discussed the *Dead Poets Society* and me. I felt ashamed. The film was Tommy's, not mine, and a stronger person would not have given the impression of wanting something for nothing by allowing himself to be interviewed. Even worse the life I had shaped and the little things I achieved seemed lost. Instead of being the books I wrote or the family I cherished, I was a creature of publicity, a nice person because the articles were generous, but a creature, nevertheless, shaped by newspapers and nurtured by an ego. On the positive side I said nothing harsh and actually corrected a misrepresentation. People had not stopped at identifying John Keating as me but had rushed on into error by assuming the head of Welton school to be Francis Carter, headmaster of MBA in the 1960s. As the head of Welton was a fiction so was his conflict with Keating. Mr. Carter was a close friend, a man whom I admired and whose family I have loved for years. Rick his son took my little boys to see their first movie, a story about a mouse named Fievel, and since Mother's death, Rick and his mother have hovered over Father, bringing him presents and inviting him to their house for meals.

Once or twice the articles made me smile. In the *Tennessean* a former student said that when my class studied Poe's poem "The Raven" I stood a boy on a chair and told him to flap his arms every time we came to the word *nevermore*. I did not remember that class, but I was lively and young when I taught at MBA and giving students the bird sounds like something I might have done. I remembered standing on desks and in wastecans. One day I went outside and taught through the window. I did such things not so much to awaken students as entertain myself. If I had fun, I suppose I thought, the boys would have fun, too, and maybe even enjoy reading and writing. In the *Tennessean* Gus Kuhn, a member of Tommy's class, attributed high purpose to my antics. "He really wanted us to think, to find our own voice," Gus said. "It's interesting that I never knew his political orientation—he just wanted us to find our own ways." Although I did want the boys to think a little for themselves, it is no wonder Gus did not know my political leanings. Even today I am not sure what they are. Some mornings I think myself more liberal than anyone I know; by afternoon I often think myself more conservative than anyone. At a school board meeting in May another member called me a Communist. When the chairman of the board said that name-calling, even in jest, was out of order, I interrupted. "Oh, no," I said, "that's the nicest compliment I've received in months. Of course," I added, "if he had called me an Episcopalian, there would be gore on the floor." Although the newspapers rarely quoted me exactly, they got down the sense of what I said correctly. Actually their changes often brushed and smoothed me over. When I said that I no longer climbed through windows to teach outside because my present classroom was on the second floor and I might fall down and "bust my ass," the reporter wrote, "His classroom is on the second floor now, making leaps through windows unwise." Only the Willimantic paper left me linty and rough of tongue, and I was chagrined to read that Keating's being a sympathetic character pleased me because "I'd rather be known as a nice guy than as a son of a bitch."

Once we reached Nova Scotia, the movie almost slipped out of mind. Our farm in Beaver River seemed beyond celebrity's schedule, the ring of the telephone, and events hurrying over each other into meaninglessness. The landscape was mild: blue and green and yellow. Near the front fence the golden chaintree bloomed. Cedar waxwings searched for bugs in the spruce windbreak while warblers hunted through the alders. Windflowers glowed like small suns; in the side meadow: buttercups, cinquefoil, hawkweed, moneywort, and daisies, white and yellow and looking like morning. In the hedge of roses hung bittersweet nightshade, petals curled up and back into purple turbans and their centers arrowheads dripping yellow. In the damp by the stone wall stood swamp candles, budded and blooming in the imagination. Along the lane toward the bluff were two-flowered Cynthia and in low spots blue flag, brightness streaming back through the petals into the stem. Along the bluff grew yellow rattle and great stalks of evening primrose while lower down in the rocks at Beaver River sow thistle was beginning to open. The calm, of course, was deceptive, for beneath and behind the yellows lay purple; in the meadows vetch and clover, its heads as big as biscuits. In the stony foundation hole of the old house on Ma's property were clumps of knapweed while behind the outlet at Beaver River beach pea sprawled garish and luxuriant. Around the pond rose shafts of pickerel weed, still narrow and green but certain to swell into bloom.

For two weeks time slowed and I busied myself with important things: at dusk and dawn studying shrews, during the day teaching the children to shoot bows and arrows and throw boomerangs, at night reading to them, first *Caddie Woodlawn* and then *The Twenty-One Balloons*. One morning, though, as I cleared Japanese knotweed from around the barn, levering up masses of damp, orange root, thick as hams, the calm burst into celebrity, purple and spiny as bull thistle. The first batch of mail had arrived from Storrs. "I've only carried that *Hartford Courant* article around for three weeks telling everyone, 'I know this person,'" Alice began and I winced. Alice's letter was one of many from former students. Occasionally the letters were not addressed to me but to Sam Pickering "Media Sensation" or "Personality." One man assured me that he had not used an exclamation point since taking a course with me seventeen years ago. School superintendents and principals invited me to address faculties and "to share," as one administrator put it, "some of your ideas about motivating and challenging students." I replied that I was not an educational theorist but just somebody who happened to teach, "a guy with a nice wife, three small children, an aging father, and a six-year-old Plymouth station wagon." Two people wanted to know how to become an essayist. Lost friends surfaced and described former wives and new loves. Strangers told stories about their school days. Three people said that although I might be the model for the character in the movie for them the real John Keating was one of *their* former teachers. A goodly number of letters contained clippings from local papers. I was relieved to see the captions of the articles were not sensational. Typically they read: "Meet the Real John Keating," "Eccentric Instructor Inspires His Students," "Model for 'Dead Poets' Hero Sees Himself as Ordinary," and "Professor Shrugs Off Comparisons to Lead Character in 'Dead Poets.'"

Much as fireweed and purple orchis seem part of July's lavish train, so telephone calls accompanied the mail. A man in Ohio asked me to become an honorary member of a Christian Dead Poets Society. I agreed although I didn't think the society would be popular. My children would prefer to join a Little Scorpions Club and would have more fun frolicking, I suspect, with Aunt Eppie Hogg and the Terrible Tempered Mr. Bang than with a schoolhouse of preachers. The director of a library where I read my essays last winter telephoned and asked to speak to "Professor Keating." From Oklahoma a woman volunteered that during the past four and a half years the right side of her brain, the creative side, had grown while the left, the mechanical side which controlled such things as mathematics and duties domestic, had shrunk. As a result, she said, "I'm a pisspoor wife." The telephone was in the kitchen, and all my conversations were public and thus open to interruption and editorial comment. During the discussion with the woman from Oklahoma, Edward, my six-year-old, tugged on my shirt and looking up asked, "Daddy, what is sex?" Covering up the receiver, I said, "It's the way men and women make children." The answer satisfied Edward, if not perhaps his mother, who dropped a beet on the floor, and I was quickly able to return to things brainy, if not intellectual. The moderator of *Straight Talk,* a television program produced in Virginia Beach, Virginia, invited me to appear on the show. I declined but I did have several radio interviews. I was in our peat bog when a woman called from a station in New Haven, Connecticut. When Vicki said I could not come to the phone, explaining, "He's in the bog," the line was silent. Finally the woman asked when I would be out, and Vicki said, "Probably in an hour. He never gets out of the bog any quicker." Vicki does not like to answer the telephone, especially when it is for me. This past spring I was at Northwest School talking to the principal when a bank officer called to discuss Mother's estate. "He's not here," Vicki said when the man asked for me; "he's in the principal's office." "Sam," the man said after reaching me the next day, "when I hung up I kept wondering what the hell you had done at your age to be sent to the principal's office."

The Associated Press article fathered several offspring. This second group of reporters were invariably curious about my philosophy of education. What they wanted was not real philosophy, problematic and deep, but aphorism. I tried to say what I believed, but everything sounded sappy. In one paper I declared that the end of education was to learn to learn, "to make decent men and women, to learn how to change your mind, to say 'I was wrong.'" "It's to be moral," I explained, adding, "I'm moral in my life, but not in my thoughts." For the interviews I changed my personality, becoming saccharine while actually I am often acerbic. At the end of this school year a student said to me, "No one can accuse you of prejudice. You've insulted every group in the country. You even insult yourself. It's a marvel you don't get in a fistfight with yourself." Eventually I reacted against the interviews and purged the sugar from my system by writing crude notes about academic matters. When a professor asked permission to quote a letter I had written about the environment, I made a single stipulation. "You can quote the letter," I wrote, so long as you don't begin, 'That turd Sam Pickering states . . .'"

Occasionally reporters contacted my friends. One old buddy supposedly said, "Pickering has single-handedly revived the familiar essay, a genre of the Romanticists of the first half of the 19th century." "Now," I told Vicki when I read the piece, "I have finally found an article that's right on the money." Of course I didn't agree with everything published. According to the *Richmond Times-Dispatch* my cousin Sherry said I met Vicki when I was a graduate student at Princeton and her father was head of the English department. Vicki was "thirteen when she first met Sam," the paper stated, "thirteen years later when she was twenty-six they married." Lest people fear to trust me with their small daughters, I must now say that I did not know Vicki until she was twenty-one. I am absolutely trustworthy around little children and everything sweet except chocolate cake. Because Mother was from Richmond, the *Times-Dispatch* wrote about her family, the Ratcliffes. Ratcliffes are often odd although I don't think they are quite so individualistic as the newspaper implied. Sherry, the paper said, remembered Mother "wrapped only in a sheet on hot nights in Hanover when the family ate on the screen porch. She would say, 'Pass the bosoms.' And Sam's father would answer, 'Say chicken breasts, Katharine.'"

As the telephone rang and letters poured in, the order of my days and thoughts unraveled. I watched for the mailman and waited for phone calls. I became crass and tried to figure out how I could use the movie to turn my books into best-sellers. Not even reality stopped my scheming. I shrugged off the royalty statement for my second book of essays. In two years, the press wrote me, the book had sold 855 copies, and during the past year there were thirty-four more returns than sales. Sometimes I even convinced myself that Disney Studios, the makers of the movie, owed the family a trip to Disney World. When Father came to Nova Scotia in mid-July and I told him that I was fed up with being a celebrity, he laughed and said, "Don't take it seriously. Just have fun. I have." Great numbers of people spoke to him on the street, he recounted, and friends whom he had not heard from in years wrote letters. Last week on the elevator in his apartment he met, he said, an acquaintance and her eleven-year-old granddaughter. "Mayellen," the woman said, introducing the child to Father, "this is Mr. Sam Pickering." "What," the girl gasped, "Sam Pickering! Why, you are famous." Indeed the nicest thing the movie did for me was to give Father pleasure. Not only that but it made conversation between us easier, and soon after Father arrived in Nova Scotia, we left the movie behind and talked about family. I learned that when Father was a boy he had a horse named Donald. During his sixteenth summer, Father worked on the highway as a water boy. The spring, he said, was a mile from the construction and as soon as he brought water up to the road he had to turn around and fetch more. He carried two buckets, for white men one with a green stripe on the outside and for black men one with a red stripe. Everyone worked ten hours a day and was paid twenty-one cents an hour, except men who were paid a bit more because they furnished teams of mules. Father told me many stories about Nashville. Leslie Dickerson, he recalled, once visited a country girl at her home in Una and stayed too late in the parlor. "Sister, is the company gone?" the girl's little brother called down from upstairs. Embarrassed and slightly nervous about having overstayed his welcome, Leslie instructed the girl to tell her brother that he had gone. "Well, then," the voice came back from above, "Ma says to pee before you come upstairs. The pot's full."

Although the movie brought father and son close together, it did not have the same effect upon wife and husband. Celebrity did not heighten my appeal, and whenever I tried to kiss Vicki in the pantry, she practiced what I call the "embrace domestic." She placed her right hand flat against my chest, the heel of her palm just below my breastbone and her fingers stretched out full length toward my throat. By straightening her arm slightly, she was able to repel all unwanted familiarity. In truth Vicki found celebrity a nuisance, something which changed a useful and perfectly good house cleaner and plate dryer into an inefficient dreamer and speculator. In early August an assistant to the president of the University of Connecticut telephoned and asked me to speak at the convocation in September. Last year's speaker was a Nobel Prize winner, and I didn't think I could refuse. "I'm honored to be asked," I answered, "and as a servant of the university I will be glad to speak." "Great God from Gulfport," Vicki exclaimed after I hung up. "Servant of the university! That makes me want to throw up." "Look, Vicki," I said, "I may have been blinded by publicity for a while, but I haven't been taken in." Then I left the house and going to the bog picked leatherleaf in order to make tea for Vicki's upset stomach.

A week later we left Nova Scotia. Waiting at home for me was a letter from a man who knew nothing about the movie but who had read my second collection of essays, the one that sold 855 copies. He, too, attended Ransom, and he enclosed a copy of the school song, observing that for best effect it required a minimum of six monotones, three breaking tenor voices, and a trio of shrill sopranos accompanied by a hollow, resonating piano, all to be performed in a room decorated in "School Board Brown." I want to write more about Ransom. Before starting, however, I must do two things. First I must address the convocation. I am going to begin with one of Father's stories. While attending the funeral of his cousin Rushton in Pleasant Shade, Tennessee, Clovis Hurlburt saw Byron Pogue, son of his old friend Peevy Pogue. Byron worked for the undertaker in Pleasant Shade, Lonnie Fedge. Sometime after he returned to Nashville, Clovis met Peevy on Union Street, just outside the Trust Building. After chatting amicably about the influenza and railway fares, Clovis mentioned Byron. "Peevy," he said, "I saw Byron in Pleasant Shade. He works for Fedge the undertaker, doesn't he? I could have sworn you told me he was a doctor." "A doctor, good Lord, no," Peevy exclaimed; "I said he followed the medical profession." I resemble Byron, I will say in my address; I am not the real thing. I am just a follower, not even of the medical profession but of that lesser thing publicity. I offer no cure-alls for the ills of society. All I have ever done is cope: digging about here and there, once or twice unearthing something interesting, but more often than not simply burying my errors. Then as soon as the convocation ends, I am going to jump in the car and go see *Dead Poets Society*. I wonder if John Keating really resembles me. If he does, I'd like to stand and say, "That's me." Of course I won't. Despite the occasional hankering, Pickerings aren't the stuff of celebrity and avoid spiral staircases and cameras, preferring instead to wander the fields and bogs of old farms, leading small children by the hand, brewing remedies for weak stomachs, and painting days yellow and purple.

Representative

"NEIL," I SAID, SHIVERING under a pile of blankets, "I have been bitten by the flu, not the political bug." "Sam, all I know is what I read," he answered. "The *Hartford Courant* says that among 'those now being mentioned' as Republican candidates in the Second Congressional District is 'University of Connecticut Professor Samuel F. Pickering, Jr., of Storrs, the model for Robin Williams's character in the movie *Dead Poets Society.*'" "Neil, I will talk to you later. I'm going to be sick," I said, adding as I put down the telephone, "I don't care what the paper says. It's wrong." For two days I languished in and out of fever. Although I was occasionally so irrational that I imagined my new book becoming a best-seller, I did not dream at all about politics. Not only had I never met a real politician, but I knew few Republicans. In the last election the Republican lost the Second Congressional District by sixty thousand votes, and even if the party was having trouble chasing a sacrificial lamb out of the fold, I couldn't imagine them nipping at the heels of an unknown, a black sheep who usually voted Democratic and said so.

Politics was rarely discussed in my family. "The right people do not run for office," Mother once said; "they are appointed." For Father political matters were the ephemeral stuff of story, not life. When he was a boy in Carthage, Tennessee, state Democrats gathered for a week every August at the Grand Hotel in Red Boiling Springs. There they picked candidates for offices, plotted legislative strategies, divided tax revenues, and parceled out rights of way for highways. The Grand was old, and Mr. Hawes, the owner, did not keep it clean. Going to Red Boiling Springs was a tradition, however, one of the few the Democrats had, and they didn't consider changing towns or hotels. Besides, Father said, politicians were comfortable with dirt; flies, though, he added, were a different matter. A few legislators from big towns like Nashville and Memphis were bothered by the fat red-eyed flesh flies that buzzed through the hotel like builders swarming over meaty contracts for state construction. One morning as he was shaving, Coker Knox, who represented a smooth, silky district west of Nashville, turned to Squirrel Tomkins and said, "I just can't stand to use the bathroom; the flies get all over me." "That's nothing," replied Squirrel, who was from Hardeman County just above the Mississippi line. "If you'll come up here at lunch or when dinner's being served, you won't find a single fly in the bathroom, and you'll be able to tend to your affairs in comfort."

For most of the year the Grand was practically empty, and when the Democrats held their yearly meeting, Mr. Hawes had to beat across Macon County looking for help, down to Gum Springs through Union Camp and Freewill and then up and over Goad Ridge to Green Tree Hollow. Although the people he hired were the salt of the earth, they were more accustomed to plain home fare than to the highly seasoned doings of the "Solons" at the Grand. Late one afternoon as he was returning to his room after drinking waters at the springs, Coker Knox, so the tale went, thought he heard the dinner bell ring. Seeing a hotel employee sweeping the walk out to the road, Coker approached him and asked, "Is that the second bell?" "No sir, Mr. President," the man said, straightening, then leaning over his broom to think a bit. "No sir, that's the second ringing of the first bell. We ain't got no second bell in this hotel."

Dividing the spoils of office went quickly as dessert, and once the platter was clean, the politicians set about the serious business of having fun. Toward the end of the meeting each year "The Mighty Haag" circus came through Red Boiling Springs. With two old elephants trailing behind four horse-drawn wagons, the circus wasn't spectacular. Its tent, though, provided the boys with an arena for antics. Each year some innocent young Methodist surprised the party bosses and got elected to the legislature. That August when he came to Red Boiling Springs, he was invited to referee a badger fight—an invitation which he was told was really an initiation into the party and which he could not refuse if he were ambitious. The badger fight was held under the circus tent. Tied to a stake driven into the ground was an old dog, rough and bony and with long, yellow teeth. Nearby was a large wooden box; sticking out from under it was a thick rope, at the end of which was, supposedly, the badger. The legislator's job was to hold the rope and control the badger so the dog wasn't killed right away. As soon as the box was lifted, the legislator was to jerk the rope toward himself and pull the badger into the fray. The preliminaries to the fight took some time, and while the young man held the rope and two circus employees sat atop the box to keep the badger from digging free, the audience bet on how long the dog would last. Finally, however, the tent grew quiet, and then Haag himself appeared, dressed in red and gold and carrying his trumpet, looking as if he were marching to Waterloo. He blew a long fanfare—sounding, Father said, like a cross between a cattle call and the *William Tell Overture*—after which the two men lifted the box and the dupe jerked the rope, pulling toward himself not a badger but a chamber pot.

Although much drinking went on at the Grand, politicians were urged to avoid drink before the final dinner. Local preachers were invited to the dinner to bless the party, and although public relations had not yet become a science, party leaders thought they ought to make a good impression upon the clergy. To this end they scheduled the dinner for three o'clock in the afternoon, so the preachers, some of whom had long drives ahead of them, the politicians explained, would not be out after dark. In private they told the truth, noting that by three o'clock serious legislators were usually just starting to drink and were not yet tumbling in the need of prayer. Much as the preachers' lessons for saving souls fell on deaf ears, so the leaders cast their plans on rocky soil, and a good many Democrats floated into the dinner buoyed aloft by drink and speaking in tongues. One year when Squirrel Tomkins was the front-runner in the race for lieutenant governor, he brought a jug with him. By dessert he was dancing on tables, and by the time the Reverend Hackett rose to give the final blessing, Squirrel had taken off his trousers and was standing on his head, waving his legs in the air. "Oh, Tomkins," Coker Knox said, looking at him with chagrin, "you have danced away the lieutenant governorship." Squirrel smiled and, kicking hard, tossed a shoe over the lectern, just missing Reverend Hackett, and said, "Squirrel don't care."

Squirrel's attitude has always seemed sensible to me, and after laughing once or twice with Neil about the article in the *Courant*, I forgot politics. Then one night a week later a member of the Republican state committee telephoned me. Would I, he asked, consider running for Congress. On my answering no, he replied that he expected such a response, adding, "That's why some people want to talk to you." For a moment I thought about kicking a shoe through the air. But then, reflecting that I wrote essays and thinking a piece on politics might be fun, I agreed to a meeting, though, I stressed, "running for office is far from my mind." We set a date near the first of February, ten days off. "Well," Vicki said when I told her, "if they read your books it's good-bye meeting." "There is little chance of that," I responded, saying that people in politics usually didn't read. Besides, I added, my sales had been so low that even if someone wanted to glance at one of my books he would have a devilish time finding a copy. And as for my life, I added, looking, wistfully off, I am afraid, into the distance, "ever since marrying you I have been a good boy, damn near a saint." "Huh," Vicki grunted, "what about that picture you got in the mail the other day?"

On my desk was a photograph taken in Switzerland twenty-six years ago. In the picture a boy lay on his back, shirt pulled up to his chest. From his belly button sprouted a bouquet of alpine flowers: yellow, purple, and pink trumpets. "Alas, dear Ellen," I wrote after receiving the picture, "the hounds of winter are biting at summer's traces. Where flowers once bloomed, weeds now thrive: goosefoot, plantain, barbed teasel, and thin strings of knotted, gray dodder." In the past I had misbehaved with little girls, but not, alas, very often. Once while playing with three girls I broke a bone. But then we were all four years old, and the game was ring-around-the-rosy. When we fell down, they tumbled on top of me and snapped my collarbone. Insofar as boys were concerned I hadn't even bruised a fingernail. One night twenty-five years ago I slept in a double bed with another student. We met on a train, traveling from London to Vienna. We arrived in Vienna late at night. The cheap hotels were fully booked, and the agent at the station could find only one decent, free room. I was exhausted and slept like one of the dead. The next morning, however, I got a single room. What bothered me most, though, about shenanigans with boys and girls was not anything I had done, but what Josh, a rough character who wandered through my writings, might say. Josh has little patience for platitudes: political, pious, or sexual. "Dammit," he said recently, bursting into my office. "I'm tired of people accusing me of being prejudiced whenever I argue with them. Hell, I am going to come out of the living room and declare that I am homosexual. Then when people differ with me, I'll accuse them of homophobia." "But Josh," I said, "you're married with three children and, so far as I know, have never had a homosexual experience. Somebody is bound to point that out." "By God, I hope so," Josh answered; "if she does I will accuse her of stereotyping. Who is she to say what I am. Limiting cultural diversity in such a manner is the most invidious form of harassment imaginable." Some other time I might have listened patiently to Josh, but I didn't want to have anything to do with him until after my meeting with the Republican committee. "Out," I said. "Out of my office. What you are saying is political dynamite."

That afternoon *Writing Home*, a newsletter written for parents of students attending the University of Connecticut, was published. A sketch of me appeared in the newsletter. The author stated that I refused to go on television, noting that my only appearance on television occurred in 1969 at halftime of the Princeton-Rutgers football game, celebrating one hundred years of college football. "Clad in a blue blazer and red striped pants and fueled by a couple of whiskey sours," I, the newsletter reported, "marched behind the band carrying a punch bowl." The article was almost accurate. Although the punch bowl has slipped from memory, I did march—though, in truth, I was fueled by more than a couple of whiskey sours. Two little nips would not have gotten me out of my seat, much less past midfield. And I marched, not alone, but with a companion, herself a field of flowers, not a posy of wilted alpine blossoms, but bluebonnets and larkspur fresh in the sun. Although the red trousers still hang in an attic closet, and I think I could fit into them without much pushing and twisting, I have not worn them in fifteen years. On bright football Saturdays, Vicki and the children and I roam the university farm. High on Horsebarn Hill we push through the long scratchy rows of corn, stumbling upon groundhogs and then watching red-tailed hawks as they wheel over the Eastern Uplands. After walking for two or three hours we go to the dairy bar for ice-cream cones: pistachio, fudge royal, blueberry cheesecake, lime sherbet, and mint chocolate chip. Whiskey sours have lost their sweetness, and rarely do I even drink a glass of wine. Only once this summer did Vicki and I share a bottle, and that was on our farm in Nova Scotia, at dinner after I was asked to speak at convocation in the fall. We drank a bottle of Canadian wine, something called Baco Noir on sale for six dollars and ninety cents. "A superior, full-bodied, rich red wine, vinted from the distinguished Baco Noir grape," the label stated. After dinner, while Vicki washed the dishes, I led the children out into a peat bog. For the first time all summer I got turned around and lost. Edward and Eliza started to cry, but Francis had a whale of a time, imagining himself poor Ben Gunn, marooned on Treasure Island. Ten minutes later we were on the kitchen porch, singing "Fifteen men on a dead man's chest" and picking spruce twigs like laurel wreaths out of our hair.

"For those booze-swilling, cigar-chomping, ass-grabbing boys in the back rooms," Josh said later when I mentioned the evening in Nova Scotia, "drinking Baco Noir would be practically the same thing as stopping cold turkey and flopping onto the wagon. Not only are you overqualified for the job, but you are too good. Forget Congress and stick to playing jokes at the university. That's a higher calling." Although the humor of some people might be elevated, my jokes usually run to the earth, much like the groundhogs we startled on Horsebarn Hill. For signing letters the head of the English department has a rubber stamp with his signature pressed on it. Two months ago I saw the stamp on a secretary's desk. I removed it and an ink pad, and going into the lavatory stamped the head's name on some pieces of functional equipment found in men's but not women's bathrooms. At least I assume such things are not found in women's bathrooms, not having explored a woman's bathroom since the third grade and then making only a cursory, terrified inspection. I removed the signatures sometime later, after a friend showed them to the head and accused him of being both unclean and addicted to graffiti. "David," I said to the head afterward, "I got rid of your signatures, but I'm not going to tell you how I did it."

Although playfulness is often misunderstood, making the serious person seem frivolous, the jokes I played didn't bother me. More damaging to my campaign, as I now occasionally labeled it, was my shaky allegiance to the Republican party. I was the worst sort of party member, a Republican not because of zeal or principle but because of tradition, and inertia. Pickerings have been Republicans since the Civil War. In 1861 my great-grandfather left Ohio University to fight for the Union. After the war he settled in Tennessee, and we have remained Republicans ever since, not because we believe in partisan politics but because we disbelieve. Thinking one group liable to be as self-serving as another, we have never felt compelled to change parties, this despite voting for Squirrel Tomkins and supporting Democrats more often than Republicans. For my part I didn't vote for Mr. Bush in the last election. Indeed I have often referred to him and his running mate as Shrub and Partridge, though when days were sunny and country things were on my mind, I whistled and called the vice president Bob White. On most issues I wasn't sure where the Republican line ran. Wherever it twisted, though, I didn't follow. Instead of gun control, I'm for gun confiscation. Little would satisfy me more than violating the constitutional rights of gun owners. I would not vote for anyone who wanted to restrict abortion. As far as possible I want Eliza to control her life. She can determine whether or not she has children, not some primitive mullah chanting high abstractions from a tabernacle. Thinking developers enemies of the people, I am such an environmentalist that I ought to belong to a weed or flower party, not a political party. As I pondered what seemed my beliefs, I realized that I should not run for office. Deluding myself into believing that I was honest, I would speak injudiciously. Even worse I would probably enjoy making people angry. Although deciding that I was a poor candidate did not make me gleeful, for no one likes confronting his weaknesses, the realization brought relief, and I pushed political matters out of mind and got on with ordinary living.

Actually the *Dead Poets Society* awakened more than politicians, and at times ordinary living seemed extraordinary. One night a real estate agent invited me to Hawaii to lecture other realtors on selling homes. The next morning the air force invited me to participate in a Civic Leaders' Tour and inspect military bases in Florida and Mississippi. A teacher from Tolland asked me to talk to 125 first- through sixth-graders on writing. The local chapter of the Connecticut Alumni Association invited me to dinner. Senior citizens asked me to speak at their yearly banquet, and a professor of education urged me to spend an evening talking to suburban school superintendents. I had already agreed to many talks; my calendar was full, and so with the exceptions of the senior citizens and the school superintendents I refused the invitations, even the military tour and the trip to Hawaii. Two years ago I spoke to young writers in Mansfield, so I did not feel guilty about not talking in Tolland. I told the Alumni Association to contact me in the fall, explaining I had spoken too often in Storrs, in the library and in churches, adding that in June I would give commencement addresses at the local high school and at a junior college in Danielson. In the middle of the week a friend telephoned and offered me the headship of a private school with some nine hundred students from kindergarten through high school. The job and its perquisites tripled my university salary, providing house and utilities, car, private school tuition for my children, and a salary of about eighty thousand a year, though this last, I understood, could be negotiated upward. In *Writing Home* I was quoted as saying, "I'm not interested in fame or money. You might as well not want the things you're not going to get." Words trap a person, forcing him to acknowledge what is important, and I turned down the headship.

That night I wrote a letter to the *Hartford Courant*. In part I refused the headship because I liked teaching at the University of Connecticut. The previous weekend the *Courant* printed a letter from a man who spent a semester teaching in our English department. In his letter the man described the poor condition of the Humanities Building, seeing its shape not simply as a "public shame" but as an emblem of general deterioration. Although some buildings at Connecticut needed repair, I answered the letter. I did so for my students. It would be sad, I thought, if critics of the university convinced students that their school and, by extension, they themselves were inferior. "Gosh," I wrote, I was sorry that our visitor found things so ramshackle in Storrs. The truth was that low-bid, functional buildings didn't function well. They required lots of maintenance and deteriorated quickly, sometimes turning those in them into functional people, gray and spiritless. Still, I wrote, I was happy in the old hulk at the University of Connecticut, even though I was one of those people who shared an office, something our visitor found particularly galling. Actually, I explained, I liked sharing an office. "For years Joe, my officemate, has laughed at me and kept me from swelling with self-importance. For a teacher pride is a danger. After writing a book or two, we sometimes get above ourselves and think we deserve the trappings of celebrity and recognition. We forget that we are, at best, servants of community and stewards of culture. We even forget how fine our jobs are. Every cultivated person in Connecticut ought to envy my job," I continued. "I spend days talking about books that thrill me. Nice young people look up to me and listen, even when they should not. Moreover, if the Humanities Building has aged into disrepair, my salary has remained sound, and I have time to write and play." Not everything at Connecticut, I said, was hunky-dory. I wrote that spending twenty-five million dollars on a basketball arena seemed "damned irresponsible." If that money had been used to put the essential plant to rights, I said, I suspected that our visitor would not have been so disturbed. Still, that was my particular hobbyhorse, one I had ridden through boredom and beyond. What bothered me more was the fear that our visitor's "gloom might become a dark litany and color the future. The University," I wrote, was not sad or shameful but good. "Some clocks in the

Humanities Building may be broken, but many classes are electric. Across the campus the range of courses taught and the expertise and dedication of the teachers are astonishing. No matter the condition of a building we will make do and we will work for better things because, sappy as it sounds, we want the best for all our children." At the end of the letter I described a walk I took late one night in the snow, two or so weeks earlier. On the way home I climbed Horsebarn Hill. At the top I stopped. Below me the campus glowed yellow. I wrote that I couldn't see or think clearly, but the soft light made me feel good. I stayed, I said, "on the hill for a long time, eating snow, and identifying buildings, and thinking how lucky I was to be teaching English at the University of Connecticut."

I mailed the letter at the airport the next morning. I was flying to the College of Wooster in Ohio to speak to scholarship students. I was glad to escape, if only for a moment, from the Connecticut me that had become political and public. Of course I couldn't completely escape. The meeting with the Republicans was three days away, and politics was back on my mind. Boarding the plane ahead of me was a woman reading a book entitled *Everyone Is Psychic*. I almost asked her if I had a chance to win the Second Congressional District. Instead I asked if she had "good vibrations" about the flight. She said she did, and I boarded and slept all the way to Cleveland. That night I spoke. The next morning I got up before dawn and explored the campus. Gray squirrels were larger and redder than in Connecticut. A flock of robins made its way across the grass, the birds' breasts bouncing like fat orange balls. Beside class-room buildings grew dogwood, while great oaks, chestnuts, and sycamores towered over the commons, their limbs bulging like muscles and seeming almost to support the rising day.

Two nights later in the rain I drove to Norwich and met twelve or so Republicans in a coffee-filled room at the Sheraton. The people were nice. Not openly partisan, they were the sort of gentle folk one would like for neighbors or relatives. No one blanched when I outlined my thoughts on abortion and development. They agreed when I said the military budget should be slashed, and they laughed when I said I got my economic ideas from the *Willimantic Chronicle*. They asked whether Vicki would enjoy an election campaign. "No," I said; "she is private and retiring, devoted to children and home, not interested in politics." She was, I added, "a pleasing person, one whom most people like immediately." I did not tell the group that as I walked out the door that night she said, "I don't approve of this meeting. I hope you make a fool of yourself and get this jackassery out of your system."

When asked if I would like living in Washington, I replied that I could not imagine raising children there. "Still," I continued, "that's beyond even slender possibility. The incumbent has this district won." Gingerly, the group asked about my past, wondering how spotted it was. No bantlings or drugs, not even a traffic ticket lurked, I responded, behind the years. "But," I said, and here I told the first lie of my political career, "but I have lived with passion and long ago was the lover of many fine women." I'm not sure why I told such a lie. Maybe the writer in me provoked it. Much as I knew my future campaign would be only an essay, so perhaps I wanted to shape a colorful and intriguing past. Be that as it may, the group was too polite to linger over love, and we pushed on to finances. How much would it cost to run, and where would the money come from, I asked. After some debate the group settled on an estimate "of somewhere between six and seven hundred thousand dollars." As for raising such funds, that was usually done by the candidate. "I have never asked anyone other than my mother for a penny," I said, "and I am too old and poor to start now." I told the group that I had no debts and would not risk my peace of mind and my children's futures for something as fleeting as politics. If I ran for office, I said, I would urge people to donate the moneys they might have contributed to my campaign to charity. That way, I explained, "when I got beat, I could at least say that I had accomplished something decent."

There may be "a tide in the affairs of men, which taken at the flood, leads on to fortune." All I know is that I clambered out of a gully and high above the wash felt relieved. The next morning I turned my attention back to summer and Nova Scotia, to little things more alluring and somehow more significant to me than politics. One morning late in August I saw a yellow jacket fly into a spider web hanging in the corner of a kitchen window. Almost immediately a small orb weaver rushed out from a retreat at the side of the window and fell down the web toward what it assumed was prey. The spider erred; the yellow jacket was not victim but hunter. As soon as the spider drew near, the yellow jacket curved its abdomen into a half-circle and stung the spider. The spider quivered; its legs curled up and then turned down and inward, much as the blossoms of wild carrot fold into small bushy cups in the fall. In a brisk, efficient manner, the yellow jacket seized the spider and, chewing rapidly through its thin, stalky middle, separated the abdomen from the cephalothorax, this being the upper portion of the spider containing its head and eight legs. The yellow jacket then flew away to its nest, carrying the abdomen as food for its larvae. The upper portion of the spider hung lightly in the web, the wound at what was once its middle gleaming and wetly orange, resembling the flesh of a bruised nectarine. Within minutes the yellow jacket or another from the nest was back. Often I had wondered why the spiders around the house hid during the day and came out of hiding only at dusk. As night approached, yellow jackets retired to their nests, and spiders were, I now saw, comparatively safe.

I followed the yellow jacket as it hovered over the porch and drifted to the side of the house, brushing through shrubs and beating against windows. The yellow jacket didn't see webs; instead it flew where webs ought to have been. Once in a web it tried to fool the spider out of hiding, initially fluttering its wings rapidly to feign panic then slowing them to simulate exhaustion. Suddenly I realized why spiders did not attack some moths caught in webs at night and instead allowed them to batter their ways to freedom, in the process destroying the webs. The vibrations the moths sent through the webs must have resembled those transmitted by predators. Out of instinct the spiders avoided the moths, preferring to give up a meal rather than risk becoming another's dinner.

From the bridal wreath under the bay window the yellow jacket flew across the side meadow to the bank of roses behind the well and around the barn. Pushing through the roses, the yellow jacket disappeared. As I looked for it, I noticed flies: gray, green, and then swarms of small gold flies. In the early sun flies sparkled as they spun through the air. As I watched them I wondered why I never noticed them before. Had dreams about the large and distant obscured my vision and led me to neglect the small and the immediate? As I stood by the roses I saw a robber fly, bearded and bristled. Ferocious predators, robber flies often resemble the creatures they prey upon, much, I unaccountably thought, as the predators of man resemble men. Wearing trousers, shirts, and shoes, our predators speak our languages and are us until they pounce and drain life and beauty away. That morning my thoughts were not deep or original, but they were thoughts, not postures assumed because they were expedient or winning. My attention soon wandered from the flies, following broad whim, not the dictates of party or campaign.

Through thorns and the swelling, heavy hips of the roses pushed spikes of long-leaved speedwell, cool and blue. Blooming pink at my feet was hemp nettle. At the edge of the meadow bittersweet nightshade twined through the roses, some of its fruit bright red droplets, others green. Out in the high, unmowed grass the dainty seedpods of willow herb split, pushing the long, winged seeds into the air and making me think of gulls riding the wind over the Gulf of Maine.

Just today I put pencils and paper and Nova Scotia aside. I walked down Eastwood and, crossing the South Eagleville Road, dropped down the slope into the marsh below. Sticking up through the ice were the horns of skunk cabbage, still green and tight. In holes in rotten trees I found two birds' nests, one filled with wood shavings, the other with moss. From the thin branches of shrubs and young trees drops of icy water hung in bumpy silver lines. I squatted down, and when I looked up toward the sky, sunlight broke through the drops, turning them yellow, then blue, then yellow again. My knees began to ache, and so I sat on the ground, the snow melting and seeping through my trousers. I wondered if politicians had time to do such things, and I was glad, ever so glad, that I was not running, just sitting.

Part Two: Messing About

Messing About

AT THE BEGINNING OF KENNETH GRAHAME'S *The Wind in the Willows*, Water Rat said to his friend Mole, "there is nothing—absolutely nothing—half so much worth doing as simply messing about in boats." Instead of sculling through experience in hopes of exploring new psychological lands, the animals played. In contrast, Huck Finn sailed down the Mississippi River with Jim, the runaway slave. Rather than traveling north, Huck headed south into the frightening world of slavery. The trip tested Huck and Jim, and the journey became a progress heavy with significance. When Mole and Ratty went on a picnic, they stayed near home. When Mole upset the boat in his eagerness to row, nothing profound was meant. Wildly happy and excited as a child with a new toy, Mole just lost control of the oars.

I have reached the stage of life in which I agree with Ratty. Nothing seems half so much worth doing as messing about. Indeed I think Hell to be a place where everything matters, a world where belief so shackles people to purpose that they spend their lives bent like slaves in the hot sun, chopping and hoeing action into significance, so ginning events that they force others into peonage, transforming them into moral and intellectual sharecroppers.

When I was young, mathematics seemed to reflect life itself. I thought hard work would enable both individuals and societies to solve problems. Much as a geometrical theorem could be proved, so truth existed. The study of mathematics created the illusion of order. Below the chaotic surface of things lay not only axioms and postulates, theorems as regular as equilateral triangles, but reason itself. Nowadays instead of mirroring life, mathematics seems matter for a sideshow at a county fair: swimming in a tank, a fish-eating calculus; a trigonometry, cloudy in a bottle of formaldehyde; and on a shelf stuffed, a spotted algebra, one of its linear equations purple, the other orange. Unlike finite mathematics variable English now seems to reflect life. Not only is language a chaos of idiom and definition, but rules of speech and grammar seem more whim than law, reducing the attempt to write "good" English to linguistic messing about. Completing the square may solve quadratic equations, but parsing sentences will not explain the workings of good prose. The real roots of fine writing lie outside formulaic scratchings.

Over the years beliefs and proofs I once thought truths have unraveled like the snail whose body peels into slime as he crawls. When Mole tumbled out of the boat, Ratty rescued him, grabbing him behind the neck and pulling him to the surface. Meaning didn't accompany Mole's return to land. Wet, not reborn, Mole did not push off into pools of significance, and smiting the tinkling current, seek "a newer world." Instead, he went home, and putting on slippers and a dressing gown, sat by the fire with Ratty. As snails crawl through time out of existence, they leave behind glistening trails. The trails are shallow; yet I enjoy seeing them wrap the ground in silver ribbons. I have grown comfortable with surfaces. Actually I think only fictions lie beneath appearances, delusions forced upon picnickers and swimmers by narrow overseers intent upon cultivating crops of meaning.

Much as rats don't associate with poor farmers, so critics leave me alone with the superficial, preferring instead to mine trails of significance which they imagine lurk golden under sentences. Everything is fleeting, of course, particularly meaning. Coker Knox, speaker of the Tennessee House of Representatives, traveled to Carthage last week to dedicate the Horton Sevier State Park. Half brother of John Sevier, one of the founders of Tennessee, Horton Sevier made a fortune trading with Indians. For a hundred years or as long as histories of Tennessee have been manufactured, scholars believed Horton's trading post was located near Castalian Springs in Sumner County. Six years ago, however, while searching for Jeddry, his mule, Loppie Groat discovered a mound in the woods behind Battery Hill. Thinking he had stumbled upon Bluebeard's treasure, Loppie returned at night and opened the mound. Instead of chests glittering with pieces of eight, he unearthed a handful of beads, two buckets of shards, and the rusty barrel of a long rifle. Since money was not involved, Loppie described the mound to the crowd at Ankerrow's Café. Not long afterward the University of Tennessee at Martin sponsored a dig, and students uncovered the foundation of "Sevier's Fort." This past spring the Tennessee legislature passed a bill establishing the park. History, Coker Knox declared in his dedicatory address, "is magical. Only ten years ago the spot where we now stand was located somewhere else." Most historical magic depends on sleight of mind. Forever being revised, the only permanent thing in history is impermanence.

My friend Josh delights in whetting his tomahawk on the skulls of historians. "In one generation the Indian of my childhood, gloriously red in paint and knife, has lost his way, going from the warpath to the sawdust trail, becoming so sanctified that if Jesus were to appear tomorrow historians would bundle him into a sweat hut and make him atone for the sins of whiteness before they would condescend to palaver about the Resurrection." "The historical Indian is so saintly," Josh continued, slicing deep into his subject, "that it's a wonder that when our ancestors arrived in the New World they didn't immediately fall on their knees and beg to be eviscerated." "Maybe, though," Josh said, pausing, "they were selfless and endured the hardship of life so their descendants could partake of the higher pleasure of being skinned alive in tribal casinos."

Josh bathes in streams a little too hot for my tepid taste. Still, neverending interpretation undercuts history, turning truth into trinket, the ripples of event no more significant than those caused by Mole's tumbling into the river. According to Josh, intellectual incubation in this country lasts fifty years. "By the time people hatch," Josh told me, "they have slept so long in the nest their brains are addled." Josh may be right. Only when I emerged from chickenhood at middle age did I stop genuflecting before the brow of history.

Age teaches a person to avoid believers. Wooden cheese and leather ham satisfy most people, even the converted, and when confronted by social evangelicals, one keeps them at idea's length by serving the prefabricated words they hunger to hear. Occasionally a Pentecostal wants to masticate more than Eukanuba. Not so flexible as folks who mess about, believers are easily duped, however. When rustlers raided farms above Carthage, Ben Meadows shot holes in the side of his cattle barn. Around the holes he drew bull's-eyes. Each hole rested in the center of a bull's-eye, making the rustlers think Ben a dead shot. Although thieves stole cattle from every farm bordering his land, Ben didn't lose a calf.

Instead of planning hours, I mess about. Generally something interesting occurs. Plans sire frustration and boredom. Like Ratty's rowboat, plans invariably go belly up, dumping their originators into cold water. So that he could adjust chores to fit his feelings, last month Piety

Goforth bought a mood ring from a peddler. "Piety would have done better to have grabbed a feather duster or a zinc-fluted washboard for all the good that ring done him," Googoo Hooberry said. "Piety forgot he was color-blind, and the next morning when he studied the ring, he couldn't see green or red, nor even blue. He just saw brown, so he shoveled manure all day." Rarely do people plan for eventualities. When fleas infested her house, Clevanna Farquarhson cinched flea collars around her ankles. "That's the most short-sighted thing I've ever heard," Clevanna's cousin Loppie Groat said later. "What's going to happen when she has to walk on her hands?"

While expectation inevitably brings disappointment, messing about leads to surprise. When Hink Ruunt's mare Centauress got caught in a barbed wire fence and ripped off four-fifths of her tail, Hink bought a jar of Growing Salve from Daddy Snakelegs, a faith doctor. Hink rubbed the salve into the remains of Centauress's tail, and the salve worked, but not quite as Hink expected. The nub sprouted and budded, not into bushy tail, but into another horse, a white stallion. Instead of a single mare, Hink now owned a team of horses joined backside to backside. A flexible and creative entrepreneur, Hink has always been able to squeeze coin out of difficulty. When Centauress came into heat, goings-on in Hink's barn were astonishing, so much so that Hink arranged dining-room chairs around Centauress's stall and charged admission. Although Hink made money, the real beneficiary of his planning was Dr. Sollows, who refused to attend a single show, even when Hink offered him a complimentary ticket. For two weeks after each estrus, the good, curious citizens of Carthage besieged Dr. Sollows, complaining of bruised withers, twisted gaskins, premature fetlocks, and detumescent pasterns. Last spring a bit lodged in Vardis Grawling's throat, and Dr. Sollows extracted it with obstetrical forceps.

No one is immune to the spirit of an age. Despite knowing that plans can only go awry, I organize days for the children. In summer I send Eliza to camp in Maine in hopes she will learn to pull a bow and build a fire. I want her to handle a canoe better than Mole so that she will be able to paddle south and journey out into whatever Mississippi's appeal to her. I also send her so that she will brush against girls who live in places wider than our backwater. Two weeks ago, Vicki, the children, and I discussed words at dinner. As usual I stressed the arbitrary nature of language. I pointed out differences between meanings of the same word in

English spoken in the United States and in English spoken in Great Britain. "In London," I said, "*fanny* does not mean bottom. It's slang for a female's private parts." Before I could continue, Eliza broke in excitedly, shouting, "So is *pussy*!" Silence erupted. The boys stared at the tablecloth, and Vicki's fork sagged, spilling a hunk of pineapple on the linoleum. After my chair settled, I asked Eliza where she got her linguistic knowledge. "On the school bus?" I asked. "No," Eliza said, "at camp. I learned lots of neat things there." "Four thousand, two hundred and fifty dollars," I said to Vicki later, "and Eliza learns the *p*-word." "What did you expect?" Vicki asked rhetorically. "That she'd learn to swim? Don't be naive."

The child of the snake isn't taught to bite. As I age, I have come to think that behavior is determined more by genes than anything else, except perhaps luck. Instead of a camp follower, Eliza is an offshoot of my DNA. Her use of strong language did not startle me. In greener days when the concept of free will seemed almost plausible, before family evolved into one wife, two dogs, and three children, I used strong words. Language has always delighted me, as it did my mother, and if I had known what *fanny* meant in British slang, the cancan would have occasionally bounced low-stepping across my conversation, so to speak.

When a teacher attributes his success to education, no one except other teachers believes him. In a world in which genes, not school, shape adults and in which messing about contributes as much to achievement as planning, education often seems more indulgent than beneficial. Because the ivied platitudes that once buttressed education have crumbled, Josh said recently, "Universities choose boosters as presidents, jumped-up Rotarians who can't distinguish a pen wiper from a post-hole digger. Forty years ago," he continued, spurning the peace pipe when I tried to interrupt him, "such people accomplished things in small towns, sponsoring spaghetti suppers at high schools and running bake sales on behalf of local hospitals. Nowadays university bureaucrats plaster faults in the mock gothic with butt-sprung words like *excellence* and *commitment*. Then before people notice the whole educational fabric shaking from intellectual palsy, administrators rhapsodize about athletics."

Although generally a man to my tooth, Josh can be zealous. He ought to mess about more. He needs to relax and enjoy athletics, and, for that matter, education. Instead of demanding that education benefit society, he just ought to enjoy the spectacle. This semester, I, for example, dallied, if not along a riverbank, at least in bleachers far from classrooms, seeing eight girls' soccer games, one boys' soccer game, three football games, two volleyball games, a swim meet, and a field hockey game. To be truthful I attended in part in order to sun myself. Age has made me cold-blooded, and if I don't absorb enough heat before writing, my prose freezes sharp and biting. "Huh!" Josh grunted. "Bleat with faculty one minute. Then roar with trustees the next. What sort of man are you?" "A happy one," I replied, "a man who thinks there is nothing half so worth doing as messing about." "Butting the times causes headaches," I added; "nothing lasts. Both foolishness and wisdom vanish in an hour." I ended my sermonette by quoting an engraving I saw on a tombstone in the Pillow of Heaven Cemetery in Carthage. "The Body born of Clay, / Blooms in a Night, / And withers in a Day."

The compulsion to find meaning distorts vision and undermines possibility. In November I attended an exhibition of Tiffany lamps held in the art museum at the university. People ought to consider art toys, like Ratty's boat and sculls, rather than propaganda or cultural icons. Insignificance is a fine conservator. Instead, say, of anger or disgust, insignificant art awakens the healthiest and most straightforward and protective reaction: covetousness. Rather than interpreting a piece of art out of identity, the person who covets wants the art itself. At the exhibition I coveted a ninety-year-old "Wisteria Table Lamp." Over the open crown of the shade, leading twisted in hard, dark branches. Soft, blue clumps of wisteria fell down the border of the shade while from the base of the lamp roots swirled outward in a skirt. In imagination I set the lamp atop the dowry chest in the living room. I dreamed of dozing beside the lamp on cold evenings. While snow shook like filigree through the street lamp outside, inside blue petals twinkled like rain. I stared at the lamp for a long time, moving only when a stranger wearing a deerstalker cap spoke to me. "Tiffany was something else," the man said. "He didn't have an insane bone or organ in his body, not even an insane pancreas." Folks who mess about are loners, wary of entanglement, slipping easily from one activity to another. When strangers approach, words curling oddly over their lips, people who mess about behave like Vardis Grawling when Loppie Groat showed her a green snake he plucked from a lilac bush. "Don't be afraid, Vardis," Loppie said, "it's only a green snake." "Yes," Vardis answered, picking up her skirt and stepping backward, "but it might be as dangerous as a ripe one."

This fall I rummaged about in the basement of the library. Entombed there are books that have not been checked out in decades. In the basement I dug through mounds of natural history books, occasionally uncovering glittering artifacts. How nice to know that larvae of the gold-banded flower fly eat aphids or that the most common gall on sweetbrier is called Robin's pincushion. Still, I am afraid I usually imitated Mole. If I didn't slide off a riverbank, at least I drifted from print to the soft edges of pages. What shone brightest from *An Almanac for Moderns* was not Donald Culross Peattie's ramble through a year, but an account penciled along the margin of three pages beginning on the sheet describing April 6 and ending on April 8. "In the morning," I read, "I worked in the greenhouse amid the varied colors and heady perfumes of carnations, poppies and calceolarias—taking daffodil bulbs from the earth that held them when they produced their beautiful yellow blooms—and putting them in crates for storage—until next Easter time when they will again come to life and gladden the hearts of people who are starved for beauty and color after a long, dark winter. In the afternoon I worked digging a ditch around the base of a foundation of a new house. I worked and smelled the earth, and I got it on my shoes and on my hands and legs."

University administrators forever preach the importance of research. Most research is simply messing about gone-uptown and gentrified. Still, I like to stick my oar in once or twice a year, just to show people that I am capable of rowing profound waters. To what Easter, I wondered, was the gardener referring when he wrote in the *Almanac?* Peattie's book was published in 1935, and the library's copy was part of the fourth impression, printed like the first edition in 1935. Because the fourth impression did not appear simultaneously with the first printing, I guessed that the gardener did not describe Easter, 1935. Still, since the handwriting was so faded, I reckoned the gardener must have written in the 1930s or 1940s. "Most likely, Easter, 1936," I told Vicki. Research, of course, would reveal the truth, and the next day I hurried upstairs to the Information Desk. On the landing outside the first floor, a stranger delayed me. He told me he owned a black cat named Binky. Three weeks ago he came home late at night and found Binky lying dead on the road in front of his house. "Smushed by a tractor-trailer, all his 'gorpals' out," the man said. So that Caitlin, his daughter, would not see Binky in the morning and become upset, the man fetched a snow shovel from his garage and after scraping the cat off the pavement buried it in the back-yard. "But guess what?" the man said. "When I opened the door the next day, Binky was curled up beside the *Hartford Courant*. Instead of Binky I buried Prune, my neighbor's pet. Isn't that just the cat's meow?" "You bet," I said. "That takes all dog."

At the Information Desk a librarian found a world almanac or book-tionary, as Loppie Groat calls it, and I researched dates of Easter. In 1935, Easter was on April 21. The following year Easter fell on April 12. Since the gardener began his description of lifting bulbs on the page devoted to April 6, I didn't think it likely he read Peattie's book in either 1935 or 1936. In 1937 Easter occurred on March 28, over a week before the man began his account. In 1942 and again in 1953, however, Easter fell on April 5, and that evening I asked Vicki's help in interpreting the research and deciding in which of the two years the man wrote in the *Almanac*. "Neither," Vicki said. "Nobody pulls bulbs the day after Easter. Real gardeners let them bloom longer." "They do?" I said. "Damn straight," Vicki said. "March 28 is the day. Nineteen thirty-seven is the year. Any fool can see that. You must be suffering from Information on the Brain."

Fashioned from words and numbers, dates have long intrigued me, seeming coordinates on planes that appear to locate everything in time and space but which actually graph little. This fall I read a shelf of books written by William Hamilton Gibson, an artist and naturalist. Popular at the end of the nineteenth century, Gibson lived in Washington, Con-necticut, and in April when the aromatic odorums of high educational talk blight spring, I may drive to Washington and saunter the byways Gibson described. This fall, though, I avoided such variables and con-centrated on grids of dates. On December 24, 1897, the library of Storrs Agricultural College purchased a copy of Gibson's *My Studio Neighbors*. The book cost $1.67 and raised the holdings of the library to 5,434 books. A modest number of people met Gibson's studio neighbors, as the book was borrowed only once in 1900, twice in 1902, then once again in 1903, 1907, 1908, 1913, 1919, and finally 1931. Gibson died in 1896. A biography appeared in 1901 and enjoyed a surge of popularity, being checked out six times in 1902. Interest ebbed quickly, though, and the book was not borrowed again until 1905. Ten years passed before another reader checked the book out in 1915. Before the next reader took out the book and the last library stamp appeared on the cover, thirteen additional years rolled past.

I did not spend the entire fall doing research in the library or dozing therapeutically above athletic fields. Reading influences messing about. In 1890 Gibson's *Strolls by Starlight and Sunshine* was published. After reading the book, I decided to wander Storrs, not by starlight, however, as no Ratty accompanied me and I didn't fancy slipping into the Fenton River some dark evening. Gibson entitled one of his books *Sharp Eyes*. Not just a lover but also a student of nature, Gibson described relationships between things. In contrast, I saw only a miscellany of discrete objects. Still, objects are good enough. One morning four bluebirds perched on bittersweet in the backyard. That afternoon a fox trotted through the dell, and a red-tailed hawk hunched on an oak, looking like an urn shelved against the sky. Above the periwinkle a hornets' nest spun out of shape into shags. After Vicki hung bird feeders on the garage, the woods shed gray squirrels, and a circus of chickadees began performing, dangling upside down on suet then flipping themselves into the air and landing upright atop the platform under the kitchen window.

Starlings careened around Horsebarn Hill, the flock billowing and wavering, floating loosely through breezes like a jellyfish, a lion's mane skidding across currents, lines of birds momentarily stretching rubbery like tentacles before being jerked back into the flock. Amid brambles a catbird's nest resembled a cereal bowl. From the bottom of the nest oozed strips of cellophane, while a serving of bittersweet berries floated above roots across the top of the nest. In woods, swatches of cedar moss resembled yellow vests, dandifying logs. Trains of cones swept out from white pines. White with dry, cracked resin, the scales looked painted. At dusk a young possum bustled along the shoulder of a broken road. In summer sunshine overflows hours. In late fall brightness seems limited. Not wanting to waste light, I wandered days. Near the Fenton River where light shimmered off laurel, I stood and let silver shake around me.

Despite my desire to absorb daylight, I also rambled rain, watching purple seep through the bark of red pine and worrying about a black racer hibernating under a sheet of plywood. A bulldozer pushed stone over the entrance to the snake's den, and the snake burrowed through a ball of grass beneath the plywood. On damp days I thought about the snake lying like a black bone, and several times I wove grass into the mound above him. On rainy afternoons sound bowled heavy across the ground instead of rising and splintering. On misty days I stood in the Ogushwitz meadow and listened to the afternoon freight, passing through town on the far side of Route 32. Not only did water press the sound of the train closer to the ground, but it absorbed it, turning it through the air in damp beads, so that the whistle echoed then rolled into gray silence. In contrast, the Fenton rushed lightly past like a streamliner. Catching on hemlocks, the water sounded like bags of air shaking against one another.

Much as Mole learned to swim and to row, so people who mess about learn to enjoy things, albeit they do not float downstream on their knowledge. Unlike Josh, I don't have contempt for history. Last week history freshened an evening. Three days earlier Francis finished a term paper that described the conflict between President Truman and General Douglas MacArthur during the Korean War. To write the paper, Francis borrowed seven books from the university library. Domestications being slightly less felicitous than usual, as Googoo Hooberry would put it, I decided to absent myself from the hearth and return the books to the library. By the Circulation Desk I met Billy. In his arms were eight books, the sources of his son's paper on Sacco and Vanzetti. "Things are cooking at home," he said. "I just thought I would bring the books back and mess around here for a while until the kitchen cools." "Good for you," I said, "there's nothing half so much worth doing."

Near Spring

ON THE FIRST DAY OF MARCH I walked through the woods in the back yard and turning south followed the cut for the telephone wires down to the small marsh next to the high school baseball field. Cattails and bulrushes grew along the third base line, and behind home plate I found horse-balm, water horehound, then a seed capsule from a single blue flag, mottled and brown and looking like an old leather football. The capsule had split and deflated, and the fibers which bound it together were white and stringy like rotten stitches. I started to pick the capsule and take it home, but I didn't. Winter no longer held me or the earth firmly in its grasp. Around the edges of the marsh ice had begun to melt, and I longed for the weeds of spring. Four days later down the slope of the long hill behind the cattle barn the children and I found pussy willow, swelling furry and silver. Turning north at the foot of the hill, we followed a brook through the woods, picking a way across ice and through briar until we came to the bottomland alongside the Fenton River, part of the old Ogushwitz farm. There in a wet spot between forest and field skunk cabbage bloomed, its red horns sticking up through the water, hooded and almost primeval. On fallen trees just above the wetland were clustered hundreds of small, gray puffballs, each with a hole in the end and swollen with spores. Two weeks later the puffballs were empty and liver-spotted, the sides having collapsed inward like the cheeks of an old woman.

The signs of spring excited us, and we roamed the field picking and collecting, the children filling their pockets with bits of clay pigeons, yellow and black, and then brass cases from spent rifle cartridges, the refuse of someone's winter target practice. Into a plastic bag I stuffed bracket fungus, mostly redbelt and oak maze gill, and then a score or so of goldenrod galls. In summer Indian corn had been planted in the field, and in the fall we gathered ears to hang on the front door and to feed to the chipmunk living under the garage. Now we wondered what animals lived beside the field and we searched for runs and burrows. Droppings were everywhere, deer and rabbit primarily. Near the skunk cabbage I found a newly dug burrow, wet mud pushed away from the entrance in piles the shape of walnuts. The burrow ran deep, and the piles were different colors, some black consisting of topsoil and others yellow from farther down. I showed the hole to Eliza, and after bending over to look into it, she straightened and said, "Daddy, we must be kind to animals, but I don't know what kind of animals we are."

At the end of the walk, we stopped at the university barns. Lambing was almost over, and we spent more time with cattle than sheep, looking at the young bulls, Hereford, Angus, and Simmental. I like to rub their thick necks and push their heavy heads, and so I called them. They came to me, as they almost always do, probably out of curiosity because my call is odd, beginning with a sound similar to that of a squirrel chattering then rising to a rolling high-pitched "hoo, hoo." Once we got home I sat at my desk and opened the galls. Most were empty; in two, though, I found fat green worms, the larvae of a small fly. Because the larvae could not live after the galls were opened, I felt guilty. I picked the galls, I think, more to teach the children respect for nature than to satisfy my curiosity. Certainly, though, I don't like destroying, and so as atonement, increasing life in one place where I lessened it in another, I ordered wildflowers for the side yard from Spring Hill, twelve Dutchman's breeches, six shooting stars, and eighteen lady's slippers.

Now that I think about it, I guess I saw the first sign of spring well before March, the day before Valentine's in fact and not on the air or along the ground but in the water at the university pool. The bathing suits worn by young girls do not resemble those worn by nice men's wives, with full backs and ruffled skirts. The girls' suits resemble skimpy exoskeletons. Hanging low over the thorax and cut away before the terga, they make wearers resemble insects, hind legs dangling out and down like those of crawling water beetles. While swimming that morning I noticed a girl with a bruise high on her coxa, so high that it was almost on the posterior epimeron. The bruise was round and mouth-sized. "Spring is on the way. I got close," Bhikhu said later in the shower, "and saw teeth marks, real teeth marks. The bruise was a Valentine's gift." I am too well-mannered and long in the tooth for nibbling. Still, I often hanker after candy, and on leaving the gymnasium and pulling my coat tight across my chest, I felt melancholy, remembering the wild sowings of springs past. How many more times, I wondered, would I see crocus push through dead grass, its leaves pursed and pressed tightly together like an arrowhead. I had only just awakened, I thought, and begun to appreciate life. To leave now would be a waste and wouldn't be fair.

Like snow flurries at the end of winter, my chill mood quickly melted. For my family February began a happy, tiring season of birth, not death. Vicki was born in February, Edward in March, Eliza in April, and Francis in bright May. On March 8 Vicki took cupcakes to Edward's kindergarten class, white cakes covered with poppy pink icing and sprinkles. Three days later on Saturday we had a party for Edward at home. That morning I took Edward and Francis to East Brook Mall. First we went to Waldenbooks where I bought a birthday present for Andrew, one of Francis's friends. Francis had trouble deciding on a present so I selected *The Dinosaur Encyclopedia,* "A Handbook for Dinosaur Enthusiasts of All Ages." Next we went to Yummy's to pick up Edward's cake, a yellow cake with chocolate icing and purple flowers, costing $9.95. Vicki ordered the cake Wednesday morning; unfortunately the order went astray, and Yummy's had only two cakes on hand, a chocolate cake with chocolate icing and a white cake with whipped cream icing and strawberry filling. Vicki was upset when I telephoned to ask which cake she preferred, so much so that my face must have changed color. "Tell you what," the man behind the counter said as he watched me on the phone, "the mistake was ours so I'll give you both cakes for five dollars."

Edward's friends arrived at half past one and after opening presents and eating cakes and ice cream—their choice of chocolate, vanilla, mint chocolate chip, or any combination thereof—we played games: Simon Says, Pin the Tail on the Dinosaur, Steal the Bacon, and Musical Balloons, after which we tossed beanbags downstairs and hunted treasure upstairs. The sun came out, and at three o'clock the children went outside, and the boys chased girls through the woods. I took Edward's "Devil Stick" away so there were no tears or cuts. At half past three parents arrived to retrieve their children, and after packing Edward's friends off with candy, balloons, and prizes—model cars for the boys and little ponies for the girls—Vicki and I collapsed in the living room. "We need another car," Vicki said, "because next year I am going to take the kids bowling." "Another car would cost twelve thousand dollars," I said, "and I'm not about to pay that for a birthday party." "You better," she began, "or else this wife . . ." She didn't finish the sentence because Edward came into the room crying. He had lost the snowplow off the front of a toy truck. Half an hour later I found the plow in the trash in the kitchen. Later that afternoon I mended the box which contained the marbles and board for his new set of Chinese checkers. Before dinner I spent twenty minutes searching for a diminutive man in a red helmet, the driver of "Mega Star," an amphibious vehicle armed with a "4XIG" rocket and decorated with a yellow hawk's head and jagged silver triangles resembling sharks' teeth. By evening Vicki was too tired to think about another car, much less dinner, so I got a pizza at Paul's, and, splitting a bottle of Miller "Genuine Draft" beer, we ate pizza and munched cake. Two days later I put the remnants of the cakes outside on the woodpile for the crows.

In March school activities resumed. The parents' club stretched after its winter nap and scheduled a night of bingo. I donated books as prizes and spent the evening eating fudge cake and drinking decaffeinated coffee. In order to pass the budget, the school board began meeting every week. When the vote finally came, I was lying flat on the floor, the muscles of my back balled like pearls on a string. "And then," my friend Neil said, "you got up only to abstain. You should have stayed on the floor; that would have been more appropriate." Money like spring was on the wing, though, and the school budget was the only expense from which I abstained. One afternoon I drove to Munson's candy factory in Bolton and sent Father six pounds of dark chocolate creams. Bulb catalogues arrived, and I ordered $284 worth of daffodils. Then I bought a piano for Francis, the purchase accomplished with my usual financial wizardry. Last fall Francis began piano lessons. Because he liked them and showed some skill and because I am musically illiterate and, like most fathers, want my children to rise above me, I suggested to Vicki that we buy a piano. In February we drove to the Piano Warehouse in Bloomfield. Before going I decided to buy a used piano and limit my spending to a thousand dollars. Like buds on a Japanese magnolia in the warm sunlight, my determination soon expanded, blooming into a new Walter piano and three thousand dollars. Despite the sudden expansiveness, however, I remained crafty and tight. "Vicki," I whispered, "don't buy now. Let's go home. In six weeks the price will drop, probably by about five hundred dollars." Six weeks later the owner of the Warehouse telephoned. A sale, he told us, was about to begin, and we could buy the oak upright which we had looked at for twenty-five hundred dollars. "That's splendid," I said, winking at Vicki. Right there is where I should have stopped. Oak in a piano or any kind of furniture does not appeal to me, however, making me imagine the back rooms of hardware stores and roll-top desks stained by soda bottles and cluttered with nails, crumbs from cheese crackers, pencil nubs, and a silver sardine can, the top peeled back and the inside stuffed with cigarette butts. "And the other pianos," I continued, "have they come down, too? I am especially interested in that dark cherry model." "Oh, yes," the owner answered; "they are also on sale, and you can get the cherry Walter for thirty-two hundred." "Terrific," I said; "that's what I want. Bring it out here and I'll have the check waiting." "Well," Vicki said later, "you're a shrewdy. By waiting six weeks for the price to drop five hundred dollars, you spent two hundred more. Thank goodness you kept your mouth shut at the school board. If you had started talking, there's no telling what you would have cost this town."

"Horseshit," I said and left the house. My response, I am afraid, was a little bold, but in March about the time robins reappear and mockingbirds begin to sing, I become assertive. When I read about spraying of pesticides on apples, I dumped all our apple juice down the drain, without Vicki's permission. The next day in the shower at the gymnasium, I said, "I poured the apple juice out last night. I hope all you fellows did the same." Basketball is the subject of most shower room conversations. In general basketball fans are not enthusiastic environmentalists, and when I stopped speaking, a man turned to me and exclaimed, "Poured the apple juice out! Don't be ridiculous. To get cancer you would have to eat twenty-four thousand apples a year for seventy years." "Oh," I said, "that's fascinating, but could you tell me more? What difference would it make in the numbers if a person ate only Winesap or Delicious apples? This is important," I continued, seeing the man look at me in an odd way. "I eat lots of apples to facilitate the easy movement of my bowels—mostly Baldwins and Cortlands, in the mornings and evenings you understand, and I wonder." I got no further; the man cursed, in the process breaking one of the Ten Commandments, and closing up his soap dish and grabbing his towel left the room. *Assertive* may be the wrong word. Last week I talked to my great-aunt Lucille; she is ninety years old and in poor health. "I asked that damn doctor yesterday," she said, "if I've got all these ailments, why I am alive. He said I was stubborn, but that's wrong. I'm contentious." Aunt Lucille is right. In March members of my family grow contentious, rather than assertive or stubborn, and contentious not simply with death but about apples.

In March I began to range out, pontificating on things about which I knew little and then roaming across the landscape. Two weeks after the children and I found the skunk cabbage, I telephoned Neil. Like groundhogs we spent the winter isolated and in hibernation, and it was time, I told him, that we dug out of domesticity. The next morning we scurried afield, walking in the woods behind the university farm for three hours. Ours was the walk of good friends. We discussed our children and wives, and the misbehavior of acquaintances. We wondered about the changes middle age brought to marriage and speculated about the future. Comfortable and relaxed and conventional, we were men with no secrets—well, perhaps one, a secret kept not from each other but from our wives. Before starting the walk we bought big ice cream cones at the university Dairy Bar. The bar had run out of chocolate, and Neil got Almond Joy and I got mocha chip. We followed the route the children and I took earlier except we crossed the bottomland and getting onto the Nipmuck Trail walked alongside the Fenton River. Ice had pulled back from the middle of the river, retreating to shelters under hemlocks and becoming loose and grainy like shavings dropped from a snowcone at a baseball game. After a while we left the trail and pushed back up into the hills through the woods toward the old turnpike. Stone walls curved cold across the hills, from a distance gray and resembling lines of pebbles tossed high on a beach by a big tide. The trees were bare, and instead of new growth I noticed decay, black knot canker on shrubs and stumps pocked by woodpeckers.

Not seeing signs of spring disappointed me. That night, though, almost as if she were trying to make me forget my disappointment, Eliza turned into a hothouse garden, washing herself with Vicki's cologne and then climbing into our bed and falling asleep. The fragrance must have affected us, for the next morning Vicki bought five pots of plants at Shop Rite, three of hyacinths, purple, white, and pink, and two of daffodils, small orange and yellow tête-à-têtes. For my part I visited the greenhouse behind the Torrey Life Sciences Building. The greenhouses were divided into rooms, some large, others small, some damp and hot, others dry and cold. Twisted over the door outside the orchid room was bougainvillea, its blossoms pink and papery. Inside the room orchids were planted in clay pots or grew in hunks of bark suspended on screens.

Despite the heat the room smelled like teaberry, and colors floated like rainbows in the air. A purple flower reminded me of high school dances and girls in stiff white dresses. I shut my eyes when I smelled it, and for a moment Randle and I swayed together again, youthful and cheek to cheek as the band played "Good Night Sweetheart."

Beyond the orchids were tables of mints: rosemary, thyme, savory, sweet woodruff, chamomile, lamb's tongue, southernwood, Jerusalem sage, hoarhound, and English lavender. Along a wall were tanks thick with carnivorous plants: Venus flytraps, bladderworts, pitcher plants, and then sundews, some resembling frying pans and others brooms. Beside a stream above a pool grew a fern garden, lacy and green; next to it was a mangrove swamp. Hanging from rafters were blossoms of angel's trumpet, long and thin like delicate orange post horns. Brunfelsia bloomed nearby, resembling a gay checkered harlequin, some of its blossoms blue and others white. Just beyond, the rich vanilla freshness of gardenia sweetened the air while the blooms of cassia glowed in the sun like scarlet powder puffs. Accustomed to woods as bare as the white aisles of a Congregational church, I was ready for signs of spring, not a lush equatorial summer. Soon I observed little, and colors and fragrances folded into each other, losing their individuality and appeal. I did not want to leave the greenhouses, so I shut my eyes and ran my hands over plants. For a while the leaves tickled my senses, but then I groped about mechanically, sensing only the familiar: saws, needles, hooks, paddles, brushes, and fans.

After leaving the greenhouses I paused to get my seasonal bearings. Not only did the cool March wind feel good on my face, but it awakened me, and looking up, I suddenly saw three small houses on top of the Life Sciences Building. In a dozen years at the university, I hadn't noticed them. Feeling curious and a little assertive, I decided to investigate. After riding an elevator to the sixth floor of the building, I opened a door with "Insectary" written on it and discovered some five hundred aquariums, all afloat with algae and small fish from Mexico. Relatives of the guppy, the fish were not so interesting as the people studying them. One woman, I learned, was an expert on animal droppings as well as fish entrails. She could identify all the animals in New England by their scats. Just recently, she said, a local police department called her into a case as a forensics expert. An intruder, it seemed, broke into a house in the middle of the night. The intruder made so much noise that he woke the owner who screamed then telephoned the police. The scream so frightened the intruder that he suffered an "accident," shortly after which he disappeared. On arriving at the house the police found no sign of forced entry, only the accident, and not sure of what they had on their hands and the owner had on the floor, they called in the fish expert. "I picked up a piece," she told me, "and passing it under my nose took a whiff and then said, 'Possum not person.'"

As white-throated sparrows appeared in the yard, so I began to chirp. Winter is too cold and summer too hot for waggery, but March is just right. The account of the opossum amused me, and when I got home, I telephoned the English department. Recently the university received some bad publicity. In going over the university's accounts, state auditors found that some moneys which should have been deposited in the state-controlled Research Foundation had instead been placed in the Connecticut Foundation, a private organization run for and by the university to get around the cumbersome state bureaucracy. Although there was no real wrongdoing, for a few days the air was rank with rumor. The English department itself kept an account in the Connecticut Foundation. In the fall the department collected twenty-five dollars from each member. Deposited in the foundation, the money bought gifts for secretaries, paid for the Christmas party, and sent flowers to funerals. When I called the department, I lowered my voice, stuttered slightly, dropped the *s*'s off my words, turned all *th*'s into *d*'s, and like a child scattering grain in a chicken yard cast agreement between subject and verb to the wind. Understanding what I said was difficult, and struggling to get at the words behind my pronunciation, people paid little critical attention to my sanity. "This is Mr. Mahmoud Burruti of the state auditor's office," I said coughing into the phone when the secretary answered; "let me speak to Mr.-Mr.-Mr.-Mr. Hankin." There was a pause. Then a voice said tentatively, "What did you say your name was?' "Mah-Mah-Mahmoud Burruti of the state auditor's office. What's the matter with you people," I yelled, then breaking into a bullfrog-like boom, belched an answer, "The earwax?" After a pause and some hurried footsteps and whispering, the head of the department came on the line and said, "This is David Hankins, Mr. Burrunder, what can I do for you?" "The first thing is to irrigate the ears. The name is B-B-Burruti-Burruti of the State Auditor's Office," I said. Before he answered, I asked if it were true that the English department had an account in the

Connecticut Foundation, adding that from the state's perspective the account looked like a party fund for "whiskey, Doritos, the onion dip, and that stuff, the boys and the girls." For a second the phone was quiet, then David said, "Mr. Burruti-Burruti, we do have an account but you must understand." "Understand!" I interrupted. "Oh, yes, I understand. I'll understand you right now. There is enough corruption in that foundation to fry your ass, and that of your wife, and fry them, not in the nice Crisco but the goose grease." And here the audit ended as Mr. Burruti experienced a cardiovascular guffaw and dropped the phone on the floor.

In the middle of March I received a letter from the "National Council on U.S.-Arab Relations," asking if I would be interested in spending July in Tunisia. I was a lover of things Arab and little would give me more pleasure than visiting Tunisia, I said when I telephoned the council. But, I explained, I was a son, a father, and a husband, and my pleasure fell at the end of a long list, behind those of family—wife, children, and parents. Instead of Tunisia, I would spend my July on our farm in Nova Scotia. In fact I had already booked passage on the ferry from Portland. Not only that but I had begun thinking about Nova Scotia stories and the inhabitants of our little area along the Gulf of Maine, from Port Maitland to Beaver River. This past summer, an old man told me why there were no poisonous snakes in Nova Scotia. Once, it seemed, poisonous snakes were widespread. They disappeared only after deer began eating them as worm medicine.

In the past parasitical worms were epidemic in Nova Scotia. One yellow, spotted variety plagued deer in particular, first breeding in the animals' intestines and then after maturing crawling up to the animals' mouths where they attached themselves to the roof. Hanging down like curtains in front of the throat, they seized food before it could be swallowed, causing whole herds of deer to starve. Because snake venom was an effective antidote, killing the worms if it were sloshed through the mouth, deer began hunting snakes, thrusting their muzzles into dens. Attracted by the heat the serpents crawled toward the entrances of their dens; as soon as they reached the surface, the deer seized them, crushing them between their teeth. The snakes tried to strike back, swarms of them attacking sleeping deer. Unfortunately for the snakes, the deer were immune to their venom, and rolling over and thrashing about killed scores of snakes, after which they ate them. Following such a struggle the heads of a few snakes remained pinned to the deer. To rid themselves of them the deer went into the ocean and, standing still, let crabs clamber over them and pluck out the heads for food. I repeated this story to a neighbor. "So far as it goes," he said, "the account is accurate." However, poisonous snakes still lived in Nova Scotia, he said, explaining that they were never seen because they spent their lives underground. After the deer killed vast numbers of them, the remaining snakes grew wise and refused to leave their dens. Instead of coming up and out of hibernation in the spring, they dug deeper and making long tunnels began feeding on mice, moles, and shrews, even blind cave fish. Spruce didn't lose leaves during winter, he cited as proof, because breath from the numbers of serpents underground warmed the trees' roots, turning them into evergreens.

In thinking about the story of the opossum and the intruder, I wondered how the fish expert came by her knowledge. Curiosity, I decided, a good, hearty curiosity must have started her sniffing. Long gone were the days when one could get occupational experience as a gold-finder or honey dipper. Of course being a plumber back before the time of the indoor necessary house could distort as well as educate the sense of smell. Certainly it did peculiar things to the nose of Bankes Mowll, who years ago took plumbing jobs in Port Maitland when fishing was poor. One afternoon after a hard day's work behind the school, Bankes ambled into Gawdry's Store just as a drummer was trying to sell Gawdry a line of perfume and bath powders. Bankes approached the counter and started to ask for something but then before saying what he wanted, Otis Blankinchip recounted, he turned a complete circle and fell out on the floor, his head just missing a keg of pickled fish. "The saints preserve us," Bertha Shifney said, "what was wrong?" "Oh, it won't serious. Bankes was just overcome with the fumes," Otis explained. "I went outside and picked up a handful of horse manure and held it under his nose and he come round right away."

As spring drew near, Nova Scotia sprouted in mind, characters budding and blooming, a few of the earliest bright as marsh marigold but most as strong and as rudely horned and red as skunk cabbage. One day a wagon suddenly appeared outside the old, abandoned, one-room store on Straddle Street in Beaver River. Driving it was a large woman with one leg, Mother Noon as she introduced herself. In the back of the wagon were a bed, two tables, four chairs, some decorations, and stock for her store, Noonday as it was called by local people. No one knew Mother Noon's real name or where she came from. She was dark, and some people thought her a Gypsy, others a Spaniard. A couple of folks claimed they knew her family. Gracious Chenoweth told Bertha Shifney she was a Watrous from Tupperville while Idella Shoup declared her to be a Purshull from Bridgewater, saying she had lost her leg in the great train wreck at New Minas. These last two claims obtained a little credence because Mother Noon was well spoken and appeared to have been a person of substance at some time in her life. Above the counter of the store she hung an old fireboard, three feet high and five feet long. On it was painted a gold grasshopper, a halo over its head and a blue ribbon around its neck. Written on the ribbon in black letters was "God's Harp." Over a shelf on one of the side walls she hung a small painting, one that provoked more controversy and mystification than the grasshopper. In the painting a naked woman sat on the back of a toad. The toad was shiny and green and had an orange eye as big as a teacup while the woman was small and so hunched over she looked like a pink nut.

Mother Noon sold herbs and dispensed folk wisdom and remedy, and Noonday was a jumble of pots, boxes, baskets, and jars. By the door were two baskets filled with dried mice and the bills of woodpeckers. To prevent toothache she recommended eating two mice a month, while bees, she said, never stung anyone who approached them with a woodpecker's bill in his hand. She sold honey, only late fall, or ivy honey, however, because it was grainy and woody and supposedly good for digestion. Behind the counter she kept earthworms in a box stuffed with damp moss. She treated burns with a salve of oil and ground up worms, and every week changed the moss to keep the worms clean and healthy. At the other end of the counter was a jar of leeches, great horse leeches for piles and blood blisters. In two other jars were spider webs sold for warts and weddings. If a web were rolled into a ball and then put on top of a wart and set afire, the roots of the wart would be killed and the wart would wither away. For warts any web would do. For weddings only webs of the house spider sufficed. If a bride drank a glass of wine containing the web of a house spider on her wedding night, she would, Mother Noon assured prospective suitors, become a frugal, patient, hard-working wife. In a woodbox on the porch were the bleached skulls of mares who had foaled. In spring farmers bought them and buried them in the fields to insure good crops. Despite the oddities, Mother Noon made most of her nostrums from the ordinary plants of field and woodland: sorrel, hawkweed, tansy, canary grass, rhubarb, lupine, yarrow, thistle. Of course like all good merchants she responded to the community and for a price accommodated her lore to individual needs.

When Jeremiah Gest suspected his wife Honoria of forgetting herself with Gideon Tannehill, he consulted Mother Noon. She suggested two remedies, Bankes Mowll later told Otis Blankinchip. If Jeremiah dried the pizzle of a red bull and then dissolved it in wine and got Gideon to drink the mixture, then, she advised, Gideon's "obscene part would lose all vigor." If, however, Gideon couldn't be persuaded to drink or Jeremiah had difficulty finding a red bull, Mother Noon said Honoria "would come to abhor venery" if her loins were rubbed with the blood of ticks, removed from the right ear of a spotted dog. Experience shapes the individual, and what impressed Bankes most about Mother Noon were not her solutions for matrimonial problems but her skill in purging and plugging—in short her ability as a plumber. In his professional life Bankes had observed many unique specimens of the crawling creation, but they were nothing, he told Otis, compared to the worms Mother Noon flushed out of the inhabitants of Beaver River. She kept the best of them in jars on the shelf beneath the painting of the woman on the toad. In one jar was, Bankes described, "a great black worm with black hair, five feet long, and big as a crane." In another was "a worm with red hair, standing straight up and long as a hand, both ends pointed like a nib." Next to it "wrapped about a ball of phlegm" was Bankes's favorite, "a very plain worm with a green head that was smooth and about the bigness of a pen with a body that was downy and a tail that was crooked like the half moon." I'm a poor plumber and a worse fisherman, and I don't have Bankes's interest in worms. Still, March has been hard on me. I'm not in good shape and all this roaming over the university farm and talking on the telephone has worn me down. Since Valentine's Day I have suffered through two colds and a sinus infection. I wouldn't mind Mother Noon's prescribing a potion to buck me up, not though, I hurry to assert, one of her love potions made out of the gall of a cat and the seeds of wild cucumber washed in vinegar. After three children and a pleasant decade of comfortable domesticity, neither Vicki nor I could endure a hard-core marriage. Daffodils, though, are pushing up in the dell; woodpeckers are knocking in the back woods; spring is almost here, and I would like some of the winter to melt off my head. According to Mother Noon if I boiled the ashes of "tender earthworms" in oil and then rubbed the mixture into my scalp, all these "hoary hairs" would disappear and then folks passing by on the road might think there was a drop or two of life in the old boy yet.

Getting It

AT MY AGE THERE ISN'T MUCH that a person gets that is good. About the best one can hope for is to slip quietly and unobtrusively through time, praying that disease and disaster won't notice him. Life did not begin this way. Years ago dreams warmed my days like the morning sun, and possibilities rang through the night like song. As a small boy I read a bookshelf of inspirational biographies about young Americans. Bound in orange and published by Bobbs-Merrill, the books pointed the way to success and indeed immortality, teaching that nothing lay beyond the grasp of the plucky and the industrious. Through impenetrable forest and desolate plain I wandered with *Daniel Boone, Boy Hunter* and *Meriwether Lewis, Boy Explorer.* With *The Mill Boy of the Slashes,* Henry Clay, I went to Washington. I was beside *Sam Houston, Boy Chieftain* when he caught Santa Anna napping and brought Texas into the land of the free and the deserving. With *Wilbur and Orville Wright, Boys with Wings,* I escaped mortal gravity and, soaring above dull earth, imagined the future bright before me like a giant apple tree, its fruits red and juicy, just waiting for me, and me alone, to pick them.

I soon learned better. Instead of beacons lighting the way to achievement, the biographies resembled the will o' the wisp, drawing youth into a wasteland pocked with disappointment. And those apples that seemed so fair in the sunny pages of biography often proved green and worm-eaten, and bitter to the taste. Not that I actually ate many. Visions rarely include practicalities like ladders and bushel baskets, and I have spent most of my adult years at the feet of trees, hands empty and tasting fruits only in my imagination. This, however, is not a state to be lamented; indeed, not getting what one dreams about may be one of life's great blessings.

Girls—silly, laughing girls—first taught me that getting what I wanted was going to be impossible. In the 1960s I was a student at Cambridge University. Tom Henn, my tutor, had extraordinarily broad interests and had written books on Yeats, poetry and painting, fishing, and German small arms. Although old and partially crippled, Tom coached one of the college crews. When I knew him, he was particularly drawn to myth and folktale. When tutorial discussions drifted toward the abstract, he brought them back to red clay, interrupting to recount a bawdy or horrifically violent story. For him boys became men on the river or on the battlefield or in the bedroom, anywhere, it seemed, but in class, and on my arrival in Cambridge, he urged me to forget books, saying, "Mr. Pickering, if you wanted to be a scholar, you should have stayed in the United States." I attempted to follow his advice but, as a bookish person, was not very successful. Still, I tried, rowing and playing water polo. One week I was so busy that I neglected to prepare an assigned essay. The simple, and true, statement that I had not planned my time well sounded priggish and would not have pleased Tom. Something more lively was called for.

"Mr. Henn," I said on entering his rooms, "I am sorry but I have not done this week's essay. I have had," I said pausing, "a problem with a brown-eyed woman."

"Well, well," Tom exclaimed heartily and, heaving himself out of his chair, put his arm across my shoulders and said, "Sam, I hope you have many more problems just like her."

I didn't. Not writing the essay was out of character. I was a good student and followed instructions meticulously, always taking *no* for *no* and *don't* for *don't*. Most of the time I never bothered to ask the question, but simply assumed the answer would be no. I was the sort of boy who, when a girl I was visiting in France called me into her bedroom and asked me to zip up the back of her dress, did—woe is me—exactly that. Even on those rare occasions when I pulled the zipper south rather than north, I later regretted it. My first real love after Cambridge was Sophy. I loved her with all the impetuosity of youth and pursued her with an energy foreign to my experience. For a while Sophy paid little attention but then she bent and invited me to spend Christmas with her and her family in Wisconsin. Late at night after her parents were safely asleep, Sophy crept out of her room, tiptoed down the long hall, and knocked softly at my door. One night while she was with me, her mother called from the kitchen. In a flash she was out of the bed and through the door. All I wanted was to pull the covers over my head in hopes the bed would become an enchanted cave out of which I could crawl and find myself safely back home in Tennessee. Alas, enchanted caves and magical doors are found only in children's books. Getting up and putting on my bathrobe, I went to the door and listened. From the kitchen, I heard the murmur of voices; then Sophy began to cry. Her tears soaked through her nightgown to my conscience. "By God," I thought, "I am just as responsible as she is. I can't let her take the blame by herself." With that I pulled my bathrobe tight and strode out of the bedroom and down the stairs into the kitchen. Determined to do the decent thing, I did not notice the puzzled expressions on the faces of Sophy and her mother.

"Sam, what . . ." Sophy began.

"Be quiet," I barked. "Let me handle this. Mrs. Currer," I said and, tolerating no interruption, shouldered responsibility for Sophy's nightly visits. "Don't blame Sophy," I said; "she didn't want to come, but I told her if she loved me, she wouldn't stay away."

"That," Mrs. Currer said after I finished, "is extremely interesting, but I wasn't talking to Sophy about that. I called her to tell her great uncle Sven died."

I wish I could say the evening in the kitchen took away my appetite for the things of this world. Unfortunately, hot youth finds it difficult to diet. Although I felt uncomfortable and was slightly down in the mouth when I sat down to breakfast the next morning, I was hungry. Stout-heartedly I took on the grapefruit, eggs, sausage, potatoes, biscuits and jam, and then the homemade apple pie that Mrs. Currer put before me. The food bucked me up considerably, and by the end of the meal, I had almost forgotten the embarrassment of the night before. Indeed, and I am ashamed to say it now, breakfast only whetted my appetites, and as I sat there, talking about the cold Wisconsin winter and sipping coffee, all I could think about was biting into soft, warm Sophy. Although Sophy gave me the it I thought I wanted as a callow youth, I never really got her, and by the next Christmas she had drifted away, leaving me feeling more alone than I ever felt in that Wisconsin kitchen.

Years and the time for mongrel love have passed. Countless disappointments and embarrassments have taught me the danger of pursuing anything. Still, humans are frail and in the passion of a moment often forget lessons driven home by hard experience. On weekends I run road races. I am remarkably slow, and in the four years I have been running seriously have not won a trophy or even a ribbon. Only once have I come close. Last year I ran in Norwich during a storm. While thunder slammed above the city and water gushed out of storm drains, sensible people stayed comfortably at home. Not me—knowing that the storm would reduce the field, I realized this was the best chance I would ever have to win a trophy, and doing my utmost to ignore the rain and thunder, I slogged through the streets. At the end of the race, I appeared successful and was given a trophy for finishing third in the forty-to-fifty-year-old age group. I was elated and fondled the trophy with as much fervor as an aging, spent runner is capable. I should have known better. Like Sophy, the things we get flow so swiftly through our hands that we are often left with nothing except laughter and the wish we had never possessed them. The trophy was mine for two minutes; then, it being discovered that someone else had actually finished third in my division, I was forced to give it up.

In truth returning the trophy saved me trouble. At home finding a place for it in the study would have been difficult. After a while, it would have become a nuisance, gathering dust and liable to be knocked over and broken by my little boys. Indeed, those things people work for, our possessions—both material goods and the immaterial past like memories of Sophy—weigh life down. That mark of success, a large house, doesn't bring pleasure. The bigger the house, the more pipes there are to burst, the more plaster to crack, the more wallpaper for children to peel off. My house has a big front yard, and friends say I am fortunate to have it for the children to play in. I am not sure. The grass not being so green as I wanted it, this spring I spent fifty-two dollars and thirty-four cents on fertilizer. Now I have the best crop of weeds in the neighborhood. Mowing accomplishes little; overnight the weeds seem to spring knee high, and now I have to buy weedkiller. Once the weeds are dead, I will harrow up the yard, rake, scatter grass seed, and cover everything with straw. Then watering begins. During the whole process, the children won't be allowed to play on the lawn.

Summer will come and go, and the children will be inside. At least they will be there if I and the things I worked so hard to get can stand them. Last week I almost had a fit when my two-year-old son, Edward, broke a cedar and mother-of-pearl footstool I had purchased in the Mideast. A decade ago I spent a year in Jordan. I bought many things, and on leaving shipped four large crates, 450 pounds' worth of possessions, to Tennessee. On their way the crates went astray. Edward's life, and probably mine too, would be more tranquil if they had not turned up. Unhappily for Edward, I determined to get what, I said, was mine.

The crates left Jordan on Alia, the Jordanian national airline, on the same day in early June that I left. I did not fly directly home but spent the summer in London working in the British Library. When I arrived in Tennessee in early September, I was astonished and irritated to learn that my freight was not there. Father traced it to New York, where Eastern Airlines had taken possession on the seventeenth of June. For a month and a half he had struggled to trace it farther. The Eastern representative in Nashville was polite but ineffectual, assuring Father "that we are doing the best we can." Upset, I sent a registered letter to the president of Eastern. Although I am a poor typist, I typed the letter myself on nondescript stationery. Three weeks passed, and then an answer arrived. The airline was unimpressed, and the man who responded was condescending rather than apologetic or accommodating. Instead of assuring me that the company would do its best to locate my possessions, he briskly requested a list of everything in the crates. At this point I should have stopped. Alas, I did not. The father of one of my closest friends was chairman of the board of a large corporation. Each year his company sent hundreds of employees to a combination convention-vacation. All the employees traveled on Eastern charter flights. The company did so much business with Eastern that the president of the airlines himself came to Nashville to meet my friend's father and spent two days as his houseguest. Upon learning this, I sent another registered letter to the president of Eastern. This time I had a professional type it on formal university letterhead stationery. Near the end was a paragraph reading, "Cormac Leighton, chairman of the board of such-and-such corporation, asked me to send you his regards. He requests that you personally look into the matter of my air freight. Anything you could do to facilitate this would be greatly appreciated." Five days later a van pulled into the driveway. In the back was my air freight, those possessions that have bothered me ever since, making moving difficult and now threatening to bedevil the lives of my children. People who strive after things often get the unexpected. Along with my possessions, I received a knowledge of influence and the workings of the world, and it left a sour taste in my mouth, one that I have never been able to wash away completely.

When I was a graduate student, I rarely participated in class discussions. Seminars were the curse of my days. Most of the talk was beyond me, and when it wasn't, it bounced so quickly from topic to topic that I was always panting far behind. No matter how well I prepared I could not keep up, and as the class steadily pulled away, leaving me stumbling and blind in a cloud of intellectual dust, I used to pray, "Oh, Lord, give me an idea. Don't make me appear such an ignoramus." My prayers must have gotten lost in the high, white ether and could not make it to heaven, for I never got an idea, at least not one I could articulate. In retrospect, I suppose I was fortunate. Not being a chosen vessel, academic or religious, one of those winged students on whom professors pin bright hopes and to whom they devote close attention, I remained comparatively free. Rather than struggling after the good things of academic life, prestigious jobs or influential editorships, I took the little bits that fell my way. And, lo, much like the miracle of the loaves and fishes, the bits have been endlessly satisfying. Instead of laboring through rain and thunder in pursuit of glitter, I have remained snug at home. Although I have won none of the trophies of the profession, grants and fellowships, I have experienced little disappointment. Perhaps my prayers made it through the pearly gates after all and have been answered—although not in the way I hoped but in the way that was best for me.

"No, my friend, you have got things wrong," an ambitious acquaintance responded when I talked to him about my career. Maybe I am incorrect, but getting things wrong often strikes me as better than getting them right. Certainly in the classroom a wrong answer is often more entertaining and memorable than a right answer. In an essay my students read recently the word *bordello* appeared.

"Steve," I asked, "what's a bordello?"

"It's," he said, "a kind of cheese, isn't it?"

Wrong, but yet bordello ought to be a cheese, wedged between the imported and the domestic, alongside the Stilton and the cheddar. Getting right answers or attaining goals too often ends things. The pleasure in getting things or having goals, be they trophies or Sophys, lies not in achievement but in anticipation. In ending the Uncle Wiggily stories, Howard Garis understood this well. What appealed to children was not the next night's story so much as it was what might happen during the day. "Now," a tale typically concluded, "if our cook makes some nice watermelon sandwiches, with maple syrup on them, for supper, I'll tell you tomorrow night about Uncle Wiggily and old dog Percival, and why Percival cried."

For my part, I don't want to know why Percival cried. Better it may be to leave tears and laughter shrouded in mystery. The attempt to get at the truth or to discover reasons for behavior is often destructive. Explanations and speculation frequently lessen life. Mr. Fenik was a handyman on my grandfather's dairy farm in Virginia. He and his wife lived in a small house behind Grandfather's garage. While Mr. Fenik was at work, Mrs. Fenik tended a garden she planted along the edge of a field near her home. She was a fine gardener, and by late summer the garden was a wonderfully green place overflowing with cantaloupes, watermelons, beefsteak tomatoes, squash, cucumbers, corn, snaps, radishes, and onions. More than anything else Mrs. Fenik loved butterbeans, and down through the middle of the garden ran four long rows like a great hedge. The Feniks were an affectionate couple, and if they had not been addicted to drink would have led a conventional life. On warm nights when she had too much to drink, Mrs. Fenik went into the garden. She always wore a blue nightgown and invariably went to the butterbean patch. Squatting down under the poles with the vines hanging about her, she sang hymns: "Bringing in the Sheaves," "Whispering Hope," and, amazingly enough, the occasional temperance hymn—"O Rouse Ye, Christian Women" or "Drink Water Every One."

Along one side of the garden grew a clump of dwarf cedar trees. Once we heard Mrs. Fenik start to sing, my cousin Sherry and I would sneak out of Grandfather's house and crawl under a tree and listen. The butterbeans were so thick that seeing Mrs. Fenik was difficult, and although we could guess where she was from her singing, we rarely saw her. When we did, Mr. Fenik was responsible. After his wife had been in the butterbean patch for a while, he frequently appeared. Instead, though, of going into the garden, he stopped at the edge and, picking up clumps of loose dirt, lobbed them high into the air above Mrs. Fenik and the butterbeans. Occasionally the clumps fell on her and Mrs. Fenik squealed and, jumping about, darted to a new spot in the patch. For a person who had been drinking, she moved quickly, and we had to be alert to get even a glimpse of her nightgown in the moonlight.

For four summers Mrs. Fenik sang and Mr. Fenik threw dirt; then suddenly they stopped. Just beyond the garden the field sloped down to a gully; across the gully grew two weeping willow trees. One dry September night while Mrs. Fenik was singing and the wind blew across the gully and over the garden, Mr. Fenik went to his car. From the trunk he took a chain saw and a can of gasoline; this time instead of stopping at the edge of the garden, he pushed through and down across the gully. There he started the saw and felled both trees. After heaping the branches into a big brushpile, he doused them with gasoline and then lit them. Immediately fire ran through the willows and sparks by the thousands flew into the air. Caught in the wind, they blew across the gully and fell like orange rain on the garden. For a moment Mrs. Fenik stopped singing and was silent; then leaping out of the butterbeans, she screamed, "Jesus," and, stumbling across the cantaloupes and the tomatoes, ran out of the garden and back into the house. Never again did Mrs. Fenik sing hymns in the garden. By the following summer she and her husband were gone, and although I have often wondered what motivated Mr. Fenik to start the fire, I have never gone beyond wonder. Why on that one night did he act so differently? What provoked him? How did the fire change the marriage? For such questions there are answers, but I don't want to know them. Instead of having the Feniks' behavior packaged and wrapped in pressed, brown explanation, then stacked upstairs in the dust beside trunks and old books, never to be thought about again, I want those summer nights to remain green, songs and butterbeans rising from the black earth, watered by a curiosity that speculates but does not dig and uproot searching for reason.

Certainly there are times when a person has to understand and understand quickly. Years ago I attended wrestling matches and cheered the villains. One evening when I was applauding the antics of two masked Japanese gentlemen who were busy pulling the hair and stomping on the hands of their fair, blue-eyed opponents, a hill of a man in overalls sitting in front of me turned around and said, "Boy, haven't you ever heard of Pearl Harbor?" Then, pausing, he glared and added, "You get me?" I got him right away, and, like the song of the lark at dawn, patriotism burst forth from my lips. Scowling and muttering evil things about Iwo Jima and Guadalcanal, I cheered our boys on to victory. By the end of the evening the big man was friendly, and as we were leaving he slapped me on the back and said, "You learn fast; you are my kind of boy."

Getting things right, however, does not guarantee acceptance. More often than not it isolates, sometimes even provoking people to behave like the big man at the wrestling match. A southern acquaintance has not been friendly ever since I interrupted him once when he was talking about "good old boys." "Good old boys," I said, determined to get something right, "good old boys—so far as I can judge—are always young and bad."

Another acquaintance and I parted after a discussion of familiar sayings. "When the going gets tough, the tough get going," I told him, was painted on the wall of the locker room in my high school gymnasium.

"I know that one," he said. "It's one of the good ones. That's what made this country great: people who refused to quit. When times were hard, they showed true grit, dug in, and held on until victory."

"You've got it all wrong," I answered. "I don't know where the tough went when times became rough. But wherever it was, if they were smart, it was somewhere soft. As for sticking around and showing grit," I added, getting under a full head of truth, "the Founding Fathers of this country were quitters, or at least their daddies and granddaddies were. Americans quit other countries by the wheelbarrow and came here hoping the going would not be so tough and they could start new lives in a good soft spot."

No, getting things right or even getting the things I think about is not for me. For years I have struggled not to want things and have asked family to refrain from buying presents on Christmas and my birthday. Besides, clothes are about the only thing people give folks my age, and I am not a sartorial high-flyer. Moreover, as a teacher I don't need much in my closet. Over twenty years ago, in June 1964 to be exact, James Neal of 71 and 72 Trumpington Street in Cambridge made the jacket I wear to most classes. In winter I wear corduroy trousers and in summer Sears Perma-Prest. Twelve years ago a relative gave me a box of J. C. Penney shirts, 80 percent Dacron polyester and 20 percent combed cotton. The shirts are indestructible and are for all seasons. This is not to say that I don't have a couple of affectations. On sunny summer and spring days, I wear a sailor's hat, brim turned permanently down, manufactured by Derby Cap Company of Louisville, Kentucky. When my students see me, they say things like, "Here comes Gilligan's Island." About every sixteen months or so, I lose my cap, and Santa Claus then knows what to put in his bag for me that Christmas.

Of course, no matter how one fights, a person cannot completely stifle desire. Sometimes after a long and dark day, I dream of meeting Sophy again. Occasionally when I can't sleep, cold years drip away like ice in March, and I imagine her tiptoeing down the hall and slipping into my room. Unlike youthful hopes, however, this is a dream that I pray will never come true. Getting caught now would lead to worse than embarrassment and take more than appetite away. Happy in the bright day, surrounded by family and all the little business of family life, I don't think much about the past, and my one or two waking dreams pertain to the future. I write familiar essays, and I imagine receiving wondrous mail. "After reading your splendid story," my imaginary letter begins, "I have decided you are the very one. Enclosed you will find a check. I hope it will be sufficient for you to take your family away to some exotic place for a year and devote your energies, full time, to your next book." Not surprisingly, the check is more than enough, and within a month the Pickerings are winging their way—and winging it first class—to Patmos or the Seychelles.

I receive quite a bit of mail, but none of it ever contains a check. Still, even though I don't get what I dream about, I do get marvelous letters. Filled with unexpected delightfully odd statements, the letters carry me to lands, I sometimes think, that Meriwether Lewis, the boy explorer, never imagined. Just yesterday two wonderful letters arrived. "As a lifetime academic," a woman wrote in analyzing one of my essays, "I also resonate to your subtext." What she meant I have no idea, but my speculations had me flying higher and farther than those boys with wings. Accompanying the second letter was a book written by Annalee Skarin, who, the editor's note assured readers, did not die but "underwent a physical change known as 'translation,' such as did Enoch of Biblical days." A man who read a piece of mine on turtles sent the book. Although the book was "not overtly relevant to that article," he sent it to me "after seeking Divine guidance on the matter." Able to communicate with the Great First Cause, the man would not have been at a loss for words in one of my graduate seminars.

Six weeks ago Eliza McClarin Pickering was born. She is her daddy's little dreamboat; unfortunately at night she does not flow out with the tide and dream. Instead she stays up, and has a fine time gurgling and kicking. The only thing that puts her to sleep is my singing to her. My voice isn't as good as that of Mrs. Fenik, but my repertoire is larger: "Good-Night Irene," "The Darktown Strutters' Ball," "Tennessee Waltz," "The Halls of Montezuma," "Battle Hymn of the Republic," "Yellow Rose of Texas," and "Daisy." I even sing hymns: "Faith of Our Fathers," "Onward Christian Soldiers," "From Greenland's Icy

Mountains." What I sing most, however, is Stephen Foster. Alas, gone are the days when my memory was young and good, and I have forgotten the words to many of his songs. As I pace back and forth across the bedroom, cradling Eliza, I find myself wishing for an album of Stephen Foster so I could get the words and sometimes tunes down right. Such a wish seems simple enough and likely to cause fewer problems than most of the things for which I once wished. Unfortunately, that is just not so. I don't own a record player, and if I bought one on which to play a Stephen Foster album, I don't know where I would put it so the boys could not reach it. If I bought an expensive record player and Edward broke it, I would be furious and probably behave worse than Mr. Fenik with his chain saw.

Magic

WHEN HORNUS ROEBUCK'S CHIMNEY began to smoulder, he didn't telephone the fire department. Instead he ran out the back door, leaped over the fence, crossed Grace's pasture, and burst into Noonday, Mother Noon's store on Straddle Street. Mother Noon was Beaver River's conjure woman, selling charms to the love-sick and nostrums to the feverish. For a damp, rumbling January catarrh she sold Hornus a cigar made from mullein leaves. The cigar cured Hornus, and so when flames flickered through cracks in his chimney, association flared like light wood, the smoke from the stove first mingling with the memory of hot mullein then rising before his vision to lead him across Grace's pasture, much like, as Bertha Shifney put it, "that cloud what led the old Jews through the Wilderness." Mother Noon did not like to disappoint customers in search of the miraculous, so she fashioned a prescription for Hornus. "Cut a branch of noisy leaf," she said, "and draw three circles around the house in the dirt, each circle nine hand lengths from the one next to it. Then lay the branch down at the east end of the house, and God will help you." As soon as Mother Noon finished talking, Hornus ran out the door and started for Grace's pasture. At the fence he stopped, suddenly remembering that only alders and red maples grew around his house and that the nearest quaking aspen was in the back yard of the Shore Grocery two miles away. "Mother Noon," he shouted, turning back toward Straddle Street, "I ain't got no noisy leaf. Do you think it would hurt if I dumped water on the fire?" "No," Mother Noon yelled back through the screen door; "it won't hurt none at all. Pour on water. In fact pour on as much water as you can."

The water put out the fire. "It was magical," Hornus later told Bertha Shifney, adding that only four bricks cracked. "Of course," he said, "if I'd had some noisy leaf them bricks wouldn't be bothering me today." Old-time magic was a staple of Noonday. For warts and bleer-eye Mother Noon prescribed a wash made from green flies and apple cider. Hanging above the counter and resembling a litter of long thin peppers was a string of lizards' tails. When wrapped in skin taken from a goat's ear and put on the mantle or, "better yet," Mother Noon instructed, "under the pendulum of a grandfather clock," a tail protected a family from fever during the winter. On the porch by Mother Noon's front door was a reed basket full of chestnuts. "If you carry a chestnut with a worm hole in it in the right front pocket of your trousers," Mother Noon told Hornus, "Cousin Bad Luck will run when he sees you." On the counter of the store sat a squat yellow jar full of what looked like feldspar, or so Hornus thought until he learned the jar contained snake stones, cut from the craws of birds which ate snakes. The stones absorbed poison, and placing one over a wound rendered the wound harmless.

Although the wares for sale in Noonday can still charm a page, they are dusty remnants, relics that no longer astonish or cure. Unlike Mother Noon's nostrums, stories rarely age into artifact. Instead of drying they swell vital and transport hearers into the magical land of Might-Have-Been. None of Hink Ruunt's mates were long-lived, and sometimes neighbors had trouble keeping abreast of the domestic comings and goings in Hink's house in South Carthage. On meeting Hink at a tobacco auction, Googoo Hooberry inquired about Hink's wife, whose name Googoo had forgotten, somewhat understandably because she was the sixth Mrs. Ruunt. Having spent the previous week in Nashville, Googoo did not know that Mrs. Ruunt had died on Wednesday. "Hink," Googoo said when he ran across Hink looking at sprays for tobacco worms, "you are looking mighty good, and how is that fine wife of yours?" "Well, Googoo," Hink replied, pausing and pushing the plunger on a spray up and down, "to tell the truth I'm kind of out of wives just now."

Not long afterward on some Caucasian holiday, Robert E. Lee's or St. Patrick's birthday, Hink went to Nashville himself. Whether the trip was provoked by grief or, as some said, a quick payment from the life insurance company, isn't known. What is certain, however, is that Hink spent much time drinking along lower Broadway in the gritty bars near the river. One night Hink wandered uptown into a better drinking establishment on Church Street. Hink was a prodigious chewer and spitter. What was fine for sawdust floors a few fathoms above the Cumberland River wouldn't do, higher up under the shadow of the War Memorial Building. And when Hink started spitting, a bartender fetched a spittoon and set it down near Hink on the floor. Hink looked at the spittoon then turned away and spat in the opposite direction whereupon the bartender shoved it closer to him. For a moment Hink looked back and forth, first at the bartender then the spittoon. But finally he shrugged and digging a hunk of tobacco out of his jaw pushed it around in his mouth, his cheek resembling the sail of a boat scudding through small-craft warnings. As Hink's cheek fluttered and billowed, the bartender kicked the spittoon right up against Hink's chair. Hink eyed the spittoon again, his cheek slack for a moment. Then he looked the bartender in the eye. "Fellow," he said, using his tongue as a tiller and steering the tobacco up under his ear, "if you don't take that thing away, I'll be hanged if I don't spit in it."

Along with being unsophisticated, Hink was lazy—spoiled, Turlow Gutheridge said, "by all them adoring wives." According to Turlow, Hink was so slovenly he wouldn't go to the door to see if it was raining. Instead he just whistled for Buster his dog, who slept under the front stoop. When Buster came into the house, Hink ran his hand along the dog's back. If his fingers got wet, Hink knew it was raining. Like many lazy people, however, Hink became energetic when he thought of an unscrupulous way to make fifty cents. Once he found a bucket of yellow paint at the dump, and when the patients from the school for the afflicted in Buffalo Valley came to Carthage for their half-yearly outing, he painted his mule and shutting it up in his barn charged the poor souls five cents to see, as the sign he hung up declared, "the camel without no hump."

The trip to Nashville changed Hink, however. Nobody knew what happened. Perhaps he drank too much or "bit off more than he could chaw," as Googoo put it. Whatever the case, on returning Hink pronounced himself a Christian and started attending Slubey Garts's Tabernacle of Love. When Pharaoh Parkus came over from Memphis to hold a baptizing, Hink was waiting on the riverbank. Hink knew almost no doctrine, and when Pharaoh asked him if he believed in Original Sin, he answered, "yes, if it's lived up to." "The cerebellum don't keep the keys to the white gate; many a plodding soul has been sucked up the heavenly flue," Pharaoh was fond of saying, and after nodding to Hink, he turned to the congregation and said, "Is there any reason why I shouldn't baptize this man?" For a few seconds the crowd was silent; then from way back came a voice. "Go ahead, reverend, but you've got aholt of an old sinner," the voice declared, "a little dip and scrub won't do him no good. You're going to have to anchor him far out and let him spend a night or two in the deep." Pharaoh was a trifle deaf, and although he smiled, most likely he did not hear the advice. In any case he ignored the voice, and turning away from the bank seized Farr Stonebridge, the man standing next to Hink, and pushed him under the water. He held Farr down for fifteen seconds, and when he let him loose, Farr flailed up, spewing water and words. "Praise God," he shouted, "I seen Jesus sitting on the great throne. All the angels was playing their harps, and the virgins and poets was dancing in their birthday suits. And that ain't all," he continued, digging a wad of red clay out of his ear, "I heard the amethysts in Hell, suffering and just crying and begging for water." After the ladies in white handed Farr a towel and led him into the shade, Pharaoh dunked Hink. After Pharaoh released him, Hink did not come to the surface right away. Instead he swam about a bit as if he were searching for something. He didn't find what he was looking for. "Hellfire," he said when he finally came up, "I didn't see no virgins. All I saw was a tractor tire, a catfish, and a goddamn big old mud turtle." What was magical for Farr was ordinary for Hink, and in truth magic may lie in the eye of the beholder. Indeed it probably resides in the plastic power of the mind, enabling a person to transform a catfish into Jesus, a tractor tire into angels, and then amid the slow wash of a river to hear the sad moans of sinners far from their God.

"When I read a book," Eliza told me last month, "when I read more than three pages, it feels like I disappear. I just go inside the book." Since Christmas Eliza has baptized herself in books, disappearing beneath the covers of Frances Hodgson Burnett's *The Secret Garden* and *A Little Princess* then swimming through a shoal of Laura Ingalls Wilder's tales. Turning pages is sleight of hand, creating illusion and transforming the self and the world. "Now you see me, now you don't," Eliza said, opening *Little House on the Prairie* and shutting the door to her room. Much as magic shines from story, so it radiates from the bindings of life. Many old ailments blind: pin and web, squint-eye, convention, and habit. Occasionally, though, one bathes in one of Mother Noon's washes, and for a moment imagines that days are stitched together not by dull task, but by a sharp wand, rippling the air and teasing glee from an hour.

I have taught for twenty-five years, and teaching has become routine. Last month at a university open house when a man asked what my students taught me, I responded automatically. "Nothing," I said. "Look," I continued, "I am fifty years old. Most students are teenagers. Even if they had something to teach I wouldn't want to learn it." The man looked disappointed and started to respond, but then he thought better and was silent. "Damn these sentimentalists, romanticizing youth and the inarticulate," I muttered to myself and turned away. My reply did not win a friend for the university, and later I felt guilty, so much so I reviewed the semester, turning memory like pages of jottings in a spiral notebook. Much as a student trying to write what his professor wanted I searched for a reply that would please the man. Suddenly halfway through the semester I found an answer, not the stuff of the old educational shell game, a soft, uplifting inspirational response, but the sinew and gristle of real learning. From Ian I learned "the rectovaginal technique of artificially inseminating cattle." "All these books we have read about nature are fine, so far as they go," Ian said to me, "but you need hands-on experience." Hands-on turned out to be hands-in. That afternoon I met Ian in the dairy barn. Over my left arm I put a plastic sleeve. Thirty-seven inches long, the sleeve reached from shoulder to fingertips. Loose-fitting, the sleeve was ten and a half inches wide at the shoulder while the distance between the end of the thumb and that of the little finger was eleven inches. Ian demonstrated the technique on a Holstein. The cow was skittish, so he suggested that I practice on another of "the ladies," a quiet, tawny Jersey with a plastic identity tag stapled through her left ear. Printed on the tag was the name Cheryl and the number 874. I lubricated the end of the glove with soap and water. Then pushing my fingers together into an arrowhead, I leaned against Cheryl and eased my hand into her rectum. For a moment Cheryl tensed and her muscles contracted, squeezing my arm, but soon she relaxed and my arm slipped deep inside her. Then I, too, relaxed. As I rubbed the base of her tail, heat from her body washed through my arm, eroding and softening the sharp pain of arthritis. "If you can't find me some afternoon," I told Josh the next day, "look in the dairy barn. I'll be up to my shoulders in arthritis cure-all." In order to find the cervix, which lay just under the "rectal floor," I scooped several handfuls of manure out of Cheryl. "Once you get that field butter out," Ian said, "push down and you will discover the cervix. It feels like a turkey neck." In my right hand I held a foot-and-a-half-long plastic rod with a plunger at one end and a dollop sperm at the other. Carefully I inserted the rod into the vagina. The going wasn't easy. I steered a slow course, but eventually I tacked through the rings of the cervix and docked at the uterine horns. "Nothing to it," I said the next morning in the Cup of Sun, "give me a mug of coffee and bring on the whole damn herd." "Artificial insemination? Did I hear correctly?" a woman sitting at a nearby table asked Josh after I left. "It won't work," she said; "it won't take. The cow's body will reject it. He ought to know better," the woman continued, pausing to chew the matter over, "he's a professor, isn't he?" "I explained to her," Josh recounted, "that you were not quite so intimately involved in the procedure as she thought. Still," Josh continued, "she was naive, particularly when it came to that bit about your being a professor. The only thing that saves the bovines around this university is that the professors are so busy screwing each other they don't have time for higher forms of life." Josh's bile was understandable. A colleague had just hammered his latest book in a big review, calling Josh himself mundane and self-serving and categorizing the book, which I thought pleasant and even sweet, as belonging to "the Obejoyful, swift-footed earthworm, cornpone school of writing."

If "learning experiences," as my questioner at the open house would label them, rarely occur in the classroom, memorable moments do happen on the campus. Not long ago I corrected a student's manners. "You need," I said, "to learn civility." The girl looked puzzled. "Civility?" she responded. "What's that? I'm not an English major." In case any of the saved needed resuscitating, Dr. Sollows attended Pharaoh Parkus's baptizing. Googoo Hooberry had recently come down with the croup, and seeing Dr. Sollows standing by himself on the riverbank, he approached, and after chatting for a while about the weather and then the state of dry unsanctified souls, he asked Dr. Sollows to recommend a medicine for croup. Dr. Sollows obliged and wrote Googoo a prescription. A week later Googoo appeared in Dr. Sollows office. "Dr. Sollows," he said, "when you prescribed this medicine you said it was good for the croup." "Yes, I did," Dr. Sollows answered; "there's nothing better." "Well, then," Googoo said, "I'm still ailing. How about you giving me something that is bad for croup. This here sickness has been humored long enough." As not all magical things said are polite or sensible, so many transformations lower rather than elevate. In spring when flowers push through the dirt and burst into bloom, aspiring almost to spiritual beauty, I sink earthwards, braying and kicking up words. People who tolerate me fall and winter bolt in the spring. A decade and a half ago the university administration decided to raise money by building an incinerator atop Horsebarn Hill. For a fee the university planned to accept and burn low-grade hazardous waste, generated initially from within Connecticut but then later, "after the kinks were worked out," from all over New England. The environmental impact would, the university assured towns-people, be negligible. Part of the incinerator would consist of a tall chimney, from the mouth of which ash would be dispersed and blow far and never near. The proposal did not fly. At a town meeting citizens burned a crate of statistics, turning the university's proposal itself into ash. The reluctant spokesman for the university's "position" was a man who after scraping the cinders from his hide became dean of arts and sciences. "Congratulations on the deanship, Frank," I said, ambling into his office one April morning, "I forgive you for trying to shrink my testicles, but, by God, don't you try anything like that again." Each spring I drop by the dean's office. Although his lights are usually on and his desk cluttered with paper, I rarely catch him in. Once I saw him through a window. He even waved at me. By the time, though, I entered the building and reached his office, he had vanished magically, leaving behind a fresh cup of coffee and a pipe full of tobacco.

Platitude often starts me bucking. In kinder moments of self-aware-ness, I think myself kicking through jargon and hollow phrase much as spring bursts clamoring and vital through the gray woods under Horse-barn Hill. In truth, however, braying is in my nature, and I enjoy burrs under my tail. I'm on the local school board, and recently when a prin-cipal said she appointed a "task force" to examine the curricula of the school, I interrupted. "Task force," I exclaimed; "I'd prefer a commit-tee. The idea of a task force sailing up and down Hunting Lodge Road and shelling Eastwood and Hillside Circle makes me damn uncomfort-able." That evening, I am afraid, I strayed far from stall and paddock. Last year the board set seven goals for the school system, one of which was to increase children's "Motivation to Learn." One principal pro-vided a list of things done at his school to increase motivation, including "Personal Safety Curriculum," "Shared Decision Making in the Class-room," "Youth Services Bureau," and "Here's Looking At You, 2000, Health, Safety and Self-Esteem Program." The word *curiosity* did not appear on the list, and most of the activities were directed toward pro-ducing happy rather than intellectual surroundings. Feeling comfortable does not necessarily make a person thoughtful, and when I saw "Greeting Students When They Arrive at School" on the list, I spoke. "What sort of greeting do you use?" I asked. "Do you say 'Good morning you little son of a bitch?'" When the principal looked startled, I forged on. "When my children get off the bus in the afternoon, I say, 'Welcome home you little bastards. How was the Hell Hole today?' And," I continued, "I'm giving my babies something important: the ability to deal with the unexpected. In contrast to all those other children who are greeted by a bland, simpering 'Good morning, Johnny' or 'Did you have a nice day, Sally,' my babies are learning to cope. Instead of being startled and knocked off stride by the unforeseeable, my children will hunker down and batter ahead, straight through to success." Often, of course, I bridle my tongue and spit the bit out only in imagination. Not long ago a parent whose child attends school in another town came to see me. In discussing reproductive matters with a seventh-grade class of both girls and boys, a teacher had unraveled a condom over a banana. I liked the parent, and knowing she was upset, I was sympathetic. "How very common," I said shaking my head, trying to confuse a small voice who was on the verge of seizing my tongue and asking, "Was the banana peeled or unpeeled?"

Always fast and loose with event, memory resembles a flim-flam artist. Still the shell games memory plays are often magical. On rainy days when recess is canceled at Northwest School, the children watch movies. "Edward," I said one night in March, "I don't care what everyone else is doing, including the teachers. When recess is not outdoors, you go to the library and read. I never saw a film the whole time I was in school. For that matter," I continued, putting down my fork, "I don't think the school owned a movie projector." "Well, then," Francis said, "what did you do when recess was rained out?" "We stayed in our rooms and . . ." I began. Then I paused. Instead of finishing my sentence with *read*, I smiled and said, "and played the eraser game." "The what?" Eliza said. "The eraser game. The greatest game in the world," I replied. "Don't they teach you anything in that school of yours?" Two children played at a time, the chaser and the chased. Both had blackboard erasers on their heads. Through the aisles they ran, one pursuing the other until somebody's eraser fell off or the person chased was caught. The winner played another round while the loser retired to his desk. "Daddy," Edward said, "were you the best in the class?" "No." I answered; "I was good, but I wasn't the best." "Who was?" Edward asked. "Hayes," I replied without pausing. "Hayes had a flattop, and he was the best." Suddenly Parmer School popped out of the past and into the present, bringing with it a classroom filled with familiar faces: Hayes, Eddie, Barbara, Alice my girlfriend, Mary, John, Jack, Bill, and Garth. The old hocus-pocus of memory made me sad. I longed to see those children again, to chase someone across the front of the room before Mr. Bass's desk, to race past the radiators, the rain ringing on the windowpanes above, no one behind me and nothing ahead except the long future and one laughing boy or girl.

At the end of March I actually saw myself running, albeit not in fifth or sixth grade but as a senior in high school. Stored in the gymnasium of Montgomery Bell Academy in Nashville were films of high school football games. For twenty-five dollars the alumni association wrote that I could buy a copy of MBA's 14–12 victory over Springfield in 1958. The showing occurred at 4:20 one Tuesday afternoon, before Vicki started dinner and just after Edward and Eliza got off the school bus. For me the film was wondrous. Thundering, or so I said, across the screen were Carl Babb, number 70, John Clay 77, George Creagh 81, Jackie Hooper 65, and, of course, good old 75. The film did not entertain the other members of the audience as much as it did me. "Daddy," Edward said, "why isn't this in color?" "Where are you Daddy?" Eliza said. "Right there on the ground," I said pointing to a pile in the lower left-hand corner of the screen. I spent most of the game on the ground. At the time I imagined that I stripped blockers from the running backs. What I now saw was that the runners were far from my grasp, and on almost every play I was knocked on my bottom, so often that the seat of my trousers was black. Still, I played, and that was all that mattered; I even played some offense. I wasn't quick or graceful; in fact Mrs. Carter, the headmaster's wife and a family friend, told me years later that "we often wondered how you managed to run without falling down." I ran because I was a poor athlete, and like many people I wanted badly to do things for which I was not suited. From football I learned that playing, not winning, was important, and through the years whenever I have coached from the front of a class, I've tried to play everybody: both the student with the agile leaping mind, and the plodder, tripping over every clod of thought. Like that field in Tennessee, the classroom is a place where games are played, a grassy area in which children tumble and block and where coaches encourage, sometimes by sprightly malice, more often by kindness.

The film was short. "Guys," I said at the end, "What did you think?" "All right." Edward answered, "but I thought this was going to be professional, or at least college." "You were wonderful" Eliza said, hugging me, "the best daddy football player in the world." "I saw a 1958 Chevrolet under the goalposts," Francis said; "it was two-toned." "My heart was just in my throat watching it, Sam," Vicki shouted from the kitchen, having left at the end of the first quarter to start dinner. That night when I snuggled up to Vicki in bed, she pulled away saying, "I am too tired to be Hovercrafted." "All right," I said, turning the other way. Soon I was asleep. I dreamed I played football. Instead of a helmet I wore an eraser. I made more tackles than anyone else on the team, and my eraser never fell off.

"Which is more useful, the sun or the moon?" Quintus Tyler asked his class in the Male and Female Select School in Carthage. "The moon," Billie Dinwidder shouted, "we couldn't get nowheres at night without it. The sun," he explained, "don't do us no good because it's naturally light in the daytime." My students are too cagey to be spontaneous, and rarely do I get such magical answers in class. Still, last Thursday Ian startled me. "I had a course with a professor who," he said, "began each class with an awful joke. I got tired of pretending to laugh, and one afternoon I went to the library and taking down the record of state employees looked up the professor's salary and the number of courses he taught. Then I estimated the time he spent grading papers, preparing lectures, and doing research, and added them to the hours he spent in class and in his office. Next I converted everything to minutes, and after dividing the minutes into his salary, I discovered that each joke cost the state thirty-five dollars." "Every man may have his price," I quipped when Ian finished, "but how many of them are worth it?" "For that wonderful joke," I said when the class looked puzzled, "the state got a bargain: nine and a half cents."

Forever pulling lively surprises out of the academic hour, Ian was a joy. Usually, however, mail and telephone startle more than the classroom. In February a writer in Georgia sent me his review of my latest book and then a selection of his essays. "I feel like a novice addressing the master," he wrote in his covering letter. "That's the stuff," I thought, picking up the article, "this review will be special." It was. "Pickering loses his way," the caption read. In the *New York Times* a reviewer discussed my being the source of the John Keating character in the movie *Dead Poets Society,* and as a result I received bundles of mail. "From the article," a woman wrote from Chicago, "I conclude you have lost your enthusiasm. Professor Pickering," she declared, "I am going to give you some free advice. Don't be afraid to be young even though you are not the youth you were twenty-five years ago and not even if you have twenty children and a harem of wives. Don't be afraid to stand on your desk again. You must give students advice. I know from the movie that the last time you gave advice you got into a lot of trouble. But don't give up. You don't have to settle for the conventional even when defeat has you by the throat." From Norfolk a man wrote saying I was his "mentor." "I was on the docks," he said, reading Walt Whitman's poetry, and rain started to fall. "It was a sign that I was destined to be a great poet. Soon I will come to Connecticut to sit at your feet." "I respond by return mail," I wrote in reply, "because unfortunately my feet will soon be out of Connecticut. By the time you receive this letter I will be in Britain. I am writing a book and must remain there for at least two years in order to do research." "Your real mentor," I stated in conclusion, "cannot be me or any stranger. Instead your mentor should be your imagination. Coupled with hard work, imagination brings success." Addressed to "Non-Finalists," a university informed me that "as of January 30, your application was removed from the Committee's file of applicants under consideration for the presidency." "We remain grateful for your interest," the letter ended, "and we wish you the best as you pursue your vocational goals in other settings." Sometimes letters are so magical that I am not sure what settings I frequented in the past, never mind settings in the future. "I was thrilled to see your name in the *Constitution* several months ago," a woman wrote from Atlanta; "I sent the clipping to my grandson and he was impressed that I knew you." After telling me about her grandson, the woman ended, asking, "Do you ever get to Atlanta any more? We'd love to see you. I remember fondly the time you lived in this house while in school at Emory University." Unfortunately I did not know my correspondent. I have spent only two weekends in Atlanta in my life, and not only did I not attend Emory, but I have never visited the campus. I was not sure how to respond. I did not want to embarrass my correspondent who seemed old and kindly. "Your letter," I eventually began, "brought back wonderful memories of days long past." I complimented the woman on her grandson's successes then concluded by thanking her for her "warm and gracious letter." To confuse one person with another is commonplace, but in the commonplace lies magic. To discover it one needs only to observe, or listen. An hour after I replied to the woman from Atlanta, KOPE radio in Medford, Oregon, interviewed me. The program lasted an hour. I talked to the host and answered questions from listeners for part of that time. Lengthy advertisements broke the show into segments, and while the advertisements were broadcast, I sat in the study, holding the telephone in my lap. At first I ignored the advertisements, but then I heard a man say "at least honk your horn" and I started to listen. At the Door and Window Store, next to the brewery in Grant's Pass, Fred waited for customers. Fred was a convivial sort; in fact, the advertisement declared, he "just loves helping you." After buying blinds from Fred, one could eat lunch at the Applegate River Ranch House, seven miles from Roque on the Applegate River. Entrees started at $7.95, and Fred's friends could chose from a wide range of "Texas Frontier and Blue Hawaii Cuisine."

Last spring I was on a program celebrating fifty years of graduate study at the University of Connecticut. Participants rode a bus from Storrs to Hartford. I sat next to Virginia Pyle, professor of music. Virginia had just begun work on Mozart's *The Magic Flute,* the first full opera ever produced by the School of Fine Arts. To bring the opera to the stage would take a year, but she was excited, she said, and looked forward to the challenge. When I said, "That's wonderful," she asked if I would like to appear in the production. Accordingly I began rehearsals the first week in March. Not since Ransom School and Nashville had I been on stage. In second grade I was a wise man in the Christmas pageant. One of the other wise men, Sarah Ann MacKenzie, froze on stage. After disappearing behind the curtain, I had to return, and creeping up behind Sarah Ann grabbed the sheet she wore and tugged her into the wings. In *The Magic Flute* Tony Dibenedetto, a chemical engineer and sometime acting head of the university, and I were "honor attendants" to Sarastro, high priest of a mysterious, quasi-Masonic brotherhood. Tony and I had "cameo," nonsinging roles. Near the end of the opera I placed a hedge of plastic privet on the head of the hero Tamino. Then in the finale I handed Sarastro a gold crown, decorated with colored glass resembling hard candies: raspberry, grape, orange, and cherry flavors. My first appearance lasted sixteen seconds; the finale, forty-eight. For my minute on stage I put in sixty and a half hours of rehearsal. While acquaintances spent spring vacations wandering white sands and sipping planter's punch, I strode the intoxicating boards. The hours Tony and I put in made us part of the company. The lead singers rehearsed for a year, and if I had devoted less time to the opera, I would have been not simply a ringer but a charlatan. The first rehearsals I attended were held in the auditorium of the agricultural school, and feeling like an outsider rather than a participant, I only observed. Pasted to the doors of the Agronomy department were bumper stickers: "Let's Stop Treating Our Soil like Dirt," then "Plant a Tree," followed by "Have You Planted *Your* Tree Yet?" Students in the cast wore the equivalents of bumper stickers, T-shirts with names or slogans printed on them: "National Music Camp," "Where the Wild Things Are" stamped in yellow under a sketch of the old library, "Greenpeace" and then across the back of a black shirt, white letters reading NINEINCHNAILS. Since the boy wearing the shirt had a long blond pony tail and looked Scandinavian, I thought the phrase Finnish or perhaps Norwegian. A student enlightened me. Nine Inch Nails was a musical group, "probably not your kind of group," the girl told me. When not performing, students read or did homework. I saw a boy race through the crossword puzzle in the *New York Times*. During two evenings Courtnay, a girl in my course in nature writing, and a tree then the belly of a dragon among other things in the opera, read John McPhee's *Pine Barrens*. Because rehearsals were new to me, I did not know how to occupy myself. To fill the hours I jotted down observations, once noting that "the role plays the person, not the person the role." By the third night, however, I began to think myself part of the production, and instead of standing aside, I was drawn into the performance. Not only did I begin to cheer the students' improvements silently, but my own small role became important, not for myself but for others. I did not want to let the cast down. I wanted to be good enough to slip on and off the stage unnoticed. Tony felt the same way, and endlessly we discussed entrances and timing. Several times we walked the stage, measuring my long stride against his short one.

Three thousand people attended the two performances. "The evening was magical," Vicki told me later. The magic resulted from hard work. As I choreograph the flow of noun and verb through para-graphs, so every moment of the performance was planned. Late each evening Paul Phillips the conductor and Nafe Katter the director dis-sected the rehearsal. Nafe spared no one, and as he churned through the rehearsal and approached my entrance, I shrank in my seat. I was back in third grade. I had forgotten to bring my homework to school, and knowing that the teacher was going to call on me, I tried to be incon-spicuous. I failed. Nafe saw me step on the train of Tamino's robe. He saw me catch my toe under the corner of a board and stumble. The day after he told me to pretend to sing, the *Willimantic Chronicle* ran an arti-cle describing Nafe's methods, noting that among other things he encouraged "English professor Sam Pickering to lip sync the arias" so I was not "the only one on stage not moving his mouth." For the next four nights I stood before the mirror in the bathroom watching myself praise Isis and Osiris. In performance I was not bad, and if the article had not appeared, friends might have thought I sang. Indeed during the week after the performance a woman came by my office. "I just wanted," she said, "to tell you what a beautiful voice you have." On my confessing that I only pretended to sing, she got huffy. "Look," she said, "anyone with a voice as lovely as yours does not have to be modest."

For the opera I grew a beard. Despite the explanation that the beard was a prop for *The Magic Flute,* friends insisted that I was making "an unfortunate fashion statement." "When the magic goes down," I told Mike, Pat, and George one Saturday at the Mansfield Parents' and Chil-dren's Basketball Game, "you guys won't be there; I will." And it was magical, in great part because it took so much work. Of course I also had fun. Printed on white tape above two hooks in the dressing room was my name. Not since football at MBA had my name appeared above a hook. Never had I worn so much makeup, and for dress rehearsals and performances I became a greasepaint native of Asia Minor. I caked "Golden Tan" on my skin, worked "Negro" through my beard and eye-brows, filled the lines of my face with black, and rubbed white on my cheekbones, eyelids, down the ridge of my nose, and over the knobs on my brow. For two evenings I strode out of the Arabian Nights, and in my imagination thundered through Tabriz and Safnarra, Kish, Dizful, and Kirmanshah, a sword whirling yellow above my head, cutting through air like birdsong. The costume also transformed me. I wore a dark blue velour tunic, trousers, and boots. Over them draped a loose sandwich board of golden cloth, decorated with bright stitching at the neck and along the sides. I enjoyed swishing about in the costume. Although the outfit was designed for the Opera Theatre of St. Louis twelve or so years ago and was battered, probably having been seen on stages in Birmingham and Knoxville, Toledo, Ames, and Bismarck, the clothes made me feel exotic, just the fellow to have a harem of wives and not twenty children but forty, fifty, maybe even seventy-five. "The flute's magic sound," as my "aria" put it, even made me think better of the university and of myself. Would that an invisible hand could have scrawled advice for all students across my sandwich board, something like, "Work hard and take advantage of the university so that when the magic occurs, you, too, will be part of it."

At nine, the morning after the second performance, I went to the Campus Barber Shop, and George cut my hair and shaved my beard. Never before had a barber shaved me. I associated such shavings with the assassination of big-city crime bosses, bodies lumpy in chairs, faces bound in towels, and blood seeping through sheets and pooling in catchments behind clots of hair. Being shaved was a treat, almost worth the inevitable bullet, I thought as George wrapped hot towels around my head, then pulled and massaged, the sharp razor mowing across my skin. Afterward came brisk wintergreen and a soothing cloud of powder. I floated home, my face and imagination tingling. Eliza, however, pulled me back to earth and to Bic and Gillette Foamy. "Daddy," she said, opening the kitchen door, "you look so dorky." Despite the shave and my ordinary outfit of sportcoat and trousers, costume remained on my mind. Three hours later I boarded a flight for Rockford, Illinois. Two rows up from me in an aisle seat sat a man wearing an expensive shirt. While the collar was white, the body was striped, blue alternating with white. After every forty stripes a broad green band appeared, slicing down the body of the shirt like a drainage ditch through a contoured field. On the empty seat beside him the man put two carousels of slides. He was a dentist, and throughout the flight he raised slides of mouths up to the light and peered at them intently. The slides were colorful and from a distance resembled coral reefs, the teeth white and glowing, black holes appearing where hunks had been whacked out. The reefs must have lain off a big city, for trash had been dumped on them, here a bicycle pump, there a pitchfork. The trash attracted fish, and the eyes of many small creatures glowed from crevices. Fish were not the only animals drawn to the reefs. Near the end of the flight a stewardess knelt in the aisle beside the man and resting her left arm on his seat, cranked her head back, opened her jaws, and with the index finger of her right hand pointed to something behind her upper incisors. Although I undid my seatbelt, hunkered down, and scanned her mouth carefully, I was able to obtain little more than a fleeting glimpse of dark enamel. The stewardess, though, and her masticatory problem became pulp for thought, returning to mind the following morning as I ate breakfast in the Geneva Room Breakfast Shoppe attached to the Holiday Inn in Rockford. I was hungry, and although I suspected I was making a mistake, I ordered eggs benedict. Alas, the Hollandaise sauce was thick and pellucid and clung to the roof of my mouth like plaque. I did not finish breakfast and left the shop bilious. Music, though, bubbled to my relief, not the "flute's magic sound" but the Rockford Alpine Kiwanis Club, singing "Ida, sweet as apple cider, sweeter than all I know." The words were familiar, and I followed my ear into a meeting room and joined the cast. This time I did not pretend. I sang: "Blue Moon," "I'm Always Chasing Rainbows," and the finale, "America, the Beautiful."

Back in Connecticut the "fruited plains" were still tightly budded, but the warm abracadabra of spring was on the wind. Two days later a red-shouldered hawk hunched on a limb above the woodpile, the cere sunny above its beak and its orange breast blowing and rippled by waves of white feathers. At the sheep barn lambs cried, and starlings hopped through the froth of wool along the backs of ewes gathered at the feeding troughs like matrons around bridge tables. Woodpeckers drummed in the woods, and, in lowlands frogs rang and snapped, sometimes sounding like castanets, other times like tambourines. Robins appeared and ran through the damp furrows of the Ogushwitz meadow. Frozen wetlands melted, the ground first cracking underfoot then spraying out into soft, sucking patties. Buds of alders turned a gentle purple, and thorns on honey locust seemed less stark. In the hills creeks lost their fangs as the ice rolled into globes resembling bright candies or bumpy platters of nuts.

The real clairvoyant does not envision the distant; instead he discovers enchantment in the familiar and the immediate. Sometimes I think I have wasted most of my life, blinded by the faraway and the unimportant. Bewitched by grades and the desire for a Phi Beta Kappa key, I collected A's, not learning in college. In April I flew to Tennessee and Sewanee to lecture. Whenever I was free, I slipped idea and thought and wandered down the Cumberland Plateau through Shake Rag Hollow. Ledges had broken from the sandstone bluffs, and unlike the smooth, almost polite hills of Connecticut's Eastern Uplands, Shake Rag was bony and arthritic with spurs. Curving beneath an overhang wind blew fast and cold. Far above buzzards glided over the valley. Pouring through cracks in the sandstone, water washed out limestone, forming caves that gaped and drew me. There are no caves in Mansfield, and lacking mystery the landscape is almost too benign, or so I thought in Tennessee. Perhaps I was spellbound. Copperheads and canebrake rattlesnakes live amid the boulders of Shake Rag, and although the weather was not warm enough for them to leave their dens, the possibility of seeing snakes made me more observant, if not careful, and increased the magic of my wandering. Except for the distant rumble of a jet airplane, the hills were silent, birdsong tagging across the slopes and the throaty rush of streams not seeming noise but notes of a visual symphony. A blue and gray flycatcher leapt off a branch and exploded in a flutter of quarter notes. A winter wren popped in and out of rocks, almost ringing. Warblers skittered through the trees: yellow throats, black-throated greens, and then a flock of myrtles, their yellow rumps clapping in the sunlight.

The steep bluffs resembled hanging gardens. Under ledges near the top were the remnants of the nests of dirt daubers, the tops eroded and the bottoms resembling the imprints of long, thin fingers. Wedged in a crevice a pod of spider eggs swelled. Ridges of iron cut like veins through the sandstone. Lower down the slope, water dripped forming lily pads of moss, and often the ledges seemed giant shells gathered about seaside pools. Lichens blossomed in bouquets of white, gold, green, purple, and rust. Grapevines tangled through the tops of saplings then stretched upward into tall oaks. Down the bluff basswood was as big as walls, picket fences of suckers rising around their trunks. Buckeyes towered in columns, their bark plates more elegant than dining room and cupboard dish. Leaves had not appeared on the big buckeyes, but about them saplings had broken into leaf to gather light before the high canopy formed a basin and caught the sun. Clinging to fists of dirt along the bluff were marginal woodfern, mountain spleenwort, and walking fern, banners of this last waving over the ground then digging tips into the soil to start new plants. Early saxifrage grew on the ledges, and I chewed its leaves and then those of sweet cicely.

A thick, wet snow fell in Connecticut the day before I flew south, and I spent the afternoon walking around Tift Pond. The snow turned twigs into soft muntins and the spaces between into panes, pulling sight into hard, clean channels. In traveling to Tennessee I quick-stepped into spring, and instead of being drawn taut my sight flowed, ebbing and spreading like a pool across the forest floor, catching leaf and flower but always lapping outward. Fernleaf phacelia covered the tops of boulders in a blue haze. Along the ground ran bloodroot, gill, larkspur, great chickweed, white trillium, geranium, violets both blue and yellow, rue anemone, crinkleroot, and toadshade, the blossoms of this last fragrant as bourbon and its red patches so dark they seemed aged. The fuzzy stems of hepatica snared sight and shined like silver fur. Under the shadow of a rock were minute shakers of pepper and salt. Along the bank of a stream wood poppies bloomed, resembling yellow saucers from a child's tea set. A blanket of dutchman's breeches wrinkled down a shady slope; through seams in its fan-like green leaves trout lilies dangled in trumpets. A white butterfly bobbed swiftly past; a brown dusky wing spread its wings in bloom. A spring azure tumbled by, resembling a fragile scrap of blue paper. May apples grew together in green puddles, the leaves spreading out and down in umbrellas.

I almost lost all fear of snakes when I saw the May apples. According to Mother Noon tea made from them purged venom. In fact the wares of the hollow could have stocked Noonday. Dutchman's breeches were good in poultices, and a wash made from the roots of toadshade cured pinkeye. Bloodroot removed warts, and hepatica cured both piles and persistent coughs. The tonic I found in the woods was not of Mother Noon's making, though, but of spring itself, not something to make me stand on desks again, as my correspondent from Chicago urged, but something to clear the eye and give a bounce to the step. I doused myself in Shake Rag Hollow, and four days later when I returned home, spring was in the house. "Daddy," Eliza said, "you *don't* look dorky any more." "You obviously had a good trip," Vicki said. "Yes," I answered, "a magical trip. But then, all this is magical, too," I added, the faces of Francis, Edward, and Eliza blooming around the kitchen table. "Mr.

Pickering," Lew said stepping into my office the next morning after class, "my father grows daffodils for a hobby. Each year he cuts at least ten thousand blossoms. Most he gives to hospitals and nursing homes. He says he likes to bring sunshine to people. Anyway," Lew continued, suddenly shy as he opened a box and handed me an armful of spring, "he wanted you to have these."

Trespassing

A HEAVY GATE BLOCKED THE DIRT ROAD. Made from pipes painted white and banded with red warning stripes, the gate hung on two iron bars. Bolted to the middle of the gate was a white metal sign stamped with black letters. STATE PROPERTY, it read, NO TRESPASSING. I took the black racer I found on the road and after wedging its mouth open with a thick twig stretched it through the pipes so that the head gaped over the NO, blocking two legs of the N from sight. No longer did the snake resemble a flattened branch. On the fence its body seemed to expand, coiling quick into odor and mood. Flies landed on the snake, and after perching for a moment on the twig in the snake's mouth, one crawled down the throat. Virginia creeper grew along the bank beside the fence. I broke off a bunch of new leaves and ground them into my palms washing off the smell of road and waste. I rubbed my hands up and down my thighs, drying them on my jeans, and then smiling, walked around the gate into the STATE PROPERTY.

For years I have trespassed. For me a closed gate is an open invitation to explore. Writers, of course, forever trespass, wandering beyond the margins of good behavior into off-limits and then converting private property into public page. Indeed much of the attraction of writing is that it opens life. A writer must stray from path and turnpike, and so I roam days, clambering over fences and pushing through pasture and wood. Occasionally I snag trousers on a barb, but the cuts never tear the rich fabric of my hours. I can find snakes at the edges of woods, and I know where muskrats live. On Monday I brought a wood turtle home to show Eliza, and so far this July I have picked six quarts of wild raspberries. They grow in the field beyond the no trespassing sign, not only red and black raspberries but a third kind which seems a hybrid of the first two. The canes billow around a small rise in the field in thick green tufts, and in the sun berries glisten by the bushel, not by the quart. Yet I am the only human picker, gate and sign, I suppose, deterring other people.

Much as I pay little attention to fences and signs, so I ignore those of decorum and push unseen into conversations. In June I traveled to Cape Cod and at a banquet for honors students talked about curiosity. Arriving early at my hotel I ordered a seafood Caesar salad at "The Pub." At a nearby table three lawyers discussed opponents in a recent case. "They have gone the sleaze route together for thirty years," one said. "Yes," the man at his left answered, "They'll stoop to anything. Phony documents, you name it, anything." Two weeks ago at 6:30 in the morning I drove to Manchester to have the brakes repaired on the Mazda. While the rear shoes were being replaced, I walked up Center Street to the Whole Donut. After I ordered a medium-sized cup of coffee and a chocolate doughnut frosted with coconut, I sat at a booth and taking out an orange pencil and a small CVS spiral notebook began to eavesdrop. Cars and dogs dominated conversation. A man in a blue T-shirt with SUPERCREW printed across the front wanted to get rid of a white Labrador puppy. His landlord disliked dogs and had hit the puppy with a rake. A young woman working behind the counter was interested. Her boyfriend owned "a greyhound and black lab mix." The dog was dopey and roamed the shore of a pond near where they lived, searching for dead fish. When he found a fish, the dog picked it up and walked around all day with it in his mouth. The white labrador appealed to her, the girl explained, because her sister once owned "a fuzzy white dog that was mostly spitz." One afternoon when she was driving near Colchester, the sister saw a man throw a bag from a car window. Curious, she stopped. Inside was the spitz. "It was a good dog," the girl recalled. "We had it six or seven years, and then one day it ran into the road and got kind of squashed." "My puppy is good, too," the man said. "I have raised her right. She eats out of a stainless steel bowl. I don't believe animals should eat off plastic. With the dog," he continued, "I'll give you the bowl, her braided rope, a rawhide bone, some puppy chow, and a bottle of Pepto-Bismol. She has a little diarrhea, and every morning I give her a dose of Pepto-Bismol."

"You and the puppy," a bearded man said to the girl, "would look good in my Camaro." "Is it a four-door?" the girl asked; "I hate four-doors. The first car I had was a Lynx that my father bought me for three thousand dollars. It had four doors." A man driving a gray pickup with a red bug shield in front of the radiator bought a cup of coffee and the day's special pastry, a cherry doughnut. Sitting down across the aisle from me, he entered the conversation, saying, "Cars ain't that cheap any more." "I ought to know. I just spent $201 getting mine fixed," a woman smoking a cigarette burst out; "I didn't have the money and had to borrow from my mother." The doughnut shop was without fences, and people jumped in and out of conversations. Maybe the real attraction of trespassing is that it confines one to the present. Alert to the moment, people don't dig up the past, as the saying goes, or tote the future. "Working?" the bearded man asked a man in shorts who was drinking coffee and eating a squat doughnut filled with Boston creme. "I worked my ass off yesterday," the man said. "I ripped a roof off, plywooded and shingled it in twelve hours. Just me and a kid. Of course it was a small roof, only seven squares, but, by God, we worked." "Did we get our hearing aids this morning?" one of the girls behind the counter asked. "I haven't seen them," the other girl replied, "or the two titsy rolls."

Many customers were in a hurry and did not talk. Often, though, their shirts spoke for them, advertising "Bob's Stores" or "The World's Largest Source of Natural Gas." Written across the chest of somebody's hall monitor was the declaration "Teachers Have Class." Above the letters stretched a line of eight ripe apples, each topped by a sprig of green leaves. Two women sat in the booth in front of me. They dressed similarly, wearing white trousers, white socks, and white sneakers. While one woman had removed the laces from her shoes, the other kept the laces in but left them untied. Both wore black T-shirts. Printed in white up the right side from waist to armpit was "Narnia 1992." Stamped on the front of the shirt was the face of Aslan, the hero of C. S. Lewis's inspirational novels describing the imaginary kingdom Narnia. Instead of a great and terrifying lion, however, Aslan resembled a rumpled fuzzy slipper. Although the women often laughed, they talked in a whisper. Still, I heard the phrase "fourth world missions." "Find people who believe in your vision," one said. The other nodded and said something I did not understand after which she added, "It's sort of lunar." "Yo," the other replied, "yes, yes."

I stayed at the Whole Donut for an hour. Then I returned to the garage. My car was still on the rack, and so I went to the waiting room. A small man, his stomach bulging like a gourd, sat on a sofa reading the morning paper. He smiled, and I nodded and sat in a plastic chair. A coffee machine gasped, and the hostess of a television show gurgled from a set high on the wall. I drank too much coffee at the doughnut shop, and the television program bored me, the hostess appearing to be one of the missing titsy rolls. Eavesdropping determined my mood, and I could not sit quietly. I wanted to hoist myself over a gate and swing uninvited through a conversation. The opportunity soon arose. A tall, white-haired man with blue eyes and a hooked nose entered the room and sat on the sofa. "What's wrong with your car?" he asked the short man. Before the man could put down his newspaper and reply, the tall man continued, providing a joint-by-joint, gear-by-gear mechanical history of his 1982 Ford. Diagnosis of the car's sundry ailments always proved difficult, and this, he informed the short man, was the eighth garage to which he had brought the Ford. The speaker was a supply house of automotive information. Having replaced most of the accessories on his car, he described stores where one could buy the cheapest parts in eastern Connecticut, places that sold lights, radios, mufflers, oil filters, alternators, and carburetors. "Last week," he said, "I found a place that will mount tires free." "Dear God," I interrupted, "who would want to do that for free? Why," I exclaimed, "I would not mount a tire for money, not even one of those cute steel-belted radials." For a moment the white-haired man paused, his eyes cloudy with incomprehension. Finally, awareness spread like the open sky over his brow, and he blinked and said, "No, I didn't mean . . ." "I know what you meant," I said. "I wouldn't mount a tire, not even one wearing chains and studs," I continued, standing and opening the door to leave the room. "The very idea."

The conventional, particularly when it is detailed into the soporific, provokes the fence-climber in my nature. In May I spoke at Rockford College in Rockford, Illinois. Resembling great mills, Pentecostal churches cover downtown blocks, their chapels, schools, community centers, and nursing homes blocking out the sun. At the beginning of my talk I alluded to the local fervor. "Never," I began, "have I seen such big churches." They were so large, I continued, that I was giving "serious thought to moving to town and opening one of God's own businesses, a rattlesnake farm, so that true believers would never run short of serpents to toss around on Sunday mornings." Such remarks are the beginning of story, and I say them, in part, because I hope others will slide under sharp propriety and follow me to tale and observation. Of course, the truth is probably that I say such things because I am a foolish and impatient person. That aside, however, rarely do people trail after me into the forbidden brush, and such tales as I fashion are always episodic and their casts of characters thin, limited to myself and a series of flat, cartoon-like individuals. In April I visited my old college Sewanee. On the road outside Murfreesboro I stopped at the Firecracker Warehouse and bought a box of block busters. The box contained forty packs of firecrackers, each pack loaded with sixteen one-and-a-half-inch "Super Charged Flashlight Crackers." That night at one o'clock I set off the firecrackers. The noise flushed students from their rooms, many of them resembling the picture on the front of the box of Crackers: a blue dragon with yellow eyes, snorting fire and smoke, its red hair curling like a nest of angry worms. Wearing pajamas I mingled with the newly awakened and nodded in agreement whenever anyone expressed disgust at "such a silly undergraduate prank." Few people delighted in the disturbance, and fashioning the next episode was left to me alone.

I did not disappoint myself. At a literary gathering the following afternoon a distinguished poet gave a public lecture. Before the poet spoke, however, I introduced him. I had done extensive research, and the introduction was detailed. The June bug was, I informed listeners, the poet's favorite insect. He drove a four-door Chevrolet Celebrity "with no bumper stickers." He owned four cats: Wanda Fay, Sammy Ray, Wayne Dwayne, and Rosebud Sue Ann. The redbud was his favorite tree, and the raccoon his preferred animal, these last being particularly fond of the cornbread the poet put out for them under his bird feeder. The poet himself fancied cornbread, and no meal made him smack his chops louder than cornbread, turnip greens, and a pot of pinto beans. At such a devouring little pleased the poet more than listening to music, especially his favorite pop songs, "Runaround Sue" and "Breaking Up Is Hard to Do." "Yes," I told the crowd, "the poet is a man of taste, discretion, and personality," although this last, I noted, "occasionally comes on a bit strong." "He is," I continued, "slightly addicted to fireworks, as some of you may have heard last night. For that lapse he has nevertheless, apologized to both me and the administration of this college. We accepted his apology willingly, and we urge you to do the same. Allowance must always be made for true genius, for like a fly it only falls upon ordure to imbibe new life."

Rarely am I asked to make introductions. The form itself is so circumscribed by convention that it resembles a pasture, fenced and far from the sharp tooth of plow and man. Acquaintances know that if I introduce someone I am liable to batter at the structure of the form and then burst into the pasture and, as the saying goes, put my foot in it. No man is consistent however. While I forgive my own trespasses, thinking they have a boyish charm, I do not tolerate the trespasses of boys themselves. I have aged, and when I climb a fence, I do so with care, unlike rude, hormonal youth. When a student says "No problem" to me when he should say "Thank you" or, better yet, "Thank you, great teacher," I immediately think of several problems to which I would like to subject him, most, I should add, of the high Aztec or Mohawk variety. In May I found a message in my box in the English department. A student who missed the final examination left his telephone number and asked me to call. I did so immediately. "May I please speak to Jim Watkins," I said when a boy picked up the telephone. "This is," the boy answered. The absence of *he* after *is* so trespassed against what I know to be polite form that I cared little for the boy's plight. Instead of murmuring long and sympathetically, I said crisply, "You must talk to the dean. The matter is out of my hands. Have a nice day. Good-bye."

In his first letter home from camp, Francis wrote that one of his counselors used "inappropriate language" and provided two scouring examples. On a camping trip the same counselor burned a leech, even though Francis asked him not to. "It wiggled around and suffered," Francis wrote, "then grew fat and wiggled one last time in agony before dying." Three minutes after reading the letter I talked to the director of the camp. In my conversation I used the expression "this is." Unlike the student, however, I forged past the verb and piled a mound of *in-* and *im-* words around the counselor's trespasses, words like *insensitive, improper,* and *inappropriate.* Thirty years ago I was a counselor at the same camp, and although boyish I did not use harsh language to children or harm the small things of this earth. The camp is a fine place, one fenced in by propriety and all those *no* signs I think necessary for the happiness of my little boys. "Bill," Francis wrote in his next letter, "is better. He is almost a different person."

To write, a person must observe, and observation often provokes questions, turning one into a crank if not a trespasser. At a recent meeting of the school board an administrator stated that dealing with a particular matter "has been a time-management issue." "If you had said 'took a lot of time,'" I interjected, "you would have saved not only time but letters, twelve letters, in fact, the difference between fourteen and twenty-six. And," I continued, "the angels rejoice in heaven whenever a letter is saved. They don't give a happy damn about people, but they are eager to convert alphas and omegas." Not only do cranks read and worry about children's letters, but they know leeches are annelids, members of a marvelous family of creatures including, among some fourteen thousand others, earth and blood worms and from the seashore bristle worms, the bodies of these last divided into more than a hundred segments. For the person willing to trespass far enough to marvel at the ordinary, days are a series of small joys, and life itself is wondrous. Late in May Vicki, the children, and I hiked up West Ridge Trail to the top of Cardigan Mountain, near Canaan, New Hampshire. The day was muggy, and in the woods black flies spun around us like cars rushing into a rotary, buzzing and sharp. I hardly noticed the flies, though, for I wandered from the path to look at flowers: Clintonia, wake robin, painted trillium, trout lilies, Canada mayflower, hobblebush, and then rose twisted stalk, its stem jutting out in jags and its flowers small pink bells. "The flies were bad," Edward said when we reached the top of the mountain, "but the view is great, and this is the high point of my life." "Yes," I answered, "3,121 feet high." "No, Daddy," Edward said, "I climbed higher than that and so did you, looking at flowers."

Observance determines remembrance. Like a fence, detail protects experience from the hurly-burly of happenings that trample event out of memory. Oddly, in wandering beyond convention the trespasser preserves not a pasture or wood lot but his own life, and, against their wills, sometimes the lives of those nearest him. Along with wayside flowers I observe the doings of my children, locking what will become their remembered pasts behind a gate of words. Because I have described the cards they gave me the children will never be free to revisit this past Father's Day and trespassing against detail create memory. While Francis forgot Father's Day, Edward made a card, one and a half inches square. On the front Edward sketched a baseball diamond. Stick men wearing gloves played the positions. Despite the small size of the card Edward created motion; the catcher leaned forward behind the plate and the pitcher rolled toward him off the mound. The drawing was not centered, though, and Edward didn't have room to draw the right fielder. Consequently my team has only eight players. "To Dad. Happy Fathers Day. From Ed," Edward wrote in pencil, neglecting to put the apostrophe between the *r* and the *s* in *Father's*. Eliza's card was bigger, five and a half by four and a half inches. "To Dad," she wrote in red ink, "I hope you will like your moskita kalectsin." Drawn on the card were two insects, the first resembling a small beetle leaping into flight and spreading its front wings or elytra, the other a fat, goofy fly with a long snout and antennae thicker than sheaves of wheat. Pasted below the drawings were the leggy remains of stilt bugs that Eliza found beneath the storm windows in the upstairs bathroom.

Although Father's Day slipped his mind, Francis will remember this year's picnic at Northwest School. The day was wet, and the picnic was held in the auditorium. A mime performed, first by himself then with children. The mime selected Francis to play an imaginary baseball game. The mime was not successful. "A ball?" Francis said later. "I thought he was throwing logs at me, and I pretended to split them, lifting the maul over my head then swinging it toward the ground." If Francis's acting mystified both mime and audience, my performance clearly irked Vicki. The first two acts went well and conventionally with grinder, potato chip, and fudge cake. Then at the beginning of the third act the woman sitting next to me said, "Oh, you're the famous Sam Pickering. I know," she said, smiling and thinking of the movie *Dead Poets Society*, "that you must get tired of people asking you." She got no further. "You're damn right I'm tired of it," I broke out; "the whole thing drives me crazy." And right here, alas, I vaulted over the gate and began to whoop and flap my arms, my voice rising like that of an owl on the *o*'s and falling with a spluttering plop on the *p*'s. "You went too far again," Vicki said later, flicking her eyes at me like a snake's tongue; "I don't know why I ever married you." Vicki married me, of course, because when she sensed the time was right for her to marry, I was the only person who asked her. And, in truth, she may have married because I trespassed. The old adage, "Faint heart ne'er won fair lady," may be the bounder's motto, but it contains wisdom.

From a distance or before marriage trespassers appeal to people who chafe at convention and hope that their lives will differ from those led by parents and acquaintances. Young dreamers, though, are not alone in hankering after trespassers. Trustees of colleges often look back upon their student days fondly, to be sure with chagrin for some of their foolishness but mostly with admiration for the boyish doings of those few years before they became corporate. Thus when trustees begin searches for college presidents they will, at first, say they are looking for someone to exert moral authority or provide cultural and intellectual leadership.

What lies behind the statement is the memory of a favorite teacher, both memory and man scrubbed and buffed by time. In the flesh, however, even the polished seem tarnished, and when a real teacher appears, he rarely shines. The real teacher educates himself by wandering and encourages others to do the same. Only platitudes come easily, and as the real teacher struggles to think for himself and fumbles through inappropriate words attempting to describe those thoughts, he makes others uncomfortable. In grasping for understanding he loses dignity and often seems a buffoon. Even worse, the attempt to be truthful can anger. Honesty threatens the fictions people erect to make social life possible. Belief, whether right or wrong, supports culture, and if people begin to wander from accepted paths and tear down *no* signs, community shatters. Then all those things done or accomplished past boyhood suddenly seem silly. In private, in an essay, one acknowledges the foolishness of accomplishment, maybe even the meaninglessness of life itself. In public one rallies to structure and buttresses the old fictions. My own explorations don't go far. Although I have tossed words over hedges, I have never really pushed through briars at the side of a path. I have not dug up a thought; instead I have wandered soft glades, places not visited by everyone but places familiar to people who read. And, of course, I have hammered *no* signs throughout my children's days. I want my babies to be happy. If they stick to well-trod thoroughfares, life will be easier for them, and maybe kinder to them, and so I batter them into correct grammar and appropriate language. Yet when they are asleep, sometimes I go into their bedrooms, kiss them, and whisper, "I'm sorry."

In my ambivalent behavior I resemble college trustees. Instead of the real teacher they select the easy manager, a person comfortable with budgets and platitudes. In May, Hampden-Sydney College began looking for a president. An all-male school with a thousand students, Hampden-Sydney is located near Farmville, Virginia. Founded in 1776 the school has enjoyed a long history of modest aspirations and quiet successes. Still, its reputation is parochial. Few people beyond Virginia know its name, and those friends to whom I mentioned the college confused it with Hampton University near Norfolk. The trustees wanted their school to be more than local, and in May I was asked to apply for the presidency. Reputation is often only bunting, and I applied not because I thought making the school better known was important but because I have a sentimental attachment to Virginia. Mother grew up in

Richmond, and I spent many summers in Hanover Courthouse. I also thought my family would like the rural South and that I might be able to lead others, not to make their school "outstanding" but to help it rise from third or fourth rank to second. Dominated by extravagant claim and promise, most educational talk smacks of advertising, and I realized that modest intention would brand me a trespasser, someone not fit to "transform" a college. Nevertheless I went to Virginia for interviews. In driving through Richmond I passed the building which housed my grandfather's store at the corner of Grace and Fifth. It was now a woman's shop called Hit or Miss. Both the surrounding streets and the store itself were empty, and the business seemed a miss, much as I reckoned my interviews would be. Still, the premonition did not bother me, and I looked forward to seeing great-aunt Elizabeth and my cousin Sherry. At Aunt Elizabeth's house Chinese chestnuts bloomed in long fingers. On a rock a river otter groomed itself. At Cumberland Courthouse I ate a lunch that the poet would have envied: snap beans, black-eyed peas, turnip greens, and cornbread. I talked to one of Mother's bridesmaids. She told me what she knew about Hampden-Sydney then asked about my children. "They are doing wonderfully," I said. "Of course they are," she said; "they are Katharine's grandchildren."

The people who interviewed me were gracious and generous, and I had fun. When asked what my personal goals were, I told the truth, saying that goals were for the young and that aside from seduction I had not had a goal since I was seventeen, adding that I wanted only to get through the rest of my days with a remnant of decorum and maybe live a little longer than an acquaintance or two. "Also I hope I won't be found out, but that," I said, "is a pipedream." On being asked over cocktails if I liked horses, I said I preferred gerbils and hamsters. A trustee took me to a picnic, and I changed clothes in a pasture. Under the trousers to my suit I wore boxer shorts decorated with small green cats. On seeing the shorts the man said, "I have seen it all now." "You've seen most of it," I responded, "but certainly not all." Or at least that's what I tell friends I said. What the truth is I don't know. I exaggerate so much that not only friends but even I think the truths I tell fiction. Indeed as I age, reality itself grows progressively vague and mysterious. Sometimes I think the things which have happened to me since my boyish days are just the dreams of a few moments. Instead of sitting at a card table writing, I know that I am stretched out dying in a ditch, my body crushed in a car wreck, and the events of the last thirty years figments of a disordered imagination. Other people have similar thoughts. "Daddy," Eliza said to me as we walked toward Mirror Lake holding hands, "life goes by so fast. I can't really believe this is my life. It goes by so fast that you don't really notice it."

Occasionally I think imagined life more real than actual life. I know that I telephoned Prince Edward Academy, a private school in Farmville, and asked about tuition, in the process learning that Latin had been dropped from the curriculum. But did I really say I would not accept the presidency unless the trustees gave Vicki a West Highland terrier? Did the man to whom I was talking answer, "Dog? Why not a Porsche? You'd like a Porsche." And did I say, "Porsche, hell! They are too low to the ground. Every time I got in and out I'd fart." What I do know is that I daydreamed about Hampden-Sydney. In my mind I roamed the campus running my hands raw across the red brick. Not only did I learn the names of all the trees on campus but I climbed some. I wrote speeches and presented honorary degrees to people whom I admired: to Mr. Rogers, heart of the best neighborhood on television, and to John Sawhill, head of the Nature Conservancy. I also awarded a degree to Little Richard because he makes me smile. Little Richard did not deliver a speech at graduation. Instead he sang "Tutti Frutti," and I joined him. Dreaming, of course, is done alone. Maybe the real trespasser is a solitary, and genuine trespassing is interior, wandering mind instead of hill and field. "Sam is too free a spirit to become a college president," a dean said to a friend recently. The dean was right. In part I trespass because I want to be alone, a desire, I am afraid, that has been passed along to the children. In June Eliza began day camp. "I don't want to make any friends," she told me before camp; "if I don't make any, I won't miss them when camp is over." "Oh, Eliza," I began. "But daddy," she continued, "sometimes I want to be solitary."

To be in the middle of life maybe one has to be solitary or at least drift from crowds and thoroughfares. Beyond "No Trespassing" wonder thrives, and after a walk I wrestle with language, not shaping phrases to win or fool but to celebrate. "You have had no administrative experience," a trustee said to me. "What makes you think you could manage Hampden-Sydney?" "Arrogance, sheer arrogance," I answered. What I almost said was that maybe the key to happiness lay in avoiding managing. Instead of channeling words into distortion perhaps the successful person allows himself to be managed, rolling with the pitch of hill and creek, following the rain and then standing silent like a root in a field, feeling sunlight clap warm through the air. For an essayist a college presidency would be a long mistake, and so I say odd things in order to remain free to wander the woods. From a worldly point of view I would have been a successful president, one of those admirable people remembered by portrait and building. In being tacked into substance by convention, though, I would have lost the ability to escape others, and myself. "Sam," Vicki said when Hampden-Sydney fell through, "I don't know whether you are a sap or not. Sometimes I think you are a jackass; other times I think you are a little right, maybe even smart, especially," she added, pausing, "when you find raspberries."

On the kitchen table was a blue bowl filled with more wild raspberries. I discovered them growing in an abandoned field. With them and the earlier quarts I picked, I brought home a peck of seasonal impressions. For the first two weeks in July I spent part of every day wandering beyond signs. For the first time I noticed moosewood or striped maple, its trunk streaked with green and its leaves big as hams and almost tropical. In the middle of a wood I found a dead white pine. The needles had turned pink and bursts of long, flames flickered through the half-light. Seeds hung from ashes in gouts, each pod a drop of water streaming upward, not down, the wing of the seed dangling behind like a damp khaki trail. At the corner of a pasture stood two old apple trees, the green fruits gnarled as character, bumpy and bent, their sides sucked inward and wrinkled into ridges. May and June were cool, and flowers bloomed late this year. Several mornings I stood in a meadow amid fleabane high as my chest, the frayed blossoms pouring around me like milk. Winter cress had gone to seed, and the pods curled up in hangers like old-fashioned coatracks. Throughout the meadow Canada thistle bloomed, its blossoms gentle above the fleabane but its leaves spiny and tearing. Vervain rose in pitchforks, the square stems green and soft in the middle but hard and molded by red on the edges. Against the light the tines on the forks seemed sharp until they bloomed and blue flowers wrapped them in aprons. In the damp, joe-pye weed was waist high. Starting at the tips, new purple leaves turned green around creamy bundles of blossoms. Tall meadow rue grew frail along the Fenton River. In a breeze the stamens of each flower swayed like a squad of long soldiers, white and straight in parade dress, yellow bonnets on their heads.

The ringing of bees rose above milkweed while on the leaves red milkweed beetles doubled themselves. From the leaf axils of nettles green flowers tumbled out in cowlicks. In the abandoned bell of hornet's nest a nursery web spider clutched a white egg. Above the fleabane white butterflies spun upward in cylinders of air. A black-winged damselfly wobbled through an elderberry, and like salt and pepper shakers twelve-spotted dragonflies turned white and black above the beaver pond. A wren bubbled as it darted from a tree to hunt bugs in brush. In a sandy field birdfoot trefoil bloomed in yellow puddles, and ground beetles hid under rocks. Along a creek skunk cabbage splayed out and melted into the ground. The ribbed leaves of false hellebore collapsed and turned yellow then brown.

I picked flowers for Vicki, bundles so big that she did not arrange them in vases but set them around the house in buckets. I found a robin's egg for Eliza and mailed snake skins to the boys at camp. One morning I spent two hours kneeling on a rock in the middle of the Fenton River watching gnats swim through the air in currents, just above the stream. Around me water hurried and dug between rocks like screws twisting through soft wood. Beside the bank quiet basins resembled wishing wells, their bottoms coppery with rocks bright as pennies. Over them royal fern swayed yellow in the light. A towhee landed on a limb and began calling. The feathers on his head resembled a black cap, and the inside of his tail a white morning suit edged with black. For a moment I thought him a barrister, rising stuffy in a British court and incessantly saying "to whit."

Rooms and words can confine. Inside I often listen to myself and occasionally have thought I sounded knowledgeable. Outside amid the quiet of bird, leaf, and stream, I know better. I decided to learn the names of grasses. How could I swell so pompous about moral authority and cultural leadership, I thought, when I didn't recognize the grasses I saw every day? "Daddy, you are very nice-looking," Eliza said one afternoon when I returned from the woods, "but very old looking." Although wandering brightened my days, I was tired, and I limited myself to a handful of grasses. Next summer, I told myself, I could wander farther afield. Like a pink mist, red top hovered near the ground by the fence and ran along the road slicing up the side of Horsebarn Hill.

Timothy bloomed lavender in the sun, its mute anthers dangling and shaking like purple clappers. By a wetland reed canary grass was shoulder high. The long panicle had expanded, and sharp purple lines cut through it like washes down a breaking slope. Smooth brome grass grew around a cornfield. Like a series of ridges rising sharp above yet shadowing those below, sandy triangles climbed the tight spikelet. From the side of ray grass, spikelets jutted stiffly out, their light green anthers yellow in the sun. Although I recognized deer-tongue, rarely did I mow through panic grasses to recognition. Much as they draw streams, wetlands pulled me, and for the first time I looked closely at rushes and sedges. With their spikelets clustered and joined by stems, the tops of meadow bulrush reminded me of bristly Tinkertoys. While the flowers of wool grass burst out in great sprays from the top of the stalk those of bog rush fell from the side. On my last walk I brought sedges home—hop, bog, and fringed sedge—and put them in a pitcher on my desk. I left them in the pitcher for several days, and Eliza asked when I was going to replace them. "Not for a while, honey," I said. "I'm resting."

Despite what I told Eliza, I won't rest much longer. Monkey flower and panicled tick-trefoil are about to bloom. Goldenrod is yellow, and I want to pick peppermint and bouncing bet for Vicki. Soon butterflies will hang on the big pasture thistles. Blackberries behind Unnamed Pond are swelling beyond green into red. By the time the boys return home from camp the berries will be black. Nailed to a tree on a hill above the blackberries is a red metal sign. Stamped on it in white letters is the warning. TRESPASSERS WILL BE PROSECUTED. Someone sprayed black paint over the last word, and from a distance the sign seems to say TRESPASSERS WILL BE. I thought about writing something over the black paint, but the words I considered seemed inadequate: *foolish, disappointed, happy, joyful*. At a time when *no* signs so stifle that people retreat from character into platitude, maybe it is enough just to assert that trespassers WILL BE.

Part Three: School Matters

Pedagogica Deserta

"DEAR MR. & MRS. PIKRING PLEAS don't get out to day after 5 in the evening." My wife and I found this note on our door one day in March after we returned from the market. Again rumor predicted trouble in Latakia and we had been warned. We stayed in our apartment that night. This, though, was nothing new; we had not been out on the streets after six o'clock since the end of December.

Each academic year the Council for International Exchange of Scholars sends some five hundred "Fulbrighters" to study and lecture abroad. Most go to Western and Eastern Europe and to, if not the westernized, at least the semi-industrialized, world. A number, however, end up in countries which drive sensitive men to drink before noon. In 1975 I taught English and American literature at the University of Jordan in Amman. This past year I was headed for Ghana. Early in the summer, though, a coup changed my plans, and in September my wife and I arrived in Damascus.

My post was at Tishreen University in Latakia, six and a half hours from Damascus by bus. A town of slightly over two hundred thousand people on the Mediterranean, Latakia is Syria's most important seaport. Before we left the United States, an official in Washington assured us that the city supported a thriving international community. Since the troubles in Beirut, he said, many people had moved to Latakia. The discrepancy between what was described and what we found was great. No native speakers of English lived in Latakia, or at least we never discovered any. Two months after we arrived we met a French couple and they became our only Western acquaintances. In the fall many Russians were present in the city. Later, after the Moslem Brothers, the terrorist organization, had assassinated a few, they disappeared into their compound, leaving us alone on the streets.

In September our embassy in Damascus tried to be helpful. Unfortunately they knew little about Tishreen University. Bloodied by violence between religious sects or "insects," as a student mistakenly labeled them in an essay, and stuck in the morass of the Middle East's internecine warfare, Syria itself is not easy to know. Policy can change like the desert wind, and rumor often becomes the only truth. Classes were scheduled to begin at Tishreen on September 29, so after a week of waiting in Damascus while the embassy tried to find out if Latakia had calmed down after recent riots, we left on a bus. Finding an apartment was easy. The assistant dean asked how much we had to spend, then told us he knew a flat for that price. Not surprisingly, we later learned that the owner's wife was the dean's cousin. Assuredly the dean received a commission, but that was all right, for our landlord was a superb man. He was an Alawite general in the army. Because they are only 10 percent of the population, Alawite Moslems from northern Syria had long been treated as second-class citizens by the dominant Sunni majority, some 70 percent of the population. Alawites have a distinct appearance. The backs of Alawites' heads are flatter and less rounded than those of the general Syrian population. This is so, Sunnis say unkindly, because generations of poor Alawites have pushed against the backs of their children's heads in order to get them out of the house and direct them towards Damascus and work. Since good jobs have traditionally been difficult for Alawites to obtain, a disproportionate number made careers in the army. When Hafez al-Assad, an Alawite, became president of Syria in a coup in 1970, the Alawite military came into its own, financially and socially. For a time this did not cause much resentment among the Sunnis. Assad brought much-needed stability, and as schools were built in, and electricity spread to, poor isolated villages, the Alawite underclass rose above servantdom. Although a Sunni town, Latakia was surrounded by Alawite villages, and many of my students were villagers seizing the first opportunity for higher education they had ever been offered.

During the past three years, however, resentment of Alawites has grown. Business has been bad and military expenditure awesomely high. Sunni merchants blame Assad for the nation's economic problems and accuse the government and army of being corrupt. Corruption is widespread in the Mideast and Syria is probably no worse than her neighbors. Much Sunni resentment focuses on the Officers' Club. Assad's brother controls it and uses its funds to finance his private army, which has a reputation for savage brutality. To do business in Syria, Western corporations make under-the-table contributions to the

Officers' Club. One businessman told me about the time he flew from Athens to Damascus carrying forty thousand dollars in his suitcase for the Club. Customs expected him and he was whisked through without his bags being touched. In hopes of destabilizing the government and bringing an Islamic revolution to Syria, the Moslem Brothers have viciously assassinated the Alawite educated elite, whether or not individual Alawites have had anything to do with the government. The disenchanted Sunni majority has not lent the Brothers active aid. On the other hand, the Sunnis have not condemned them either. Since there are few Moslem Brothers, the Sunnis reason that when the government falls they will be able to brush them aside and establish a government of their own. During the past year, hatreds have boiled. The good are silent, and violence has spiraled as the government's secret police have viciously repressed dissent or potential dissent. At times during the year, Aleppo and Hama seemed foreign countries brought back under Damascus's rule only by tank law. "You don't know," a student told me with tears in her eyes; "the people die like rain."

As a general, our landlord was well guarded. Three to seven soldiers lived on the third floor of our building. So when bullets began to fly in Latakia in the spring, we felt almost safe. Growing accustomed to automatic rifles, however, is not easy for a teacher used to nothing more violent than the correspondence column of *PMLA*. Sometimes when we climbed the eighty-three steps to our fifth-floor apartment, a new guard would greet us gun in hand. Frequently visitors received escorts up to our flat. Most took it in stride, but some never returned.

Tishreen University consisted of four faculties: engineering, medicine, agriculture, and letters. For years construction of a new university has been under way. Unfortunately the end is not in sight, and the faculty of letters is, and will be for many more years, housed in a secondary school building just beyond the freight entrance to the port. Unlike the United States, where the shortcomings of education are obvious, Third World countries seem to believe that education will provide the answers to all problems. Consequently governments in such countries, in part because rational dissent is stifled, confuse themselves with the Great First Cause and create universities by decree. The planning comes later—if indeed it ever comes. Tishreen University as it is now is not the gleam that shone in the eye of its creator. In my first day at the faculty of letters, I asked to see the library. The assistant dean showed me an empty room and said, "This is the library, but we don't have any books yet." Since the English department itself was only two years old, the absence of books, although unexpected, did not unduly startle me.

In Jordan, when I was asked what I wanted to teach, I tried to be a good advertisement for my country, and, trusting to the fairness of my colleagues, said I would teach what the department needed. As a consequence, I, like everybody else, taught one elementary and two upper-class courses each semester. In Syria, when queried about courses, I responded as I had done in Jordan. I made a mistake. Dignity is important in Syria, and the accommodating man is often seen as a person of no consequence, to be used and abused at will. First-year classes at Tishreen contained large numbers of students, sometimes two hundred. By the second year many had left the university, so that frequently classes had only forty students. In the first semester I taught sixteen hours of courses. Unlike my three Syrian professorial colleagues, as I later found out, I had all first-year students. Six hours a week I taught prose and ten hours a week I taught composition. The chairman, a "specialist" in prose and poetry, taught only second-year students; the assistant dean, a specialist in drama, did the same. Most of the first-year courses were taught by two demonstrators, recent graduates of Syrian universities, and me. This almost graduate-assistant kind of treatment did not initially make me resentful. To obtain a Ph.D., my Syrian colleagues had to work harder, make compromises, and suffer indignities which I knew I could not imagine. Theirs was a real achievement, one that marked them out in Syrian eyes as not merely different from, but better than, others.

My wife and I were the only Americans the majority of my students had ever met, and our style of living was different from that of the Syrian professors. Instead of buying a car or taking a taxi to the university, I walked across town. Unlike Syrian professors, who dressed carefully and kept themselves immaculate by never erasing a blackboard, I wore corduroy trousers, a corduroy sports jacket, and blue topsiders to class. When I erased my own blackboard and got covered with chalk during a two-hour class, students were astonished. Since the lowest workers, porters in the harbor, wore sneakers, my shoes provoked much discussion. Six months after classes began a student told me that he and his friends had been puzzled by my shoes at first. "Every Doctor of Language in the university considered himself a minister," he said, "but you did not. We honor you for your shoes. You come to work." Since I did not appear as a minister, confusion about me and my position lasted throughout the year. In April a student who had attended almost every class but whose English was poor asked me if I were an elementary school teacher in America. Numerous times surprised students told my wife and me, "Americans are so simple and humble."

These students meant to compliment us. Complexity often implied corruption or favoritism. Our accessibility or simplicity or democracy was thought admirable. In contrast to the typical Syrian faculty member, though, I must have appeared as a man who carried himself in a manner unbecoming his position. By doing so I cut the ground from under the faculty member's hard-won achievement and obliquely undermined the hierarchical structure of university life. No wonder first-year courses were loaded on me and I was never consulted about my timetable. I only began a slow burn, however, when I learned that while I taught six days a week, my fellow professors were teaching four. Although I began to teach on September 29, the chairman did not appear until two and a half weeks later. The third full-time Ph.D. member of the department did not arrive until November. The random appearance of the faculty members was paralleled by the students' attendance. Tishreen was an open university. Many students never attended classes because they held jobs, quite a few teaching in remote villages. Given eight years to pass the required courses, other students pursued relaxed courses of study. As in secondary schools, university education depended primarily upon rote learning. Class discussions, particularly those discussions which raised ideas different from the professor's, were discouraged. At the end of term, professors' lecture notes were mimeographed and sold for seventy-five cents a course. If a student memorized these, he had a good chance of passing. To some extent the notes took the place of assigned texts. The university did not have a bookstore; often local booksellers were not informed what texts were needed for courses until it was too late to order them. As a result, many students never had books, and one member of the department even suggested that books were an unnecessary expense. He proposed that all professors have their notes printed before lectures started. That way, he explained, students would not have to buy books like *The Old Man and the Sea* or *The Penguin Book of English Verse*.

With new students appearing even on the last day of class, December

24, teaching was a tedious matter of repetition, careful enunciation, and slow speech. In mid-November a latecomer sent me a note asking for help. "The nam of gud. Dear my teacher: Good morning," he began. "I am very later in my lossons," he continued, "pleas help me if you can help me and I promsed you, I will read my lossons in this tim. I wrote this wards becoues the time of examniisoins are not very long. Pleas help me, I need this helps very much. If you help me I am thankful you very much. pleas/pleas/pleas." Although all my students were majoring in English, and this meant taking eight to ten courses in English a year, like this boy few could actually speak much English. In most cases, secondary schools provided them with little background. Of the approximately two hundred and fifty people who taught English in the Latakia school province, fewer than a third were full-time teachers, and these taught other subjects as well. The rest were part-timers. Most of these part-timers were my students, usually poor boys and girls who knew almost no English and could not write a simple sentence.

Long and narrow, with 150 students clustered on benches, my classroom was at the front of the building. Tractor trailers loaded with weapons from the Soviet Union or consumer goods from China thundered by at two-minute intervals. Teaching was impossible while a truck passed. Eventually I obtained a microphone. Unfortunately it was stuck together more with hope than tape and was usually broken. When it was repaired, either I couldn't use it because of static in the system or the electricity was off. As a result, I lectured by cupping my hands in front of my mouth and shouting. Throat sprays and pills quickly became more necessary to my teaching than paper and pencils.

The students themselves were a diverse group of boys and girls—rich and poor, religious and nonreligious, young and old. For many it was the first time they had attended class with members of the opposite sex. English was extremely popular; French was taught, but only fifty or sixty students each year majored in French in comparison to the three hundred and fifty or four hundred who majored in English. Enrollment numbers were never exact; faculty members never received a roll, and the president himself was not sure how many students were in the university.

My students dreamed of going to America. Despite Syria's close military ties with the Soviet Union, Russian was not taught because students refused to study it. If language is the greatest propaganda instrument in the world, then the West has won massive propaganda victories in the Middle East. Indeed America's cultural hegemony over Syria is amazing. Although our trade with Syria is not large, and ignorance of America is widespread, Syrians equate American with modernity and opportunity. Many students had cousins in the United States and studied English in hopes that it would provide the key which would magically open doors to America and golden treasures. "Go to America," a boy told me, "and shine shoes. Return to Syria a merchant." Recently I received a letter from a student who had been raised in a small mountain village. He does not know where America is but he wants to come here. This past summer he went for a daylong trip in the Mediterranean. The man who took him told him that they were near America. "I have acquainted on somebody from Saudane," the boy wrote; "he took me in a sojourn with him in the sea. We were about to reach AMERICA. I asserted him to do so but he didn't do it. He was always in a hurry and for this I hated him."

Countries in transition from an agricultural to a mixed economy often overvalue modernity and suffer from what in effect are cultural inferiority complexes. In Syria even those who hope that the resurgence of Islam will enable them to retain some traditional mores recognize that the forces of modernization are practically impossible to oppose successfully. "The eastern," a conservative Moslem girl wrote, "now are hanging by the western's tail. The westerns have the progression in working, living, eating, but the easterns haven't. The westerns have also the dissoulution. And by the time we will have it so." Syrian secondary schools drum in the "dissoulution": the failings of America and capitalism. Occasionally attacks on capitalism cropped up in student essays. "The capitalist people," a boy wrote, "believe in all kinds of stealing in order to ern much money. They built their happiness on other's misery. Money made them unhuman creatures as if they live in a forest." For most students such attacks did not take. *Capitalism* like *socialism* was a word used in politics rather than life. The vast majority of students wanted wealth and their own businesses. In developing countries in which tribal and traditional ties are being shattered, money confers both dignity and identity. Much is made, however, of our racial problems. On several occasions—and this must appear somewhere in a secondary school textbook—students asked me if it were true that a black man had to bow down whenever he met a white man on the street. Questions about race, though, seemed to come more from curiosity than belief in racial equality. Students greeted interracial marriage with disgust, and blacks, I was told, had smaller brains than whites. Students had little knowledge of American government or politics, though one boy did predict that Ronald Reagan would not be elected president because "he will be 70 after erection."

The abilities of first-year students varied, but at the beginning of the year most were at a third- or fourth-grade level in English. They could not speak or write a sentence, and in first-term composition I taught primarily simple and compound sentences. During the second term I made students write three- to five-hundred-word essays, and I read and marked more than eighteen hundred of these. Much improvement was made, but I am certain that this coming year the deluge of rote learning will wash away the effects of my classes. The students were my joy. We had no adult friends aside from our landlord and his wife, neither of whom spoke English; the French couple; occasional American visitors from Damascus; and one teacher who lived an hour and a half away. The faculty at Tishreen was not sophisticated enough to realize that the only Americans in Latakia were just a teacher and his wife. Two members of the faculty told us they had been warned to avoid us because we might work for the CIA. When the cultural affairs officer from the embassy delivered our air freight, he visited the assistant dean. As soon as he left, the dean asked me if he was a spy. From that date in early October until mid-February, the assistant dean avoided me and we did not speak. I soon had a huge following among the students and was not always sure I enjoyed it. After classes every day, students walked uptown with me to talk and practice their English. In the mornings they waited to catch me on the way to the university. My wife and I rarely went shopping without running into students. During the break between terms we went to Jordan and Egypt. Unable to find us, students left notes at the stores we frequented. When we returned in February, a bookseller gave me the following letter: "I havn't ability to express about my feelings. is it correct that a man need to see his brother again? if you have, or if you would like. When you catch this letter, said to my friend, who is the owner of library, when I can see you Because I need to see you. I am eager to see you. Your effectionate friend."

Many students invited us to their villages, and the days we spent visiting were the happiest and also the most tiring—because no one spoke

English well—that we spent in Syria. At the beginning of the year when they could not speak English, students communicated by notes which they labored over like sculptors. A girl who had worked on her simple sentences invited us to her village, writing "I live in a Beutiful town. It is called Jable. I want you to visit it with your waif. In jable my family will BE happy when you and your waif visits us. my mother also want me to calld us. Then if you came Y feel too happy. I writ theses composition Becaus Y respect you. And Y admir very much of your waif. It is a gentil and Beautiful woman, what you said, yes, or no. A simple sentences."

Early in the year a teacher warned me that professors did not talk to students outside the classroom or office. I paid no attention to the warning and must have been a disturbing influence. Vague cultural assumptions support the Fulbright scholar program. Generally it is assumed that academic exchanges build bridges between peoples and cultures and, in the case of American grantees, broaden their horizons. What the Council for International Exchange of Scholars does not say, but what the State Department correctly assumes, is that the Fulbright program is a propaganda effort. In Syria the State Department seems interested in establishing links with, and presenting a favorable picture of America to the people who have or will have influence. Emphasis is not on the masses but on the elite, and with Syrian-American relations at an ebb, the cultural branch of the embassy avoids disturbing the sensibilities of those who have power. In contrast, the Fulbright program, as it developed in my case, was educationally revolutionary. American simplicity and democracy go counter to the Syrian educational system. By encouraging class discussion and original thought, and by treating the students seriously, I implicitly criticized the methods of other professors. Fresh educational air is not necessarily pleasant educational air, and instead of attracting the educational elites, I put them off. Although the nation is ostensibly socialist, people in Syria are not equal. Money and position shape castes, and tribal, village, and religious ties often determine success in the university and outside it. At the end of the first term, the assistant dean lost his post. The ways of Syrian university politics are complex but I was told the student association had complained repeatedly that he was arrogant. During the second term, the man cultivated student leaders. Outside the cafeteria was a battered Ping-Pong table. One day the former dean appeared with a pair of sneakers. He put them in his desk and wore them when he played table tennis with students. Dignity mattered a great deal to him; associating with students was bad enough but wearing porter's shoes must have been hateful. What he thought about me, my shoes, and my easy ways, I shudder to think. As propaganda I think my year was successful, but not in the way it was intended to be. Since returning to the United States I have received many letters from students. These students are comparatively poor and will never become cabinet ministers or Ph.D.s, but will instead be housewives and village schoolmasters. None will ever be singled out for cultivation by our State Department. Instead of building cultural bridges with the people who politically or educationally matter in the Third World, perhaps the Fulbright program undermines such constructions.

Syria exhausted me emotionally. Syrian students, with their society in transition from a conservative rural Moslem culture to a modified urban Western culture, face confusing problems. Rarely do they express their confusion or frustration publicly because they believe it will be interpreted as political disenchantment and they themselves will disappear. In private, they ask for personal advice and voice their disgust with the state of the nation. Private revenge, although discouraged by sophisticated urbanites, still exists in villages. One boy, for example, after recounting a harsh tale to me, asked if I thought he should kill the villain of the piece. Some people in his village thought he should, he said, but he wondered what a Westerner would do.

For women, Western feminist concerns about equal job opportunity are beside the point. In Syria women are not equal to men. The birth of a girl is often an occasion for unhappiness rather than celebration. "I was the second girl in my family," a student wrote; "my father went out for three days when I was born in spite of he already had a son." Because I was the representative of a progressive society, students frequently believed that I could solve problems which involved a conflict between conservative family or community traditions and modern individualism. Traditionally, a girl's father chose her husband for her. "But the great wish is to meet my love and to live with him forever," a girl wrote in an essay; "I pray for him. And I implore God to gather us one day. I Love person sine when my age was six years . . . Each of can't live without the other. But the great problem is my family. They did not agree to marry him . . . and there is another problem takes place now. A lawer came to my hous. And he became friend of my family. He want to engage me. All my family agree with him. But I refuse. Because I want to marry my childhood friend whom I love. I hate that Lawer. I wish I did not see him. But he always comes to our house. This is my problem. So I ask professor pickering to advice me. But not at the class. And God bless you."

Amid what would be considered harsh repression from a Western feminist point of view was a great deal of joy. The girls in my classes forever gathered in the hall and giggled and laughed. When I assigned telling a typical Syrian story as an essay topic, many more girls than boys turned in broadly funny tales. "In Lattakia," one wrote, "when women meet other's they began to talk and talk in many speech and sometimes they tells special jokes like: Once two old wife and husband wanted to ceremony at their eighty marriage feast. The old woman wore her Soiree dress, then they brought the great dinnar to made their party more beautiful. The old woman bent to put the soup for her husband her pap loll out of her dress and they nearly touched the vessel of the soup. The old man said: I want the soup without meat."

Until they came to know me, I was a cartoon figure to many students. Their perception of me, like the Third World's perception of America and Americans, had in great part been shaped by television, advertising, pop music, and B-grade films. If Westerners are not thought immoral, they are certainly believed to be enlightened, and this led to embarrassing moments. Having received many invitations, I suspected nothing when a female student invited me to a cake party after class one Thursday in the school cafeteria. When Thursday afternoon arrived, the girl told me that the authorities would not let her have the party at school; consequently, she had changed its location to her apartment and said her cousin would drive us there. A white Mercedes picked us up at the front gate. As we roared through Latakia at what seemed fifty miles an hour, the girl added that none of her friends had been able to come to the party, and she hoped I would understand. Perspiration and understanding broke out simultaneously. Resembling a set from an Egyptian film, the apartment was furnished in "Louis Farouk," gaudy and expensive gold and silver. Between two sofas in the living room was a low table. On it were several kinds of luncheon meats, trays of nuts, assorted cheeses, oranges, apples, lemons, chocolates, two types of imported beer, a bottle of Johnnie Walker, two bowls of pink and white carnations, and a three-layered cake covered with whipped cream. When I sat on a couch, the girl sat next to me. The cousin started to sit opposite, but then he looked at his watch, said he had an important appointment, apologized, and left.

When I am nervous, I talk. For an hour I talked incessantly while the girl stared into my eyes. When I slowly slid to the end of the couch, she followed, serving me cake and urging me to drink. When half my backside hung over the edge of the couch and I was in danger of falling on the floor and undergoing I knew not what, I stood up and asked to see the apartment. Politely I complimented the bathroom; my hostess responded by turning on the water and asking if I would like a bath. An imitation tiger-skin blanket covered the double bed in the bedroom. If ever I wanted, she said, I could spend the night there. This was Arab hospitality carried to an extreme. Finally, after I had inspected all the rooms, I felt unable to face the couch again. I thanked my hostess and cut and ran—not, however, without presents for my wife: the carnations and the remains of the cake.

Although it may seem obvious, I was never certain what the girl wanted. Rich and living alone—something unique among the students—I suspect she may have fallen prey to the cinematic depletion of Westerners. Maybe she simply wanted a high grade. Perhaps, however, this was an attempt to compromise me. As the only Americans in Latakia, my wife and I suffered from paranoia. People stared at us wherever we went and we could not fade into a crowd. By December we began to think we were watched. Our mail had been routinely opened; often letters did not arrive, and occasionally odd things happened. When my wife's parents opened one of her letters, they found a snapshot inside. They assumed it was our landlord's family. It wasn't; the people were strangers. The person reading the mail probably had several letters open on his desk, and when he re-sealed them he mistakenly put the picture into my wife's letter.

According to rumor, there were nineteen secret police organizations in Syria. I knew of five in Latakia, two having their local headquarters on streets immediately behind our apartment building. In the spring, an acquaintance who had a friend in one branch of the secret police obtained copies of reports on me. In all university classes there were spies—students paid to report on professors to branches of the secret police. Although this process did not bother me, because I was a foreigner and able to leave the country, it frightened and inhibited Syrian teachers. Only one aspect of the reports about me was interesting. It was alleged that I favored girls in my classes. Supposedly I cultivated their friendship, not for "sexual relations," but because I wanted to discuss politics with them. While at the "party" in the girl's apartment, I had asked her many questions about the problems in Latakia in order to keep us talking. Showing little interest in sex, I must have shown an immoderate concern about politics. Perhaps she was the source of the reports. Most probably she was not, but it is rather nice to think she might have been.

A student whose parents forced her to attend university wrote an essay in which she described her dislike of studying. "I always," she wrote, "asked our God to rest me from this calamity. I want to sleep without any think of the studies." This Fulbright lecturer seldom thought of studies. Grading compositions at home took much time, but class preparations were minimal. Day after day I repeated lessons in composition, trying to teach my students basic grammar rules. In prose I taught *The Old Man and the Sea* and the first forty pages of George Orwell's *Coming Up for Air*, this latter being a terrible choice for first-year students whose reading was frequently at the primer level. In composition I spent most of my time explaining idioms and defining simple words like *green* or *blue*, *living room* or *dining room*. Rarely was I able to venture very far into thematic topics; when I did, two-thirds of the class got lost. Similarly, my colleagues and I never discussed literature. The university and Syria itself did not provide the kind of atmosphere in which such thought could flourish. Good books in English could not be bought in Latakia, and since I was not an Arabist the possibility of research did not exist. Consequently every night I went to sleep as my student wished, "without any think of the studies."

For the Fulbrighter in Syria and perhaps in the Third World in general, what happens outside class influences the academic experience more than what happens in class. During the first weeks, thoughts abdominal replace thoughts intellectual; the anatomy changes and one becomes more bowel and less brain. Once things internal are acclimated, however, then external events and conditions determine the quality of the experience. Although my wife and I saw much of Syria, and although many nights in Latakia were filled with the sound of music—the *1812 Overture* with mortar and Kalishnikov effects—we were usually bored. The cinemas showed either broad Egyptian comedies or gory Italian and American gangster films. There was only one good restaurant in town, and it was frequently closed because of the troubles. To survive we bought a radio, listened to the BBC's Middle East service, and planned vacations. We had a television set, and once a week saw *The Virginian*. Sometimes *Switch* appeared. Those were evenings to be savored. In general Syrian television was a dreary patriotic affair. Throughout the year party functionaries opened power plants and Assad accepted flowers from masses of cheering schoolchildren. The patriotic drumbeat never stopped, and on the evening news, the words *America, Israel, Zionism*, and *Camp David* were intoned like a litany as the government blamed the country's troubles on external enemies. Few people took the propaganda seriously. According to a shopkeeper in Latakia, the mayor called the merchants together in order to explain why there was inflation and trade was poor. Camp David was behind everything, the mayor explained. When the mayor finished speaking, a merchant stood up in the back of the room and said, "You are mayor. When Camp David came to Latakia, why didn't you order the police to arrest him and put him on a bus to another city?"

When the Iranians first took the embassy personnel in Tehran hostage, and the State Department conducted a token evacuation of Americans from eleven Moslem countries, our feelings of isolation and vulnerability grew. We were out on a limb far from Damascus and communication was difficult. Our landlord had a telephone, but the link between Latakia and Damascus was often disrupted. In class, students who were nervous because I might leave Syria assured me that my wife and I had nothing to fear. "We Moslems love you," students said, and promised to take us to their villages if danger developed. One acquaintance, whose brother-in-law was a general, declared he would transport us to his village in a tank if necessary. The first time I heard such things, they made me more comfortable. But after I had been reassured some forty times, nagging worries and feelings of vulnerability began to grow. Where there was so much smoke, or concern, there must be a little flame.

The only member of the English department whom I considered a friend indirectly fanned our worries. A Syrian and a brilliant student, he had completed his Ph.D. in Britain, published essays in good academic journals, and returned to Syria to teach. Apolitical and perhaps the most honest man I have ever met—and in Syria to be completely honest is practically impossible, and even dangerous—he suffered from the accidental disability of being an Alawite. He had taught at the University of Damascus but had left, among other reasons, because he feared for his life. Now as assassinations spread to Latakia—two streets behind our apartment a man was murdered—my friend became convinced that an attempt would be made on his life. Although he lived an hour and a half from Latakia, he spent two nights a week in the city. In the afternoons he would visit and confide his fears to us. His was the only literate conversation we enjoyed in English, but since his fears were all-consuming, our subject matter was limited. In our isolation—feeling under siege because of Iran, hearing America violently attacked on television as President Assad tried to blame Syria's internal troubles on external forces, and talking with our friend about little except his fears—we began to get the wind up. With no one to help us put our foolish anxieties into reasonable perspective, we retreated more into our apartment and marked off on the calendar the days until term break. Eventually, the embassy called us to Damascus to inform us about the state of affairs in Syria and Iran and to reassure us, but it is in the nature of a diplomat's existence, in Syria at least, that form and circumstance separate him from what is happening in the country. He reads scores of informative reports and dines with important people, but these are no substitute for being able to move about freely. Knowing that we felt isolated, the ambassador suggested that we move to the University of Damascus or the University of Aleppo. Aleppo, he said, was a particularly appealing city. Because I felt responsible for my students at Tishreen and because of a perhaps adolescent dislike of appearing a quitter, we remained in Latakia. This was fortunate; two months later disturbances shattered Aleppo's appeal, and the university, to all intents and purposes, closed for the year.

Like scholars, diplomats depend upon sources for their knowledge. Aside from us, the embassy had no sources in Latakia or at least what they had been told about the city was inaccurate. After we returned, the embassy's assurances, which had sounded so good in Damascus, evaporated like rain on a hot sidewalk. On those days which my frightened colleague spent in Latakia he went to the university by different means and different ways. By mid-December I, too, varied my route to the university. The end of term brought great relief. Almost immediately my wife and I left for a month in Jordan and Egypt, where we would not stand out but would be just two more nondescript Westerners. There we could escape the shackling authentic experience and enjoy the comfortable tourist experience.

We returned to Latakia in late January, relaxed and ready for whatever came our way. I graded five hundred exams, and when classes began ten days late, on February 19, I was eager to start. I was also pleased because I had demanded and gotten a second-year course: Shakespeare. The chairman, a man with vast resources of cunning, invited us to his home for tea and urged me to teach nineteen hours—prose, composition, and Shakespeare. I had learned my lesson the first term and was not accommodating; composition and Shakespeare were enough. Once classes started, the term quickly became chaotic.

Although Syria suffers from a dearth of trained teachers, no exemptions—legal ones—are made for military service. University professors must serve like everyone else. Frequently, this is done after they finish their graduate education and are teaching at a university. Usually after they complete their basic training, they are seconded back to the university, where they teach as second lieutenants, distinguishable from civilians only in that they receive military pay instead of the much higher university pay. Basic training begins in the fall and spring, not in the summer, so that universities are often left with half-taught courses on their hands. In March my friend who had been frightened for his life left the university to begin his military training. At the same time, the chairman, who was also liable for military service, came down with an attack of diabetes and disappeared to Damascus for two or three weeks. In April one of our two demonstrators left Syria on an AID fellowship to work for his Ph.D. in the United States. The only persons left to teach courses were the assistant dean (recently demoted to an ordinary teacher), the second demonstrator, and I. Courses were piled on the demonstrator, and the assistant dean's wife taught part-time. The department muddled through the term. Many courses, however, went untaught for long periods and the students suffered.

Even more inhibiting to the students' progress than the absence of professors was the state of the nation. In February violence in Syria grew geometrically. By the end of the month Aleppo was a little Beirut, and the Fulbright lecturer at the University of Aleppo had left the country. Latakia was not so violent. Assassinations occasionally occurred in the daytime, but most trouble happened at night. Dynamite bombs exploded practically every evening. Counting them became exciting and addictive; in May, when a temporary calm descended, life seemed less intense and we were bored. Because they did not want to be on the streets at dusk, students avoided classes that met after four o'clock. My colleagues received notes and telephone calls threatening their lives. My teaching timetable changed radically. No one consulted me; I learned about the changes only when I went to class at the wrong time. Eventually a reason for the changing timetable became apparent as my morning classes became afternoon classes. A foreigner was safer on the streets late in the afternoon than was a Syrian professor. Guards armed with tommy guns had guarded the faculty of letters twenty-four hours a day throughout the year. Now there were more guards. And on some days when there had been much trouble the night before, guards seemed to outnumber students.

Gun battles began to occur at night between the Moslem Brothers and their sympathizers and the secret police. In Aleppo and elsewhere, Russians were murdered. This caused us some worry because many Latakians who had never seen Americans assumed we were Russians. People often said "Russians" in a derogatory tone when we passed them on the street. "My God, sir, my God," a nervous girl burst out in class, "you look so like a Russian." Acquaintances became worried, and one of them took matters into his own hands. Meeting us in town, he informed us he had done us a favor. He said he had discovered that many people thought we were Russians. To prevent a mistake, he said, he had spread the word to people who in turn would inform those behind the violence that we were not Russians but Americans. For such a favor I was not grateful. Nobody gets things right in Syria; it is better for one to lie low and say nothing than to have attention called to one.

The troubles came to a head in March. Elite commandos appeared in Latakia, and together with the secret police they attempted to crush the terrorists. From the balcony of our apartment I watched gun battles. For two weeks life in the university slowed almost to a halt. Students stayed away from class. Out of 150 students in a class, 2 or 3 who lived nearby might show up. Walking to school was nerve-wracking yet intoxicating. From behind sandbags, soldiers guarded street corners; often streets were completely empty or sealed off. In its disregard for truth, rumor waxed poetic. Although the violence subsided—it never died out—classes did not return to normal. It would have been abnormal if they had. Alawite students from the villages were frightened and in some cases embittered. Sunnis became more opposed to the government while Christians damning both sects withdrew into their own community. The only assurance that the future seemed to hold was that someday there would be more and worse violence.

During the period of the worst troubles, I taught *Hamlet* to those members of my second-year class who attended. The parallels between Hamlet's rotten Denmark and Assad's Syria were marked. Corruption from the head of state infected the nation. Many of the people resembled Hamlets or Rosencrantzes and Guildensterns. Either, like Hamlet, they found their world and responsibilities bewildering, or like Rosencrantz and Guildenstern they were little spokes joined to a big wheel which if it broke would destroy them. Obliquely I drew comparisons between Denmark and Syria. Some understood and were knowingly silent; others studiously and carefully avoided understanding. The majority were not linguistically good enough to move beyond language to theme. If, however, most of my students did not see, or refused to acknowledge, the contemporary significance of *Hamlet,* I could not avoid it. During the first term I faced no important academic questions. Although I was teaching at a lower level than I had taught before, I knew that what I was doing was useful. English was the language of science, medicine, business, and diplomacy. Like a technician I was teaching a skill my students could use. In contrast, *Hamlet* forced me to confront the relevancy of literature to one's spiritual or moral life, a subject which I had always avoided in the United States because it seemed beside the point. Was my teaching *Hamlet,* which universalized and indirectly examined the problems Syrians faced, one of the most meaningful things I had ever done in a classroom? Or was teaching literature and discussing Hamlet's inaction while people were dying on the streets one of the most meaningless things I ever did? I never decided.

Throughout the turmoil, my relationship with the students was constant. On Easter I received several cards. My Moslem students knew that it was an occasion for a Christian feast, but most were not sure which one. One card read, "Merry Christmas to My Sincerely Teacher." When my wife became ill in late April, eight Moslem girls, all wrapped in scarves and long coats, came to our apartment with armfuls of flowers. On the last day of class, students asked me to autograph their books. There were tears, reluctant farewells, and assertions of lasting friendship. The year had been difficult; I made almost no adult friends. I had done no research. The seven hundred examinations I graded in July convinced me that three-quarters of my students would never complete their studies and the bright dreams and hopes they shared with me would wither. No Fulbright lecturer would follow me to Latakia the next year and most of what I had accomplished with even my best students would be swiftly erased.

I went to Syria when my professional career seemed at a crossroads. A university press had accepted my second book. My articles appeared in the better literary quarterlies, and journals were beginning to write me soliciting essays. When I was in Syria, my professional work had to be shunted aside; unseized opportunities passed on to other people. Was the year worth it? I am not sure, but when I left, a student presented a poem she had written to me. Although it was embarrassingly fulsome, its sentiment touched me and almost made me glad I had spent the year in Syria. "Like the effect of sunset," she wrote,

Like the gone of the moon,
Like shadwos spreading in space,
Like storms which destroy everything
Like all these things your leaving will be.
Your leaving will fill our hearts with sadness and dullness.
Your leaving will take the dynamic thing from our life.
Maybe my words is very big for the situation,
But that is really what I feel and the truth.
So you have the right by getting back home again,
But we havn't the right to possess whom we loved.
God bless you, our wonderful teacher.
God help you with your coming life.
God take care of you and your wife fore ever.
I want of you just to remember that there are
Students loves you and think of you forever.

At Cambridge

"WE TAKE AMERICANS FOR MANY REASONS. Either they are scholars, which you are not," Tom Henn began after I had been in Cambridge four weeks. Tom was right. I had not come to Britain to study. I had been a student at Sewanee, so disciplined that classmates called me "Machine" and sometimes made whirring or clanking sounds when I entered a room. Tom did not explain clearly why St. Catharine's admitted me. The college's reasons were probably as vague as my reasons for applying. In part I applied because I did not receive a Rhodes scholarship to Oxford. Although I never expected to win a scholarship, I didn't think I would be rejected either, and until December of my senior year, when I was interviewed by the Rhodes Committee, thoughts of green quadrangles, madrigals at dawn, and strawberries and cream for tea occasionally drifted through my dreams. Unfortunately, I bored easily and interviewed poorly in those days. Bromides did not bubble naturally and smoothly from my lips, and when asked a hackneyed or ponderous question I had trouble keeping my tongue in check. When asked about the mission of the United Nations, I tried to liven up the interview and said, "On the radio the other night, I heard a preacher say 'U.N. or U.S.—what's it going to be? We have to choose.' That struck me as interesting." That, alas, did not interest the committee, and drawing wit and wisdom from a highland preacher, I must have appeared remarkably provincial.

In truth, I was provincial, not, however, because of preachers. Only rarely did I hear preachers on the radio, and, when I did, I paid little attention to idea, listening instead for colorful language. In part I applied to Cambridge because I suspected that I had received a narrow education. At Sewanee I was a bookworm, studying seven days a week, thinking little, and observing less. Moreover, at that time Sewanee itself was provincial. Ten thousand acres atop the spur of a mountain, the college was contained both physically and intellectually. Among students cults of the South and the Christian gentleman flourished, and form often seemed more important than substance. "Our glorious mother ever be," students sang in the alma mater. Sewanee was a kind of mother, nurturing and protecting but also smothering. Much as first- and second-year courses in English were restricted to "great writers"— Homer, Sophocles, Aeschylus, Dante, Lucretius—so the whole university seemed turned toward the past, not a past of butchery and injustice, a past to anger and quicken, but a past of tradition empurpled by sentiment, a past so superior to the present that it sapped vital curiosity and led to cool satisfaction.

Even when problems beyond the mountain touched the college, Sewanee transformed them into the quaintly anecdotal and thus reduced their significance. Until my last year Clara's, the lone restaurant at Sewanee, was segregated. Then some people from Chattanooga staged a sit-in that coincided with the annual meeting of a secret college society. During the meeting students drank heavily, after which they roamed about waving lanterns and singing songs about George Washington. More raucous than melodious, the singing disturbed the early evening nap of an ancient relic of a bishop of Arkansas. "Jerry, what's that noise?" she asked a student who rented a room in her house. "Oh, it's nothing, Miss Amy," he said. "It's just a bunch of men from Grundy County, going down to Clara's to hang the sit-iners." "Dear me," Miss Amy replied. "I don't mind the men hanging those people, but I do wish they would give them a trial first."

I didn't know to which college to apply at Cambridge, and since no one at Sewanee seemed able to advise me, I chose St. Catharine's on a whim. Because my mother was named Katharine and once went to St. Catherine's School in Richmond, Virginia, and because a girl named Catherine was on my mind, I picked St. Catharine's. Realizing that the deadline for formal applications had long passed, I wrote a letter to Tom Henn, who supervised English studies at the college. I decided to read English at Cambridge because I had majored in English at Sewanee and didn't want to study hard for examinations. Tom agreed with me. "If you wanted to be a student," he told me shortly after my arrival, "you should have stayed in the United States." My letter to Tom was honest. I said that academic matters played no role in my wish to attend St. Catharine's. I explained that I wanted to travel and learn more about life. I also mentioned that I was over six feet tall and weighed about one hundred and ninety pounds. More than anything else, I said, I wanted to row. Although I didn't know it at the time, Tom was a fervent rowing man. Two and a half weeks after I mailed my letter, I received a note from the senior tutor. Although the application period had expired, he explained, the college might have a place for someone like me and he asked me to send testimonials and a transcript. I attended Cambridge on the "Pickering Fellowship," not one my parents had expected to fund. Recently I had won a three-year scholarship to law school at Virginia. Winning the scholarship gratified me, but I wasn't ready for law school. At Sewanee I made only one B. Even father called me a drudge, and when Virginia agreed to hold the scholarship for me while I studied at Cambridge, my parents underwrote the Pickering Fellowship.

When I went to Cambridge, becoming a teacher was far from my mind. Some of my teachers at Sewanee had been cranks, appealingly eccentric but wildly irresponsible. During the sit-in at Clara's, Abbo, my favorite teacher, brought a copy of the *National Geographic* to class. Opening the magazine, he held up a picture of bare natives gamboling along the banks of some dark African stream, and then, snorting and shaking his head, said scornfully, "These people want to go to school with you." No one spoke; Abbo's prejudices were legendary and so all-inclusive that most students shared at least one of his dislikes: Germans, Yankees, ignoramuses, pushy females, the newly rich, Catholics, and teetotalers. Also, we didn't take his pronouncements seriously, knowing that they flowed more from bottle than heart. Abbo drank heavily, and, one afternoon before an examination, he saw me in the hall and called me into his office. "Pickering, I am indisposed. Take this," he said, handing me the examination, "and go and write it on the blackboard." I wrote the examination on the board and when I finished took the copy back to Abbo. "Thank you, Pickering," he said. "Here is fifty cents. Go to Clara's and have a beer." Not wanting to take the money, I told Abbo I didn't drink. "I must do something for you, poor Pickering," he said. "Just take half the examination." I did as he instructed. The next week Abbo stopped me on campus. "Pickering," he said, "do you know you took only half the examination? I gave you an A because I am kind. But you must learn to follow directions or else there will be no hope for you."

The more outrageous Abbo's behavior, the deeper the impression he and his classes made upon me. Against what I then thought was my better nature, I grew almost to love the man and have not forgotten the authors read in his classes. While the matter of other, more respectable, courses soon fell like tired leaves into the brown mulch of college days, Abbo's Wordsworth, Byron, Carlyle, Ruskin, and Bagehot have remained green. Seeing, however, that successful teaching depended not upon the platitudinous virtues in which I wanted to believe—tolerance, sensitivity, even rectitude—but instead upon that lower thing personality, I decided that I would not teach.

Along with the knowledge that I would not be a teacher, I arrived in Cambridge believing literary criticism was mostly trivial, if not silly. As far back as I can remember, I have distrusted words, written or spoken. As a teenager at Sewanee sitting in classes often taught by men, I had been told, with national reputations, I suspended distrust, and until my junior year accepted the ingenious, buttressed by learning, for the actual and the true. Then one day a distinguished teacher called attention to some mistletoe appearing in a short story. "What," he asked, "is mistletoe?" "A parasite, probably in the same family as Spanish moss," answered a boy from Louisiana. "No, no, a hundred times no," the teacher answered. "Mistletoe is the sperm of the gods." Normally I wrote down everything the teacher said in class, but this time I paused. Before Christmas each year I went to my Aunt Lula's farm in Williamson County, Tennessee, and shot mistletoe down from the tops of trees. The plant I hung in the front hallway at home had little to do with gods or sperm. "If I kiss anybody under the mistletoe this year," I whispered to the boy next to me, "I am going to wear a rubber." Thinking myself wonderfully witty, I paused before I added "hat." From that moment on I suspended belief, and lectures which earlier I would have thought heavy with fertile learning struck me as barren.

Despite disenchantment with literary discourse, I attended class and took thorough notes. I liked making A's, not because they were signs of learning or because they were necessary to winning scholarships, but for themselves. I liked to add them up, much as I did the baseball cards I owned as a child, and one semester in which I made seven A's pleased me immensely. Out of habit and because I lived in a boarding house outside college and didn't know what else to do, I attended lectures my first year at Cambridge. Under no pressure to make a grade and suspicious of literary criticism, however, my attendance was spotty. Although Raymond Williams and George Steiner tried to bind literary criticism to moral choice, I was unconvinced, and the only course of lectures I attended regularly was a twice-weekly series given by a prominent female don. Although the lectures were informative, I attended more on compassionate than on intellectual grounds. Over three hundred students appeared at the first lecture. The don's delivery was dull, however, and despite her learning, the audience dropped off rapidly, so rapidly that by the time I wanted to stop attending myself the number of students was so low that I would have been missed. Rather than risk hurting the don's feelings, I stayed in the course. Only three students, including me, were present at the final lecture. Living in college my second year, I was closer to the lecture halls and might have attended more often had I not come down with a terrible cough. For weeks at a time, I heaved up blood at night. I tried all sorts of remedies, finally settling on milk, keeping a quart by the bed and sipping some whenever I began coughing. During the day I rarely coughed, except in lecture halls where the heat made me retch. Not only did the cough prevent me from attending lectures but for a while it made me think myself a second John Keats. Sensitive and doomed, I wrote a sheaf of fleshly poetry, adorned with wraiths, grapes, urns, breasts, and autumnal sighs.

More stimulating than lectures were the weekly tutorials with Tom Henn. Tom impressed me because along with critical studies he had written about fly fishing. During the Second World War, he had been a brigadier and wrote a manual describing German small arms. Tom was a character and institution like Abbo. Instead of dislikes which led Abbo away from literature and toward politics, Tom's enthusiasm for myth and Irish politics pulled him toward literature. Anglo-Irish, Tom told tales about the troubles of 1916. Three of the five boys he traveled home with from school that year, he said, were killed. The night his family's estate was slated to be burned, the raiders destroyed a house across the valley, not before, however, cleaning out the wine cellar and rendering themselves unfit for further mischief. With the exception of a paper considering whether or not a novel could be tragic, I recall nothing about the essays I wrote for Tom. Whatever I did, however, was undistinguished, and after the first term Tom passed me on to another supervisor.

Although my paper on the novel did not impress Tom, it affected me. Knowing my argument had to focus on specific books, I began reading Faulkner. Although I soon saw that his books contained the traditional elements of tragedy, I did not understand Faulkner until one afternoon in Bowes and Bowes I ran across Cleanth Brooks's *The Yoknapatawpha Country*. I looked at Brooks's book because Father once mentioned being at Vanderbilt with him. Brooks wanted, Father told me, to be a good trackman and most afternoons could be found circling endlessly around the football field. *The Yoknapatawpha Country* was a model of elegance and good sense, and reading it raised my opinion of literary criticism. The book did not lead me to make large claims for criticism, however; in fact, I thought debate over whether or not a novel could be a tragedy was silly. Interest in the form of a work seemed to me to ignore vital content and like an emphasis upon manners focused on the inessential.

That aside, though, Faulkner bewitched me, and I started writing a Southern novel. Not restrained by courses, I wrote rapidly. Speed and skill, though, are very different, and after finishing the novel, I threw it away. The tale began with a young Confederate officer returning to wife and home in Mississippi at the end of the Civil War. Although the man had lost his money, he had his wife and looked forward optimistically to building a new and better life. His wife was little more than a girl. He had married her in 1864 during the lull which followed Forrest's victory at Brice's Crossroads. The day he arrived home was hot and dusty. No one ran out to greet him, and only cicadas answered when he called his wife's name. Seeing the door pushed out of the frame, he hurried across the porch and into the front hall. There at the foot of the grand staircase lay his young bride, clothes torn away and body broken and swollen in decay. A long black line of ants streamed across the floor, and climbing across the girl's left leg, dipped down and entered her body through her private parts, making them quiver lasciviously. As the soldier paused, the name "Maryellen" dying on his lips, an opossum stuck his face up through her belly and, seeing the man, thrust himself up and out of the body and scurried heavily down the back hall leaving clotted brown footprints behind. Such a sight would have broken a lesser man but not my hero. He had ridden with "that Devil Forrest" and was made of sterner stuff. Pulling a long knife out of his belt, he strode across the room and sliced a lock of golden hair from his beloved's brow. Then he set the house afire, burning not simply his bride but the past and all hopes for the future. With smoke billowing like night behind him, he rode down the lane, jaws set, eyes frozen, on the trail of the marauders who had savaged his world. From this point on, the novel really became violent and graphic, as my hero tracked his men across the South and

West, catching them one by one and subjecting them to fiendishly imaginative deaths.

At Cambridge I read a great deal. During my second year, when I lived in college, I went to the student lounge each morning after breakfast and read the daily newspapers and weekly and monthly magazines: *Times, Guardian, Listener, Spectator, New Society, Field,* and *Country Life* among others. After finishing the papers, I walked to a bakery across Trumpington Street and bought a chocolate cake. Then returning to my room, I brewed tea, ate cake, and read. I went through mountains of books, most of them novels. At Sewanee I took many English courses, more than most majors, but I never read a novel. Translations of Greek literature, the poetry and drama of the Renaissance, and the Romantic poets of the nineteenth century were the core of the Sewanee curriculum. Tainting the novel must have been remnants of nineteenth-century moral criticism which condemned novels for intoxicating the imagination and leading young people astray. Although Faulkner certainly intoxicated me, the regimen of reading I pursued sobered me. I read through the eighteenth and nineteenth centuries from Fielding to Henry James. Not only did I read famous authors, but I read shelves of Marryat, Bulwer-Lytton, and Lever. Dickens became my favorite writer, and I read his novels twice. In reading novels I got the sort of literary education which suited me. Dickens's novels were too richly involved for an eighteen-year-old student, forced to cut his days into classes and life into courses. To appreciate the three-decker novel takes hours, the sort of expanse of time usually only available to adults in the evening and now to me at Cambridge. Much more suited to the American college curriculum are the lesser forms: essay, short story, and lyric poem.

Whatever the case, however, my reading roamed far from the texts set for the examinations, and before the last six weeks of my second year, Dick Gooderson, my tutor, called me into his office and said, "Sam, don't you think it's time you read some of the books on the Tripos?" I had not been quite so lax as Dick thought. One of my papers was on Dickens, and for another I had reread Greek tragedy. What I had not looked at and what I never prepared were the texts for the required French paper. Studying for the French paper would not have taken much time, and I didn't prepare it, most probably because I had lost interest in grades and knew that I could do well enough on the other papers to receive a degree. Additionally, having to study something because it was required, not because it appealed to me, may have stuck in my craw. I am quietly willful. Happily, my willfulness manifests itself only rarely, and then it is usually because I have balked at some requirement. When I taught in Jordan years later, an official told me that I could not receive wages until I provided the university with a stool sample. The government had to know, the official explained, if I had parasites. "I wouldn't shit in a pan for the president of the United States, much less for pay," I said, getting up and leaving the office. It being unlikely that I brought dangerous parasites with me from America, my salary was paid two days later without further ado.

Toward the end of my second year at Cambridge I decided against going to law school. Before leaving Tennessee I visited Wilna, an old woman who had worked for my parents for many years. Wilna was ill, and, when I pulled a chair close to her bed, I saw my picture on the bedside table. As we talked, she asked me what I planned doing when I came home from England. "Oh, Mr. Sammy," Wilna exclaimed, half raising herself from the bed when I told her I was going to law school, "Mr. Sammy, don't you be a lawyer. Lawyers don't do right." In my first term at Cambridge I met an American lawyer on sabbatical. During the struggle over equal access to public accommodation, he had originated the argument that requiring the owner of a restaurant, for example, to sell food to people whom he didn't want to serve was a form of involuntary servitude, or slavery. The argument was clever and had received much publicity, but it wasn't right, and when Wilna died, I decided law was not for me.

Still bewitched by Faulkner, I wrote the University of Mississippi, requesting an application for graduate school. Initially all went smoothly. After reading my preliminary statement, the head of graduate studies wrote, promising me a fellowship. All I had to do, he explained, was complete the required forms. Dutifully I filled them out until I reached the health form. On one side was a sketch of a mouth; I was instructed to draw an X through my missing teeth. On the other side were questions about my physical and mental states. I did not mind revealing that I had had the measles and that my tonsils had been removed, but I balked at saying whether or not I got car sick or wet my bed. When I posted the application back to Mississippi, I did not include the health form. In a letter to the director of graduate studies, I explained that the form was in poor taste. He answered sensibly, agreeing that the form was intrusive but stating that the law required it and urging me to fill the form out, "creatively" if necessary. Dickens and Faulkner were never far from my mind at Cambridge, and I wrote back, wilfully quoting *A Tale of Two Cities* with its "age of foolishness," saying I would never complete such a form. Thus my scholarly studies of Faulkner ended before they began.

While at St. Catharine's, I attended a few meetings of the college literary group, the Shirley Society, named after the seventeenth-century playwright James Shirley. One evening Norman Mailer spoke and much to most people's dismay comported himself with dignity. A poet was better value, tearing off his shirt, urinating out an open window, and ending the evening by asking me to sleep with him. He is the only poet, male or female, to issue me such an invitation. Of course, I have not known many poets. In any case, with a day on the river ahead of me, I didn't have time for such foolishness. My appearance at Shirley Society gatherings was, I am afraid, as occasional as my attendance at lectures.

In contrast, I never missed rowing. Six afternoons a week I was on the Cam. Above Cambridge, the Cam was sweet and cool and muskrats lived among the reeds lining the banks. Below Cambridge near our boathouse, the water was brown and clotted, thick with duck feathers, newspapers, tin cans, and bicycle tires. Farther down, past the gasworks and near the lock, the countryside opened and the river broadened out, sweeping under willows and alongside flat fields, on the borders of which swans nested. Here, when the going was good, one could slip through time almost as easily as through the water and imagine days of Beauty and Certainty. For my friends, the golden days were not medieval or gothic, but the Georgian autumn before World War I, the age of Rupert Brooke and Grantchester with the old mill and "church clock at ten to three." A boatmate organized the St. Simeon Stylites Society, named after a man who supposedly spent thirty-three years sitting on top of a pole. Although our patron was benighted, the society was romantic, rather than bitingly satiric as might be expected. Once a term we donned dinner jackets and punted up to the Red Lion at Grantchester, where we drank and ate and for the moment probably saw ourselves like Brooke, unsuited for "the long littleness of life."

Sentiment played only a small part in the rowing day. After the first term callouses so covered my hands that they looked and felt like feet.

Because I often jerked the oar into my chest, all my T-shirts were blood-stained. Despite the rich low country and the green willows, tipped with silver in the spring, the lock was not romantic. Just above it, treated sewage from Cambridge poured down a sluice into the Cam in a thick brown broth. One wintry day a friend and I rowed down to the lock in a double scull. We drew alongside the bank and stretched the oars out over the towpath, thinking they would hold the shell while we walked about. The current, though, was stronger than we imagined and it spun the shell off the bank and swept it toward the lock. As the shell hung on the lip of the lock, I stripped and, diving through the sewage, grabbed the shell. I had not noticed anyone about other than my friend until just before I dived into the river. On the other bank of the Cam, black against the green grass and blue sky, stood a young nun. She watched me swim to the boat and pull it back to shore. She even watched as I climbed out of the water and slipped back into my shorts and shirt. Over the years I have not forgotten that nun, and occasionally I imagine lifting the mantle off her head and her hair slipping like waves through my hands and over my arms.

Life may be composed more of images linked by association than by events bound by cause and effect. Nuns have appeared throughout my schooling. When I was five, my parents sent me to a kindergarten run by nuns. I shrank before their black habits and hard discipline and begged to go elsewhere, to a place of light and laughter. My parents listened, and soon I was in Miss Little's kindergarten, playing the tambourine. Not until Sewanee did I cross paths with nuns again; then one night while I sat in an empty classroom studying, a group of friends rushed in and grabbed me. Stripping me to my underpants, they bundled me off to a car and drove eight or so miles across the mountain where they dropped me halfway up a drive leading to a nunnery. Much to their surprise, I didn't turn around and start back to Sewanee but walked up the drive and knocked on the door. When a nun opened the door, I explained why I was in my shorts and asked to use the telephone. The nun invited me in and led me to a sitting room. As I sat there waiting to use the phone, two nuns came in and chatted with me, and a woman who worked there volunteered to take me back to Sewanee. She wasn't needed. When I went into the nunnery, my friends became frightened, thinking the dean would frown on their prank. Saying that they had followed the boys who had torn me away from my studies, they appeared at the nunnery, posing as saints to take me back to Sewanee. After urging my friends to turn the car heater on while driving me back, the nuns sent me off. In class the next Monday Abbo looked at me and then said, "Pickering, I understand that you lost your trousers at a nunnery. In Papist states, there is a long tradition of such things, leading, so I have been told, to the origin of the Foundling Home." "I do hope, poor Pickering," he concluded, "that you are not thinking of going over to Rome."

In Cambridge I lost my trousers on several occasions, usually near the college on King's Parade, though, and never at a nunnery or in the company of poets. Contrary, perhaps, to expectations, being debagged was a sign of affection, not dislike. The danger of such affection, however, was not that it led to a cold and pneumonia but that it could warm up considerably. Standing around a bonfire feeling particularly good-natured after a boat club dinner, several members of my boat decided to broil me. Chanting "Burn the American," they tossed me into the flames. Fortunately youth does not know its strength, and I flew over the top of the fire and rolled down and out the far side, singeing a shoe and burning holes in my dinner jacket. Drink flowed at boat club dinners, and by dessert most of my friends were smoldering, just on the edge of spontaneous combustion. Nowadays drink disagrees with me. In restaurants I sip water, not wine, and the only time I have beer is at home when Vicki cooks tacos. Age has diminished my exuberance, and, aware of the frailty of everything, I shun dislocating drink. Years ago at Cambridge when mortality was a word I confused with morality, drinking was fun. Too young to think bright promise could be washed away, my friends and I wandered along Trumpington Street and across the Silver Street bridge, faces aglow, cups in hand, singing and laughing. The occasional tailor's bill was but a small price to pay for such gaiety.

After a beery evening, several of us returned to the college late one night. After stumbling across an unlocked bicycle propped against the front gate, I began cycling around the main courtyard, singing "Daisy, Daisy"and making a fine hullabaloo. Lights came on around the courtyard, and the porter ran out of the lodge and tried to catch me. Since only fellows were allowed to walk on the grass in the courtyard, the porter had to chase me around the sidewalks. Around and around we spun, me ahead, weaving and singing on the bicycle and the porter behind puffing and shouting "Stop." My friends stood by the gate and watched until I ran out of song and crashed into a rose bush beside them. Only a torn trouser leg for the worse, I ran through them toward the old Bull Hotel, by then part of the college, yelling, "Run, run, or you will be caught." Even among the innocent, guilt spreads rapidly, and my friends followed me into the Bull. Making a thundering noise like buffalo on the plain, they ran up the steps and down a corridor to one boy's room. I stopped almost at the door, turning aside into a washroom where I crouched under a sink. As could be expected, the porter followed his ears and missed me. The next morning the dean fined my companions five shillings apiece. Later that afternoon when I went into the lodge to check my mail, the porter asked, "Didn't I see you last night, sir?" "Most probably," I answered. "There was a scandalous commotion in main court and I came out to investigate." "I assume drunken louts were misbehaving," I continued, shaking my head and walking out the door, "rugby players, most likely; such things should not be allowed. I came here because I thought this was a scholarly community." Fond of a glass of sherry himself, the dean was not hard on students who drank too much. At twelve o'clock the gates of the college were locked. If a student was outside the gates and wanted to return to his room without having to pay a fine, he climbed in. A protocol was attached to climbing in. The easiest place to climb in was over the fence around the Master's Garden, but the master asked students not to come in through the garden because his flowers might be destroyed. The students respected the master's wishes and climbed in over the old wall bordering King's Lane, an alley running between King's College and St. Catharine's. Sometimes, most probably when one glass of sherry after another led to thoughts of adventure, the dean tried to catch students climbing in. He enjoyed the sport and bought a powerful sealed-beam light for the purpose. The wall was ten feet high, and, as soon as a student was dangling down into the college with no place to go but the ground, the dean sprang out of the shadows, shined his light in the student's face, and shouted, "Don't run away from me; I've got you. If you have been drinking, it's all right, but if you have been to a brothel, you are in trouble."

On moving into the college, I obtained a room on E-staircase, facing the Walnut-tree Court. E-staircase was out of the way and inconvenient. The toilet was across the courtyard in the basement of another building while the nearest tub was two courtyards away. Inconvenience mattered little to me, for E-staircase was the oldest part of the college. First occupied in 1634, the building was weather- and history-worn. I liked the staircase for being narrow and crooked. Above fireplaces in the rooms dark oak was carved in the shape of Catherine wheels. I had just settled in when college authorities decided to remove everyone from E-staircase. There had been little rain in Cambridge for several summers, and the thick heavy mud on which E-staircase rested had dried, shifting the building and making it unsafe. While the other inhabitants of the staircase happily moved into the ceramic world of sinks and tubs, I stayed put. I have always liked old things, not because they teach truth, but because they endured. For me history is a battered trunk bulging not with the slate and chalk of instruction, but with the patchwork of story, beginnings and endings side by side like scraps of cloth stitched on a quilt. I liked climbing the cramped, narrow stairwell and running my hands along the old newel posts. The staircase resembled an attic, dusty and cluttered but alive with story.

I petitioned the fellows of the college, asking permission to remain in my rooms, declaring that if the building tumbled into Queen's Lane, I would ride it down like a cowboy breaking a mustang. The fellows agreed to my request, and I was the last student ever to live on E-staircase. To celebrate I bought a case of brandy and invited friends over to my rooms after dinner. The labels on the brandy were covered with stars, and soon most of us had blasted off dull ground. For some reason there were tall, thick stacks of newspapers and magazines in the hall outside my room. These we took inside and shredded, with the result that the paper in the room was eventually waist-high. Over the course of the night some of us found the fuel too rich and crashed back to earth, slipping heavily under the paper like meteors falling into desert sands. Not high flyers by nature, others dug down like moles, and burrowing across the room tossed up paper and assorted snorts and howls. My celebration was just the sort of volatile, high-octane affair the dean enjoyed, and I was ready when he knocked at the door at one-thirty. While my friends dropped down and tossed paper over their heads like hermit crabs escaping the sunlight, I poured a big glass of brandy. Then, opening the door, I handed the dean the glass before he could speak. "Here is a little something for you, old horse," I said. "We have been waiting for you." Then, putting my arm over his shoulders and kicking paper aside, I pulled him into the room and began singing "Should Old Acquaintances

Be Left Out." The dean looked around, blinked, took a belt of brandy, and was right at home.

My friends at Cambridge had gone to grammar schools or minor public schools. St. Catharine's did not attract many students from prestigious public schools, and the few about were clubby. My rumbustiousness, at best hardy and at worst insensitive and vulgar, did not appeal to clubmen. Toward the end of my stay at Cambridge, I started a rumor that led to my being approached by several clubmen, most not from St. Catharine's. When days became too routine, I often tried to spice them up, much as I had tried to liven up the Rhodes scholarship interview, by saying or doing something to provoke a reaction. What I did was harmless, arising out of playfulness rather than the chilly desire to reduce individuals to dissectable reactions. Some mornings I walked down King's Parade greeting strangers by saying things like "I prayed for your soul last night." Other mornings I hopped about in the shadows of the church at the corner of Trumpington Street and Botolph Lane, cackling like a hatchery full of Orpingtons or Wyandottes. My chicken imitation has always been good, and, after passing by, often on the other side of the road, people stopped and listened. Once a man began to crow like a rooster; I answered him, and together we sounded like poultry house at the Tennessee state fair. The rumor hatched during my last year, however, was a different sort of bird. When an inquisitive, gossipy friend asked how I could afford to attend Cambridge, I responded that although I hesitated to talk about such things the fact was that my father was the Coca-Cola Company's third largest shareholder. Four days later I received an invitation to dinner from a clubman who had never spoken to me before.

Not being a good oarsman contributed to my enjoyment of rowing. If I had been better, I would have probably taken the sport and myself more seriously, and, amid technique and triumph, fun would have disappeared. Giving me almost as much pleasure as rowing itself was the bicycle ride from the college to the boathouse. Weaving in and out of cars, three or four of us would race down King's Parade, Trinity Street, St. John's Street, then across Bridge Street in front of the Round Church to Park Street, and finally across Jesus Green and Midsummer Common. We rowed hard during our outings; afterward, though, all was laughter and song. Every day for a month in the shower until number 7 threatened to quit the boat, a friend and I sang, "There are no flies on us.

/ There are no flies on us. / There may be flies on some of you guys. / But there ain't no flies on us." Repeating the ridiculous has always appealed to me, particularly when the repetition irritates someone. Every morning for three years at Sewanee I began my day by singing, "Open up your mind and let the knowledge shine in. / Face it with a grin. / Bookmen never lose. Students always win." Nowadays when Vicki comes outside while I am working, I break into "I'm my own yardman. / I rake the leaves when I can." Although she often goes back inside, Vicki has not threatened to quit the crew, yet. The summer bumping races were the highlight of the rowing year. All the colleges filled boats, some of the larger colleges filling eight or nine. The boats raced in divisions, and a boat's position within a division depended upon the previous year's finish. Thus the second St. Catharine's boat would start where St. Catharine's number two had finished the summer before, although the boat was composed of an entirely different crew. For a race itself a division rowed down to the lock where the boats turned about and lined up along the bank with slightly over a length of water between each shell. When a cannon was fired, each crew tried to overtake and bump the boat ahead before being bumped by the boat behind. If the two boats immediately ahead were involved in a bump, the following boat rowed by in pursuit of boats still farther ahead. Once a crew picked up a rhythm, the races were great fun. The banks were lined with spectators, drinking, eating, and yelling. Coaches cycled along the towpath beside the Cam, shouting encouragement and firing pistols loaded with blanks as a crew pulled closer to the boat before them.

The start was tense, though, and to loosen us up, I always told the story of P. M. Coatsworth Wallingford, who rose to glory behind his oar, stroking Cat's to Head of the River. Although Coats died at Haling Way, just before the Long Reach, he didn't stop rowing. All heart, he even raised the tempo to thirty-eight strokes per minute near Ditton Meadows, eventually pushing into a sprint so that Cat's bumped 1st and 3rd Trinity opposite Stourbridge Common and went Head of the River. When the crew pulled to the bank to celebrate, Coats refused to release his oar. Not even the big men in the middle of the boat could pry his hands loose, and when the crew lifted Coats out of the shell and stretched him out on the grass for the celebration, bow and number 2 unlocked the oar and carrying the blade gingerly and reverently put it on a flat, bare spot so Coats could row comfortably. Cat's had never gone Head of the River before, and cigars were passed around, and champagne flowed. While the crew danced about, boozing and thumping each other on the back, Coats lay on his side in the grass, thrusting and grunting, and puffing on a cigar the cox had stuffed in his mouth. The crew knew they could not have succeeded without Coats, and they wanted him to enjoy the celebration. When the ambulance came to tote him away, they gathered around him, taking care of course not to be hit by his oar, and sang "For He's a Jolly Good Fellow." Not until rigor mortis set in eight hours later did Coats stop rowing, and the undertaker, a St. Cat's and rowing man himself, said that just before Coats let his oar go forever, he raised the rhythm to a magnificent fifty-four strokes a minute.

"Mr. Pickering, if ever you have an overnight visitor," my bedmaker told me when I moved on to E-staircase, "just put a flower in the door and I won't disturb you." On the walls of my room I had hung Hogarth's *The Rake's Progress*. The prints gave the bedmaker the wrong impression. Rowing and reading took most of my time, and I did not entertain overnight visitors. Rarely did I go to parties, and, even though I bought a ticket or two, I did not attend a May Ball. Perhaps because I was an only child, I have always been self-sufficient. Instead of enriching, girls complicated experience at that time of my life. Four years earlier, like an anchorite seeking the calm of the desert, I left Vanderbilt and coeducation for Sewanee. Girls, however, are born trackers, and despite my monkish leanings and the out-of-the-way location of my cave on E-staircase, I had occasional visitors. During my first term at Cambridge several Swedish girls found my boardinghouse. For many days running two of them came to my room and ate peanut butter, almost half a jar each visit. At the time I wasn't imaginative enough to think of anything that I could do with two girls and peanut butter, other than make sandwiches, and eventually the girls left me alone. At Cambridge my mind rarely even strolled, much less ran, to things sexual. During one Christmas vacation I met an American student in a café in Amsterdam. After I told her about the trip I planned, she asked to come to my hotel room and see the map I had drawn up. Thinking that she was curious about places to visit, I showed her the map. She glanced at it then suggested that we travel together. At the time I did not realize that she meant our trip to include some crunchy doings with peanut butter, and I refused to travel with her, saying I could see more if I went by myself.

Lovers are very different from readers, especially a reader like me. No overnight visitor could brighten E-staircase like a Victorian novel. An ardent reader ambles, toying with interpretation and rolling motive through his mind like a rich sauce on the palate. In love quickness is all, and he who pauses to ponder motive loses the girl. By the time a reader realizes that the soft calls ringing on the breeze were for him, spring and love have flown off to warmer climes. During the summer after my first year at Cambridge I worked for a travel company and for eight weeks conducted twenty-four American girls through nine countries. I was twenty-two, and the girls ranged in age from nineteen to twenty-three. Since I was the only boy on the trip, a couple of girls became infatuated with me. I was so conditioned by reading, however, that when awareness poured over me like a hot shower, the time for action had turned cold. Late one night toward the end of the tour I was awakened by knocking at my door. "Good Lord," I thought, "something terrible has happened to one of the girls." My pajamas having disappeared in Berlin, I snatched a pillow and, sticking one end between my legs while holding the other over my navel, I hobbled across the room and opened the door. There stood Elena. "Elena, what is it?" I said when she didn't say anything. "What has happened?" "Nothing has happened," she answered. "I just wanted to see if you were in." "Obviously, I'm in," I replied, irritated at being awakened. "Well," she said, pausing, "is there anything you want?" "At one-thirty in the morning, sleep, that's all I want," I exclaimed. "Good night," I added, then shut the door. "What was that about?" I thought to myself as I wiggled back under the covers. Sixty seconds later I was out of bed, pillow forgotten, breathing hard, and opening the door. Alas, Elena had disappeared.

Blaming Sewanee for my provinciality is unfair. Education has little effect upon character—at least education doesn't seem to have had much influence upon me. As a child, I always stood apart in a kind of provincial state of mind, refusing to become deeply involved in anything. At Sewanee contemporary history passed me by, not, however, because I consciously avoided it. I had been on the edge of things so long that I was incapable of recognizing important events. When the sit-in took place at Clara's, I ignored it. Instead I tromped about, waving a lantern and singing silly songs. Naively I thought that by going to Cambridge and changing place I could change myself. That didn't happen, and while history rolled by, wet and uncomfortable, I remained a sometime observer, high and dry on E-staircase, surrounded by books. When John Kennedy was killed, the other American at St. Catharine's wept. I remained untouched, and when curious friends came by the room to observe my reaction, I didn't react. "Look," I said, "no matter who the president, I am going to brush my teeth before I go to sleep tonight, and tomorrow I am going to eat a big breakfast." While at Cambridge I attended some meetings sponsored by the Campaign for Nuclear Disarmament. Completely unconcerned about nuclear war and not having the slightest interest in world peace, I went to the meetings for the spectacle. Clownish characters appeared, and the atmosphere was entertainingly circuslike. Nowadays I look back on that unconcerned boy with a kind of fond and horrified awe. I have three small children, and when I think about what may lie ahead of them, I am frightened. I wish I could do something, but I have never been a political activist. The closest I ever came to political action occurred in London some years after I left Cambridge. I attended the hundredth anniversary celebration of Gilbert and Sullivan's Savoy operas. During intermission I found myself standing in the bar next to Harold Wilson, the former prime minister. Suddenly an overpowering urge to goose him swept over me. All I had ever wanted to say to a politician seemed to force its way into my thumb, and Bunthorne and Jane's duet from *Patience* ran through my head. "Bah to you—Ha! ha! to you," I would say as I goosed him. Luckily one Gilbert and Sullivan always leads to another, and *The Mikado* popped into mind. Not wanting to be put on "a little list" of scholarly offenders who "never would be missed," I balled my hands, crammed them into my trousers, and putting political action behind me ran out of the bar.

After graduating from Cambridge I returned to Tennessee and taught high school for a year. Through the British Council, I had obtained a post in Sierra Leone; my parents, however, objected so strongly that I gave it up. Over the telephone Father said, "They must have turned you into some kind of liberal over there." After Father finished his say, Mother told me not to pay attention to him. "He is so upset about this Africa thing," she explained, "that he doesn't know what he is saying. He is almost crazy with worry, and it is making him sick." Behind the desire to go to Africa lay childhood reading, not political consciousness. When I was a boy, my favorite author was Edgar Rice Burroughs, and in elementary school I swung out from many a drab civics or health class into an Africa of the imagination, a green viny place of blooming adventure, a place where I was free to drop myself and the close world of textbooks, chalk, and blackboards.

I left Cambridge with a bang. The day before sailing from Southampton I rowed in a regatta at Marlowe. That night so I could catch the boat train the next morning a friend drove me to London in his old Austin. On the way we almost had a wreck. As we started up a long incline, we saw a car at the top pull out from behind a line of traffic. Speeding toward us in our lane and passing all the cars on his side of the road, he did not turn aside. Just before the collision which would have sent me to a place rather colder than Africa or Tennessee, my friend swerved off the road and we bounced over the shoulder into a field. The driver of the other car did the same thing at almost the same time. Both cars ended in the field, his down a slope behind us. The other driver was drunk; he retained enough presence of mind, however, to lock his doors. Almost before we stopped moving, I was running toward his car. Once there I battered it, kicking in the sides and smashing the hood and trunk with my forearm. By the next morning when the boat train left Victoria Station, all traces of my anger had vanished except for an abrasion and a couple of bruises. Although battering the car satisfied me then and the memory still satisfies me, the incident was a warning. Instead of traveling down main roads, I was better off, uninvolved on the physical and cultural edge of things.

In Tennessee I spent a slow happy year living at home. I applied for a Woodrow Wilson fellowship in order to study English in graduate school. At the interview I talked about Dickens and didn't quote any preachers. After winning the fellowship, I applied to Princeton and, being careful to complete the health form, was admitted. I went to graduate school not because I wanted to teach or because I believed the study of literature benefited society, somehow broadening people and making them more humane. I went because I enjoyed books and thought four years reading at Princeton would be pleasant. Before leaving Tennessee I drove to Sewanee to see Abbo. He had slipped. Although I introduced myself, he did not remember me. He looked absently off into the distance and said, "I have just been singing with the church choir." Then he walked away.

I did not keep up with my Cambridge friends. Only people immediately successful keep up, measuring themselves against and competing with contemporaries. The pressure to be a notable success often makes the person who lives an ordinary life feel guilty. Reading about the triumphs of former classmates, he thinks he has squandered his talents, be they real or imaginary. For such a person, keeping up disturbs and dissatisfies; for him, anonymity is far more comfortable. I was almost forty when I started writing, and by the time I achieved a small success, I was aware of the mortality of words and self, and rivalries seemed beside the point.

Despite knowing little about the doings of my contemporaries at Cambridge, I still wear my college scarf. Claret with two pink stripes running its length, the scarf is practical, not stylish. Thick and warm, it goes well with stocking caps, baggy down coats, and Connecticut winters. On the wall above my desk are two prints of "Catherine Hall." Both are views of the main court, the larger taken from the *Cambridge University Almanack* of 1814 and the smaller produced and colored by R. Harraden and Son in 1809. When I notice the prints, which I rarely do because I have grown accustomed to them, I find it difficult to believe I went to Cambridge. Somebody who spent two years there ought to gleam with polished civility. He ought to revere things British, dreaming of trekking by blue lakes in Cumbria or living in a deeply red eighteenth-century Georgian row house. Unpolished, I often seem foolish and abrasive; last week Vicki called me an "arsoon," the offspring, she explained, of an illicit coupling between a buffoon and an arse. When colleagues in the English department wax sentimental after reading about places they visited in Britain, I become exasperated. "Britain," I want to say. "That's not your life. Windham, Willimantic, and Danielson are."

Yet despite the years and lack of contact, I sent announcements to the *St. Catharine's Society Magazine* when my children were born. I am on leave this spring and for a while thought about taking my family to Cambridge and living there. I imagined riding a bicycle through the streets and coaching a crew. I saw myself thoughtless and full of fun, a younger me not burdened with worries about the future. I stayed in Connecticut and did not return to Cambridge, however, because my mother and father who are old and ill need me in this country. I did go back once though. Ten years ago I attended an old-boy dinner and stayed overnight in the college. At the dinner I drank too much. The next morning I could not find the pants to my suit. Although the pants had to be in my room, searching for them was beyond me. Putting on the gray flannels which I had worn up from London the day before and which I had hung in the closet was all I could manage. On my way out of the college I stopped at the porter's lodge and, giving the porter my address in London, asked him to have the pants mailed to me when they turned up. Having been at St. Catharine's for many years, the porter recognized me. In fact he was on duty the night I bicycled around the main court, singing and shouting. "Lost your trousers again, sir?" he said as he took down my address. "Things don't change much, do they?" "No, they don't," I said, tipping him and walking out of the lodge. When I reached the street, I turned around toward the college. Wondering if the rose bush into which I crashed was still there, I stepped back and leaned to my left in order to see around the gate. In doing so, I tripped and, stumbling to the side, fell heavily into a nun.

Occupational Hazard

LIKE THE INDISCRETIONS OF YOUTH, some ailments are too boring to be bandied about in medical journals. While a thousand scalpels would leap from operating rooms to preserve the honor of cholera morbus, hardly a lancet would be raised in defense of tennis elbow or housewife's knee. Yet if such ailments do not inspire articles too profound for seriousness, a survey of academics from Maine to California would reveal that occupational hazards spare no named chair. In the paneled halls of ivy lurks pomposity.

Rarely fatal, the virus usually leads to a comfortable mental state in which the sufferer becomes inaccessible to thought. What the disease lacks in virulence, however, it makes up for in epidemic proportions. Even the brightest, blue-eyed, fit young instructor fresh from an exhilarating jog through graduate school eventually slows, swells, and sickens. No antidote has been found for the corrupting effects of being treated by undergraduates as one of the wise men of the ancient world. Slowly the belief that one is Delphic gets under the skin and becomes incurable. But if medical science has found no vaccine for those sensations so warm to the ego, it has at least marked the stages of the disease's progress. Soon after his first book meets with friendly critical nods, the young assistant professor becomes susceptible. Giving the lie to the old adage that clothes make the man, the sufferer strides into pomposity's deceptive sartorial stage. Paunching slightly with confidence, he wraps himself in a tattered afghan in the winter and lets his toes dangle through the slits of Rhodean sandals in the summer. When reversed his paisley tie delivers a full-fisted message, matched in its rough whimsicality only by the lavender shorts he wears to the president's tea party. To the outsider this would seem a young man on the way out. But to the cognoscenti, this is clearly a man on the way up. They know that it is only a short step from afghan to Brooks Brothers. The paisley will be weeded out and Bronzini and Sulka will blossom in its place. The sandals will languish in the closet while those sweet harbingers of spring

Whitehouse and Hardy wingtips will escort a new associate professor to that tenured land where scotch and water purl against ice cubes like the Afton flowing gently to the sea.

Not long afterwards, our subject becomes "Guggenheimed" and flies away for a year in the British Library. A penchant for Gauloises and Harvey's amontillado and the appearance, much anticipated, of *the book* mark the disease's inexorable progress. After the return from Bloomsbury, Vanity Fair prints of willowy John Whistler and languid Lord Leighton decorate the sufferer's office walls while the poster celebrating the annual rattlesnake roundup in Sweetwater, Texas, curls in the wastecan. In the classroom a great vowel shift occurs as our not-so-young young man sounds like he lost his youth on the playing fields of Eton or under the shadow of King's College Chapel. On the title page of *the book,* L. Stafford Brown rises like the phoenix from the ashes of Leroy Brown, Jr.

Alas, university life is imperfect. Unlike the happy bovine, the graying academic cannot forever graze in green pastures blissfully ruminating over the cud of learning long digested. Before our sufferer answers the great cattle call from above and assumes the mantle of a named chair, he becomes aware of his illness. While perusing the shelves of the bookstore and pondering a list of books to be read during summer vacation, he hears a student confuse him with Balaam's inelegant long-eared beast of burden. At a colleague's Christmas party, he harangues the pert helpmate of a junior member of the department with learned jocularity. Certain he had left her in the living room like Saul on the road to Damascus blinded by light, he returns from the Necessary House in time to hear her compare him to that befeathered creature whose cackling saved Rome from the Gauls. Awareness sweeps down upon him and he vows to take a cure.

Unfortunately diagnosis is easier than treatment. Several remedies are available; and although each may cause a temporary remission, none can completely eradicate the disease. First our sufferer grows long sideburns and begins frequenting the society of the young and ignorant. With enthusiastic joie de vivre, he puts off the old and selects a new wife from his seminar on the Age of Reason. Sadly he discovers that ignorance charms only at a distance and youth like okra rises on the cultivated stomach. The days when he could burst from bed to greet the sun like a morning glory are over. Before the bottoms of his jogging shoes wear thin, his wife decamps. The shoes join the sandals in the back of the closet, and our professor places his hopes for a cure in canine informality. When the leaves turn gold above the autumn mists, our professor comes to the office carrying a large blanket and leading a small dog. Alas, as little acorns grow into big oaks, so small dogs grow into large beasts. By the summer all the days are dog-days. And when Kim suddenly develops heartworms, the professor openly weeps but privately mixes a decanter of martinis. Our sufferer's Indian summer of heartiness is over. Elevated to the department chair, he ignores the petty world scrabbling below and nods into graying dignity. Pomposity brooks opposition no longer, and the professor becomes a wonderful old boy in whose presence ideas flap heavily and fall to the ground like dying swans. Alumni recall his incompetence fondly. And when asked to speak at their annual dinner, he charms away fret from their busy lives by stumbling about sleepily. In his presence hardened men of the world drain their cups and recall that splendid time when they were boyish "Sons of old Cayuga."

On the campus stories describing his terse "ah ha's" and thoughtful "um's" abound. His enrollments swell as gentlemanly B's are bestowed with grand largesse. While students dream of girls as sugary as peppermint, the old boy puffs his pipe, rolls his *r*'s, and discusses the Immortal Bard's "Ring of Rightness." Time seems to doze until one long noon when pipe smoke gathers about the professor like cumulous clouds rolling to a storm. Suddenly there is a puff and he is gone. Some say he went above and now sits near the Great White Throne impatient to be promoted out of his number 2 wings and into number 3 wings. Some say he went to a warmer place. Others say he never left and that his spirit haunts the university waiting to capture a bushy-tailed young instructor.

Whatever the truth may be, the L. Stafford Brown Reading Room is dedicated at the next commencement. The walls of the room are paneled in rich walnut, rescued from a mildewing English country house. Large stuffed red leather chairs cluster here and there. Along one wall stands an eighteenth-century mahogany and rosewood bookcase. On its shelves are the professor's collection of cream pitchers. From above the mantlepiece, a mantlepiece on which, it is rumored, Dr. Johnson once rested a weary elbow while expostulating with Boswell, stares the professor himself. He appears walking across the Cotswolds. Sheep frisk behind him while in his right hand, he carries *the book*. In his left he holds a pipe. There are always a few bleary-eyed students in the room. Soon it is known as the Cave of the Old Sleeper.

From My Side of the Desk

NOT MANY CHILDREN STUDIED LATIN at the Male and Female Select School in Smith County. To get enough students for the first-year class Quintus Tyler visited Sunday schools around Carthage. Some of Jesus' best friends, Quintus told Sunday scholars, knew Latin well. In hopes of arousing interest Quintus described Pompeii on the first day of class and passed around an old *National Geographic*. Over the years the *Geographic* became tattered. One September Carolynne Foshee sneezed on the photograph of the House of the Silver Wedding at Pompeii while somebody stuck chewing gum on *Hercules and Telephus*, a wall painting from Herculaneum. The gum covered Hercules' behind. A stringy bit resembling a fishing line trailed down across the lion beside Hercules' right foot, then ran out to the end of the page before curving around and upward, back through the picture, ending in a small plop over Telephus's left eye. Although Quintus suspected Laney Scruggs, he never discovered who stuck the gum on Hercules. What he was certain about, however, was that the gum was Spearmint—Wrigley's, he told Turlow Gutheridge. "I pushed it about with a protractor and sniffed before it hardened," he explained.

Eventually the *Geographic* got so dirty that Quintus retired it. Although he searched the attics of Carthage, Quintus was unable to find another copy. A man of settled habits and years, Quintus enjoyed describing Pompeii, and so instead of changing the class, he decided to replace the *Geographic* with a volcano, one of his own creation. He bought a box of colored chalk and arriving early the first day of school covered the blackboard behind his desk with an extraordinary volcano. Big hunks of orange stone and a gray cloud of ash exploded toward the picture of George Washington hanging on the wall. Red lava gushed through a green countryside. Just ahead of the lava stick people fled along a road: two men in a pink chariot and a woman in a long blue bathrobe the end of which had caught fire. On the shoulder of the road lay an abandoned crib, two little paw-like hands tossing a spotted white ball into the air. Quintus was proud of the drawing, and after the first bell when students filed into the class he stepped from behind his desk, striding over to the corner of the room near the stand holding the Tennessee state flag. Pointing to the picture with a yardstick, he asked, "What do you think this is?" When the children looked puzzled and did not answer, he persisted. "You don't know?" he said. "Look at this red flame. What does it remind you of?" For a moment the silence continued, the children studying carvings on their desks and the curious patterns dirt made under their fingernails. Suddenly awareness erupted. "Mr. Tyler, Mr. Tyler," Billie Dinwidder shouted, waving his hand and speaking before Quintus recognized him, "it looks like Hell."

Billie and Quintus sat on opposite sides of the desk, and their views were not the same. The perspective from outside the classroom differs even more. Often people interview me about things educational. Although the questions asked are usually similar, they focus on matters I rarely think about. "What teachers influenced you?" reporters invariably ask. Because people want to believe education is a high endeavor shaping both moral and financial success and because reporters expect a platitudinous response, I mention one or two teachers. The truth is that home, heredity, and luck, not the classroom, have determined the course of my life. The question which ought to be asked is what teachers did I influence. Was fourth grade ever the same for Miss Bonny after I left, and how did I change Mrs. Harris's life in the eighth grade? Reporters interested in universities presuppose conflicts between teaching and research when the truth is that research invigorates my teaching. Between classes I roam wood and field collecting insects and wildflowers. One day early this past October I filled the pockets of my sport coat with animal droppings. "Tiffany," I said walking into a creative writing course and handing a furry hunk of raccoon scat to the most carefully perfumed student in class, "look at this." "John," I said, turning to a skinny boy wearing a T-shirt with the Grateful Dead on the front, "smell this. Take a bite if you want. It tastes sweeter and is better for you than tobacco." The nitrogen I spread that day enriched the class, and during the semester essays bloomed bright, fragrant with natural observation well into December.

Escaping educational platitude is impossible. "Whatever you do," I heard a school psychologist say to kindergarten parents, "be consistent. When you make a decision stick to it." For a moment my stomach sank.

Francis was five at the time and had long since battered me out of decisiveness. Suddenly, though, I realized that the psychologist got his ideas from a textbook, not from life. Firm decisive parents, I decided, raised quitters, children who taking *no* for *no* buckled under when the going got tough. I, on the other hand, was instilling drive, intensity, persistence, and the great American virtue of stick-to-it-tiveness. When the going got to no, Francis clamped down, and no matter how I or anyone else shook or twisted, he hung on until yes.

"How has television influenced students?" a writer asked me recently, expecting me to answer that television undermined literacy and morality. "Look," I said, thrusting my hand into my coat pocket, "a hundred years from now people will long for the good old days when children watched television and stayed out of serious trouble. Besides," I continued, discovering an owl pellet in a fold in the pocket, "television is more dangerous to adults than children. How many children leave husbands or wives seeking the fleshly pastures of soap operas? Never have I heard of a child trying to perk up his domesticity by putting candles around the bathtub and then singeing his private parts when he tried to slip in alongside a mate. Ever since actors started bathing en flambeau on television, Dr. Jurgen here in Willimantic tells me," I said, "that sauteed bottom has become a culinary hazard of wedding anniversaries."

All too frequently reporters quiz me about teaching. "What," a writer asked last week, "makes a good teacher?" I did not answer. Blended in a good teacher are knowledge and personality. Both knowledge and personality, however, are various and the blend is mysterious and volatile. The person who is a wonderful teacher at thirty may be terrible at forty then good again at fifty-five. The teacher who stirs the top quarter of a class might not be effective with the lower quarter. Moreover, students often don't recognize good teaching until they have left school. The teacher who seemed incandescent to the twenty-year-old can appear ashen from the perspective of middle-age. Likewise the teacher whom the young student damned as dull and unimaginative might later be remembered as responsible, maybe provocative by the forty-year-old alumnus. Complicating attempts to define good teaching is the fact that the effects of a class vary according to students' personalities. The word one student does not hear echoes through another, ringing a carillon of associations. "Six years have passed since I was in your class," a girl recently wrote me from New Britain, "and I want to tell you that you handled me the right way. I did not think so then, but now that I am older and have thought about it for a long time I realize you were correct. Thank you for doing me such a service." I did not recall the girl until I looked at my grade book. She was one of fifty-four students and received a B in the course. She wrote three B+ papers, then a B, and finally a C paper; she made 86 on the final examination. In class she was silent, a faceless gray student who never talked. Indeed the semester passed without my speaking to her except when I returned her papers. From my perspective the handling that I accomplished so memorably did not occur. From her side of the desk, an offhand remark of mine must have seemed aimed at her and started thought striking across the years.

Last spring I taught a course in the short story. On the back row in the right-hand corner of the room beneath a window sat a hard boy. He always wore a blue baseball cap with an orange bill. Printed across the front of the cap was "Danbury." Instead of removing the cap when class began, he pushed it around so that the bill pointed toward the wall. Then he leaned forward on his elbows and glared at me for fifty minutes, his scorn luminous and his expression never changing. This month he came to my office. He wore the same cap, but in his right hand he carried an empty tin can, the top of which had been sliced off. The label still remained. Printed in yellow and white letters against a blue background was "Colossal Pitted Ripe Olives." Underneath the words were six dark olives and the trademark of Shop Rite stores: an overflowing black grocery cart, a commercial bullseye on a round red and yellow target. "Hope you don't mind," the boy said, sitting down then raising the can to his mouth and spitting into it. "I chew. I'll bet," he continued before I could reply, "you thought I was from Puerto Rico. I work at the beach in the summer and get dark. I am from Bridgeport, not Puerto Rico. I came to tell you," he said, "that your course was the best I had in this university. Funniest damn course in the world. Thought I would bust a gut laughing. Told all my friends to take it. I won't forget you," the boy said, abruptly standing and shifting the olive can to his left hand in order to shake hands. "I won't forget you either," I said, mechanically. Actually, now that I think about it, I know I will forget him, for my memory works as strangely as association does in the minds of students. "Incidentally," a man wrote me in February, "the story of you, the Dartmouth English department chairman, and the visiting Englishman has been in my repertoire for years." What story, what Englishman, I thought as I read the letter. I barely recall the years I spent at Dartmouth, much less any, if there were any, visiting faculty.

To know the effects of a class upon students or rather how students think a class affects them would be disturbing. Twenty years ago if I had known how my class affected Gail, my children would not be named Francis, Edward, and Eliza. I was young and unmarried. All I remember about Gail was that she had brown hair, sat in the first row, once wore a yellow dress, and that I was in love with her. I was so in love I could not bear to look at her, much less speak to her. Whenever she missed class, the room seemed empty. The semester ended, however, and Gail vanished. At a reunion eight years later George, another student from that class, visited me. "Sam," he said as we sat in the living room, "do you remember a girl in your class named Gail? She sat in the front of the room and had brown hair." "Yes, slightly," I answered, feeling uncomfortable. "God," George exclaimed, "was she in love with you! The whole class knew it. Some days she couldn't face you and wouldn't attend. Isn't that the darndest thing." "Yes, George," I answered, "the darndest thing."

The desk stood between Gail and me. Although I have long since emigrated from Youth and the volcanic landscape of passion, the desk still separates me from students. I have changed, however. Missed connections hold no allure for me, and I am thankful the barrier exists. If someone my age, I warn students, wants to be your friend, watch out. I urge them to think of me as a father, kindly but stern. Although many have lived through rich joy and sadness, students are too young to frame the narratives of their lives. Consequently, they don't interest me as much as adults. In part research attracts me because it enables me to wrestle with mature thought and pushes me to see and think, thus indirectly influencing the classes I teach. To students I pontificate, hoping for good discussion but rarely getting it. How effective an argument can an eighteen-year-old, no matter his intelligence, make to a middle-aged teacher who, more than likely, has heard the same points a dozen times before? Moreover the students' world does not attract me. "Go to Huskies," a girl suggested the other day, speaking of a hangout at the edge of campus: "Wednesday is New Wave night." Instead of music the mention of waves brings death to mind. I don't imagine Bud Longnecks dancing with the St. Pauli Girl but Tennyson's sunset, evening star, and friends being swept across the bar and out to sea. Only then do I imagine the students, children drinking and misbehaving at Huskies, silly and unaware of the fragility of life.

One cold December Slubey Garts invited Pharaoh Parkus to preach at the Tabernacle of Love in Carthage. Pharaoh was a water-and-fire evangelist, and when he asked folks to "step out with Jesus," whole congregations waltzed toward the altar. At the Tabernacle of Love when Pharaoh called folks who had been smoking and drinking and staying out at night to come forward, half the congregation stood. "Tell it, Reverend," Dora Ludnum hollered from the back of the church; "preach it, Reverend. You're getting them." After Pharaoh asked men who had burning sinful thoughts about women and those women who had hot thoughts about men to come forward, almost all the rest of the congregation rose. "That's right, Reverend," Dora shouted; "you just preach it." When Pharaoh called those "captives" stung by bad thoughts about boys to come to Christ, Mr. Billy Timmons left the organ and joined the horde at the altar. "That's right, Reverend, amen," Dora shouted, sitting in her pew and waving her fan; "you done it at last. You done got them all." Pharaoh was silent for a moment. Then after eyeing Dora up and down, he said, "Now, I wants to see you old sisters who've been walking around this here church, full of snuff and gossiping." "Dammit, Reverend," Dora shouted, "you done stopped preaching and gone to meddling."

Instead of men and women I see students as boys and girls, during the semester almost my adopted children. Last week Vicki and I were late for a meeting at Northwest School, and Vicki urged me to drive faster through the campus. I refused. "Vicki," I explained, "these students are other people's babies, and I have to be careful." Like Pharaoh I have gone to meddling, straying beyond textbook and assignment to sermon. On most days I am behind the desk fifteen minutes before class begins. As students drift in, I preach, warning them that I will lower their grades half a letter if I see them jaywalking. Riding a motorcycle without a helmet gets an F. "Fools," I say, "don't deserve to pass, no matter their test scores." I bring knives and forks to class and lecture on table manners. I harangue smokers. Dangling modifiers and comma blunders might hurt a person's chances to get a job, but they don't cause lung cancer.

Because English is not central to the curriculum of the corporate university, I am free to meddle. No bridge collapses if I misinterpret Jane Austen. Still, I wish universities thought liberal studies valuable. Would that knowledge was more significant than credentials, all those certificates attested to as weighty by faculty committee but which float and tinkle like tinsel when real learning blows across them. "Don't be so down," my friend Josh said. "To be sure, these are lean times for English departments, but fattening things up would be easy. There is gold in mortars and pestles," Josh said, taking a deep breath and starting a sermon of his own. "English should change its name to Literary Sciences. Departments which once skimped by on scraps have grown round and sleek after changing names. Once the butt of jokes about stutterers and Dale Carnegie, speech has been treated with high seriousness ever since it became Communications Science. No pork-barrel bill could ever contain the crackling that Political Science has brought to Government. Gone is the seedy picture of back-slapping, booze-swilling witch doctors. In its place is the image of white coats, stethoscopes, decency, sound learning, and constitutional law. Even Home Economics has come out of the kitchen and gussied itself up as Human Development and Family Relations. If you'd quit stuffing your pockets with manure in Valentine Meadow, you would see that the world has changed. Go to the library, but don't expect to find cheery Miss Puddleduck smiling behind the Reference Desk or old Mr. Bookbinder poking about in the Rare Book Room. Computers have replaced them. In fact if you say library, people will think you live out where the buses don't run. Libraries are extinct. Born-again educators have brought the Learning Resource Center to the university."

Once Josh bites into a subject, not even gristle slows him. Smacking of pipes, rumpled tweeds, argyle socks, and flatulence, the title *professor,* he said, ought to be dumped and something more tony like *facilitator* take its place. Unlike professors, facilitators don't fumble about but impact and interface. "Graduate students," he stated, "should be facilitators in training and the courses they teach practicums." Course names also needed changing. Bonehead English should be transformed into Interactive Elements in Informational Systems. The contents of the course would not change, he assured me; students would still learn parts of speech and compose simple sentences. In the catalogue, though, students would become clients and the word *simple* would be dropped. "In fact," he added, "the catalogue should be filled with mystifiers and awe-inspirers, words like *kinesiology, morphology,* and *taxonomy,*" explaining that big words chopped money trees down faster than chain saws.

"Good buddy," he said, "make the clear obscure. Don't be satisfied with half a fog. Import a northeaster. Between semesters baptize the Freshman English Committee and don't just dip it like some tottering weak-kneed serf or country-club Episcopalian. Toss it out into the shining river with the silver spray. Then watch it rise, wearing a golden crown and white robe and speaking in tongues, calling itself an Ongoing Curriculum Laboratory with a directive to emphasize Prethinking and Conceptual Complex Function." For a moment Josh paused and looked dreamily off in the distance toward the university's new twenty-eight-million-dollar basketball court. "Sam," he said, turning back toward me, "with a little effort the Literary Sciences could become Revenue Producing Agents, brokering the services of facilitators. Suppose the university franchised Diagnostic Centers calling them Mr. Sentence Shops. Folks having misplaced Elements in Informational Systems could visit a center. For a modest fee weary businessmen or inarticulate, lovesick swains could have their prose repaired while they waited."

Josh started to say more, something about turning the Ph.D. into a Doctor of Literary Science and then establishing a licensing board to police Learning Resource Centers and prosecute lax facilitators. "Prosecute them," he said, "with the same fervor that the American Medical Association pursues delinquent members of the medical profession." Before Josh explained the workings of the board, however, a student appeared in the doorway and interrupted him. Since she didn't know what jaywalking was, she blurted out, she didn't think it fair for me to lower her mid-term grade. Josh looked at her, shook his head, and went to class. I told the girl that if she stayed off motorcycles, did not jaywalk, or smoke cigarettes for the rest of the semester, I might consider an adjustment to her final grade. The girl left, and I walked down the hall to the seminar room for lunch and the daily meeting of the Rump Parliament. Membership is not difficult for anyone over forty. First, the rumps of sitting members must measure at least fifteen inches from flank to flank. I, incidentally, better the minimum standard by two inches. Second, members must have been rendered powerless by academic trend. At ease with one another, Parliament enjoys good talk about real books. No member is ludic or dourly brilliant, and the house is pleased to let those more ideological run the university. "The happy geldings," Josh labeled us, but then Josh is thin and ardent. His outspokenness makes the house uncomfortable, and we wince when he rushes into the seminar room and interrupts debate to repeat one of his witticisms. "This morning I told the dean," he shouted, "that the whole of the English department was less than the sum of its private parts." As might be expected most members of Parliament are male. Indeed when recently asked to describe my approach to literary criticism and then being provided with a formidable list of forty or more approaches, most of which I could not pronounce, I simply wrote "white, middle-aged daddy approach." Family life reduces ideology to insignificance. Fears for my children and those other children whom I teach clang so loudly through my thought that I rarely hear the din of literary controversy.

Unlike me some members of Parliament observe trends, and on occasion Parliament discusses contemporary critical doings. Since our discussions like those of the British House of Lords will not influence matters in the English department or the corporate university, our chat lacks zeal and is pleasantly bloodless and genteel. All members of Parliament are effective teachers, however, and we keep abreast of student concern and activity. Managers of the university declared the second week in February "Sexual Awareness Week," and according to the student newspaper, a member of "the Health Education staff" said the purpose was not simply to "promote awareness of sexuality" but also to "introduce alternatives to sexual intercourse." Thinking this last subject provocative, Parliament went into extraordinary session, one extending fifty minutes, far past the usual quick bagel and cream cheese or sliced carrot sticks and tuna sandwich. Although many alternatives to intimacy were discussed, three rose to the top of the poll: Waldorf Salad, Parcheesi, and the foxtrot. Reaching a consensus in Parliament is rare. In general Parliament does not vote or sit in judgment. Instead members enjoy the higher pleasure of collegiality, benefiting from friends' worldly expertise. Last week a distinguished member showed us how to make a paper water bomb. The process was too intricate for most of us, so another member made a cootie catcher, in the mouth of which he drew four fat cooties.

The parliamentarians have served many honorable years behind desks, and I am very fond of them. They have aged beyond ambition and small loyalty to idea. For them, as for me, people and place are more important than guild. When I teach, I often look out the window. Horsebarn Hill rises swollen and mottled like old bread, reed grass growing moldy up the slope beyond the parking lot. In Valentine

Meadow Morgan horses gather in dark clumps, blowing steam. Lambing has begun in the sheep barn, and the bawls of the newborn crack the air. Seeing is not enough. I want to inhale place and transform it into muscle and bony thought. When I was young, I turned through libraries of books. Now I turn over rock and log, struggling to read the land. I want students to see beyond idea to particulars, rather than abstractions, clouds rising not like dream or hope but instead resembling sheep: the low, woolly clouds, southdown; the tall white ones, Dorset; the dark, black-faced ones Shropshire. I have modest expectations for my classes. Not for me high truths about existence but only the hope to fan curiosity. If students leave my courses willing to pause and turn over word and low stone, then I will have done enough.

After class I step from behind my desk, not to talk to students but to wander Storrs and find matter for the classroom. The past two winters have been Bluebird Winters, so called because the weather has been mild and bluebirds have thrived in eastern Connecticut, a flock of six living amid the brush and broken trees in the cut for the power line running behind my house. In February after classes resumed, I started roaming Storrs and Bluebird Winter. A tawny hunting cat prowled the sweet fern above the marsh behind the high school baseball field. Binding dried leaves to cocoons with dung, the orange larvae of small moths dozed through the winter in the fern itself. On cherry trees in front of the speech building were the eggs of tent caterpillars. In spring they would build nests, filling them with their droppings. The droppings discourage most predators but not green stinkbugs who bore through the dung and suck the juices out of the caterpillars.

This winter I spent days looking at trees: the hawthorne with its chalky limbs and spiked twigs topped by glistening green buds, the bold, stubby buds of the ginkgo, the fringe tree, its modest buds giving no sign of May's white bunting. In the middle of February pussy willows became noticeable, silver fluff creeping out from under the dark beetle-like scale. After I started looking, I realized that for years I had walked blindly past forests on the way to class. Never did I notice the katsura, for example. Along twigs remnants of seed pods swayed upwards in groups, swelling at the upper end like minute cobras bewitched by the cool music of a mild winter. Occasionally identifying a tree took a long time. For a while I thought the green, rolled calyxes of witch hazel were early spring blossoms instead of the remnants of fall flowers. Although I walked miles, I often sat still in the woods, typically studying lichens filling pits in granite rocks with orange or just looking at a hornbeam, a few pink leaves hugging branches and folded inward making fragile, papery pockets.

Near the end of February the wind freshened; gray drifted out of the gunny sky, and days turned blue. The light seemed tinted with spring, first colors that brought plants to mind, followed by the plants themselves: peach and cherry, dogwood, shadbush, and autumn olive. On the first of March the last winter snow fell. Heavy and wet, it caked trees and shrubs. At 10:30 at night I went for a walk with George, my dachshund. We climbed the side of Horsebarn Hill and then dropping down along the horse trail behind Bean Hill wandered the Fenton River. Shrubs drooped low over our path in thick, moist patties, obscuring the familiar, and twice I lost my way. The night was silent and blue, and the pain in my arthritic hip throbbed, more noticeable than in the day. Early the next morning I explored the campus. The snow that turned the big ashes into lattices clogged highways, and people seemed out of sorts. For many snow was an inconvenience. Instead of changing the landscape so that one saw and maybe thought anew, the storm disrupted schedule. I crossed the Gurleyville Road and followed the creek through Valentine Meadow. Against the snow vervain stood out dark and wiry, goldenrod galls bulged, and reed canary grass gathered the meadow in rippled tufts. The snow pushed brambles over into half circles, exposing highbush blueberry, winged euonymus, red seed pods still spotting its branches, and then nannyberry, the flower buds resembling the dried skulls of diminutive crows, swollen at the base but tapering long and beaked.

In the low pasture behind the sheep barn was the body of a deer. In leaping a fence the deer snagged its right hind leg between woven wire and a strand of barb wire, twisting then cinching woven wire around its ankle. I tried to free the deer, but the wire had cut through the hide and into bone. The deer had been dead a long time; animals had eaten its entrails and white oak leaves had drifted and piled up under its ribs. Later that morning on a stony slope just north of the abandoned ski tow, I found the skull of a small animal, lodged between a rock and a fallen tree. Unlike the deer the skull was fresh. In the eye sockets specks of red shone, and the brains were uneaten. I thought about taking the skull to class and identifying it, but the snow was deep and some creature, I knew, could make a meal out of the brains. The snow remained on the ground only two days. Bluebird Winter was almost over. On the eighth of March I noticed that red maples had broken into bloom. That afternoon I saw a dead groundhog on the Chaffeyville Road. For weeks I had seen bodies of raccoons and opossums. Their bodies revealed little about the weather. That of the groundhog, however, told me winter was over. Above the groundhog a flock of starlings pulled across the road. Resembling a question mark on its side, the flock flowed suddenly up in a hump over the pavement then rolled downward, sliding rapidly through the stem of the question mark across a field bristly with corn stubble.

"What makes a good class?" a reporter asked me last month. In discussing education tough, sensible people become soft. Instead of honesty they want sentimentality. Knowing the writer expected a vague scientific metaphor describing a reaction between student, teacher, and material, I poured him a beaker of palatable humbug, a simple, ideal mixture glowing and syrupy. The truth is that the success of a particular class depends upon my mood, something that texts and students rarely influence. My knowledge of the books I teach is thorough and constant. What varies is the topography of my days, the hills and long, low creek beds not simply of the Eastern Uplands but of life itself, the very ages of man—dreamy youth imagining a light at the end of the tunnel and happiness beyond, middle age knowing that the only thing at the end of the tunnel is the end—and then more fleetingly those little happenings that blow across an hour turning mood green toward the blushing south or blue toward the pale north. Three times a week I swim before class. During winter many people swim, and the pool is crowded. Four weeks ago as I was leaving the pool, I noticed an older faculty member walk out of the men's locker room, step on to the tile, and stride toward me. Over his shoulders hung a red towel. The towel was gathered neatly and was almost dashing. Clearly the man arranged it carefully. In his left hand he carried a striped athletic bag. The man's air was jaunty, and he was pleased with himself. Unfortunately, he had forgotten to put on his bathing suit. "Well," I greeted him as he approached, "aren't you the bold lad?" He looked puzzled, and I continued, "You are doing something I have wanted to do but have never been able to muster the nerve for." When he looked irritated, almost contemptuous at my unexpected familiarity, I said, "Only a real man would be brave enough to come out here bare ass and fancy free." An hour later my class was a success.

Not all unexpected events are jolly. Last Saturday the local newspaper interviewed me. My birthday was mentioned in the article. Monday morning when I was in the Cup of Sun, pouring half and half into a coffee mug, a stranger introduced himself. "We have the same birthday," he said, "September 30. Have you ever thought," he continued, "that you were conceived on New Year's Eve and your parents were probably drunk as Hell?" Although the thought had never before crossed my mind, it beat a path through my brain during class thirty minutes later. No matter what students said I could not push the picture of Mother and Father out of my imagination, eyes glazed, tossing streamers to the ceiling, little red party hats falling down over their ears.

Because I write essays I study my life. Many of the ordinary events I press into memory might drop silently out of another person's mind. Not only does the clutter influence my courses but sometimes it prefaces the books I teach. Today before class and Sherwood Anderson's *Winesburg Ohio,* I described yesterday's conversation with Eliza. "Daddy," Eliza said, pulling up her leotard, "I want to be a famous ballerina." "Oh," I said, having just returned from a speech in Colorado and feeling full of myself, "as famous as your daddy?" "Well, not exactly," Eliza said slowly, "a little more famouser than you." For the teacher the classroom can be unhealthy. Treated as an oracle the teacher can lose perspective and maybe humanity. At home I'm daddy: a silly, flawed, ordinary man, a realization which accompanies me to the classroom. In my writings I celebrate the everyday; in my teaching I urge students to notice the ordinary. In January Vicki, the children and I visited her parents in Princeton. Roads were icy and the drive back to Storrs was difficult. Recollection of the drive, however, warmed my mood yesterday. Aside from the usual family doings, nothing happened on the journey. A Roadway truck broke down on the George Washington Bridge, and traffic backed up into New Jersey. We sat on the bridge for twenty-five minutes, and Eliza's allergies bothered her. "Jesus," Vicki exclaimed after Eliza sneezed for ten minutes, "this is like living in Booger City." "Booger City, where?" I said trying to inch in front of a silver Volvo in the left lane. "Booger City, South Dakota, where else?" Vicki answered, reaching into a sack on the floor and pulling out an apple. "These are Empires, good for the nerves. Do you want one?"

Not long after my father died, a family friend said Father envied my life. "Roberts and I," Father told her, remembering his college roommate, "always wanted to be free spirits like Sammy." Father was wrong.

Affection and its consort responsibility have bound me so close to others that the concept of freedom has always seemed beside the point, an abstraction too cold for Bluebird Winter. The love and fears I have for my children make me worry about students. Dawn suffers from bulimia and after eating a meal often forces herself to vomit. The bile she throws up burns her skin, and dark channels run searing from the corners of her mouth over the sides of her chin. Last week she wrote a story describing a girl suffering from bulimia. One afternoon the girl went to the grocery store and, starting to shop, lost control of herself. Frantically her hands crammed food into the grocery cart: Lender's raisin bagels, Philadelphia cream cheese, a six-pack of Reese's Peanut Butter Cups, a bag of double-stuffed Oreos, an Entenmann's cheese danish, a half gallon of Ben and Jerry's Dastardly Mash ice cream, sacks of Barbara's Pinto Chips and Stateline potato chips, a box of Pepperidge Farm Chesapeake Chocolate Chunk pecan cookies, and lastly a quart of diet Sprite. While driving back to her apartment, the girl ate the Oreos. Once home she gorged, aware of nothing except "a buzzing in her head" until she noticed her stomach was distended. Stumbling into the bathroom, she balled her left hand into a fist and with her right forced it into her diaphragm. She pushed until she vomited. To make sure no food remained in her stomach she guzzled a quart of water and punched herself again. She repeated the cycle until all she vomited was yellow bile. The story ended sadly. On the last page the girl prepared a celebratory banquet for herself. After setting out silver and covering the table with a lace tablecloth her grandmother brought from Germany, she put on the white dress she wore to her senior prom in high school. Then she lit a candle, played a recording of "We've Only Just Begun" by the Carpenters, and began to eat. "Savoring every bit," she ate everything. Afterward she walked into her bedroom and sat down on the bed, smiling at her reflection in the mirror. Then she opened the drawer in the bedside table and took out two bottles of Nytol. She removed the tops and "one by one swallowed the sweet tablets." The story frightened me, and I came out from behind the desk. That night Edward had a nightmare and woke up crying. "I've lost my daddy," he said, "and I can't find him." "I'm here, Edward, honey; I'm here. Daddy's here," I said pulling him to my chest and rubbing his head, almost as if I were trying to squeeze fear out of him, and me, forever. As I held him, I thought of Dawn, her left fist hard against her stomach, and I wondered if I had done the right thing.

The next morning was bright and clear. It was Edward's birthday; he was eight years old, and Vicki had stayed up late blowing balloons and hanging them in the kitchen and dining room. When Edward awoke, he bounced downstairs. He had shadows under his eyes, but he did not remember the nightmare. That afternoon Vicki and I picked him and Francis and Eliza up at Northwest School. Edward had invited ten of his friends to a bowling party at Lucky Strike Lanes in Willimantic. The car was packed, and the children barely had room to sit. Piled in the trunk were party favors, napkins, plates, balloons, ice cream, popcorn, and trash bags. The cake was on the floor of the back seat under Eliza's feet. We were late, and I drove quickly through Mansfield's winding roads. As I turned on Route 32 toward Lucky Strike, Eliza suddenly grunted and then threw up on herself, Edward, the back seat, and the top of the cake box. "Oh, Jesus," Vicki cried, turning around and grabbing the box then wiping the top with a Soft & Dri. I made a U-turn and took Eliza home and washed her in the tub. Vicki and the boys went to the party. "How was it, gang," I said three hours later. "Great," Edward said, "just great." "Great," Vicki echoed, smiling wanly as she sat down and asked for an apple. "Well," I said after the children vanished upstairs, "how was it really?" "I survived," Vicki said. "Didn't anything awful happen," I asked. "Not really," she said. "The son of the second-grade teacher threw a bowling ball at the school superintendent's son, knocking him over the ramp for the ball return. He's a big boy, though; he bounced and wasn't hurt. In any case it was all in the school system, sort of like family."

Part Four: Bookish Matters

Book Tour

READING OCCASIONALLY INFLUENCES LIFE. In the *Hartford Courant* I read an article describing a book tour made by Kaye Gibbons. To publicize her novel *Sights Unseen*, Gibbons visited thirty cities. *Walkabout Year*, my latest collection of essays, appeared in early October. "Damn," I said to Vicki, putting the paper down on the kitchen table, "I bet my Australia book would sell better if I went on a tour." "Then go on one," Vicki said, bending over and slipping a tray of cinnamon buns into the oven. I followed Vicki's advice. I walked out of the kitchen into the hall. From a hook in the closet, I removed the Akubra hat that I bought in Cairns three years ago. Then I strolled through the woods to the Cup of Sun, the first stop on my tour. I drank two cups of coffee, ate a bran muffin, and talked to Mary, Ellen, George, and Roger. Later that morning Eliza played soccer at Spring Hill. I wore the hat to the game. "Just in from the outback?" Chuck said when he saw me. "No," I said, "I'm on a book tour and this is my second appearance." "Oh," Chuck said, pausing before asking, "do you think the girls will win today?" "Yes," I said. I watched the game. The girls won 4–0. When I returned home, I hung the Akubra back on the hook in the closet. The tour was over, or at least the actual tour ended. My imaginary tour, however, was in full swing, stretching not just through thirty cities but through all my days, not only shaping sights unseen but so quickening them that they cast bright shadows across the hours.

Children force parents to see clearly. In a family the sun often rises and sets at high noon, preventing parents from dreaming, and transforming shadows into the stuff of life. Recently the president of the United States spoke at the University of Connecticut. "Daddy," Eliza said at dinner one night, "the parents of lots of my friends received invitations to meet the president. You write books. Why weren't you invited?" Before I answered, Edward spoke. "Many people write books," he said. "Dad's not important." Edward told the truth, something that brings book tours to abrupt ends. Because my applications are always rejected, I no longer apply for literary fellowships. Now, instead of becoming gloomy as I fill out forms and realize that no matter my words, the applications will fail, I only dream of success. I imagine the pages fellowships will enable me to write. When I get up from my desk after not completing an application, I feel invigorated. I am ready to wander hill and field and spinning loops through the air turn falling leaves into necklaces, strings of jewels: yellow sugar maple and black locust, crimson red maple, orange hickory, and bronze beech. Keeping imagination vital is not easy. This fall I turned down two speaking engagements because the fees offered were modest. In contrast I agreed to speak on four occasions for free. "The honorariums were so low they made me feel ordinary," I explained to Vicki. "When a person doesn't receive a fee, he is free to create an imaginary self. Money does not define him and reduce him to the everyday." "But," Edward said when I finished the explanation, "if you made the speeches, you would earn enough to buy Mommy the new refrigerator she wants."

Writers whose tours take them to faraway places meet lots of literary folk. On my tour I met only one other writer, and that was Eliza. On Eliza's desk I found an account of Hungry Bert, a young vole who spent his summer playing games instead of stocking a larder for the winter. During the first week of winter Bert stripped the shelves of his store-room. Forced to leave his burrow to search for food, Bert suffered from the cold. "'Just look at my hands; they are frozen,' Bert exclaimed; 'even the marrow of my bones is blue from cold!' 'That's what you get from playing kick-the-acorn instead of collecting insects for the winter!' cried a goose, flying south." Luck enabled Bert to survive "the winter of '93," as Eliza phrased it. Early in the fall a squirrel abandoned a flea-infested nest. In a corner of the nest Bert discovered a cache of acorns.

In late September fleas infested our yard. In jumping from the grass to George and Penny, they hopped into dinner table conversation. From there they bounced into Eliza's writings. While cleaning Eliza's room, I found a poem under the bed. The poem was entitled "Poppies." "The poppies grow gaily out upon the green. / Their colors are sapphires and a rosy sheen. / They bob and dance so gracefully in the blowing breeze, / While listening to the music and singing with the fleas. / If I were but a poppy in a field of grass, / I know a flute I'd play, not a horn of brass."

After book tours writers often get mail. Despite the appearance of *Walkabout Year*, I received few letters this fall. Only long after my tour ended did the mail bring letters that touched on writing matters. One day I received two letters. Announcing the publication of a magazine devoted to elementary school matters, the first letter began, "Dear Literature Professional." An old friend and a literary amateur who had written a box of books wrote the second letter. Some time ago he suffered a stroke, and I wrote him, wishing him good health and describing the happy hours I spent watching the children play soccer. "Your soccer-parent days remind me of my son and me years ago," my friend said. "Now all my grandchildren are college graduates and ready to improve an imperfect world. Alas."

Unlike most writers on tour, schedule did not buckle me tightly to place and time. "Your tour," Vicki said, "sounds more like a detour." "Yes," I said, "that's the best kind of tour." One morning I drifted through Carthage, Tennessee. I didn't sign copies of my book, but I learned that Alice Blair, the fairest bud ever to bloom in the gritty soil around Mayflower, had married William Whicker from Nashville. Whicker was from a wealthy family. He grew up in a big house on Craighead and graduated from Wallace School after which he spent two lean years at Vanderbilt. Rich men often make poor husbands, and Whicker did not appreciate Alice, thinking her roots ran shallower than those of people blossoming in West Nashville. One night after she labored over dinner, Alice asked, "Darling, do I cook as well as your mother?" "My dear girl," Whicker responded, turning his fork sideways and digging at a kernel of corn lodged next to the first premolar on the left side of his face, "I come from an old and distinguished family. My mother was not a cook." Old and distinguished the Whickers may have been; brainy they were not. Before the wedding Whicker's brother Baxley visited the Blairs in Mayflower. Alice's father Nunnley was a deacon in the local church. On Sunday night Baxley accompanied Nunnley to a meeting of the church vestry. A parishioner had left the church a substantial bequest, and the vestry debated whether to spend the money on a chandelier or on a piano. Out of courtesy the vestry solicited Baxley's opinion. "If I was you," Baxley said, excavating a seam of golden wax running through his inner ear, "I'd buy a piano. You are mighty deep in the country, and you aren't going to find anybody out here who can play a chandelier."

Carthage itself enjoyed Indian summer, that quiet time between the last of the summer camp meetings and the first of the winter revivals.

Taking advantage of the theological calm, Slubey Garts started a collection of sermons. "Folks tell that you are writing a book," Googoo Hooberry said to Slubey one afternoon. "Yes," Slubey answered, "although I'm just a poor weak worm creeping after Christ, I'm trying to do a little something at it." "Well," Googoo said, "keep going. You have just as much right to make a book as them that knows how." Slubey had not progressed far when I visited Carthage. He had decided on a title, written part of an invocation, and filled a spiral notebook with jottings. The title was *Like to a Saltlick,* the phrase being taken from "Come back to Christ like to a saltlick," an invitation Slubey often issued during services at the Tabernacle of Love, spreading his arms wide, gazing upward, and staggering slightly, looking like, Turlow Gutheridge said, "he was carrying a giant turnip to the Smith County Fair."

Slubey liked music. He often said, "You can lead a congregation to the collection plate but without some whooping and hollering they'll just stand there." In the invocation Slubey combined his affection for music with what he thought was the dangerous spread of Catholicism in Tennessee, particularly in Nashville. "After Nashville, Carthage; after Carthage, the world," Proverbs Goforth declared one Sunday. In the invocation Slubey stated that *papist* and *Romanist* disagreed not only with his soul but also with his ear. In order to make his prose more euphonic and more pleasing to God and man, he was changing, he wrote, the *-ist* ending of *papist* and *Romanist* to *-ite,* thus producing *papite* and *Romanite.* "Christ did not build his cathedral on a cabbage stump, but on words," Slubey said, explaining that in changing *-ist* to *-ite* he was following "the divine pencil." "Edomites, Moabites, and Ammonites," he said, wandered the Holy Land, "not Edomists, Moabists, and Ammonists." "Elijah was a Tishbite, not a Tishbist; Ephron was a Hittite, not a Hittist, and Bildad was a Shuite, not a Shuist." I told Slubey that I didn't think linguists would adopt his changes. But I could be wrong. After I told Josh about Slubey's proposal, he embraced the notion wholeheartedly and immediately began calling Communists, Communites, and feminists, feminites.

Despite the invocation Slubey's notes implied that the book would contain only one critique of papite practices. Under the heading "Relics and Bamboozle" appeared a list, "pickled tongues, candied noses, and ears in aspic" followed by "the hook that caught the great fish which swallowed Jonah, the bag from one of Pharaoh's lean kine, and three hairs from the tail of the ass that Jesus rode into Jerusalem." The rest of the sermons appeared to be standard moral fare. Under "Anger," Slubey wrote, "Describe the red-mouthed man." Beneath "Spewing Hate" *Humility* appeared, followed by "Bowing to a dwarf will not prevent a man from standing up again." On another page, one that I assumed referred to gluttony, he wrote, "John the Baptist fed on locusts, but today people are not satisfied with chocolate-covered raspberries or strawberries; they want chocolate-covered watermelons." "Lazy folks," he wrote on the next page, "water the horse with the milk bucket. In spring they don't drain fields, and instead of corn they raise frogs." Under "Ravages of Cupid," he warned, "Bedroom slippers are made out of banana skins. Only wingtips can ferry the soul over the bottomless ocean of corruption." Watery metaphors lay beached throughout Slubey's notes. "Many lewdsters," he wrote, "awash on the flood of sin consider sending a note to God in a bottle, begging for help and forgiveness. Alas, wine fills all the bottles in their basements, and instead of praying to God they worship drink, and sink under the waves." On the same page appeared an anecdote. Although Slubey ran a pencil through the names, I was able to decipher "Horace Armitage" and "Enos Mayfield's Inn." Horace, it seems, appeared at the inn late one Saturday night. Drunk and short of money, he slapped a Gideon Bible on the bar "as security for drink." When Enos refused to accept the Bible, Horace was incensed. "Why you refuse God's own word!" he shouted, staggering toward the door. "You must be an infidel."

My tour did not flow smoothly. Fatherhood forced me to return to Storrs for soccer games. On the Sunday of Columbus Day weekend, I got up at six o'clock in order to drive Edward to Lebanon for a tournament that began at eight. I returned home at 6:45 that evening, Eliza's last game having started in Willimantic at 5:10 in the afternoon. Sarah Dorr was Eliza's best friend. Sarah played on the same team as Eliza, and often I drove the girls to games. Afterward they enjoyed insulting each other, Eliza calling Sarah "doorknob" and Sarah responding with "nosepicker." When soccer did not kick books out of mind, Josh burst into my office. "Great God!" he exclaimed last Tuesday. "The woods are full of men in drag and carrying guns. Don't think about going on one of your inspirational little rambles now." "In drag?" I asked. "Yes," he said, "flaming queens in gray and green outfits." "Camouflage," I said; "the men are hunters dressed in camouflage." "No!" Josh shouted. "Soldiers wear camouflage, and no war is being fought in Mansfield. The men are queens." Early in October myth was on Josh's mind. "Remember Pygmalion," he said, "the sculptor who carved a statue of a beautiful woman and then fell so in love with his creation that he kissed it, whereupon the gods blessed him and turned her into flesh and blood?" "Sure," I said; "supposedly, Pygmalion and his bride lived happily ever after." "Well," Josh continued, "that wouldn't happen in today's feminite environment. Now the statue would accuse Pygmalion of sexual harassment and sue him for kissing without permission."

Josh is fond of silly stories, and yesterday he insisted upon my listening to an account of a mother snake and her nineteen snakelings. The snakelings spent days practicing hissing, perfecting their technique in a pit dug for them by their mother. One day when the mother had to slither out to crawl a couple of errands, she sent her children to the den of Mrs. Pot, a neighbor. Mrs. Pot was out of her den, but when she returned and found the snakelings hissing in her pit, she sent them home. When they crawled through the front hole, the babies' mother asked why they came home so soon. "Mrs. Pot sent us," the snakelings cried. "Why that ungrateful coluber," the mother exclaimed. "Who assisted her the last time she suffered from ecdysis and couldn't see? Who nursed her when she bruised her fangs against the heel of man? Who does Mrs. Pot think she is? Her family is new to this range. Who showed her all the vole runs? Why I remember when the Pots didn't have a pit to hiss in."

I had heard Josh's story before. Instead of boring, however, repetition reassures, implying that life is comfortably circular, not linear. Yesterday's event will be tomorrow's happening, and no regimen of zeal or moral earnestness can alter the cycle. Rather than thrusting forward into the unknown, carrying banners proclaiming "progress" and "development," the person who believes life circular can relax, and riding the wheel of days, marvel at the dust pitched up by spinning time. On my tour I traveled a familiar October landscape. Fields appeared shaved, the corn stalks chopped into silage. From Horsebarn Hill the land rumpled outward in embers, trees flaming red and orange through ashy mists. In depressions between rows of stalks, lamb's quarters glowed, the stems claret and the flowers purple. Low bush huckleberry spilled down a slope in a red haze. In woods hayscented and New York ferns crumpled.

Color leached out of fronds, transforming them into ghostly remnants of the green that rolled like water through spring. Down the hill behind the sheep barn cinnamon ferns turned ochre, looking as if they had been burned by a damp fire, cindered and rusted at the same time. Bundles of satiny sweet everlasting glowed in the dull light. Bushy and purple-stemmed asters drifted across vision looking as fragile as cirrus clouds. Canada geese honked overhead, the sound almost too familiar to hear. In contrast calls of crows jerked into awareness like wrenches tugging frozen bolts. A collar of alders pressed against the woods. Resembling gauze bandages, woolly aphids wrapped around twigs. The larvae of striped alder sawfly clung in circles to the margins of leaves and on cold mornings glistened like glazed doughnuts.

Leaves bunched across the forest floor in shag rugs. The foliage thinned. The woods turned yellow, and shadows became wispy. As sunlight sifted through black birch and sugar maple, it lost body and absorbing color floated lightly over the understory like a throw of weary lace. Thickets of spicebush turned hollows yellow. Along the border of the woods, green dried out of beaked hazelnut. For a moment the leaves turned yellow. Then splotches spread across them like measles, at first appearing red and proud but then shrinking into brown crust.

Because I had no appointments, I drifted across days. Instead of signing books, I looked for, if not the signatures, at least traces of others. On a dead star-nosed mole flies laid eggs in clutches, resembling bundles of shiny white spindles. Sagging on a spicebush were three heart-shaped balloons, all with "Happy Anniversary" printed on them. A hedge of pink hibiscus blossomed across the front of one balloon. On the second balloon horticultural artists forced peonies out of season and into the company of chicory and goldenrod. A wicker basket opened like a ventricle on the last balloon. Roses burst over the rim of the basket in scarlet spurts while in the middle of the basket a dove huddled on a nest, an anniversary being a time when home is where the heart is and when feeling pulses stronger than thought.

I followed whim through days. One damp morning I watched leaves drizzle into the Fenton River. Some surfed the air, riding up over a finger of breeze then quickly dipping and coasting into the water. Others swung through circles resembling drops tossed out by a sprinkler. Some leaves from red maples turned like corkscrews. Others with long stems fell like arrows. The river was low, and leaves drifted slowly downstream, bunching against rocks and ledges, and in worn bends rumpling together, resembling quilts pushed against headboards. Hemlocks grew along the riverbank, and needles hooked leaves, seeming to reel them in and wear them as ornaments. I walked up from the river to the raspberry field. A woodcock broke cover and flying low circled behind me. A flock of yellow-rumped warblers hurried through the scrub. Sulfur shelf fungus bloomed on a log. The leaves of staghorn sumac resembled artists' palettes running with color, green near the stems, deep orange in the middle, and red at the tips. Northern red oak grew at the edge of the field. Color swept out from then drew back into the big leaves, shimmering, making me think Neats Foot Oil had been rubbed into them. White pines towered behind the oaks. Tops of the trees were green, but nearer the ground branches had broken off, and the trunks resembled heavy culverts, at their bases needles oozing out in an overflow of orange.

To see how season signed October, I toured at different times. Early in the morning fibrous mists floated over lowlands. A tuft of reed canary grass resembled a scythe, the panicle bending the stem into a blade. Inside the curve hung a spider web, droplets of water silver on the silk, creating the illusion of motion, making the grass swish through the air. A bumblebee quivered chilled and dying on top of a field thistle. Seeds spilled out of milkweed in damp mats, resembling sheets of water that had frozen, melted, and frozen again, this last time into cloudy sheaves. At midday I forced my hands into open milkweed pods. The pods felt warm and oily. Sometimes I shook stalks, and a frolic of clouds blew out of the pods. Below the white hairs seeds hung swollen, arches of yellow at the bases of the hairs curving over them like minute rainbows. On Queen Anne's lace umbrels folded inward so seeds could dry. Lady bugs nested in the umbrels, the prickly seeds blankets around them. I did not tell Josh or Slubey about touring early October. Queen Anne's lace, Josh would have warned, was just the bit of nifty to spice up the gowns of men trolling the woods with guns and dressed fit to kill, hoping for a slice of the old venison. Slubey would have preached to me, accusing me of turning nature into god. I can hear Slubey now. "Instead of listening to the rustle of leaves, harken to the rustle of angels' wings."

Book tours, as Slubey might have put it, "pry open the portals of the head." At the end of a tour writers return home, having seen and heard the stuff of new stories. One evening during the middle of my tour, I drove Eliza to soccer practice. As I drove along the dirt road past the town dump, Eliza asked a question. "Daddy," she said, "what is Communism?" "Communism was," I said, "a theory of government. Like all theories it promised people better lives." I explained that the gap between theory and practice was vast, primarily, I said, because humans were flawed creatures. Self always got in the way when people tried to implement theory. "Instead of being our brothers' keepers," I said, "we have become our brothers' exploiters." "Communism," I continued, "promised a fairer distribution of income. If the United States were a Communist country," I said, "I would not have the money to send you to Camp Wohelo in Maine each summer. But then some of the poor children in Hartford might have better lives." "That doesn't sound bad to me, Daddy," Eliza said. "I don't know why Americans hate Communism so much."

The practice field was four miles from our house, so I stayed at the field and talked to parents. Most parents were threads from the same financial and social fabric: doctors, teachers, lawyers, and artists. A few parents did not have means, however. On the weekend Eliza's team was scheduled to play in a tournament. The entrance fee for the tournament was fifteen dollars a child. "Is Sally looking forward to the tournament?" I said to a mother. "She'd like to play," the mother answered slowly, "but we can't come up with the fifteen dollars. Bill broke his arm six weeks ago. He hasn't worked since, and we don't have insurance." Sally played in the tournament. Afterward she baked me an apple pie. The pie was sweet. Still, as I ate it, my mind scrolled back to the conversation with Eliza. "Fifteen dollars," I thought, "from each according to his abilities. To each according to his need. Communites could teach us a lesson."

The narrative weather changed rapidly during my tour. While some stories were cloudy, others were sunny. The morning after the tournament I went to the Cup of Sun, and Ellen told me a story about Robbie, the five-year-old son of a friend. This fall Robbie started kindergarten. When he got on the bus the first day, he asked the bus driver his name. "Just call me Mr. Bus Driver," the man said. "Isn't it wonderful, Daddy," Robbie said to his father later, "that Mr. and Mrs. Driver named their little boy Bus, and when he grew up, he became a bus driver?" "Yes, son," the father said, "that's wonderful." As children age, stories told about them remain wondrous, albeit the tone changes.

Edward's soccer team played most games on a field below the middle school. Parents parked cars at the school. We sat on a railing at the edge of the parking lot, watched the games, and talked about our children, then life itself. Twelve and thirteen, the boys on the team had grown prickly. "Ryan," a mother recounted, "never wears shoes out of the locker room. Last Wednesday when the temperature was below freezing, he walked barefoot across the parking lot. When he got to the car, he said, 'Boy, I'm cold.' 'Maybe, if you wore your shoes, you would be warmer,' I suggested. 'Why are you always trying to ruin my life!' he shouted, getting into the back seat and slamming the door."

Halloween is a week away, and at the Cup of Sun this morning, friends and I dallied through muffins and coffee, talking about costumes. One year when I was a graduate student, I bought several pairs of inflatable buttocks. I strapped them to my chest and backside and went to a party as an ass. Another time I purchased a plague of rubber flies. I glued a swarm to my face. Afterward I attached threads to the wings of another swarm and hung them from the brim of a battered Cavanaugh hat. Then I went to a party as Fly Face, a character from the Dick Tracy comic strip. "Costumes are fun," Mary said; "years ago a friend convinced his sweetheart to dress like a Girl Scout for a Halloween party. She put the outfit on in my friend's apartment, and they never got to the party." "Sort of like your book tour," George said; "you never got out of Mansfield." "Still, I bet you had almost as much fun as that Scout master," Ellen said. "More," I said. "I had much more fun."

Road Warrior

AT 6:30 I DROPPED EDWARD at the Dorrs' driveway so he could ride to Loomis-Chaffee with his friend Geoff. The Gurleyville Road curved around Valentine Meadow like a hard rib. In the meadow mist pillowed fatty, near the lip blowing in straps. Along Route 44 fog whitened hollows, forcing me to drive slowly. Not that I drove fast— my flight to Baltimore didn't leave until 10:15. I always get to airports early. This morning I was starting a book tour, promoting my new collection of essays, *A Little Fling,* traveling initially to Greensboro then to Knoxville, Sewanee, Chattanooga, Savannah, and Nashville. Not only was the tour my first, but it was also the first sponsored by the University of Tennessee Press. In June the publicity director of the press resigned and went to work for AT&T. Overnight the tour tumbled onto the desk of an intern, an undergraduate unaccustomed to brassy hawking and selling. She worked hard, mailing sheaves of letters to radio and television stations urging them to interview me. Her tone was differential, however, that of a student begging favors from a crusty professor. "We feel that this book would be of interest to your listeners and hope that you will consider publicizing his appearance," read a note to the program director of Nashville Public Radio.

The program director ignored me. Before I left Storrs, though, three reporters telephoned. "I want to tell you up front that I haven't read a word you have written," a man stated at the beginning of an interview. "In fact I've never heard of you." "Now, how do you spell your name?" another reporter said before asking, "Have you ever written anything?" "Well," I said, "I am going on a book tour." "Oh, yeah, that's right," the reporter said, "I scribble lots of stuff, and I forget things." The third reporter sounded like a child, and I asked if I should address her as Miss or Mrs. "At 2:30 this afternoon," she said, "I will have been married nine whole months." "That's wonderful," I said. "I do hope your husband's a nice fellow." "Oh, yes," she answered, "he's a good Christian man."

Finances of the tour smacked of autumn, change falling from my wallet like leaves. The Press paid for my room in Greensboro, $112 at the Koury Convention Center at the Holiday Inn; two plane flights, the first from Providence to Greensboro, the second from Nashville to Providence; and then for a car, a blue Chevrolet Malibu I rented from Avis at the Knoxville airport at nine o'clock the night of October 3 and which I left at the Chattanooga airport at 7:15 the morning of October 7. I drove the car 305 miles, initially around Knoxville then to Sewanee by way of Chattanooga, the next morning returning to Chattanooga. The car cost $347.73. Early in September, the intern scheduled a book signing at six in the evening in Memphis, planning for me to spend a day driving from Sewanee, some 310 miles away, 90 miles from Sewanee to Nashville then 220 more miles to Memphis. I'd never been in Memphis, and I would have arrived as afternoon traffic clogged streets. I changed the plan, noting that at most I would sign six books. Instead of grinding back and brain to gravel, pounding the interstate, I suggested spending the day in Chattanooga.

I kept the Press's expenses low. Flights from Providence were cheaper than from Hartford. Although Bradley Airport is only thirty-five minutes from my house and driving to T. H. Green in Rhode Island takes an hour and fifteen minutes, I flew from Providence. The flight to Greensboro and the return from Nashville only cost the press $252. In fact flying from Providence cost me money. I left my Toyota at Thrifty Valet Parking on Post Road early on October 2, retrieving it at 6:24 the evening of October 10.

While parking at Thrifty cost $63.82, as a state employee on "literary business," I could have parked free at Bradley. For the tour I was $679.34 out of pocket, big items being rooms: two nights at the Fairfield Inn on Alcoa Highway across from McGee Tyson Airport in Knoxville at $132.46, and two nights in Nashville at the Marriott on Fourth Avenue costing $249.88.

The other major expense was $80.11 for two pairs of orange and white athletic warm-up trousers, purchased as presents for Eliza and Edward at the University Book and Supply Store in Knoxville. Eliza liked the trousers and wore them to volleyball practice two days after my return. Edward's trousers were too big, and after trying them on, he dumped them in the upstairs hall atop a heap of dirty clothes. During the tour I taught a class at the University of Tennessee and gave evening talks at Sewanee and the University of Tennessee at Chattanooga. Rarely do I speak for less than $1,500. When a talk requires me to fly, I charge at least $2,500 plus expenses. On the tour I spoke for free, "cheapening the wares," Vicki said. Sewanee, however, surprised me, giving me $500, thus reducing the cost of the tour to $179.34. During the tour I sold approximately 172 books. The book was priced at $26, my royalty being 10 percent of the net. After deducting 40 percent of the price for booksellers' profits and another 15 percent for additional discounts, I earned a tenth of $12.48 or $1.248 a book, the royalty thus amounting to $214.656. In short, after subtracting expenses, the trip earned $35.31. Or to put the finances another way—I was away from home nine days. Calculated on the basis of an eight-hour working day, a figure that deceives, for I spent more than eight hours each day traveling, visiting, and signing, I earned an hourly wage of $0.49. "But you haven't added in sales on Amazon.com," my friend Josh said when I cited the statistics. Josh was wrong. The figures included Internet sales. Before the tour Amazon had not sold any copies of my book. I have now been home for three weeks and six days, and Amazon's sales have remained zero.

Because the tour lasted nine days and I had to wear a tuxedo in Savannah, I carried two suitcases and a backpack. I crammed tickets, money, eyeglasses, schedules, talks, then a toothbrush and toothpaste into the backpack. At USAir in Providence, I checked the two bags to Greensboro. My first flight was on MetroJet, and I asked the clerk at the counter to describe the airline. "Greyhound of the sky," he said. At the Paradies Shop, an airport bookstore, I bought Patricia Cornwell's *Point of Origin* for $8.55. Butchery flies well, and I read Cornwell on planes. Before buying the book, I skimmed the first chapter. Cornwell's characters reappear in book after book, and I was not sure if I'd read the novel. Still, I bought it, reading eighty-seven pages on the flight to Baltimore.

At Ocean Coffee Roasters I purchased a medium-sized cup of coffee for $1.34 and sitting at a table studied my surroundings. Anton Airfood managed the food court, a group of franchises that shared a kitchen, these including Newport Creamery, Godfather's Pizza, Narragansett Grill, Del's, as well as Ocean Coffee Roasters. Del's peddled fruit juice, especially "soft frozen lemonade," a small glass costing a dollar, a large, two dollars. Pizzas at Godfather's were small, cheese costing $3, pepperoni $3.95, and also for $3.95 "breakfast" pizza. Priced at $4.25, the most expensive pizza was Humble Pie, loaded with pepperoni, sausage, onion, and green pepper.

Often during the tour, time stretched like a desert, and I spent hours trudging mirages sandy with small observation. After drinking the coffee, I walked to the departure gate. From Baltimore my plane continued to Orlando. Beside the gate idled a train of wheelchairs, seven cars lumpy with old people. Sitting in rows near the check-in counter were families traveling to Disney World. I sat and waited for my flight. On the row behind me a small bear in a red jacket dozed in a valise. A little boy cradled a polar bear, and a khaki elephant curled in the lap of a freckled girl. Seventeen years ago I bought Francis a gray elephant in London. The elephant had a broad white tongue and white tusks two inches long. He wore a blue pale suit, across the chest of which chugged a toy train, a red engine pulling two cars, one yellow, the other green, both rolling atop black wheels. Francis named the elephant "Ellie," and although years stuffed Francis's room with a zoo of animals, Ellie remained his favorite. This September Francis entered college. I packed the car and drove Francis to New Jersey. Before leaving Storrs, I asked him if he wanted to take any animals to school, "maybe Ellie," I said wistfully. I knew what Francis would say before he spoke. Yet, when he said no, I felt sad. "Damn," I muttered as I looked at the little girl's elephant, "damn." I didn't mutter long. My plane landed, and I watched passengers disembark. A daughter rushed up the gangway and hugged her mother. Large and top-heavy, both women had thin legs and, wearing dark trousers, looked like pears standing on black stems. For ninety-two seconds the women hugged. Then they stepped back, looked into each other's eyes, and hugged again. Because a clerk began to bustle passengers onto my flight, I didn't time the second embrace.

On reaching Greensboro, I telephoned the Holiday Inn, and the hotel sent a courtesy van to the airport to fetch me. I checked into the hotel at 2:40, my room being on the twenty-sixth floor, far above the top rung of any fire ladder. On the flight from Baltimore to Greensboro, I refused the peanuts Piedmont Airlines served as a snack. I was hungry, and after dropping my bags in the room, hurried downstairs to the Guildford Ballroom, a forty-thousand-square-foot bowling alley, lit by chandeliers and with a stage at one end. The room housed the trade show of the Southeastern Booksellers Association. Two hundred and eighty-eight exhibitors displayed wares on low lunch tables, books stacked heavy in columns or leaning akimbo on racks, looking like doors slipping hinges. Before examining books, I rummaged for food, cadging a square of dark chocolate from the University of Alabama Press, two nubs of Swiss cheese from Chariot Victor, then three crackers spread with "Dilly Shrimp Dip," the dip made by a member of the local Junior League. Culinary pickings being slim, at five o'clock I dodged cars in the hotel parking lot, crossed an access road, and for $5.24 bought a chicken teriyaki dinner in the Four Seasons Mall. Salty, the bird rose to my crop, and after the meal I roosted in my room and finished *Point of Origin*.

Earlier that afternoon, I searched the ballroom in hopes of discovering writing friends. Not until the next morning did I see anyone I knew. Then I met Connie May Fowler, author of *Before Women Had Wings* and most recently *Remembering Blue*. Each winter the Jacksonville Public Library sponsors a literary festival. Six years ago Connie May and I participated. After returning to Storrs, I never heard from the festival again. "Sam," Connie May announced, "we are banned from Jacksonville." "What?" I said. "Banned," she said, "and I thought we were having a lovely time." Writers attending the festival stayed in a motel several miles from downtown. A van ferried us to events. Connie May, her husband Mika, I, and others, including Kaye Gibbons and her husband, sat in the rear of the van and chatted. Another participant at the festival who, so far as I could tell, liked neither men nor women who liked men sat in the front seat next to the driver. Unknown to us, she jotted down our conversations. Later, she sent transcripts to officials of the library, saying we were not people who should participate in literary festivals. "I can't believe that," I said. "Yes," Connie May said, "we are banned from Jacksonville."

While roaming the ballroom, I collected souvenirs: a book bag from Tennessee, on one side a white square, in the middle blue letters declaring "The University of Tennessee Press Advancing Knowledge for 60 Years, 1940–2000"; from the University of Alabama Press, a church fan with a wooden handle shaped like two ice cream spoons glued end to end; then a rack of ballpoint pens, advertising Ingram, Southern Book Service, and Hill Street Press. An editor at Florida gave me a copy of *Florida Wildflowers in Their Natural Communities*. During dark moments on the tour, I opened the book and plucked bouquets bright with red basil, dog hobble, pine lily, and Osceola's plume. Ambling aisles between tables, I studied presses. Because people in the room were strangers, I talked to myself, praising my observation, noting that Peachtree had forsaken southern literature for children's books and that Longstreet had pitched humor for business and self-help.

In front of the stage stretched a row of tables. Behind the tables sat authors autographing books, ten authors at a time. At eleven Sunday morning I signed. The books were free. An author was not allowed to sign unless his publisher donated a minimum of one hundred books. "Chum to stir waters," explained Gene Adair, marketing manager at Tennessee. Booksellers lined up to receive copies. Most were sharks who sold the books at their stores. People who intended to sell my book asked me not to inscribe the title page, instructing that I only sign my name, sometimes requesting that I date the signature. The greed irritated me, and several times I said, "Since you are buying this book free, why don't you send a nickel to charity?" A few booksellers returned to the line for second copies. "Would you inscribe this one," a man said. "I'm not going to sell it. I skimmed the book. I liked the essays, and I want the book for myself." "I'm not taking this to sell," a woman said. "I'm giving it to my daughter for her birthday. She likes essays. Would you write, 'Happy Birthday, Louise. Your Mother never forgets you when she buys books.'" At the end of the show, booksellers packed libraries into cardboard boxes, rolling them out of the Holiday Inn on dollies. Having paid for travel, hotel rooms, and registration, store owners, I suppose, viewed the books as perquisites. And in truth I picked up a handful of books in hopes of finding something to read at night.

After finishing *Point of Origin,* I went to a party sponsored by Algonquin. I arrived just as food ran out. Still, I scooped up a Heineken's beer, a crab cake, three cherry tomatoes, and a biscuit stuffed with ham. I didn't talk to anyone, but I got advance proof of Louis Osteen's *Charleston Cuisine: Recipes from a Low Country Chef.* "For Vicki," Osteen wrote on the title page, "who needs to know about Southern Cooking—Come to Charleston." Since the proof was "uncorrected," I wondered if proportions listed in the recipes were correct. Still, because southern cooking does not appeal to Vicki, matters of cup and tablespoon were beside the point.

I sleep fitfully in hotels. Later that night I watched *The Twelve Monkeys* starring Bruce Willis, a movie I'd seen in Storrs. In Knoxville the following night I watched Kurt Russell in *Soldier,* a film about space soldiers. I thought I would watch a movie every night. My room in Sewanee did not contain a television, however, and after the visit to Sewanee I was too weary to keep abreast of plot. At the Koury Center, the Fairfield Inn, and the Marriott, mirrors papered bathroom walls. The cheaper the room, the more mirrors in the lavatory. The more mirrors the less I sleep. Moreover I loathe walking into a bathroom and no matter where I turn seeing my saggy self, meat swaying from me in dewlaps.

At the start of the tour, cadging food became a game. At eight the first morning in Greensboro, I attended the Millennium Breakfast sponsored by a gaggle of publishers. I didn't have a ticket to the breakfast. A woman collected tickets at the entrance to the dining room. I told her I left my ticket in my room on the twenty-sixth floor. Before she spoke, I strode into the room. Food was dreadful. I drank three cups of coffee, buttered a cold croissant, and munched red grapes, fingerprints of waitresses clear on the damp skins of the fruit. I joined eight booksellers at a round table. Sitting with us was a writer, her plate and coffee resting on a glass-bottomed tray, a raised wicker edge surrounding it. Before coffee appeared, she listed the virtues of her new book. For five minutes she spoke without stopping, after which a woman at a nearby table stood and shouted, "Change tables." Quickly the writer vanished, and another author appeared, tray in hand and mouth full of words. One visitor to the table said she would sign her book at any bookstore in the country, this despite living in New York. "Signings thrill me," she gushed, "and I love bookstores. The people who own them are just my favorites." "What a nice woman," an owner said after the writer shifted to another table.

Early Sunday afternoon Gene dismantled the Tennessee exhibit, and he, his wife Leslie, and I left for Knoxville in a gray van. Gene drove. I sat next to him on the front seat, and Leslie sat on the seat behind. The trip took six and a half hours. So that Leslie was part of the conversation, I turned sideways, in the process so corkscrewing my back that for the rest of the tour sitting caused pain to jangle up my spine. Before entering the interstate, we stopped at Chili's, a chain restaurant. Leslie and I ordered Cajun chicken sandwiches, for a fifty-cent charge substituting a salad for french fries. On the plates a boy fetched from the kitchen were lumberyards of potatoes. "These people didn't order those fries," the waitress said brusquely, jerking the plates off the table. When she returned, the potatoes had vanished, and my sandwich had been bashed out of its roll, the contents scattered across the dish like feathers. "I've never seen a waitress behave like that," Leslie said. On the tour I expected to blow past people like a freight rumbling through whistle-stops. But I grew fond of Gene and Leslie, seeing them in Greensboro, Knoxville, and later Nashville, the affection saddening, emphasizing the fleeting nature of acquaintance, even of family and love.

The drive to Knoxville exhausted me. Signs splotched the highway proud as acne, and trucks rumbled past abrasive and unshaven, reducing day to shadow. Only rarely did I notice sunlight breaking green through the Smoky Mountains. When I picked up my car in Knoxville, I was too tired to explore mazes of knobs and handles. Not until the next morning did the handle that locked the Malibu leap to hand. After parking the car and leaving my bags at the Inn, I trudged the shoulder of the Alcoa Highway to Wendy's. For $2.91, I bought a Kid's Meal. "You look tired," the manager said, staring at me. "Give him a big Frosty and a large coke, and toss in three orders of fries," the man said, addressing a boy in the kitchen. "We've got to perk you up," the manager said, turning back toward me. "Thank you," I said.

At lunch Gene had handed me a packet put together by the intern at the Press. The next afternoon I was scheduled to teach writing at the university. Later I appeared on WBIR television, on a program called *Live at Five*, after which I read and signed books at Davis-Kidd bookstore. In the packet was a map of Knoxville. The distance between bookstore and television station was fourteen and a half inches, as the ruler measured. Seven lines of directions steered me from the university to the station. "Gene," I began. "Sam," he said, reading my expression, "I'll navigate. Even I'm not sure what's the best route across town."

My room at the Fairfield Inn was a box within a box, the only window looking down at an enclosed pool. I slept poorly. At seven the next morning, I ate breakfast in the lounge on the first floor: a bowl of corn flakes, two slices of toast, and two and a half cups of coffee. A television tilted down into the lounge from a nook in the ceiling. While I ate, a blond woman babbled on screen, her voice rising and falling, a smile slicing her jaw. Four business travelers sat at a table to my left. They wore dark trousers and white shiny shirts, creases stamped into leg and arm. I overheard snatches of conversation: "when the rubber hits the road," "our two key points," "offer different opinions," and "it's the money after the fact. That's the problem." The men depressed me. How sad it would be, I thought, if my children had such jobs, staying at airport motels, televisions drizzling words on them at breakfast, their conversations flat as asphalt.

Although I didn't teach until much later, I drove to the Tennessee campus after breakfast, parking in Area 9 across from the football stadium. Streets along the river had been named for coaches and athletes, Phillip Fulmer Way for the football coach, Pat Head Summitt Street for the women's basketball coach, and for a woman basketball player Chamique Holdsclaw Drive. "The people who run the University of Tennessee," I thought, "must be long-necked, google-eyed peckerwoods. How embarrassing."

Throughout the campus Gideons stood on corners, distributing small volumes containing Psalms, Proverbs, and the New Testament. Ahead of me lay 210 empty minutes, so I talked to the Gideons. Seventy Gideons spent the morning handing out books. "We could use ten more people," a man told me. I assumed Gideons came from the lower middle class, at least financially. I was mistaken. I chatted with six Gideons: a retired electrical engineer, the owner of a medical equipment store, a pediatrician, a certified public accountant, an entomologist, and the owner of Wildwood Cabinets, a manufacturing firm in Maryville, Tennessee. This last man founded Wildwood thirty years ago. "I'm retiring this year," he said. "I am selling the company to my employees. They helped make the business, and they should own it." In the right lapel of his jacket, the man wore a pin, two small silver feet, the heels pressed together, balls spread slightly forming a V. The pin, the man explained, represented the feet of a six-month old fetus, "I'm against abortion," he continued. "But that's not a Gideon stance. It's just my view." "I'm on the other side," I said. "That's all right," he said. "People differ." "Gideons are not confrontational," the accountant said later. I talked for a long time with the entomologist. He had worked for the Tennessee Department of Agriculture for thirty years. We discussed hemlock and balsam woolly adelgids, fire ants, deer ticks, and gypsy moths. "Don't do anything if gypsy moths appear," I advised. "Spraying does more harm than good." "That's what I have heard," the man said. "I have been told," the doctor said, "that people spit on Gideons up north in Maryland and New Jersey." "That's not true," I said. "I live in Connecticut. People in the North are just as nice as they are in the South."

After talking to the Gideons, I explored Hodges Library. The university owned a dozen of my books. "Gideons are everywhere," I said to a reference librarian. "That's because southerners go to church," she said. Offices of the English department were in McClung Tower, a stobby, functional building. Chalked on the building's brick facing was "What's SHAKEN? Romans 15:13," *shaken* being slang for *happening*. On nearby steps lay a Gideon New Testament. I looked up the verse. "Now the God of hope fill you with all joy and peace in believing, that ye may abound in hope, through the power of the Holy Ghost."

Not sure where to eat lunch, I explored the building, trusting to happenstance. In a cramped room on the third floor, a representative of Longman's and Addison-Wesley publishers exhibited textbooks. "Eat with me," he said. "Coke and pizza are going to arrive any minute." I drank two cups of Coke and ate two slices of pizza, one plain, the other measly with pepperoni. After teaching, I roamed the campus again. I listened to a mockingbird singing atop a dawn redwood. A ladybug lit on the back of my hand, crawled to the tip of my index finger, and launched herself into the air. At the Daily Grind in the Presidential Court, I ordered a small coffee and a piece of chocolate cake. "You look beat," the woman said who took my order. "I'm going to give you a large coffee and two pieces of cake for the price of one."

At four o'clock Gene and I drove to the television station. Outside the studio grew a tulip tree with leaves big as fire shovels. "From what tree does this come?" I asked the receptionist, holding a leaf in my right hand. "I don't know. A maple?" she said, adding, "Who are you?" "I'm the love doctor," I said. Several guests appeared on *Live at Five*, the nun who wrote the film *Dead Man Walking*, and from Dollywood—the theme park underwritten by Dolly Parton, a country music singer—two men, the food manager and a cobbler who made pegged shoes. Each fall the cobbler worked a month at Dollywood. During the rest of the year he made Civil War reproductions. "Ninety percent of Civil War antiques are fake," he said. "Don't buy any." The food manager cooked buffalo burgers. I ate one, wrapping it in lettuce and tomato. The last person interviewed, I sat through news, weather, sports, and bubbly chatter read from a monitor. The "Big Question" of the day was, "What is the largest number of clothing changes ever made in a movie?" The answer was eighty-five, the record set by Madonna in *Evita*. A chubby man and a blond woman interviewed me. We sat on couches in front of false windows, eighteen panes to a window. Outside the panes a street reached like a forearm up to a white steeple. Shops lined the street, trees green before them, leaves heart-shaped. On a shelf in front of the window stood nine empty leather magazine cases, all labeled to contain issues of the *National Geographic*. The case of numbers published from January through June 1983, stood upside down. "Did you know that one of the cases in the window is upside down?" I said to the woman during the interview. "No," she said. My interview ended the show. Afterward the hosts stood, removed their microphones, and without saying a word hurried off the set. Gene and I got in the car and headed for Davis-Kidd.

At the bookstore, Barbara, a friend from childhood, met me. "Howdy and I saw you on the news, and we had to say hello." Also in the store was Townsend, a classmate at Sewanee whom I had not seen for thirty-seven years. Once a superb golfer, Townsend had aged into a rock gardener. "Flowers are wonderful," he said. After the reading, Townsend treated me to barbecue. A woman's book club met at the store. On my starting to read, they suspended their discussion and listened. "What fun," one of them said later. None of the women, however, bought my book. I inscribed a dozen books then signed thirty more for the store manager. "Don't worry," he said. "I'll sell them."

During the reading Gene went home, Townsend having assured him he would direct me back to the Alcoa Highway. I checked out of the Fairfield Inn at eight the next morning. I'd been on the road three days. "Was your room all right?" the woman behind the desk asked. "Yes," I said. "Next time you are here," she said, "y'all come back to see us." "Well," I said, "if I'm ever on another book tour, I'll come back. Right now I am a bit too weary to think about returning." "Oh, me. Bless your heart," she said. "You get some rest."

From Knoxville I drove south on Interstate 75 for 113 miles. Then I turned north for 51 miles to Sewanee. Trucks swept along the interstate, pushing cars beyond the speed limit. Once I stopped and drank a Pepsi to knit frayed nerves. At Sewanee, George Core, editor of the *Sewanee Review* and godfather of Edward, my second son, met me. I stayed in the Chancellor's Suite at Rebel's Rest, the university guesthouse. On my arrival George handed me a stack of books to review, most reprints of rollicking sea stories, among others, Frederick Marryat's *Percival Keene* (1842) and Michael Scott's *Tom Cringle's Log* (1834). Three years ago I visited Sewanee and stayed in Rebel's Rest. Unable to sleep, I strolled into the dining room and from a shelf removed a mystery, E. Phillips Oppenheim's *The Last Ambassador; or, The Search for the Missing Delora*. I didn't finish the book that night, so the next morning the *Delora* became airplane reading, going missing in my backpack. The ship novels were frigates, heavy as hearts of oak. Lowering them into the holes of my suitcases forced me to lighten the load, and I jettisoned five books I'd carted away from Greensboro. Although paperbacks, the books were autographed, a good swap for the *Delora*. In the dining room I stood Fred Bonnie's *Detecting Metal* beside Margaret Maron's *Storm Track*, the title pages autographed but not inscribed. Writers inscribed the three remaining volumes. "For Sam Pickering," Tom Corcoran wrote in *Gumbo Limbo*, "Can't Put It Down." "To Sam, who probably lived this version of this time," Nancy Kincaid wrote in *Crossing Blood*, an account of growing up in the South. On *Mr. Spaceman*, Robert Olen Butler wrote, "For Sam. It was great meeting you."

I spent the afternoon at the Sewanee Book Store, chatting with students and signing thirteen books. I also signed books after my talk that night then again the next morning at the bookstore. The manager of the store coached rowing at the college, and he gave me a white cap with "Sewanee Crew" stitched across the back, and two T-shirts, one purple with white letters stamped on the chest, the other white with purple letters, both shirts reading SEWANEE CREW.

That evening George and Susan Core took me to dinner at Pearl's, a restaurant midway between Sewanee and Monteagle. I ate fried green tomatoes and crab cakes. The dean of the college and his wife ate with us. They did not attend the talk. I spoke to two hundred people in Convocation Hall, not one a member of the college administration, a slight that irritated since Sewanee touted me on the school's web site. After the talk an older woman said, "I want to thank you." Her father died slowly and painfully. While bedridden, he read my books. "They made him laugh, great belly laughs, and cheered his final days. Thank you." The woman did not purchase my new book. "What would she have done with it?" Josh said later in Storrs. "Plant it on her father's grave? Dead people aren't great readers. In fact most of them, even graduates of Harvard and Yale, are illiterate."

The next morning after eating patty sausage with George at the Smokehouse Restaurant and listening to flickers yelp through oaks in front of Rebel's Rest, I drove to the University of Tennessee at Chattanooga. Much as George managed my time at Sewanee, so Bill Berry, provost at Chattanooga and a friend from graduate school, organized my visit to Chattanooga. I stayed at the Adams Hilborne Mansion on Vine Street, a bed and breakfast set on a hill overlooking the university. Once the mayor's residence then later a funeral home, the house was, as a journalist put it, "one of the best inns in the South." I stayed in the Presidential Suite, so named because a signed picture of Lyndon Johnson hung on the wall. The owner's father served as ambassador to Pakistan. A silver sheet hung above an end table, letters pressed into the metal. "To Ambassador Benjamin H. Oehlert, Jr.," the sheet read. "We, the members of the official American Mission in Pakistan at Rawalpindi, Dacca, Karrachi, Lahore, and Peshawar, wish to express our appreciation for the privilege of serving under your inspiring leadership since August 15, 1967. Our admiration is heartfelt. We offer our warmest and best wishes to you and Mrs. Oehlert upon your departure from Pakistan."

Across the room on the opposite wall was the photograph of President Johnson. In short sleeves with his collar open and the top and second buttons of his shirt undone, Johnson stood at the entrance of a stone building, weight teasing mortar from between blocks and wood framing a doorway white. Before the president was a dark wooden lectern, the seal of the United States pasted on the front and three microphones twisting upward like snakes. I studied Johnson's handwriting. He wrote hurriedly, the signature one line, the *n* at the conclusion of *Lyndon* sweeping up slanted to the right, joining the top of Johnson's middle initial, the circle at the bottom of the *b* then rising up in a scoop to the top of *J*.

The concierge told me my room rented for $225 but that the university paid the corporate rate, $125. That night I spoke to two hundred people. In the talk I said the price embarrassed me. "'$125? $225? My friend Sam,' Bill should have said, 'is a $350 man at the minimum. To pay less for his room would insult not just Sam but the whole academic profession.'"

The furnishings of the room were originally purple, but sunlight had baked them brown. Not until I glanced into the bathroom did I feel presidential. The second biggest tub I'd ever seen filled half the room. Although I showered at Sewanee that morning, I decided to bathe, clambering into the tub at 1:50 in the afternoon. The sides of the tub were pink and high, and I climbed in carefully. Inside, I sank and stretched out, shoals of chest and belly rippling unappealingly in front of my chin. That night during the talk I described the bathroom. Later a woman said, "You should share the tub and a bottle of champagne with a new friend." "Alas," I said, "two baths a day are all I can manage."

Bathing invigorated me. Afterward I ambled down Vine Street to the university bookstore. I sat in a rocking chair opposite the front door behind a portcullis of books. Few people broached the barrier, and I signed seven copies, all for faculty members. On the way to the store I visited Lupton Library to see how many of my books the university owned—two, both scholarly, not collections of essays. Chalked across a terrace below the library was LAUREN TURNER U ARE OWLSOME, the *Owlsome* blue, the other words yellow. An owl, a student in the bookstore informed me, was the mascot of Chi Omega sorority. Lauren Turner pledged Chi Omega. "I'm a Chi Omega," the girl said, "and Lauren is really nice."

The tour provided little opportunity for exercise. In hopes of loosening the binding around a bale or two of cellulite, I sauntered Vine Street. The neighborhood had once been Chattanooga's best. The street clung to the side of a hill, houses on the river and lower side of the hill dropping off behind, their backs pounded into the slope. On the opposite side of the street and the upper side of the hill, walls supported lawns and porches behind the bulging trusses of stone and cement. Businesses were moving into the neighborhood, lawyers having recently paid $450,000 for the house across the street from the Mansion. The day was warm, yet smoke billowed from a chimney. "The home of an old person burning coal. The next house to be sold," I thought. A woman walked a ratty dog on a leash. I asked her about real estate and discovered she was a member of the Board of Trustees at Sewanee. In June an alumnus nominated me for the presidency of Sewanee. Before the tour I cantered out of the race, pleading intellectual spavins.

I ate dinner with the English department at the faculty club. The main course was chicken Kiev. Stains displease Vicki. Because chicken Kiev squirts butter and garlic like a water pistol, I slung my necktie over my right shoulder and down my back. Bill Berry was wearing a new tie, and he did the same, explaining that we belonged to a secret society, draping ties over right shoulders being part of the society's culinary hocus-pocus. Later my speech went so well that I was foolishly ebullient. John, a classmate from Sewanee, attended. John is now a circuit judge. As a result when I signed a book for him, I didn't write what I really thought, "John, I am proud of you, and I love you." Instead I scribbled, "I'm glad the payment took care of things. If you ever need a little something special, just mention my name to Tiffany." At the signing following the talk, a man gave me a cigarette lighter. A metal band circled the lighter; stamped on the band was the face of Jesus and the capital letters WWJD, standing, the man explained, for "What would Jesus do?" I had not seen the abbreviation before, but from henceforth, it appeared throughout the tour: on a bumper sticker glued to a black Mercedes in Savannah, on a yellow wristband worn by a burly man flying from Atlanta to Nashville, and scrawled across the sidewalk in front of the Bennie Dillon Building in Nashville.

On the seventh I was scheduled to fly from Chattanooga to Atlanta at 10:15 and from there to Savannah. Nervous that morning traffic would make me miss my plane, I got up early and drove to the airport, so early that after returning the rental car, I caught the 7:35 flight to Atlanta. Savannah wasn't strictly part of the tour. Last April I agreed to address the thirty-fifth anniversary dinner of the German Heritage Society, a gathering of four hundred men, 150 members and 250 guests. The Society paid my way to Savannah from Chattanooga then from Savannah to Nashville. I also received a $2,750 honorarium, the last $250 tacked on to the fee to cover the cost of a tuxedo.

I stayed in the State Suite in the DeSoto Hilton. Furnishing the suite were eleven chairs, eleven tables, two television sets, three bathrooms, four hair dryers, seven lamps and one chandelier, three sofas, eight hand towels, nine bath towels, then twelve toilet bottles containing things such as shampoo and mouthwash. I stuffed the bottles into my overnight kit and carted them away when I left Savannah the next morning. On my arrival I filched an apple from a bowl in the lobby, the first fruit I'd eaten on the tour. After depositing my bags in the suite, I roamed Savannah for an hour, circling squares near the hotel: Chippewa, Orleans, Pulaski, Chatham, Monterey, Calhoun, and Lafayette. Spanish moss draped from trees, but I was too tired to notice much. "Some day," I thought, "I'd like to return and see this town." The apple not proving breakfast and lunch enough, I snacked at Cleary's Restaurant. I asked the waitress if spinach salad was tasty. "I ain't never had it, but some have," she said. I should have ordered what the waitress ate. The salad was terrible.

Until the speech in Savannah, I'd never made a talk that pancaked. "Don't tell me about it," Vicki said when I returned to Storrs. "Didn't you feel terrible while you were speaking?" she asked. "You bet," I said. I began at ten in the evening. The audience was male, most middle-aged or older and, if they resembled me, used to being in bed by 9:30. Before I spoke, they had pledged allegiance to the "Flag of the United States of America" and sung "The Star-Spangled Banner," "Dixie," "Edelweiss," and the national anthem of the Federal Republic of Germany. They'd consumed paprika cod on vegetables, oat dumpling soup, loaves of buttered pumpernickel bread, hearts-of-palm salad, lemon sorbet, herb-stuffed pork loin with chanterelle sauce, spaetzle, braised red cabbage, and lastly a six-inch beer mug made from chocolate and frothy with "Berry Mousse." Most had drinks before the meal. During the meal they drank two wines, a liebfraumilch and a Schwartz Katz; a stein of beer; and peach schnapps. I stood behind a lectern along one wall, the ballroom extending almost beyond my peripheral vision to the left and right. Even worse, the program labeled me a "humorist." What started out as a forty-minute address collapsed into twenty-five. Stories that never failed to stir tempests of laughter provoked doldrums, bringing a rain of perspiration from my forehead. At the end of the speech two people said they enjoyed the talk. I fled the ballroom and hid behind an ornamental pillar close to a block of elevators. Sitting nearby was an old man. He had attended the banquet, but he didn't recognize me. The man had a game leg and was waiting for the lobby to empty before he took an elevator to his room. Under the guise of Good Samaritan, I waited with him. Once the lobby was clear, I helped him, and myself, creep into an empty elevator. My flight left Savannah at 7:30 the next morning. I arrived at the airport at 6:15, sneaking out of the hotel before anyone who attended the banquet got up.

I changed planes in Atlanta. In Terminal A, my spirits revived. At the Country Western Bar opposite Gate 27, I bought a cup of coffee. No cream being visible on the counter, I asked for milk. "You'll have to buy it," the woman at the cash register said. "We don't provide milk for coffee." The woman pointed at a plastic glass containing packets of Coffee Rich. Circling the lid of each packet were two lines of minute type, listing the ingredients of Coffee Rich. "If I dumped this powder in my cup, I'd fail urinalysis and be banned from next year's Olympics," I said. "What?" the cashier said. "He means," the woman standing behind me said, "that he's not turning his mouth into a landfill. Neither am I. I'm buying coffee elsewhere."

I sat down to wait for my flight. Across from me were four women, volunteers who helped cancer patients. The women were flying from Jackson, Mississippi, to Nashville for a meeting at Opryland. A smiling woman gave me a brass pin, the word "Mississippi" stretching across it. Never again, I decided, would I speak to an all-male group. Middle-aged men are not so lively as middle-aged women. Women hear better than men, and they buy more books. Two nights earlier, the husband of one of the women baked chicken. "The bird only had one arm," he told his wife when she came home from work. "I looked in the oven," she recounted, "and sure enough the chicken had one arm." "The other arm did not flutter into sight," she continued, "until we sat down at the dinner table and I poured ice tea. The arm was swimming in the bottom of the pitcher." The women were peppy. Instead of speaking to the Southern Festival of Books, they suggested I address their meeting. "We'd be a terrific audience," they said.

A festival volunteer met me at the Nashville airport. After checking into the Marriott and autographing a program for the desk clerk, I walked four blocks to the Hermitage Hotel where the Festival hosted a Hospitality Room on the second floor. In the room I ate lunch: a croissant, coffee, green grapes, and two hunks of chocolate cheesecake. Afterward I buckled on cheerfulness and visited publishers crowding the War Memorial Plaza. Sixty presses set up booths, many exhibitors familiar from Greensboro. I talked to Gene and Leslie at the Tennessee exhibit. My book stood on a stand. "In Nashville," I said, "I will sell the copies you brought and more." Next day proved me right. After my talk, Gene quickly ran out of copies. Two years ago the University of Georgia Press published one of my books, and I talked to Mary Beth, the Press's marketing manager. That evening Reynolds Price gave the Robert Penn Warren Lecture on Southern Letters. A ticket to the lecture and the meal beforehand cost fifty dollars, not something for which I budgeted. "Sam," Mary Beth said, "I have an extra ticket. Would you like to attend as Georgia's guest? The food will be filling, and you look like you could use a big meal."

After wandering exhibits for two hours, I returned to the Marriott to shower and change clothes. I telephoned Vicki from the hotel, using a calling card for the first time. Since June Eliza had lost twenty pounds. When I left Storrs, she was five feet nine inches tall and weighed ninety-eight pounds. Eliza ate well and was fit, playing on the junior varsity volleyball team at high school and running on weekends. Weight had slipped from her mysteriously. The morning I arrived in Nashville, Vicki took Eliza to Dr. Dardick. "Things don't look good," Vicki said on the telephone. "Ken found proteins in Eliza's urine. He is running more tests, but there is a chance her kidneys are failing." I did not reply. Before I went on the tour, Eliza cut two hearts out of red paper. On them she wrote, "Have A Good Trip!" and "Good Luck," signing them "Love, Eliza." She buried the hearts beneath clothes in my suitcases. I discovered them when I unpacked. Eliza is the only family member who likes me. Before going to sleep, she kisses me goodnight and says, "I love you, Daddy." Neither the boys nor Vicki show affection. Busy at college, Francis has shunted me onto the every-other-Sunday family email schedule. As for Edward, I so disrupted his days by pushing him into private school that he hasn't spoken to me in three weeks, this despite my driving him to and from school several times each week. And Vicki? Twenty years of marriage have changed her affection to tolerance at best, and at worst, minor irritation.

Scribbling essays colors my days, transforming straight lines into loops. If Eliza were to become terribly sick, not only would I stop erasing and distorting, but I'd also put a period to myself. Sitting on the bed after talking to Vicki, I remembered a tale that appeared in *Early Piety*, a children's book written by George Burder and published in 1806. In September I read the story to students. A hermit, Burder recounted, set out to discover if Providence guided men's lives. A "beautiful youth" joined the hermit on the pilgrimage. The two spent a night at the home of a benevolent old man who was the father of a baby boy. After dinner, the youth and the two men discussed religion. The next morning before he and the hermit departed, the youth "went to the cradle, in which was a pretty infant, (the pride of its aged father) and broke its neck." After witnessing the youth's cruelty, the hermit fled. The youth pursued the hermit, and after catching him on the road turned into an angel and justified his action. "The child of our pious friend," the angel explained, "had almost weaned his affection from God; but to teach him better, the

Lord, to save the father has taken the child. To all but us, he seemed to go off in fits, and I was ordained to call him hence—the poor father now humbled in tears, owns that the punishment was just." "Horseshit," I said aloud. To escape melancholy I went to the dinner early and bought a glass of red wine for $4.50, the first wine I sipped on the tour. The dinner slipped quickly past. A man in a brown suit introduced Price. The next thing I heard was applause. I had fallen asleep and missed the lecture.

The next morning was rainy. I didn't want to pay eight dollars for breakfast in the hotel, so I put on wrinkled khakis and a worn shirt and walked streets, searching for a place to eat. Because the day was Saturday, restaurants downtown were closed. Eventually I walked down Fourth Avenue to Broad Street. A group of men gathered outside Robert's Western Café, waiting for the door to open at nine o'clock. I joined the group. All smoked and had lived rough, their faces red and pocked, clothes gritty, in places worn shining from losing their grips on life. The men addressed me as "Sir." After unlocking the door, the owner of the café jabbed his right hand at a man with watery eyes and commanded, "You! Leave!" The man obeyed. The restaurant was long and narrow, resembling a hall. To the left of the front door was a small, elevated bandstand. A shelf ran the length of the room, pairs of cowboy boots lining it like books, toes pointed outward. Tacked above the bar were dollar bills, all signed. I ordered sausage and eggs sunny side up. When the waitress poured my coffee, she handed me a packet of Coffee Rich. I didn't ask for milk. A man in a blue jacket sat next to me. Many years ago in Indiana, he began, a dispute over parking turned violent. A drunk attacked him and his brother, shooting the brother with a twenty-gauge shotgun. The drunk fired three times then his gun jammed. The brother raised himself off the ground, blood pooling over him, pulled out a forty-five magnum, shouted, "Now, it's my turn," and killed the man. The brother, himself, almost died, spending fourteen days in intensive care. "The man with the shotgun was crazy," my breakfast companion said. "We tried to reason with him. We told him to put the gun away. I told him we kept a pistol in our truck. But he wouldn't listen. If my brother hadn't shot him, I'd be dead. What else could my brother have done?" "Nothing," I said. "He didn't have a choice. He did the right thing."

After breakfast I walked back to the hotel to change clothes. A beggar hunched in a doorway, his body reedy and alcoholic. He wore an orange jacket, "Volunteers," the nickname of athletic teams at the University of Tennessee, sewed on the back in white. The man begged change. I said that I had none and climbed the hill. Seventy-five yards later, I turned around. The man had stood, and drifting around a parking lot, searched for cigarette butts. I hurried back down the street. "Here," I said, giving him five dollars, "get breakfast," thinking all the while, "maybe this will help Eliza." "Thank you, sir," the man said.

At one o'clock that afternoon I gave my final talk, speaking in the Senate Chambers in the Capitol Building. The room was spacious. The ceiling was forty feet high, and a dozen red columns supported a gallery. As I waited outside the chamber, I thought about Eliza, and wondered how I'd perform. But then Elizabeth Proctor, the eighty-two-year-old mother of Bill Weaver, my oldest friend, appeared. "I couldn't miss you," Mrs. Proctor said. "I love you." I pressed worry into the back of my mind, and the talk succeeded.

I began eleven minutes late, the moderator of the previous session having lost track of time. C-SPAN, the television channel, filmed my presentation. The producer instructed me to wait ten minutes before beginning. "No," I said, "enough time has been wasted. I'll speak for eight minutes after which I will stop for the introduction. Eight minutes and several paragraphs later, Brad Gioia, a friend and headmaster of Montgomery Bell Academy, introduced me, and although stitched together haphazardly, the talk ran smoothly, finishing so that the next presentation, a speech by William Frist, Republican senator from Tennessee, began on schedule. Many people saw me on television. Because the day was rainy, I borrowed an umbrella from the Marriott. Before speaking, I laid the umbrella on a dais behind me. At the end of the talk, I forgot to remove the umbrella. An hour later as Senator Frist finished talking, I returned to the chamber for the umbrella. "I didn't hear your speech," my cousin Ann recounted, "but I watched you get a white umbrella. You did it with style, creeping behind the senator, in your blue blazer looking like a big, friendly cat."

That night at the Country Music Hall of Fame, the Tennessee Humanities Council sponsored a party for festival participants. Worried about Eliza, I didn't stay long at the party, long enough, however, to inhale a plate of barbecue, a dish Vicki never serves, and also long enough to covet. The first thing I wanted was a green suit worn by

Jimmy C. Newman and decorated with sequins, white flowers that seemed crosses between magnolias and snowdrops, and then alligators, these last red with yellow backs, bellies, and jowls. The second item I coveted was Webb Pierce's 1962 white Pontiac Bonneville convertible, cow horns on the front bumper, a leather saddle riding the axle and dividing the front seat into halves, piggy banks of silver dollars glittering from doors, and an arsenal of guns, a rifle atop the trunk, and racked here and there at least seven pistols. "If I wore that alligator suit and drove this car around Connecticut," I said to a man, "the ladies would go wild." "And so would the gentlemen," he said. "Hell, yes," I said, "especially the men."

My flight left Nashville at one, Sunday afternoon. In Pittsburgh I changed planes. In the seats next to the one I'd been assigned sat a young married couple holding a baby girl. "If I see an empty seat," I said after I sat down, "I'll move." "I understand," the man said. "Children can be nuisances." "No," I said, "it's not that, not that at all. Your little girl is lovely. Hug her. These years are wonderful." Then I stopped talking, fear turning words to tears. I reached Storrs at 8:15. "Good news," Vicki said. "Eliza's kidneys are fine. She has thyroid trouble, and Ken wants her to see an endocrinologist. You make the appointment." Eliza saw the doctor at two the next afternoon. "The best way to understand the problem," he explained, "is to think about it as mumps of the thyroid. A virus made her lose weight. The virus is gone now, and she should start regaining flesh."

In the lives of the middle-aged, nine days are nothing. Most members of the English department didn't notice my absence. Don noted it, however. On Tuesday in my mailbox appeared a review of my travels, entitled "An Innocent and Broads." "Sam Pickering," Don wrote,

> takes us to the musty back rooms of country book-stores to discover what really causes that musty smell. In his wake he leaves reviews of his readings in newspapers with circulations of 2,000. Pickering is known and loved as a Southern Raconteur, and his narrative pauses often to remind readers that shaggy dog stories have always swapped fleas among themselves, and that many of his anecdotes resulted from his having hunkered down on the front porches of country stores with a bottle of Dr. Pepper and a few oldtimers. "Why," he drawls, "if'n all this was true I couldn't

hardly drag myself home and my wife wouldn't let me in any-ways." In fact Pickering is now in the fourth month of an extended tour to promote sales of *An Innocent and Broads*. But he says he calls home at least once a week, just to see which way the wind blows.

"Lordy," I thought, holding the review. "My tour is over. How good it is to be home."

Split Infinitive

"MR. PICKERING," THE REPORTER FROM THE *Hartford Courant* began, "the new edition of the *Oxford American Desk Dictionary* accepts the split infinitive. What's your reaction?" When the reporter telephoned, I was pushing my foot down the left leg of a battered pair of trousers. Earlier I cleaned the air filter on the lawn mower, readying myself to mulch leaves, not verbs. As I pulled up the trousers, I almost said, "I don't give a fart about infinitives." Then for a moment I pondered a serious answer, saying the vitality of English depended upon democracy. Rules changed with seasons. Like mushrooms in fall, words suddenly appeared, some spilling spores through the language, others vanishing overnight, being cropped by the voles and squirrels of usage. English sprawled vulgar and alive, unlike French, which academicians labored to freeze into propriety, deadening it cryogenically at the top in hopes of insulating it against change. Because people skim newspapers, however, I jettisoned the thoughtful for the brisk and said, "I do not dine with those who split infinitives." And that remark, I thought, slapped a declarative end on the subject. I was wrong. The last week in October an article on the infinitive appeared on the front page of the *Courant*. My picture also appeared. Percolating in black type under the photograph was my gastronomic assertion. The statement made people bilious. My friend Josh reported that the quotation provoked indigestion in the business school, "that stew," as he put it, "of short-order cooks able to fry numbers but in whose skillets fine language clumps in unpalatable heaps of comma splices and dangling participles." So many people bearded me about the infinitive that I fashioned shaggy remarks. To some people I said, "Oral transgressions such as the split infinitive and the misuse of *lie* and *lay* betray out-of-grammar conceptions." "In this age of family values, patriots must not turn deaf ears to illicit couplings." "Youth and the aristocracy," I told others, "forever fornicate across linguistic strata," adding that for an aristocrat, dining with the illiterate was another matter. "Can you imagine," I asked, "sharing a meal and conversation with someone who placed gerunds where participles belonged and who forked through agreement oblivious to the nominative and the objective?"

My tone stopped acquaintances from ruminating endlessly about usage. Alas, the statement in the *Courant* turned transitive. The Associated Press reprinted my quip. *Newsday* made it "Quote of the Day," and a score of radio programs interviewed me, including the Voice of America. Rarely do remarks on radio constitute a sound byte. Almost before I opened my mouth, I was off the air. Form determines content, so I cooked up several crisp statements. I began interviews with "To be or to not be, that is the question." "Republicans," I asserted, "had mulled making me an independent linguistic prosecutor." On some shows I declared my patriotism, asking why an *Oxford* dictionary. "Why not a Nashville, a Wichita, or a Peckerwood Point dictionary containing apple-pie American speech?" Unfortunately my literary petits fours rarely sweetened interviewers. Nobody recognized the paraphrase of *Hamlet.* "Is that a quote?" a man asked. "Yes," I answered. "What's it from?" he continued. "It sounds good. But what does it mean?" "I've heard of Nashville and Wichita," a woman said, "but not Peckerwood Point. In what state is it located?" Even worse, talk-show hosts took my statements literally. "Wow," a woman said, "I didn't think people in Congress cared enough about speech to appoint a prosecutor."

The day after the Associated Press printed my remark, I received a transformer of electronic mail. I shouldn't have been surprised. Discussions of language short-circuit common sense. Near the end of September, Turlow Gutheridge wrote me from Carthage. Piety Goforth's son Reuben, Turlow reported, eloped with Hymettus Clopton. The Cloptons being Pentecostal, Piety disapproved of the marriage. Later when he saw Reuben outside Barrow's grocery, Piety said, "I heard tell that you is married. Is you?" Not expecting to meet his father at the grocery, Reuben paused for a moment then said, "I ain't saying, 'I ain't.'" "I ain't asking you, 'Is you ain't?'" Piety responded, "I'm asking you, 'Ain't you is?'"

Unlike Turlow's story electronic mail did not celebrate language. Many correspondents were angry. Several urged me to get a "real life." "In some place," Josh said, "smoky with erasures where sentences are fragments and people double negatives." I crafted an answer to one message rough with inappropriate demonstratives. "Dear Anonymous," I wrote, "you didn't sign your name. What a pitiful chickenshit you are." Eliza saw my reply. "Don't send that, Daddy," she said, "the person is such a pitiful cackler that he is liable to flutter into Storrs and lay addled eggs on the front stoop."

Several correspondents hugged the remark to their bosoms. "I'm glad someone maintains high standards in the classroom," a man wrote. "Standards are so low today that a one-legged grasshopper could bound over them." Under the heading DISAPPOINTMENT, a woman wrote, "it has come to my attention a horrible quote attributed to you in a recent AP news update regarding the latest edition of the OED. The article quoted you as saying that you do not dine with those who split infinitives. I would hope this is not true and if it is, it was in jest. How crude it would be to say such a thing in real life, removing oneself from opportunities to dine with those who would benefit perhaps from your life experiences. Have you ever taken it upon yourself to dine with children or young adults who would benefit from educated mentors and perhaps imbed a spark in a young mind to succeed in life? Would that be possible if you were only to dine with those who avoid splitting infinitives? How unaccomplished your life must be to be so haughty and removed."

In contrast to notes written by people suffering from fused intelligences, several messages flickered good-naturedly. "I saw your remark about the infinitive in *Newsweek*," a woman wrote. "In June I heard you give a commencement address. In the speech you mentioned a son but not a wife. Might you be single?" "Seven years ago," another woman wrote, "I bought one of your books. On the title page you wrote, 'May your garden be green with children.' I just wanted you to know that I think of that comment often. I am married now, and Bill and I are looking forward to starting our garden." A sophomore in high school wondered if there were sentences in which an infinitive might sound better split. That question out of the way, the sophomore asked sixteen more questions, among which were: what are some of your main interests, do you enjoy your current job, how would you describe yourself, could you list some important events of your life along with the dates, and lastly, what is your opinion on war.

Every morning I have coffee with friends in the Cup of Sun, a café near the university. As I was reading the student's questions to Ellen, a stranger approached the table. "I saw your statement in the *Courant*," she said, handing me a sheet of paper. "I'm not sure what an infinitive is, but I know you'll like this story." Yellow with age, the paper had been folded into tenths, a crease running smudged down the middle. Written in blue ink in a firm upright hand was a tale of low usage. A preacher who wanted to earn money for his church learned that a fortune could be made racing horses. Consequently he decided to purchase a horse and race him at the local track. Because prices were steep, "the preacher ended up buying a donkey." "He figured that since he owned the donkey, he might as well enter him in a race." To his surprise the donkey finished third. The next morning the headline on the sports page declared, "Preacher's Ass Shows."

The preacher was so pleased by the donkey's performance that he entered the animal in a second race. This time the donkey won. The next day the headline proclaimed, "Preacher's Ass Out in Front." Publicity about the races so upset the local bishop that he ordered the preacher not to run the donkey again. Having already registered the donkey for a third race, the preacher immediately withdrew the animal. Accordingly, the next day the headline stated, "Bishop Scratches Preacher's Ass." The headline gave the bishop high blood, and he demanded that the preacher get rid of the animal. The preacher wanted the donkey to go to a good home, so he gave it to a nun living in a nearby convent. The next day the paper announced, "Nun Has Best Ass in Town." On reading the paper, the bishop fainted. As soon as he recovered, he told the nun to rid herself and the parish of the donkey. The nun sold the donkey to a farmer for ten dollars. The next day the paper reported, "Nun Peddles Ass for Ten Dollars." "Twenty-four hours later," the story concluded, "the bishop was buried."

"And all of this," Ellen said after reading the story, "because of your asininity. What a period the story puts on the split infinitive!" Ellen is a novelist, not a grammarian. For her, the end of a story is "The End." In contrast linguistic matters stretch through endless run-on sentences. Instead of a period, the story was a colon. That afternoon I received a packet of letters.

In nineteen lines a woman used twenty-two split infinitives, ending her letter with a postscript explaining, "to quickly come up with so many infinitives to wantonly split was not easy, but it was fun to hardly try." From Toronto came an advertisement for a "Diksionari uv Kanadan" written in something akin to phonetics. "Prof Pikrin," my correspondent explained, "Yu ar a linggwistik aktivist. Dherfor, I hoop dhat yu will organaiz ful, staffd diskussiones uv Kanadan, dhe fiinal tranzformasions uv ingglis." "I well remember," a man wrote from Vermont, "that nothing caught a teacher's eye like a split infinitive. My cousin would deliberately include one deep in any lengthy report he wrote as a test to see if the teacher actually read it with attention." At the end of the letter appeared a list of questions. Why, for example, "when English was being codified, did the academics involved decide to make the infinitive two words?" Suddenly, I tired of the parenthesis life had become. Condemning the infinitive to the pen, the page, and the dictionary, I split. I dropped the letters into the recycle bag, and slamming the door behind me, headed for wood and field.

Below the sheep barn the afternoon sun planed through sugar maples, painting the scrub orange. Along the cut for the power line, ferns curled bony and bronze, and green drained out of barberry, turning leaves orange then red. Early the next day silver halos leached from the leaves of northern red oak, buffing the sky. Along an old road a breeze streamed cool as water. At the edge of a marsh a female osprey perched atop a shattered tree, clutching a fish. I had never seen an osprey in Storrs. The bird's white breast and epaulettes gleamed in the light. Later that day in the English department, Tom asked, "has there been any reaction to what you said about the infinitive?" "Yes," I said, "but this morning I saw an osprey."

Selecting a Past

MY RIGHT ARM HAS BECOME WEAK, and recently I have spent many hours in Boston undergoing tests at Massachusetts General Hospital. As I sat in waiting rooms, the names of diseases spinning through my mind, I realized that I had little control over my future. What choices I might once have made would now be made for me by luck or illness. The realization depressed me, but not for long. If I couldn't control the future, I decided riding the bus back to Willimantic one afternoon, so be it; I would select a past. Besides I was middle-aged, and behind me lay almost fifty years of experiences—experiences like a mountain of marble, not Carrara or Pentelic, but marble seamed by veins of lively imperfection, green, pink, and yellow. From Providence to Danielson I imagined myself a master stonecutter, and the landscape which rolled past my window was not that of Rhode Island and eastern Connecticut but that of Attica and the Apuan Alps.

No man, alas, with a bad arm could ever be a stonecutter, and after arriving in Willimantic and eating a pizza, I stopped considering my past as raw material for a St. Peter's or a Parthenon. I did not, however, stop thinking about selecting a past. In fact I pushed ahead. The sense of a past, I decided, banished insignificance from life, creating the fiction that one was more than just a minute part of long biological and geological processes. A past provided identity and I began to shape mine, not in Greece or Italy but at home in Storrs. The past one left behind, I soon realized, was more often than not a matter of chance. In the attic, I knew, were boxes stuffed with old clothes, toys, papers, the detritus first of childhood and then more recently, of happy married life. Initially I considered pruning the attic, stripping away branches I did not want to be part of my past and then grafting something green into a trunk to be discovered in the future. Unfortunately I got no closer to the attic than my study. Opening boxes in the attic, I suspected, would upset Vicki and so I kept putting off the chore. Then on the day I finally decided to climb to the attic, the children asked me to help them explore the woods behind Horsebarn Hill.

In walking through the lowlands toward the Fenton River, I recognized flowers: purple trillium, marsh marigold, bluets, wood anemone, Solomon's seal. Later that night I realized that for me the landscape was a flower garden. Because I have never been able to associate names with leaves and barks, I hardly noticed the trees, the most conspicuous part of the woods. Another person would have recognized trees and not flowers. Going to the attic, I suddenly concluded, would probably resemble the day's walk. I would see a few flowers, but no trees, and what pruning I did would be arbitrary. Far better was it to concentrate my energies on things more limited and less strenuous. Because I knew biographers usually described what their subjects read, I decided people curious about my past would examine my reading. Moreover if the attic was beyond my energies and control, bookshelves in the study were not. By the quick and simple process of shifting books, I could influence how people would read my reading, thereby sketching in part of a past. Most books in my study were ordinary: paperbacks of the happier Victorian novelists, Dickens and Trollope, and then leather-bound sets of Charles Lever and Bulwer-Lytton, gifts from friends. Two shelves contained studies of natural history, mostly beginner's guides to birds, flowers, insects, and rocks. Books by essayists filled other shelves: Montaigne, then from the nineteenth century Charles Lamb and William Hazlitt, and from the twentieth century E. B. White, A. J. Liebling, John McPhee, Joseph Epstein, and Edwin Way Teale. Books so conventional would, I decided, have little effect upon a past, and I couldn't imagine drawing conclusions from them. Perhaps someone bent upon interpretation might note the essayists and then searching for frustration speculate about the difference in quality between my reading and writing. But that I decided was pushing conclusion too far. What would influence a past would not be the ordinary books I owned, stretching in long lines around the room, but the few oddities, scattered and dusty at the ends of shelves. So that a past would be convenient I gathered the oddities together.

Given to me as a birthday present twenty years ago by a lively spinster who knew I was interested in eighteenth-century things, the first book I picked up was ONANIA; or the Heinous Sin of Self-Pollution, And *all its frightful Consequences in both SEXES, Considered. With Spiritual and Physical Advise for those, who have already injur'd themselves by this Abominable Practice.* Printed by John Phillips in Boston in 1724 and "Sold at his Shop on the South side of the Town House," *Onania* had enjoyed great popularity in Britain, over fifteen thousand copies of earlier editions, Phillips claimed, having been sold. "Self-pollution" is, the author explained, "that unnatural Practice, by which Persons of either Sex, may defile their own Bodies, without the Assistance of others, whilst yielding to filthy Imaginations, they endeavour to imitate and procure to themselves that Sensation, which God has order'd to attend the carnal Commerce of the two Sexes, for the Continuance of our Species."

Although he warned "all Masters of Schools" to keep a "strict Eye" over their boys to prevent "the Commission of this vile Sin," the author emphasized that self-pollution was not limited to adolescent males but ran the gauntlet of sexes and ages. The governess of "one of the most eminent Boarding-Schools," he recounted, had surprised one of her scholars "in the very Fact; and who upon Examination confess'd, that they very frequently practis'd it, cum Digitis & Aliis Instrumentis." Although noting that both married and single men practiced "this abominable Sin," the author was particularly hard on females, not simply, as he put it, widows and "Married Women that are Lascivious" but upon pious, proper ladies. Unlike other kinds of "uncleanness" which needed a "Witness," self-pollution could be undertaken alone. "Some lustful Women of Sense," he elaborated, made outward shows of virtue and morality. "In the midst of strong Desires," not only did they reject "disadvantageous Matches" but they also refused to betray "a Weakness to any Man living," preferring instead to abandon themselves to self-pollution.

Onania, the author argued, was the unacknowledged source of many common ailments. In men it brought on phymesis, paraphymosis, stranguries, priapisms, "gonorrhaa's," fainting fits, epilepsies, and consumptions. For men who desired heirs it had sad consequences, causing both the "Spermatick Parts" to "become barren as land becomes poor by being over-till'd" and "a Weakness in the *Penis,* and loss of Erection, as if they had been Castrated." Not only did it affect women's complexions, making some pale and others "swarthy and hagged," but it caused "Hysterick Fits," consumption, and barrenness, or if not actual barrenness "a total ineptitude to the Act of Generation it self." Even if people who had recklessly indulged in self-pollution managed to conceive children, such children would not live long, being puny and lingering, "more brought up by Physick than Kitchen diet."

Even more terrible than the physical were the moral consequences of self-pollution. While one could lead only to the grave the other led to Hell, and the author urged readers to discipline the imagination and resist temptation, writing, "When Man grows stout and courageous, Satan grows cowardly." Once the barrier that fenced chastity was broken, however, "the enemy to Purity and Holiness makes daily Inroads, and ranges through every Passage of the Conquered Soul."

Besides being a hearty moral tract, *Onania* was a self-help manual, and the author suggested many ways to keep self-pollution beyond arm's length. The best antidote was early marriage, but if marriage was not practical, he urged sufferers to eat sparingly. Particularly to be avoided were beans, peas, and artichokes because, the author wrote, they make "those Parts more turgid." Also banished from the diet was salt meat. "A learned Physician of our own observes," the author explained, "that in Ships which are laden with Salt from Rochel, the Mice breed thrice as fast as in those Ships laden with Merchandize." In bed, men, in particular, were urged to sleep on their sides, not backs "for that heats the Reins, and causes irritations to Lust." Additionally, the author noted, neither men nor women should "handle those Parts at any Time, but when Necessity of Nature requires, for handling of them puffs up, irritates and raises Fleshly Inclinations." If after following all the suggestions regarding diet and domestic habit, a man committed "involuntary POLLUTIONS" in his sleep, the author proposed a fail-safe remedy. "I would advise you," he declared, "whenever you are apprehensive, or in fear of them, to do what Forestus, a noted Physician in his time, lays down, as certain when every thing else has fail'd, which is, to tie a string, when you go to Bed, about your Neck, and the other End of it about the Neck of your *Penis*, which when an Erection happens, will timely awaken you, and put an effectual end to the seminal Emission."

I realized *Onania* could almost single-handedly distort my library and me. In truth I am not the kind of person who for medicinal reasons must sleep on his side and avoid peas and artichokes. My library is a cool place. I think people ought to behave themselves, and I own almost no books in which people misbehave. Long ago I jerked Emma Bovary off the shelf because I didn't want her around radiating heat. The only book I keep which contains warmish parts was written by a friend, and since he visits occasionally I cannot throw it away. I have, however, buried it deep on a damp lower shelf and only dig it up and plant it in the sunshine just before his arrival. One scene in the book does, as the author of *Onania* put it, raise fleshly inclinations, and when my friend's mother-in-law read it, she immediately dropped the book to the floor and kicked it out of the living room, down the hall and out the front door into the snow, after which she called her daughter, shouting into the telephone, "You have married a pervert. Come home."

Lest *Onania* make me seem a pervert or literary peeper, I surrounded it by other, more respectable oddities, cooling it down with leather-bound copies of the *Arminian Magazine,* on the left by the volume for 1787 and on the right by the volume for 1788. I bought the volumes fourteen years ago in London because they contained the autobiography of one of my favorite characters, Silas Told, a friend of John Wesley and an eighteenth-century Good Samaritan. Born at the lime kilns near the hot wells in Bristol in 1711, Told was the son of a wealthy physician, who, unfortunately being a "great schemer" lost thirty-three hundred pounds in building a wet-dock at Bristol after which he was forced to work as ship's doctor on "a Guinea-man" where in the course of his first voyage he died. At fourteen Told himself was bound apprentice on a ship sailing from Bristol to Jamaica. On the trip the ship was becalmed, and the sailors ran out of food and were forced to drink water alive with maggots. In nine years at sea Told endured worse than maggots, however, suffering through beatings, shipwrecks, pestilential fevers, and service on a slaver captained by a sadist. At twenty-three he escaped the sea, becoming first a bricklayer, then a servant, and finally in Wesley's service, head of a charity school. Ultimately, after a second marriage which brought modest means, he devoted his last years to visiting "malefactors in the several prisons in and about" London. He nursed the sick, prayed with debtors in Newgate, and converted the condemned, often riding with them in the cart to the place of execution. Told's charity did not stop with deathbed conversions, and he aided the families of those executed, finding jobs for widows and children. Unlike many spiritual autobiographies, Told's is filled with both the grit of hard living, nights during which forty-one out of eighty slaves suffocated in a "loathsome den," and the grainy surface of cruel justice which condemned one Anderson for stealing cloth worth sixpence to feed his starving family. After talking to Told, however, Anderson embraced the gallows, declaring, "This is the happiest day I ever saw in my life! Oh! who could express the joy and peace I now feel! If I could have all the world, I would not wish to live another day!"

The quiet assurance which enabled Told to endure the scorn of turnkeys and persist in helping his fellows did not come easily. Even after meeting Wesley and taking up schoolmastering, he doubted himself. Despondent, he went for a walk early one morning after preaching. Near Ratcliff Row he met a cow. So troubled was he that he wished to be transformed beyond thought into the cow. A little later he noticed a disreputable man some yards away and thought, "That man would afford me the greatest happiness I ever before experienced, if he would put an end to so wretched a life." In part because he was depressed Told wandered into a lonesome corner of a field. Once there, a hand struck him on the head whereupon he cried, "Praise God! Praise God!" Looking up he saw the "air and sky, full of the glory of God," after which all became black for a moment. Before opening his eyes again, Told beseeched God to let him know if the event signaled the remission of his sins. Feeling "an unspeakable peace," he dared to look up. Before him the heavens opened into a seam, tapering "away to a point at each end." The center of "this sacred avenue," Told recounted, was "about twelve feet wide, wherein I thought I saw the Lord Jesus, holding up both his hands, from the palms of which the blood seemed to stream down. On this, the flood of tears gushing from my eyes, trickled down my cheeks and I said, 'Lord, it is enough!' From that hour I have not once doubted of my being freely justified."

Our age seems to focus on matters sexual almost to the exclusion of all else, and so I drew a line down the margin beside this part of Told's autobiography and in bold letters wrote "N.B." Still, I wasn't sure it was enough to mortify *Onania's* fleshiness. Consequently, beside the first volume of the *Arminian Magazine* I put *Lois Dudley Finds Peace*, a tract published in 1923 by the Bible Institute Colportage Association of Chicago and telling the story of an orphan girl's accepting the Lord as her "personal Saviour." Beside the other volume of the *Arminian Magazine* I put T. A. Faulkner's *From the Ball Room to Hell and the Lure of the Dance* (1922). "Tell me, you dancing Christians," Faulkner asked, "how many lost souls have you led to Jesus?" According to Faulkner dance polluted more souls than any other activity, and in chapters typically entitled "Christ at the Ball" and "The Dance and White Slaves," he cited statistical and anecdotal proof. "*Eighty per cent* of the thousands of the denizens of the underworld," he noted, "have been members of some church where dancing was permitted." From California a Catholic priest wrote, saying he had interviewed 200 girls who were "inmates of the Brothel." "Dancing schools and ball-rooms" directly caused the downfall of 163 of the girls, the priest reported, while "Drink given by parents" ruined 20, "Willful choice, caused by low wages," 10, and "Abuse and poverty," 7.

Today the lure of interpretation is greater than that of the dance, and I realized someone could conceivably bind the carnal to the spiritual on my bookshelf and thereby reach a conclusion about my past, a conclusion which, like Lois Dudley's peace, would pass "all understanding." In selecting a past, however, one cannot forestall perverse interpretation. After having made "the Outward Shew of virtue," all I could hope for was that whoever examined my library would do so with an eye less rancorous than that with which the author of *Onania* oogled "lustful Women of Sense." In any case the library constituted but a chapter of my past, and after finishing it I picked up the bigger signature of memory, not initially, though, my own but family memories. On Mother's side of the family, the Ratcliffe side, many people do not marry. Single and singular, they only occasionally approve of each other and almost never approve of outsiders. Just recently, I learned that my great-aunt Betty almost married. When youngish, she fell in love with a man from Pennsylvania, and fleeing family and spinsterhood left Richmond with him on the evening train, rolling toward Philadelphia and matrimony. She got as far, I was told, as King William or Caroline County, where the train was shunted onto a siding and she was pulled off by relatives armed with virtue and pistols. For his part her lover was encouraged to continue to Philadelphia and advised not to return to Richmond. Finding Virginia courtships a little too passionate, he remained in Philadelphia and married there, not before, however, suing the Ratcliffes for alienation of affection, a suit settled out of court by my grandfather, who, despite not being involved in the railway incident, was the only member of the family at that time with means.

Although the story of Aunt Betty's elopement appeals to me I wish I knew it were true. Even if it were, I'm not sure I should include it in my past. One of the problems with selecting a past is that the past is always vital. Not only can it shape perceptions of the moment but it can influence futures. Grandfather Ratcliffe died when I was small, and after his death, Mother often described the things he and I did together. I was, she said, a source of amusement to him. Once while he lay napping in the back parlor, I burst into the room, having tried unsuccessfully to build a toy box. "Big Ga," I shouted, waking him and holding out my hands, "get the axe and chop these arms off. They are no damn good!" Even thinking that such an anecdote could influence a child's development seems perverse, yet I have never been good with my hands. The workings of a hammer, a nail, and a wall are just as mysterious to me as those of a microprocessor. And once or twice over the years, I have thought that if Mother had not told me the story about my hands and the axe I might have tried harder to learn about tools.

What bothers me in the account of Aunt Betty's elopement is the violence. Although family tale has it that my great-great-grandfather Pickering gave up schoolmastering to fight in the Mexican War, eventually becoming a lieutenant colonel, rarely have either the Pickerings or the Ratcliffes been violent. In general we labor to avoid being drawn into conflicts. During the Vietnam War when I stopped teaching in order to attend graduate school, my draft classification changed to 1-A. If drafted, I don't know what I would have done. Leaving the country was not something my friends did, and I suspect I would have enlisted in the navy. In any case I didn't face the dilemma. Various universities had awarded me scholarships, including a couple of National Defense Act Fellowships. Gathering the fellowship offers together, I made an appointment to see the clerk of the local draft board. For the appointment I put on my best suit and smoothest manner. After reading through my materials, the clerk turned to me and said, "Mr. Pickering, I cannot tell you what an honor it is to have you registered here."

In thinking about it now, I suppose I should not include this account in my past. It makes me appear smug and cunning when the truth was that at twenty-five the possibility of my being called up, manners and fellowships aside, was almost nonexistent. Of course by taking word or event out of context, selecting distorts. Years ago when I asked Vicki to marry me, she hesitated, explaining that she did not know whether to marry me or become an ornithologist. To find out she volunteered to work for the Wildfowl Trust at Slimbridge in Gloucestershire. After she flew off to Britain, I thought there was little chance of her roosting quietly in my domestic nest. Three months later Vicki called me. She was in Princeton. "I'm back," she said, "and I'll marry you." "That's great," I answered, "but what brought you home." "Ducks," she said. "Ducks shit a lot"—with the inference being, I suppose, that my performance in such matters was somewhat more satisfactory. A decade of affectionate family life and three fledglings later, all inferences seem beside the point, and smacking of a flightier, migrant time, the story has little to do with the woman who moves through my days softer than birdsong. What the story does, however, is underscore the problem raised by time when one selects a past. Mentioning the Vietnam War makes the 1960s seem important in my past when actually the sixties, like the war, did not touch me, not the music, the drugs, the social protests, not even the sexual revolution. I think I read through the sixties, but I am not sure, for never have I had a clear sense of time.

Not just in January but throughout the year I date checks incorrectly. Connecticut Bank and Trust is so used to my mistakes that instead of returning the checks they correct them silently. Of course selecting a past may decrease the importance of time, forcing one to view time not as a series of discrete historical units but as a continuum, a line on which date is less significant than mood. A person finding the initial notes I took for this essay could conclude that I lacked any sense of ordered, historical time. Instead of jotting down ideas as I normally do in a hundred-page, eleven-by-nine-inch yellow spiral notebook printed for the "UConn Co-op," I wrote ideas down in a small, four-by-six-and-a-half-inch "Vanderbilt Notebook Student Series," taken by my father to lectures in the 1920s. On the cover Father wrote his name several times in blue ink then drew scores of whirling attached circles, shaped like Slinkies. Inside he recorded remarks about Thoreau, Emerson, Whitman, Melville, Twain, Lanier, and Poe. His teacher spent much time discussing Puritanism and things southern, and Father's notes referred again and again to H. L. Mencken and Stuart Sherman. For my part I started my notes on a page at the top of which Father had written "For Saturday—a paper" and "Thursday week—a quiz." Underneath he drew an anvil, on the side of which he wrote the first ten letters of the alphabet in capital letters.

I don't mean to imply that time or, better, the times are unimportant in selecting a past. The spirit of the present may actually influence selection more than conditions of time past. I spent childhood summers on my grandfather's farm in Hanover, Virginia. Hanover was rich in country things and country people, both black and white. As the dirt roads wound about between farms, so people's lives twisted together, endlessly supplying matter for stories, some poignant, some gentle, and a good many racist—or perhaps not racist so much as racially aware, for the tales often revealed intimacy and affection. In the late 1940s William the oldest son of Molly, grandfather's cook, left Virginia for New York where he became a successful undertaker. "Oh, Miss Katharine, William is doing just fine," Molly answered when Mother asked about him; "he's so light people think he's a spaniel." Mother and Molly were good friends, loving, if not each other, then the world in which they grew up. For years after the farm was sold and we stopped visiting Hanover, they talked on the telephone. I must have heard the story of William's success a score of times, for Mother told it to me after each conversation with Molly. Yet if William were to become part of my past, he would have to be even lighter—whitewashed out of time and beyond offense.

In the class notes he took on Mark Twain, Father wrote, "Dangerous to carry humor too far in dealing with great subjects." Not only does the present force one to shun particular subjects but it also distorts the past by compelling avoidance of certain types of anecdotes. Importance is often equated with solemnity, and the light treatment of any subject, great or small, is dangerous. No matter the selection, if I write humorously, chances are I will have no past, at least not one judged worthy of thought. Consequently, I was tempted to select mostly cosmetic, serious anecdotes for my past, in the process distorting daily life. This weekend I talked on the telephone to Aunt Elizabeth in Richmond. She asked if I remembered going to Uncle Wilbur's office one day when I was eleven or twelve. After learning from the receptionist Mrs. Lane that Uncle Wilbur was busy removing wisdom teeth, I burst into his office and turning to him looked him up and down before saying, "Well, Dr. Ratcliffe, it's so good to see you almost sober for a change."

Although I would not want such knowledge to become part of a past, the truth is that for as long as I can remember I have been outspoken. Recently the University of Connecticut condemned four hundred acres of farmland and established a research park, and yesterday in the campus mail I received a letter inviting me to become an associate of the Science and Technology Institute of New England, a consortium of faculty members interested, as a friend put it, in "enhancing earning potentials." Although ostensibly written to the entire university, the letter was really addressed to the science faculty. For some reason that lodged awkwardly in my sensibility, and I telephoned the secretary of the institute. I appreciated his letter, I said, adding that I wanted to become an associate of the institute. The institute, I continued, when he paused on learning that I taught English, would need people to write propaganda and reports. In fact, I stated, I had considerable experience with the legal side of business writing. "Let me give you an example of how I would write a contract for you," I said: "The party of the first part, hereinafter known as greedy sons of bitches, contracts with the party of the second part, hereinafter known as sell-your-birthright-for-a-dime bastards."

The conversation with the secretary did not last much longer, but walking home, I felt good. That evening I realized my remarks sounded remarkably like something Mother might have said, and I wondered if thinking a person could select a past was only delusion. Maybe a past, even the very words I used, had already been selected for me by heredity. Instead of being free to speak my mind, perhaps I was hung in a groove which had rolled round through generations of minds. Two weeks ago in class I tried to explain how the birth of children changes romance. After the appearance of children, I said, romance lost its dreamy appeal, quickly becoming a practical matter of schedules and consequences. My students were, alas, too young even to want to understand. "Just because of a moment of pleasure," I finally broke out, "just because of a passing thing like chewing Teaberry or Juicy Fruit gum, I haven't slept a night in seven years." What I said was, of course, almost true. Since Francis's birth seven years ago, I haven't spent an undisturbed night. At least once, and more often than not two or three times a night, a child awakens me or I wake on my own and go look at the children to be sure they are still breathing. What was also true was that what I said in class Mother had said to me years earlier in a slightly different way. "Great God!" she exclaimed in exasperation. "Because of you I haven't slept in a single night in twelve years."

Despite the possibility of heredity's selecting one's past, I want to believe that a person has at least some freedom of choice, in my case freedom enough to distort the past consciously. I do not want my past to have a great influence upon my children's futures, forcing them to live contrary to their inclinations, endlessly measuring themselves against steep, high standards. I don't want my life to weigh them down. Instead I want them to feel superior to me. Superiority brings the freedom to dismiss. And although I hope the children will occasionally remember me lovingly, I nevertheless want them to forget me and live natural, self-assured lives, unburdened by my past. To this end I have distorted my life, selecting a past which reflects a me, often silly and always odd. No person is ever consistent for very long, though, and while selecting a modest dismissible past for myself, I have tried to shape the children's futures.

If my lack of mechanical ability stems from Mother's recounting my desire to have my arms lopped off, then perhaps the tales I tell about the children will influence their lives for the better. To some extent I guess I am selecting pasts for them, pasts, I hope, though, of mood not abilities, pasts soft and gentle and smiling. Edward who is five admires G.I. Joe and everything military, and although Vicki and I refuse to buy him toy guns, he fashions them out of sticks and Legos. In contrast Eliza who is three likes dolls and is forever having tea parties or staging ballets with them. One afternoon last week Eliza and Edward were playing quietly upstairs until Eliza suddenly appeared crying. "What's wrong, Peanut," I said when Eliza came into the study. "Crystal Star and I were having a party in my room," she sobbed, "and then in came the army." Lest this story someday give Edward a wrong impression of himself, I ought to add that Edward's army is usually composed of peacekeepers. Rarely does he invade tea parties because he generally walks about the house with my pillow on his head, sucking his left thumb and rubbing the edge or the pillow case between the thumb and index finger of his right hand. Four nights ago while I read him a story in my bed, I asked him to massage my weak arm. "I will, Daddy," he said, putting the pillow on his head and beginning to rub the case, "but first I have to fill up with gas at the pillow station." After rubbing the pillow case for ten or fifteen seconds, he started massaging my arm. Because his hand is small, it, evidently, could not hold much gas, having to return to the pillow case and be filled several times.

Under the heading "Things associated with the South by People" Father listed six items in his notebook. The first was Sentiment, about which Father wrote, "Passes too often into Sentimentalism." Part of the southern past sixty years ago, sentimentalism is part of my past today, and I cannot help being sentimental about the children. In fact if I examined the present closely I would probably discover that sentimentalism pervades my days. In contrast to time, particular place matters to me, and when I thought about selecting a place for my past, sentiment influenced me, pushing me toward childhood and the South and away from maturity and Connecticut, a stage of life and a place in which I have been wondrously happy. For a while I thought my place would be Carthage, Tennessee, Father's hometown. I even did research, learning that Grandma Pickering bought her home on November 5, 1909, paying $4,000. She sold it in 1952 for $15,500. This past Easter, though, Mother died and was buried in Carthage, and suddenly Carthage seemed a place of losses, both homes and joy. In Connecticut I own almost no land, and after Mother's death I suddenly wanted a place rich with acres and possibilities. Recently I reread Teale's *A Naturalist Buys an Old Farm*, and after following him across the hills and streams of Hampton, Connecticut, I returned to Hanover and the Virginia farms of childhood, farms I had roamed like Teale's Trail Wood, observing and naming: Sliding Hill, Red Barn Creek, Piney Woods, The Circle, Bamboo Forest, and Turtle Pond. I remembered the way along old Route 614 from Cabin Hill to Etna Mills: down a long hill and around and over Norman's bridge across the Pamunkey River into King William County. Just on the Hanover side of the bridge was an old house in which Gypsies stayed every summer. One August Grandfather took me there and I watched them dance, skirts spinning yellow and red in the green shade. Across the bridge we once stopped so a mother skunk could escort her kits across the road. On the left farther into King William was Hornquarter, a farm Grandfather tried unsuccessfully to buy. At Bleak Hill Fork we turned right, passing Gravatt's Mills Pond and then reaching Etna Mills.

In turning toward childhood for place, I turned toward the past itself, selfishly neglecting both the present and those about me. On sunny weekends my family and I often walk in the woods, down behind the university's barns or through Schoolhouse Brook Park. On the walks I behave much as I did as a child, overturning rocks, digging out the rotten hearts of fallen trees, and wandering off to climb small bluffs or explore marshy lowlands. "Gosh," I said to Vicki last Sunday, "this is great. I don't envy the Weavers scuba diving in Montego Bay." "That," Vicki said after a pause, "that would be fun, too." Although Grandfather Ratcliffe owned twenty-seven hundred acres, his farms seemed small to me, not so much in size, as I now think about it, but in mood and pace. The city's fast pace probably lay behind my not placing my past in Nashville. The elementary school I attended has been torn down, and so much is new in Nashville, even the old, that the place seems to have no past, or at least little sympathy for a past like mine, not crisp Scalamandré roped off in a museum but frayed kitchen oilcloth.

As I want simplicity to be a great part of my place in the past, so my past itself should be simple. In arranging the books in the study, I may have made interpretation needlessly and confusingly complex. With the chest of drawers upstairs I did better, only putting an eighteenth-century Pennsylvania spice box on top. Eighteen inches tall, fifteen wide and twelve deep, the spice box has thirteen drawers, surrounding a keyhole opening. While ginger, nutmeg, and cloves were kept in the drawers, the mortar and pestle for grinding spices probably sat in the opening. When I found the spice box in Mother's attic, it was almost empty, containing needles and thread and three blue buttons. Since putting the box on the chest, I have filled two drawers. In one I put a small silver locket, seven-eighths of an inch in diameter. The locket was given to Vicki's grandmother when she was a student at Wellesley, and engraved on the back are her initials MFJ and the date 1908. On the front is the orange and black crest of Princeton University. Vicki's father was an undergraduate, and I was a graduate student at Princeton, so the school is part of our family's past, and perhaps like my southern sentimentalism, it will crop up in the future. At least I hope so, and to this end, I put the locket in the spice box as a sort of seed. Someday, maybe the children will find it, and becoming aware of the past, will consider going to Princeton.

On the other hand my family is various, and if attending Princeton is part of my past, so is not attending Princeton or for that matter any college. After applying to and being admitted to several schools, Mother refused to go, choosing instead to spend months hunting and riding in Arizona. "I'd had enough school," she said; "books are only part of life." To balance the austere Princeton locket, I put two pieces of Mother's jewelry into the spice box: a heavy gold ring in the middle of which sat an amethyst as big as a tangerine and then a pin shaped like a salamander, its body greenish-blue malachite, its eyes rubies, and diamonds glistening at the tips of its fingers. I had the jewelry because Father insisted I bring it to Connecticut after Mother's death. I stuffed it into the bottom of a handbag, on top of which I crammed four or five purses which Father also asked me to take. At the airport the bag was certain to be inspected, and I envisioned being arrested as a masher or cat burglar. "Well," the woman opening the purse at the airport said, "you certainly have a lot of purses." "Aren't they divine," I answered, inspiration twisting about like a hot salamander; "I never travel without a purse for each outfit. Wait until you get to the bottom of the bag and see my jewelry. It is just scrumptious." "So it is," the woman said looking at me out of the corner of her eye and drawing back. "Just scrumptious," she said, cursorily pushing a purse aside before handing me the bag and adding, "Have a nice flight."

I haven't put more family jewelry into the spice box, partly because I'm not sure I can blend the austere and the flamboyant in a way which won't affect my children's futures. Moreover I have almost come to believe in an accidental past, one smacking more of the geological than the rational. The effects of glaciers can be seen all over my part of Connecticut. When the ice melted, glacial drift remained behind. Here in the Eastern Uplands, the drift is till, sediment of all sizes jumbled together: pebbles, stones, clay, and boulders. Whenever I dig in the yard, I hit some kind of rock. Perhaps that, too, is the way of a past. Scraping across then withdrawing from the surface of time, a life leaves till behind, and if someone starts to dig, he's sure to hit something with his shovel. Although I have put nothing more in it than locket, ring, and pin, the spice box has begun to accumulate till: paper clips, pencil nubs, a pearl button, and then mysteriously the buckeye and shark's tooth Mother kept for good luck and which she put in the overnight bag she took with her to the hospital that last time.

Composing a Life

LAST MONTH I RECEIVED A LETTER that began, "Are you the Samuel Pickering that went to Sewanee twenty years ago?" I did not know how to answer the letter. A boy with my name once attended college at Sewanee, and although I knew him fairly well and think I liked him, that boy had long since disappeared. Some good things happened to him at college, and I have often considered writing about them. The trouble is that I am not sure if the things I remember actually happened. Did that boy actually carry a hammer into Professor Martin's class one day, and when an old roommate Jimmy asked why he had it, did that boy really say, "For nailing hands to desks." And did he tell Jimmy to flatten his hand out on the desk if he did not believe him—whereupon, trusting a friend, Jimmy did so. Shortly afterwards when Professor Martin asked Jimmy why he had screamed, did Jimmy answer, "Pickering hit me with a hammer"? And did that boy stand up and say, "I cannot tell a lie; I hit him with my little hammer."

No, no—the person who I have become certainly didn't do that. This person lives in a world without Jimmys, hammers, screams, and exclamation points. For fifteen years I have taught writing. For ten of these years writing has taught me, and I have labored not so much to compose sentences as to compose my life. Hours at the desk and countless erasures have brought success. I haven't committed a comma blunder in almost five years, certainly not since I married Vicki. Happily I have forgotten what participles and gerunds are, but then I have forgotten most things: books, loves, and most of my identities. At my dining room table, dangling modifiers are not mentioned, and I ignore all question marks as my days are composed, not of lurid prose and purple moments, but of calm of mind and forthright, workaday sentences.

Rarely do I use a complex sentence, and even more rarely do I live with complexity. In a simple style I write about simple people, people born before the first infinitive was split and the wrath of grammarians fell upon mankind. Occasionally I write about a small town in Virginia where I spent summers as a boy. In the center of the town was the railway station. Clustered about it were the bank and post office, Ankenbauer's Café and Horace Vickery's store. Mr. Vickery was a big man; alongside him, his wife, whom he called "Little Bitty Bird," seemed no larger than a sparrow. Mrs. Vickery spent her days in the domestic nest over the store where she delighted in rearranging furniture. One night Mr. Vickery returned home late from a meeting of the Masons; and if the truth be known, he came home a trifle "happy." Not wanting to wake Mrs. Vickery, he did not turn on the bedroom light. He undressed in the dark and after hanging his clothes up, silently slipped into his pajamas then leaned over to get into bed. Alas, the bed was not where he remembered it; Mrs. Vickery had spent the evening moving furniture, and as Mr. Vickery reached to pull back the covers, he fell to the floor in a great heap. "Oh, Little Bitty Bird," he sang out once he got his breath, "what have you done?"

By rearranging her few possessions Mrs. Vickery was able to create new worlds for herself. Distant places did not appeal to her, and when her husband took the day train to Richmond, seventeen miles away, she stayed home, content to shift a chair or dresser. As I think about Mrs. Vickery now, her life seems almost ideal. In my seven years in eastern Connecticut, I have lived simply, rarely traveling to Hartford thirty miles away. Years ago simplicity held little attraction for me, and I traveled far afield seeking the confusion of mixed metaphors and long, run-on sentences. Dashes marked my days, and I dreamed of breaking through the tried and the safe into the unknown. Once in Baku on the Caspian Sea, Soviet police dogged my footsteps, and I retreated into the twisting byways of the old town where I would suddenly disappear and then just as suddenly reappear, much to my pleasure and, as I thought, to the amazement of the police. When I began to write, I was taught to vary my style. "Use different sentence structures; be different people," teachers told me. And for a while I did that, meandering along slowly then darting forward only to turn back abruptly like the boy in Baku. Here I would insert a compound sentence, there a noun clause, here a gray man of mystery, there a colorful eccentric. For years experimenting was good, and although I didn't publish much, I had many styles and identities. Now the older and simpler me stays home, and as my car is a family station wagon—an American-made Plymouth Reliant—I have only one style, the solid, economical, fifty-thousand-mile-warranteed reliable style of the short declarative sentence.

Other kinds of sentences offend me and seem unsound and unsettling. Words, rules, and life confuse people. The simple style orders confusion, at first producing the illusion of control and then, after time, the reality. When pressure makes a person bear down so hard that he or his pencil breaks, he should struggle to write simply. By doing so one can regain composure. For years shots made me faint, and I shuddered whenever I entered a doctor's office. Then one day I found myself in a small room waiting for a blood test while another man sat on a couch outside. When the nurse appeared and saw me and the man outside, she called a companion on the telephone. "Mary," she said, "you better come down. There's two here waiting to be stuck. I'll stick the one inside, and you stick the one outside." What a wondrously insensitive thing to say, I thought, certain I would soon topple over. I was wrong; suddenly my nervousness vanished as I pondered sticking the nurse's remarks into an article I was writing. And that shot and those that have followed have passed without a tumble. Thoughts about writing never fail to contribute to my composure. Whenever I visit a doctor now, I don't walk into his office trembling in expectation of the worst sort of parsing. Instead I am ready to turn the experience into a story and thus control it. Once while in the Mideast, I picked up an exotic fungus. Although the fungus was out of sight, it grew on a part of my body that made me uneasy, and as soon as I returned to Connecticut I went to a dermatologist. "Good God," he exclaimed when I showed the fungus to him; "I have never seen anything like that." Then pausing for a moment, he added cheerfully, "All I can say is that I am glad it is on you and not on me."

I am not always successful in composing things. Sometimes words get out of hand and, carrying me beyond the full stops I plan, spill over into the tentative world of the colon and expose parts of life that ought to remain buried. Some time ago I decided to write about my summers in Virginia. The essay didn't turn out to be the hymn to golden days that I envisioned. When it appeared in print, I read it and was disturbed. None of my periods worked. "Good country people," the essay began, "scare the hell out of me. Once I liked the country and thought that the closer a person was to the soil, the nearer he was to God. I know better now. The closer a person is to the soil, the dirtier he is." The essay bothered me until I read a note a boy handed in with a story he wrote as an assignment for a course I teach in children's literature. The students were told to write cheerful stories with positive endings. "I am sorry this is such a terrible story," the boy explained, "but I just couldn't think of a good one. They all kept coming out the other way around with Evil triumphing. I am a very disobedient person by nature." All people and sentences are disobedient; and after reading the note, I realized that words, like human beings, occasionally violated the best outlines. All one could do was erase, rewrite, and hope that evil would not triumph in the final draft.

As a person has to struggle with words to make them obedient, so one has to revise life. The effort to become simple and perhaps boring is difficult, but I am succeeding. At least twice a week I tell my wife Vicki that she is fortunate to be married to such a conventional person. "Stop saying the same simple-minded things," she replies; "you are hopelessly repetitive." "Ah, ha," I think, "a few more years and my full stops will block everything unsettling." In passing, I should add that as one grows older and better able to master simple thoughts, he will, nevertheless, violate many rules of grammar. I, for example, am over forty and don't have the energy I once had. Despite suggestions that urge me to use the active rather than the passive voice, I am afraid I live in the passive. Let young writers attempt to manage lively active verbs and do all sorts of creative things to predicates. For my part I am content to be acted upon. Occasionally I ponder taking a forceful part in life but the fit passes. As one grows older, material goods become less important; as one learns the virtues of the oblique approach, direct objects disappear from life.

Age has taught me the value of a familiar, relaxed style and life, beyond direct objects. On weekends I run races. My goal is never to complete a race in the first 50 percent of the finishers. Unlike top road racers, my performance never disappoints me. Sometimes I am tempted to thrust ahead but I always resist. Last weekend as I trotted down a street, a young woman yelled, "You are so cute." To be honest, after hearing that I heisted my legs up a bit and pranced for a while, but then as soon as I was around the corner and out of sight, I settled back into a slow, comfortable rhythm and let a crowd of younger active runners rush by, chasing celebrity and trophies.

Age and the experience it brings lead a person to break many grammar rules. Students in my writing classes always confuse *its* the posses-sive with *it's* the contraction. When I first began to teach, I railed against the error, attributing ignorance about the possessive to a left-wing con-spiracy that was sweeping the nation and undermining the concept of private property. Nowadays I don't give a hoot about the possessive, in great part because I no longer have anything that is mine and mine alone. My two little boys, aged three and one, have converted me to socialism, something no learned text or philosopher was able to do. What I once thought belonged to me, I now realize is theirs too. My papers are pushed aside and my desk has become a parking lot for Corgi Juniors, Hot Wheels, and Matchbox cars. At night Vicki and I don't sleep alone; we share our bed with an ever-changing group of visitors including Little Bear, Big Bear, Green Worm, and Blue Pillow.

Like a good essay, the composed life has a beginning, middle, and definite ending. Youth can dream about the future and imagine a multi-tude of endings, and as a result usually can't write well. After forty, dreams stop and one buys life insurance. Instead of evoking visions of idyllic pleasure, the ellipsis that looms ahead leads only to an erasure and an empty notebook. For the writer beyond forty the end is clear and nothing can change it. In contrast the past is infinitely malleable, and I often write about it, trying to give shape to fragments that cling to mem-ory. In classes I tell students to write about the small things in the first paragraph of life and not worry about the conclusion. It will take care of itself. All writers should avoid shadowlands where things are not clear and simple. Occasionally, the complex and mysterious tempt me, and I consider writing about such things as a train journey I made on Christ-mas Eve, 1964, from Bucharest to Sofia. Guards with tommy guns paced up and down inside the cars while outside the train whistle blew haunt-ingly through the night. Near the Bulgarian border snow began to fall, and I joined a funeral party that was drinking sorrow away. At the bor-der when guards began to pull people roughly from the train, I opened the window in my compartment and serenaded them with Christmas carols. I got through "Hark the Herald Angels Sing" and was just begin-ning "The First Noel" when a somber man entered the compartment and grabbing my jacket, pulled me back inside to the seat. Without say-ing anything, he sat next to me. The funeral party looked at him, then left, and the two of us rode all the way to Sofia in silence. I often wonder what went through the man's mind as we travelled through Christmas morning together. Yet whenever I begin to speculate, my thoughts soon turn toward summers and trains in Virginia. Men sat on the porch of Vickery's store, and as the trains passed through, said things that I remembered, simple things that now seem more important and more lasting than all the mysterious silences I have known. "She's a long one," someone would invariably say about a slow freight; "on the way to Richmond," somebody would add. Toward evening when the coal train to Fredericksburg was due, a man was sure to look at his watch and say, "About time for the coal train." "And for my dinner," someone else would say and then get up and start home.

The reading I assigned students in writing courses once created difficulty for me. Anthologies always contain a few pieces by well-known writers, people that students will hear about someday. Setting myself up as an authority when I was unknown bothered me. Even worse I knew I would always be unknown. Aside from writing an essay that would find its way into an anthology and thrust me out of anonymity, something that was impossible for a person so passive, I did-n't know what to do. A little thought and some labor at revising, how-ever, worked a change. I wrote a piece in which I celebrated anonymity and as a consequence am now wonderfully content. Oddly enough, being unknown and being satisfied with a passive, simple style has brought me attention. Not long ago the *Willimantic Chronicle,* our local newspaper, began an article on road racing by quoting me. Unfortu-nately, or perhaps fortunately, for fame can disrupt a simple style, the article began with a typographical error. "Ass Sam Pickering has noted," the paper stated—I have forgotten the rest. After such a begin-ning, it seems unimportant.

A problem arises after one turns life into a series of balanced, short declarative sentences. Well-placed modifiers and proper subordination do not lend themselves to startling essays. The run-on life, like the sen-tence, breaks through propriety and occasionally stumbles into interest-ing constructions. I wondered if I would be able to write once my sen-tences were under control and my life simple. I should not have worried. Almost every day the postman brings me matter for essays. "Good going old horse," a former student wrote after he read something of mine. "My Dear Samuel Pickering, Jr, I have read your brilliant book and found great satisfaction in it," a woman wrote after reading an arti-cle of mine in a quarterly. "Our universe is rolling on in an endless chain of miseries and misfortunes," a man wrote from Syria; "it is the law of our land that we all should die one day; we die when children, money, profession, fame either, can do us nothing. We stand alone, stripped out of everything, in a contest, without spectators, without glamour and hope of win or fear of loss—with much delight and disbelief in our competitor's right and still less confidence in ours. My father died 20 days ago dreaming in the world to come."

As transitions link fragments of life and enable one to escape despair, that terrible sense that nothing matters and chance determines everything, so they bind my disparate letters into articles. Many years ago, before the first sentence of my life was conceived, my grandfather owned a dairy. Although grandfather had several businesses, Henry Hackenbridge his herdsman assumed the dairy was the most important. Every day Henry came to grandfather's house and in great detail described the mood of the herd. When grandfather went out of town, Henry wrote him letters daily. Once after breakfast at the old Ritz in New York, grandfather went to fetch his letter. "Yes, sir, Mr. Ratcliffe, there is something for you," the clerk said and started to hand grandfather a letter. Suddenly a look of concern came over the clerk's face, and he said, "Oh, dear, I am so sorry." Grandfather was puzzled until he saw the letter. Under the address in big, clear letters, Henry had written, "P.S. Grandma slipped last night." Although the clerk did not know it, Grandma was not my grandfather's mother or wife. She was an old cow, and the night before she had not fallen on the stairs or in the hall, but had in the language of the dairy, lost her calf. When I search for the right transition, I often think of this story. If I can find the right word and am able to keep my life and sentences simple, chances are good that I won't slip too often.

Picked Up

POD MALONE WAS THE WORST STUTTERER in Smith County, Tennessee. One evening after a meeting of the Knights of Pythias, Dr. Sollows, who had just read about a new treatment for stutterers at Vanderbilt Hospital in Nashville, met Pod outside Read's drugstore. "Pod," he said, "have you ever attended a clinic for stutterers?" "No," Pod answered after pulling his left ear and thinking a bit, "I just pi-pi-picked it up on my-my own."

Most learning is like Pod's, picked up informally beyond the high rail of rule and regulation. Bound by focus, formal education forces one to crop a narrow path and by preventing a person from ranging leads not so much to thoroughbred intellect as to absurdity. It just so happened that one night, so the old but illustrative story goes, a long-haired professor, a bald-headed man, and a barber were traveling together through a forest inhabited by packs of ravenous wolves. Before dusk the travelers stopped, gathered wood, and built a fire to keep the wolves away. To insure that the fire would not die during the night, they set up a watch. The barber agreed to watch from eight until midnight. Then, he said, he would wake the professor, who would tend the fire for the next four hours. Finally, the bald-headed man was supposed to watch the fire from four until the sun rose the next morning. Traveling through the forest had been difficult, and by eight o'clock the bald man and the professor were sound asleep. Quickly the barber grew bored. No wolves appeared, and made out of hard, dry wood, the fire burned easily and did not need much attention. To pass the time, the barber propped the professor up against a tree and shaved his head. When he finished, he laid the professor back on the ground. By midnight when it was time for the professor to stand watch, the barber shook him. Tired from the day's journey, the professor sat up slowly then rubbed his hands across his face and back over his head to help him wake up. As he pushed his hands across his head, the professor noticed that he didn't have any hair. For a moment his face was blank and he looked puzzled, then suddenly, as knowledge seemed to break upon him, he nodded and spoke. "What a fool you are, barber," he said. "You have awakened the bald-headed man instead of me."

If the professor had spent more hours in the woods and less in the office, he would have grown accustomed to odd things and the absence of a little hair would not have confused him. Grazing unblinkered across years, a person doesn't pick up ideas so much, though, as he does facts. As he grows older, many of the facts are, alas, necessarily medicinal. By fifty, one usually knows more medicine than an intern. I have spent much time roaming through libraries, reading books more neglected than the most forbidding part of any forest. In the process I have accumulated a medical school of knowledge, much of it, I am afraid, pertaining to digestive matters. "Great harmes have growne, and maladies exceeding," John Harington wrote in 1624, "By keeping in a little blast of *wind: / So Cramps, & Dropsies, Collicks* have their breeding / And *Mazed Braines* for want of vent behind."

In gathering medical knowledge I followed the lead of Henry Lyte, who in 1619 wrote in the introduction to *A New Herbal* that "a good thing the more common it is, the better it is." In *A Rich Store-house or Treasury for the Diseased* (1596), A. T. suggested that one who was "costive and bound in his body" should take a suppository of "boyled Honny and little fine Powder of Salt." If this did not work, one could, *The Treasure of Poore Men* (1550) advised, "take a morsel of Larde as much as thy finger" and powder it with sage and "put it to the fundamente." For the opposite sort of stomach affliction, I found many remedies. "The doung of a Camell dried & dronke" or "the liver of ani beast sodden in vinigar," Humphrie Lloyd (1585) wrote, "doth binde the belly mightely." The best thing for a pain in the side, Lloyd thought, was "the doung of a Wolfe, if it bee newly made." According to William Warde (1560), the best way to cure "the paine of the side" was to keep a dog in a chamber for ten days "and give him only lambes or motton bones to gnawe, then take of his excremendes and drie it in the sunne, and make thereof a powder, and give the patient to drinke of it every morning halfe an unce in white wine hote." If one didn't have a dog handy, "the like effect" could be achieved by making a "warm glister." "Take the dung of a blacke asse as hot as you maie find it whan it commeth from him," Warde instructed, "and seeth it in white wine that is not sweete, wringing well the dunge into the wine."

While searching for cures for various digestive ailments, I came upon useful remedies for all sorts of afflictions. For "leprosie," T. Bright (1615) recommended "*Hedgehogs* dryed and drunke"; for cankers, "the flesh of *Snayles* boyled, *Crayfishes*, greene *Frogges*." For "the stone," L. M. (1588) recommended the "Oyle of scorpion," while "Millipede, the loop, or the worme with many feet drunk in wine cureth the Jaundice." Often, of course, one remedy is about as good as another. Some years ago a drummer appeared in Carthage and, setting up a table on the courthouse lawn opposite the Smith County Bank, started selling bottles of flea powder. With each bottle came a page of instructions on how to kill fleas. For best results, the drummer explained, reading the instructions, the flea was to be held in the left hand between the thumb and index finger. With the thumb and index finger of the right hand, one was to take a pinch of the powder and apply it "to the flea's trunk or bloodsucking proboscis." Afterward, the drummer declared, "if any flea to which this powder has been administered can be proven to have bitten the purchaser, I will give that person another bottle of flea powder free." Vester McBee, a country woman from Gladis, a hill and hog hamlet up the road from Carthage, bought the first bottle. Vester listened carefully while the drummer explained for a second time how to use the powder. When he finished, she raised her hand slowly and then innocently asked whether—when she had caught the flea and had it in her hand between her fingers—killing it with her nail wouldn't do as well as the powder. "Yes," the drummer said, folding up the table and packing his bottles away, "that's a good way too."

The person who ambles through days picking up out-of-the-way learning rarely sets goals for life. Content to idle along without a purpose, he is usually not ambitious and collects observations, rather than possessions. For such a person, experience is an end in itself, the stuff of tale and conversation, not the means to advancement or growth. Along with medical knowledge, I have picked up many creatures during my wanderings, including a flea or two during my dog days. Much as some people return from travels with clothes or jewels, I bring back memories of creatures. Years ago I visited Kos, the birthplace of Hippocrates, the great physician. Early one morning I bicycled out from Kos Town to the ruins of the Asklepion, the medical sanctuary built in the fourth century B.C. in honor of Asklepios, the god of healing. As I walked through the terraces, I hoped to see a snake. Asklepios himself was represented as a serpent and the serpent is still, of course, the sign of a doctor. I climbed through the pine woods to a hill behind the sanctuary. Below me the pines were yellow in the sun. Beyond them lay the blue sea and to the northeast Bodrum, a white speck on the horizon. In the pines cicadas chattered, but on the hill all was quiet until something on the ground rustled. I looked down expecting a snake; instead a large tortoise crawled out from under some briars. He stopped at my feet and wagged his head back and forth. Then he scraped one side of his head through the grass. The right side of the tortoise's head puffed out, and the eye was shut, buried beneath a pillow of proud flesh. Seeing something sticking out at the corner of the tortoise's eye, I reached down and, wrapping my hand around his neck, held the head steady while I pushed back the swollen skin. In the corner of the eye was a thorn. At first when I tried to pull it out, the thorn would not give, but then it slipped free, hard and glistening. Behind it burst a thick brown cream, spotting my shirt then dripping down the tortoise's neck and over my hand. I held him while the sore drained. It took a long time, but when it stopped the tortoise blinked his right eye. Seeing the eyeball had not been damaged, I freed the tortoise, and he crawled noisily away through the grass. Unlike Asklepios, I had not restored life to the dead, but I had saved a tortoise's eye, and, walking back through the sanctuary to my bicycle, I felt in harmony with time and for a moment thought myself part of a natural process, green and healing. Snakes have attracted me since childhood, and I was disappointed not to have seen one on Kos. Over the years, though, I have collected a den of memories. My interest began when I spent summers on my grandfather's farm in Virginia. A dirt road passed in front of the farm, and occasionally cars ran over snakes. Because the road was soft, the snakes were not badly crushed. Whenever I found a fresh one, I took it back to the house and, when Mother took her afternoon nap, I carried it upstairs and curled it in the hall outside her door. Nowadays when I explore ruins, I look for snakes. Their presence quickens the dead rock and invigorates me. Just before going to Kos I saw two snakes in Syria. Early one morning as I walked sleepily through a maze of gray fallen columns in Palmyra, I stopped and unaccountably looked at the ground. A step ahead a snake lay partly buried in the sand. For a moment the snake was still, then it slipped silently under a column. Initially I thought the snake a Palestinean viper, but later I realized it was too long and was probably a harmless whip snake.

For the rest of that morning, though, I was alert and little in the ruins escaped my sight. Three days later I explored Marqab, looking out over the sea above Baniyas. Marqab is made from black basalt and on overcast days seems to hang above the coast like a heavy cloud. Inside the castle the keeper had a one-barrel shotgun beside his desk. He used it to shoot snakes, he explained and warned me that the castle was infested with kufi, the Arab name for the Levantine or blunt-nosed viper. Stout and sometimes five feet long, the kufi is dangerous, and the thought of coming upon one excited me. If I walked softly, I thought, I might see one, and sure enough, as I crossed stone fallen from a broken rampart in the middle of the castle, I found one sunning himself. I tried to creep up on him, but as soon as I got within four feet, he wrinkled and sliding off the rock disappeared into a patch of yellow flowers.

I am not sure why snakes attract me. Not only do I look for them in ruins, but I pick up stories about them. According to ancient account, Noah is responsible for there being snakes in the world today. Although God told him to take some "of every thing that creepeth upon the earth" into the ark, Noah disobeyed. Because of the serpent's treachery in Eden, Noah refused to allow snakes on the ark. As a result, all the snakes on earth drowned during the flood. When the waters receded, Noah immediately started building a new and better world. Over six hundred years old, he did not know how many years he had left and he did not want the lesser things of life to distract him from plowing and planting. Above all he did not want to fritter time away pursuing fleeting pleasure. Despite resolution and age, however, his penis kept obstructing his plans, drawing him toward sweet grapes and ripe music. One day while sowing grain, he had thoughts so amorous and distracting that he became disgusted and tearing off his penis threw it into an acacia tree. Immediately the penis turned into a giant viper, thorns from the acacia its fangs and its belly swollen with young.

Although I often try to catch the snakes I see, the truth is that I am relieved when a snake glides out of sight. Other creatures, though, I pick up and bring home. One October several years ago, I found a monarch butterfly lying in the grass in the front yard. Because the butterfly's wings were still intact, Vicki said we ought to revive him. I took him into the house and put him on a bowl of chrysanthemums in the living room. In the kitchen I dissolved cane sugar in boiling water and, taking two small cup-shaped ketchup containers from Wendy's, I made "honey pots." After placing them under the chrysanthemums, I urged the butterfly to drink. For a while he seemed to regain strength. That night I told Vicki that we would probably find Mr. Butterfly sitting on the mantlepiece the next morning. Instead I found him on the rug, lying on his side and slowly wiggling his legs. I picked him up and carried him over to a honey pot, where he drank a little. For six days Vicki and I fed the butterfly. No matter how we "stuffed" him, however, he was always on his side in the morning. Finally on the seventh morning I found him on the rug dead, lying on his back, legs drawn into his body. Vicki put him in a red matchbox, and after breakfast we buried him beside some goldenrod.

"That's the last wild creature I bring home," I said after crumpling the honey pots. Three years passed, and Francis and Edward were born. One night six weeks after Edward's birth, Vicki and I sat at the kitchen table eating chocolate chip cookies. Suddenly Vicki glanced outside, then jumped up and jerking open the back door ran into the yard. The dog next door had broken up a rabbit's nest and after scattering the baby rabbits was trotting home with one in its mouth. "Damn it, Coke," Vicki yelled, "drop that rabbit; drop it right now." Seeing Vicki rushing after him, Coke paused, then dropped the rabbit and ran home. Vicki picked up the rabbit; at the same time I looked out at the road. Crouched in the middle was a baby rabbit so little and awkward it could barely push its way along. Thirty minutes later the two rabbits were buried under a pile of shredded paper in a box under the kitchen table, and I was at the mall in the CVS drugstore buying an eyedropper and cans of soybean baby formula. Every four hours, night and day, for nine days I fed formula to the rabbits. Vicki wasn't able to help because she was busy with Edward. At two and six every night Edward woke up wailing. After handing him to Vicki, I staggered downstairs and warmed up formula for the rabbits. Once they were fed, I took Edward from Vicki and put him back in his crib. At the end of nine days the rabbits had grown considerably and were trying to jump out of the box; I then fed them clover and grass along with the formula. After eighteen days the rabbits were fat and vigorous and too much to handle. The next morning Vicki and I with Francis afoot and Edward in a Snugli walked to the university farm and turned the rabbits loose under the briar patch at the edge of a wood.

Since feeding the rabbits, I have avoided close involvement with neighborhood wildlife. After roving cats destroyed the nests of catbirds, I chopped down two yews which stood in the front yard. Hearing noises outside the bedroom window one night, I rushed into the yard and managed to save one fledgling from the cats. I wrapped the bird in a heating pad, but it died the next day. In thinking about it, I suppose I am more inclined to pick up animals than most things, particularly things mechanical. For example I dislike cars. I walk to my office at the University of Connecticut and have refused good positions at other universities because I would have to drive to work. I don't know how to use a computer and recently have stopped answering the telephone. When I started writing, I eagerly answered the telephone, hoping that someone was calling to praise a piece I had written or, better, to ask me to write an article or book. Years have passed and I have received little praise and no invitations to write books. So much time has passed that I don't want anyone to call me. A call now would only awaken resentment. Instead of being pleased with the present, I would think about the barren past and my day would be ruined. To insure no one telephones, I insert stories into my writings in order to keep people from taking me seriously.

Although I pick the stories up everywhere, from magazines and books or from conversation, I usually place them in my father's hometown, Carthage. Not long after she bought the flea powder, Vester McBee became housekeeper for Mrs. Hamper, widow of Morris Hamper, who sold lard and grease and manufactured linseed oil. Mrs. Hamper lived on Main Street in Carthage in a big Victorian house with purple and yellow stained glass in the door and above the front windows. Active in the Eastern Star and Ladies' Book Club, Mrs. Hamper was one of the grande dames of Carthage. She wore heavy hats with thick black ribbons and even put on perfume, something Vester had rarely smelled in Gladis. "Has that toilet water come?" Mrs. Hamper asked one morning when she was getting ready to call on Mrs. Eaves, a neighbor and treasurer of the Book Club. "Yes, ma'am," Vester answered from the kitchen. "I put it on the back of the commode." "Was it scented?" Mrs. Hamper asked, adjusting a ribbon on her hat. "No ma'am, it won't sented," Vester said. "I went to Read's drugstore and brung it home myself."

The person who ambles along informally picking up learning and other things is usually content. Generally such a person has few wishes. Focused on actual objects, wishes lead to dissatisfaction, for failure to obtain a wish often brings unhappiness while a wish achieved frequently turns out to be a wish lost. With no desire thrusting him forward toward a goal, the "picker-upper" begins each day curious and expectant, and relaxed. Always willing to poke about in this and that, such a person can be a meddler. Two years ago an acquaintance in the English department spent nine months in London. Before returning he mailed a cart of books back, and for a week each day's mail brought six or seven packages to the English department. Curious about what my acquaintance was mailing, I sorted through the packages and read the customs declarations. Most boxes contained books; one or two, though, contained items less academic. On one declaration my colleague stated that the box contained "Books, Running Shoes, Sweat Suit." After the words "Sweat Suit," there was a gap on the customs form. The space offended my aesthetic sense, so I took out my pen and to the declaration added "One Jockey Strap (Very Small)." I put the box on top of the other boxes and made sure it stayed there until my colleague appeared to remove his belongings.

Things of interest turn up almost everywhere. Besides reading customs declarations, I listen to conversations. Much that I overhear is dull, but occasionally I hear something useful. This past summer after we had been in Nova Scotia for eight weeks, I read in the local paper that a ten-kilometer road race was going to be held that afternoon in Yarmouth, twelve miles away. Although I had not run all summer and had put on ten pounds, I decided to race. Since my running clothes were in Connecticut, I wore a white undershirt, a purple bathing suit, a pair of brown, stretch, knee-length, insurance salesman's socks, and the pair of battered tennis shoes which I wear when mowing the grass. "I might not be fit," I told Vicki, "but Yarmouth is flat. I might even win a prize. Not many hotshots are liable to show up here." For three kilometers I bounced along, but then my feet began blistering, the bathing suit started chafing, and a summer of shortcake afloat in cream and wild strawberries began percolating. Although I wobbled toward the end of the race, I was alert enough to hear a boy say to his father as I passed, "Daddy, look at that man. He is going to fall. He shouldn't be running." The boy was right. I put away my socks and bathing suit after the race and have not run since. Despite finishing ninety-third out of 102 runners, I retired in style, however. Because I was from Connecticut, I was awarded the medal for the runner who lived farthest from Yarmouth. Unfortunately, the medal was not inscribed. McDonald's sponsored the race, and instead of the date of the race on one side of the medal appeared Ronald McDonald, his hair crinkly like fungus on damp wood.

The discipline and the labor necessary to complete a task or master learning often stamp impressions upon memory. In contrast, things which are picked up informally or require little effort to learn can just as easily be put down and forgotten. Occasionally being able to drop something quickly is convenient. Not long ago I decided to write an essay about my hometown, Nashville, Tennessee, and in a conversation with my father mentioned the idea. "That wouldn't be nice for your mother and me. We have to live here," Father said. "Besides," he added, "Peter Taylor has already written about Nashville and he has done it better than you could ever do it." Father was right. That night I tore the page with "Nashville" written at the top out of my notebook and began taking notes for a piece called "Horse Sense." "You can find more horse scents in a stable than anywhere else," I had read recently and thought I might write about the relationship between Nature and Reason. I didn't write the essay; something interrupted me and by the time I returned to the subject a fresh breeze had blown my thought away. Actually, most of the ideas and learning which I pick up get away from me, even medical knowledge. Having heard that I knew something about stomach problems, a friend came to my office in the English department last week. He told me he felt poorly and then after describing his symptoms asked me if his difficulties originated in his stomach or his liver. I had nothing to say. If I had remembered Wynkyn de Worde's *Judycyall of Uryns* (1512), a book I read four years ago, I could, however, have helped him diagnose himself. "Uryne thyn and somewhat reade and cleare with a bright cyrcle," de Worde wrote, "betokeneth a bad stomach."

The loss of learning does not bother me. Rarely do I regret forgetting about a book like de Worde's *Judycyall;* most of the time I don't remember such books well enough to realize that I forgot them. What does bother me, however, is the loss of the gentling effect of culture. At best culture is a veneer, but it is one which took effort for me to acquire. Sadly, anger can melt it in a moment. Three years ago I attended a performance of *La Traviata* at the Royal Opera House in London. The rich music moved me, and I left the opera thinking that if human beings could produce such beauty we were not doomed.

"Maybe someday," I thought, hope ringing through me like music, "good really will triumph over evil." Even the descent into the Underground and the loud, dirty ride on the Northern Line to Hampstead did not affect my feelings. As Germont's "Who hath won thy heart away from fair Provence's sea and soil" played through my mind, I imagined rock roses pink and rich with myrrh and didn't see the metallic cars, cigarette butts stamped out on the floor, and advertisements for temporary jobs pasted around the ceiling. At the Hampstead station, I got out and walked along the platform almost oblivious to the crowd around me. Suddenly noise broke my mood. Near the elevator four drunken louts leaned against the wall, screaming obscenities. While we waited for the elevator, one of them urinated. Then another swayed into us and put his arm around the waist of a woman beside me. All traces of the music died out. Grabbing the man's arm, I jerked him through the crowd and, spinning him like a child playing crack the whip, I slammed him into a wall. "I'll throw the next bastard that moves," I yelled, turning to the others, "down the goddamn elevator shaft." They didn't move, and when the elevator came the passengers got on silently. Halfway up the woman turned to me and said, "Thank you." "Forget it," I said, not wanting to talk. Outside on the street, I took three or four deep breaths, hoping cold air would bring the opera back, but like the hopes of Violetta and Alfredo, beauty had died, and I strode aggressively down the street to my apartment on Rosslyn Hill Road, spoiling for a fight.

As one grows older, he realizes life is fragile. Time seems to pass quickly and one is no longer willing to commit years to mastering a subject. Instead one learns names, in my case the names of flowers. Not only does learning names create the comforting illusion that I have learned deeply and well but it makes me feel less temporary. Instead of being an alien, insignificant being, I feel part of larger enduring nature. Most flowers have had many names. In the past the common yellow and white daisy, today generally known as the ox-eyed daisy, was called, among others, moon penny, dog blow, butter daisy, and poverty weed. Names change perception, creating character and stimulating observation. Not until I learned its many names did I pay attention to the yellow mullein growing in a ditch along Eastwood Road, not far from my house. Now, whenever I walk along Eastwood, I stop and looking at the mullein marvel at the appropriateness of torches, hare's beard, velvet plant, Jacob's staff, shepherd's club, and Adam's flannel. A pink and white member of the morning glory family, hedge bindweed is one of my favorite flowers. Because the name hedge bindweed did not appeal to me, I refused to plant it until I learned that the plant has also been called bell bind, harvest lily, Rutland beauty, creepers, and lady's nightcap. In general I prefer older to newer names. Contemporary names often reflect advertising glitter. Recently Breck's sent me a description of their "Exclusive New Premier Daffodil Collection." For me the daffodil is a wholesome, homey flower of bank and brook and, no matter how ornate the blossom, it should not be named Palmares, Ambergate, Oriental Express, and Paola Veronese. Instead of budding spring, swelling with light and life, Breck's descriptions smacked of Hollywood and titillating lingerie advertisements. "For the first time ever a Butterfly Daffodil," Breck's wrote about Palmares, "with a diaphanous apricot-pink frilly cup subtly accented against pristine petals." I will probably order bulbs from Breck's but I won't call them Paola Veronese or Oriental Express. I will plant them in the side yard near the squill and Jacob's ladder and call them something familiar like girl's love or bright-eyed Eliza after my little daughter.

In learning the names of flowers, I also picked up remedies for stomach ailments. To cure "windy outgoings," John Gerarde (1597) recommended the "marsh mallowe." "Whosoever is troubled with breaking of winde and weakness of stomack," Barnaby Googe suggested in *The Whole Art & Trade of Husbandry* (1596), should "use *Betony*, either the hearbe and flowre boyled in wine." Flowers even provided cure-alls for injured snakes. Being run over on the dirt road in front of Grandfather's farm was not certain death. To survive, a snake had only to drag itself off the road and stretch out on moneywort or, as it was once known, herb twopence, yellow myrtle, creeping Joan, and wandering tailor. I even discovered what to do if I fell asleep while exploring ruins and a snake crawled down my throat. On waking, Googe suggested, I could not do better than to drink "destilled water" of the "blessed Thistle." "A boy," Googe recounted, "into whose mouth as he slept in the feelde happened an Adder to creepe, was saved by the drinking of this water, the adder creeping out behind, without any hurt to the child."

Despite my interest in things digestive, most of my picking up is not done in libraries. I spend more time bent over in the front yard picking up sticks than I do hunched over old medical books. My trees, alas, are professionals and manufacture woodpiles. I sometimes think that if American industry would send workers to study my hickories and maples, domestic productivity would shoot up and hundreds of plants in the Far East would wither. Actually, I have learned a lot picking up sticks. Unlike facts discovered in libraries, this knowledge has resulted from experimentation or field work, as I say to acquaintances with scientific bents. When I bought my house and began research, I naively thought a lawn mower would grind most sticks into mulch. I was wrong; the lawn mower only broke big sticks into small sticks and scattered them over the yard. The way to get rid of sticks, I then decided, was to cart them away. Parking the lawn mower in the garage, I went into the house and got a sheet from the linen closet. I took it outside and, after spreading it on the ground and carefully placing rocks on all four corners so it would not take flight, I dumped a vast quantity of sticks on it. Even if I had been able to pull the four corners together, getting the sheet off the ground was impossible. I kicked two-thirds of the sticks back on the grass and managed to carry what was left into the woods behind the house; unfortunately, I only made two trips to the woods. Sheets are soft and thin, sticks hard and sharp; after my second trip the sheet was ready for the rag bag in the basement. This, I am afraid, led to some domestic discomfit as experience proved me unable to distinguish a good from a bad sheet.

Next I bought a tarpaulin. Thick and sturdy, tarpaulins are stick-resistant. They are also heavy, and unless one is young and fit and believes a hernia is a bird that lives in marshes and eats frogs and minnows, and the occasional baby snake, he ought to avoid tarpaulins. After the tarpaulin I purchased a wheelbarrow. A red wheelbarrow looks good sitting next to a lawn mower in the garage. On a late spring evening when the tulips are blooming, the poppies swelling, and the rabbits nibbling, I feel competent and wonderfully handy when I look in the garage and see my wheelbarrow and lawn mower nestled side by side like eggs in a nest. Unfortunately, wheelbarrows nest better than they carry. At every mole run, my wheelbarrow lurched, tipped, and dropped a stick or two. By the time I dumped a load of sticks in the woods, the wheelbarrow was half empty. I did not lose heart, however; in field work, failure and improvisation are the parents of invention. In the garage was a plastic garbage can in which I had once kept grass seed.

The can was not handsome; part of one side and both handles had been torn off. Its faults, however, proved virtues. Because carrying the can was awkward, I could not overload it and strain a muscle. Actually, the temptation to overload did not exist. If I put too many sticks in the can, they fell out through the side, pulling handfuls of other sticks behind them. I now keep the can by the garage door, and, whenever my trees start turning out groves of sticks, I trundle it out, load it, and drag the sticks off to the woods.

People who wander through life picking things up informally rarely develop obsessions. Mastering one yard of knowledge, however, can affect behavior. Last May a limb fell into a patch of poison ivy in my backyard. I did not know there was poison ivy near the house, but, allergic to it since childhood, I should have stayed away from the limb. Having mastered sticks, I was not about to worry about a little poison ivy, and, mumbling "Mind is superior to matter," not only did I carry the limb away but I ripped up the poison ivy bare-handed. Two days later I was in bed, swollen and itching. Of course, if wild touch-me-not or jewelweed, as it is often known, grew on Eastwood, I could have cured myself. Not only do the plant's juices stop poison ivy from itching, but they dry it up.

Eventually people themselves are picked up. Blown from the tree of life, they fall to the ground where they are gathered then carted off through the sky to that town with jasper walls and golden streets. While tarrying here, however, most folks get picked up for many things and in many ways. Perhaps the most common thing people are picked up for is driving too fast. I was once stopped for speeding; happily, some of the language I picked up reading hymnals got me out of the ticket. I had driven from Nashville to Hanover, Virginia, to spend Thanksgiving with my grandmother. We ate our Thanksgiving meal on Saturday rather than Thursday and instead of turkey had goose with relatives in Louisa. The goose must have hung too long and lost its patience, for soon after lunch it began honking. By midnight I was certain I had been poisoned and longed for angelica, a sure remedy not only for poisons but for the plague. There being no angelica in the yard, I had to endure until dawn when the goose suddenly rose, circled once, and headed south. Once the goose was out of sight and body, I recovered rapidly and at nine o'clock left for Tennessee. Leaving four hours later than planned, I drove faster than usual and near Cumberland Courthouse whipped through a radar trap eleven miles above the speed limit. Despite the goose, I was ready when the patrolman pulled up behind me. "Praise the Lord," I said, getting out of the car to shake the policeman's hand, "God's in his heaven this Sabbath." When the policeman stopped and looked at me, I knew he was as good as in the collection plate, and I launched my appeal.

"Brother, do you follow Jesus?" I asked. Then before he could reply I answered my question. "Yes," I said, "you do. From your soul the sun shines more glorious than that glowing in any earthly sky. In that bright sun isn't there pardon for me?" "Don't you think, Christian brother," I continued, stepping forward again, opening my arms, fingers outspread in benediction and familiarity, "don't you think that on this the seventh day you could rest and forgive me? When your summons comes to meet the blessed Savior and you put on the Crown of Glory, no jewel will shine brighter than that of Forgiveness." At first the policeman did not speak. He glanced at his watch and then as I took another step forward said hurriedly, "The Justice of the Peace has gone to church, and she won't be out for two hours, so you can go." "Hallelujah," I exclaimed, raising my hands and rolling my eyes heavenward until the whites showed. By the time I looked down, the policeman had gotten in his car, turned around, and was racing back along the road toward the world, speed traps, and sanity.

Vicki and I have three small children. This fall when one entered kindergarten and another started nursery school, we began talking about education. Rarely did we mention courses or technique. What we talked about were the children's abilities and characters, specifically what they picked up from us and our families. Although there has been some disagreement on the matter, I think it fair to conclude that the children inherited good looks, generosity, and genius from their father whereas any tendency toward the untoward probably broke off from their mother's family tree. At dinner last week Edward, who is four, announced, "In my house there will be no coffee, no tea, no beer, no alcohol, no drugs, no Coca-Cola, no smoking, no hamburgers, and no french fries." "Almost as discriminating as his father," I said to Vicki when Edward completed the list. Francis, who is five, is a thread off the old cashmere too. Just yesterday he refused a bathing suit which Vicki bought him, explaining it looked like Hawaii. Francis resembles me a great deal. When I was a sophomore in high school, I went to the state mathematics contest in Algebra II. Not only has Francis completed first-grade math, but he is interested in the computer, and the school has set up a special class for him. Although most of my colleagues own computers, I don't have one. In truth, I am not comfortable typing and have been afraid to touch a computer. Still, if Francis can use one, then the ability is in the blood. Come the fall I am going to pick up one.

Part Five: Familial Essays

Faith of the Father

ON WEEKDAYS VICKERY'S STORE was the center of life in the little Virginia town in which I spent summers and then Christmas and occasionally Easter vacations. The post office was in a corner of the store, and the train station was across the road. In the morning men gathered on Vickery's porch and drank coffee while they waited for the train to Richmond. Late in the afternoon, families appeared. While waiting for their husbands, women bought groceries, mailed letters, and visited with one another. Children ate cups of ice cream and played in the woods behind the store. Sometimes a work train was on the siding, and the engineer filled his cab with children and took them for short trips down the track. On weekends life shifted from the store to St. Paul's Church. Built in a grove of pine trees in the nineteenth century, St. Paul's was a small, white clapboard building. A Sunday school wing added to the church in the 1920s jutted out into the graveyard. Beyond the graveyard was a field in which picnics were held and on the Fourth of July, the yearly Donkey Softball Game was played.

St. Paul's was familial and comfortable. Only a hundred people attended regularly, and everyone knew everyone else and his business. What was private became public after the service as people gathered outside and talked for half an hour before going home to lunch. Behind the altar inside the church was a stained glass window showing Christ's ascension to heaven. A red carpet ran down the middle aisle, and worn, gold cushions covered the pews. On the walls were plaques in memory of parishioners killed in foreign wars or who had made large donations to the building fund. In summer the minister put fans out on the pews. Donated by a local undertaker, the fans were shaped like spades. On them, besides the undertaker's name and telephone number, were pictures of Christ performing miracles: walking on water, healing the lame, and raising Lazarus from the dead.

Holidays and funerals were special at St. Paul's. Funerals were occasions for reminiscing and telling stories. When an irascible old lady died and her daughter had "Gone to Jesus" inscribed on her tombstone, her son-in-law was heard to say, "Poor Jesus"—or so the tale went at the funeral. Christmas Eve was always cold and snow usually fell. Inside the church at midnight, though, all was cheery and warm as the congregation sang the great Christmas hymns: "O Come, All Ye Faithful," "The First Noel," "O Little Town of Bethlehem," and "Hark! The Herald Angels Sing." The last hymn was "Silent Night." The service did not follow the prayer book; inspired by Christmas and eggnog, the congregation came to sing not to pray. Bourbon was in the air, and when the altar boy lit the candles, it seemed a miracle that the first spark didn't send us all to heaven in a blue flame.

Easter was almost more joyous than Christmas. Men stuck greenery into their lapels and women blossomed in bright bonnets, some ordering hats not simply from Richmond but from Baltimore and Philadelphia. On a farm outside town lived Miss Emma and Miss Ida Catlin. Miss Emma was the practical sister, running the farm and bringing order wherever she went. Unlike Miss Emma, Miss Ida was shy. She read poetry and raised guinea fowl and at parties sat silently in a corner. Only on Easter was she outgoing; then like a day lily she bloomed triumphantly. No one else's Easter bonnet ever matched hers, and the congregation eagerly awaited her entrance, which she always made just before the first hymn.

One year Miss Ida found a catalogue from a New York store which advertised hats and their accessories. For ten to twenty-five cents ladies could buy artificial flowers to stick into their bonnets. Miss Ida bought a counterful, and that Easter her head resembled a summer garden in bloom. Daffodils, zinnias, and black-eyed Susans hung yellow and red around the brim of her hat while in the middle stood a magnificent pink peony.

In all his glory Solomon could not have matched Miss Ida's bonnet. The congregation could not take its eyes off it; even the minister had trouble concentrating on his sermon. After the last hymn, everyone hurried out of the church, eager to get a better look at Miss Ida's hat. As she came out, the altar boy began ringing the bell. Alas, the noise frightened pigeons who had recently begun to nest and they shot out of the steeple. The congregation scattered, but the flowers on Miss Ida's hat hung over her eyes, and she did not see the pigeons until it was too late and the peony had been ruined.

Miss Ida acted like nothing had happened. She greeted everyone and asked about their health and the health of absent family members. People tried not to look at her hat but were not very successful. For two Sundays Miss Ida's "accident" was the main subject of after-church conversation; then it was forgotten for almost a year. But, as Easter approached again, people remembered the hat. They wondered what Miss Ida would wear to church. Some people speculated that since she was a shy, poetic person, she wouldn't come. Even the minister had doubts. To reassure Miss Ida, he and his sons borrowed ladders two weeks before Easter, and climbing to the top of the steeple, chased the pigeons away and sealed off their nesting place with chicken wire.

Easter Sunday seemed to confirm the fears of those who doubted Miss Ida would appear. The choir assembled in the rear of the church without her. Half-heartedly the congregation sang the processional hymn, "Hail Thee, Festival Day." Miss Ida's absence had taken something bright from our lives, and as we sat down after singing, Easter seemed sadly ordinary. We were people of little faith. Just as the minister reached the altar and turned to face us, there was a stir at the back of the church. Silently the minister raised his right hand and pointed toward the door. Miss Ida had arrived. She was wearing the same hat she wore the year before; only the peony was missing. In its place was a wonderful sunflower; from one side hung a black and yellow garden spider building a web, while fluttering above was a mourning cloak, black wings, dotted with blue and a yellow border running around the edges. Our hearts leaped up, and at the end of the service people in Richmond must have heard us singing "Christ the Lord Is Risen Today."

St. Paul's was the church of my childhood, that storied time when I thought little about religion but knew that Jesus loved me, yes, because the Bible told me so. In the Morning Prayer of life I mixed faith and fairy tale, thinking God a kindly giant, holding in his hands, as the song put it, the corners of the earth and the strength of the hills. Thirty years have passed since I last saw St. Paul's, and I have come down from the cool upland pastures and the safe fold of childhood to the hot lowlands. Instead of being neatly tucked away in a huge hand, the world now seems to bound erratically, smooth and slippery, forever beyond the grasp of even the most magical deity. Would that it were not so, and my imagination could find a way through His gates, as the psalm says, with thanksgiving. Often I wonder what happened to the "faith of our fathers." Why if it endured dungeon, fire, and sword in others, did it weaken so within me?

For me religion is a matter of story and community, a congregation rising together to look at an Easter bonnet, unconsciously seeing it an emblem of hope and vitality, indeed of the Resurrection itself. For me religion ought to be more concerned with people than ideas, creating soft feeling rather than sharp thought. Often I associate religion with small, backwater towns in which tale binds folk one to another. Here in a university in which people are separated by idea rather than linked by story, religion doesn't have a natural place. In the absence of community, ceremony becomes important. Changeable and always controversial, subject to dispassionate analysis, ceremony doesn't tie people together like accounts of pigeons and peonies and thus doesn't promote good feeling and finally love for this world and hope for the next. Often when I am discouraged I turn for sustenance, not to formal faith with articled ceremony but to memory, a chalice winey with story.

Not long ago I thought about Beagon Hackett, a Baptist minister in Carthage, Tennessee. Born in Bagdad in Jackson County, Beagon answered the call early in life. Before he was sixteen, he had preached in all the little towns in Jackson County: Antioch, Nameless, McCoinsville, Liberty, and Gum Springs. Although he was popular in country churches, Beagon's specialty was the all-day revival, picnic, and baptizing, usually held back in the woods near places like Seven Knobs, Booger Hill, Backbone Ridge, Chigger Hollow, and Twelve Corners. Beagon made such a name that the big Baptist church in Carthage selected him as minister. In Carthage, Beagon tempered his faith to suit the mood of the county seat. Only once a year did he hold a meeting out-of-doors. For his first four or five years in Carthage, he led a revival near Dripping Rock Bluff across Hell Bend on the Caney Fork River, the spot being selected for name not location.

The narrows of the river were swift and deep, and crossing Hell Bend was dangerous, a danger Beagon celebrated, first reminding the faithful that Jesus was a fisher of men and then buoying their spirits up on a raft of watery Christian song: "Shall We Gather at the River," "The Rock That Is Higher Than I," and "In the Sweet By and By." Beagon's meetings across the Caney Fork were a success, with people traveling from as far as Macon and Trousdale counties to be baptized. But then one spring Gummert Capron or Doodlebug Healy, depending on whose memory is accurate, became frightened in mid-river and tipping over a rowboat changed "Throw Out the Life-Line" from word to deed. If Hosmer Nye had not grabbed Clara Jakeways by the hair, the dark waters, as the hymn puts it, would have swept her to eternity's shore. As it turned out Clara's salvation turned into romance, and three months later she and Hosmer were married, much to the disappointment of Silas Jakeways who owned a sawmill and the Eagle Iron Works and who disapproved of Hosmer, until that time an itinerant bricklayer. Clara, Silas was reported to have said, "would have been better off if love hadn't lifted her from the deep to become the wife of a no-account." Whatever the case, however, Beagon never led another revival across Hell Bend; instead, he stayed dry on the Carthage side of the Caney Fork, once a year holding a temperate affair, more Sunday outing than revival, on Myers Bottom.

After Beagon had been in Carthage for twenty years, he grew heavy and dignified. No longer would he preside at river baptizings. In his church he erected, as Silas Jakeways said, "a marble birdbath," a baptismal font, copied from one he had seen in an Episcopal church at Monteagle. In Carthage, though, pretension was always liable to be tipped over, if not by simple-minded folk like Gummert Capron or Doodlebug Healy, then by daily life. Addicted to drink, Horace Armitage, the disreputable brother of Benbow Armitage, occasionally cut hair at King's Barber Shop. One morning after a long night of carousing at Enos Mayfield's in South Carthage, Horace was a bit shaky, and while shaving Beagon cut him slightly on the chin. "That's what comes of taking too much to drink," said Beagon, holding a towel to his chin. "Yes, sir, Reverend," Horace replied, "alcohol does make the skin tender."

The account of Beagon and Horace is itself tender, making me feel good about religion. When religion is a matter of people and story, it attracts me. In contrast regulation has often repulsed me. In grammar school I was the only one of my Episcopal friends who did not become an acolyte. Years later at Sewanee I disapproved of compulsory chapel and each fall semester attended church for seventy days in a row to rid myself of the year's requirement. I approved when students read the *Daily Worker* in church to protest compulsory chapel. They went too far, however, when taking scotch, soda, an ice bucket, and silver mint julep cups to Evensong, they sat in the back of the church and mixed drinks. No longer does Sewanee require church attendance, and the

Episcopal church itself has changed, too much, I'm afraid, for my liking. No one's character is consistent, however, and despite my disapproval of hard rule and line some structure, particularly that which increases familiarity and makes a person comfortable, seems good. Before the latest revision of the Prayer Book, I could enter almost any Episcopal church in the country and feel at home. Now as I stumble through the prayers, resisting change and breaking prose on every line, I feel out of place, a stranger apart from community, resentful and eager to criticize. For my children I approve structure and send them to Sunday school. He was satisfied, Josh Billings wrote, that every man who lied for fun would eventually lie for wages. Some discipline and a few lessons early in life will help the children. Although they won't become acolytes, maybe habit will be stamped upon them, and they won't lie or do worse for wages.

Sometimes I think the Episcopal church like the landscape of our country is in the hands of developers. Wetlands are drained, and crisp, functional buildings rise where cattails once bent in the breeze, dragonflies clinging to them like ancient liturgies, awkward but somehow rich and alluring. In part, I suppose, my disenchantment with religion resembles that of the dreamer, disappointed to discover that his beloved is mere flesh. I wanted more than religion could accomplish. I wanted religion to make man better than he is capable of being. Even worse, commitment to a faith, I saw in the Holy Land, more often than not does not elevate but lowers. Crushed between the ideals of stony doctrine, people bleed. "We saw the buildings pulled down," wrote a Syrian student who fled the Golan Heights in 1973; "we saw the people killed. We saw our house pulled down. We left the city. We left everything there. Our city was occupied. I was so sad. I left my dolls. I left my small room. I was afread. I could not forget this picture. It left a bitter wound in my heart. I could not recognize it at the time. I was too young. It is afread me a long time later."

Not simply religion's inability to patch up pitiful, flawed humanity, but its tendency to destroy community, crushing dolls under the mechanical tread of doctrine, has long been lamented. In almost tacit recognition of such weakness, divines have preached otherworldliness, urging the downtrodden and the suffering to look to heaven for justice and decency. Too often whatever is is wrong and when doing research for a study of early children's books, most of which were religious, time and again I was bothered by tales preaching stolid acceptance of misfortune. In Samuel Pratt's *The Paternal Present* (1795) appeared the story of Nahamir, an account which taught children to be satisfied with their lots in life because they were ordained by God. "Old, hunch-backed, lame, crippled" and "half-starved," Nahamir, Pratt wrote, begged alms before the gates of Bagdad. Nahamir had once been handsome and had a wife and six children, but suddenly his family died and a "hideous bunch of superfluous flesh" appeared on his shoulders. Then in an accident he lost an eye; following this misfortune, he tumbled down a stairwell and broke a leg while going to aid a small boy who was being beaten. Later feeling compassion for an old man slumped over by the side of the road, he stopped to offer assistance. When Nahamir bent down to help him, the old man drew a sabre and sliced off Nahamir's right arm. Finally Nahamir's business failed and his friends forsook him.

Somewhat understandably, at least from my point of view, Nahamir thought himself unfortunate. One day as he lamented his fate, an angel appeared and rebuked him, telling him his torments were blessings. When Nahamir asked for an explanation, the angel observed that Nahamir survived when his family died. In truth, the angel said, the deaths of Nahamir's wife and children were examples of "the benevolence of heaven." If they had lived, the children would have been disobedient and Nahamir's wife would have betrayed him. Moreover, the loss of his good looks had preserved Nahamir's life; if he had remained handsome, the angel said, he would have been involved in "a scandalous intrigue" and on its discovery would have been impaled. Even the loss of his eye was fortunate; unknown to Nahamir, the Caliph wanted to make him a harem guard. "Certain ceremonies would have been necessary," but the Caliph rejected the idea when Nahamir lost an eye. In falling down the staircase, the angel next recounted, Nahamir had been fortunate to break only one leg. The loss of his right arm was also a blessing; at a feast sometime later, the angel reminded Nahamir, he had been insulted. If he had not lost his arm, he would have drawn a sabre and committed a mortal sin. Even the bankruptcy was fortunate, for Nahamir would have used wealth in a detestable manner and become "an horror to thyself, and a disgrace to human nature." "Suffer patiently," the angel told Nahamir. "After death, thou shalt commence a new career, where every happiness shall be complete and uninterrupted." The angel convinced Nahamir that he was fortunate, and, satisfied with his lot, Nahamir returned to begging, thanking "heaven with all his heart that he was old, deformed, blind and crippled, and limping, without fortune, without a wife, and without children."

Strangely although the tale bothers me, it has some appeal, particularly as I look about and see a society rushing madly to lay up treasures where moth and rust corrupt. Blessed, I want to believe, are the poor in spirit, if the phrase refers to those who seem dull and unambitious because the simple satisfies them and glitter does not attract them. Vicki and I and the children spent New Year's with her parents in Princeton, a town in which everything seems for sale. Between Washington Road and the home of Vicki's parents on Linden Lane, a matter of three or four short blocks, I counted the offices of eight realtors. Like bees about a hive, Mercedes cluster around Palmer Square, its cell-like shops fragrant and dripping with expensive honey. With imported tea kettles marked at eighty-five dollars, prices in Kitchen Capers are too highly seasoned for the Bible's "salt of the earth." Thoughts focused only on raiment, white hunter impersonators wander through Banana Republic, planning expeditions to Bucks County, Pennsylvania, for dinner. Across Nassau Street even the university, its buildings stony and heavy, seems insubstantial. Faculty appointments are "media events," and instead of a community of teachers, some of whom are scholars, the university promotes itself as a galaxy of stars, the stuff of publicity not people. The sweets of Princeton are ever-alluring, however, and resisting them is almost impossible. Munching on a chocolate muffin, I told Vicki that I wanted the children to attend Princeton, although the school is priced far beyond our means. "Princeton will give them tone," I said, "and make them aware of possibilities." And in truth not all Princeton is show. Apart from the bustle of shops, the chapel stands, empty, but nevertheless dignified and substantial.

Of course a community of people and tales still exists in Princeton. Unfortunately it resembles St. Paul's, a part of my childhood rarely touching everyday life. Almost as tender as Beagon's chin are memories of the classes I took, taught, to be sure, by learned but still ordinary folk: the man from Texas who pushed Dr. Johnson aside one day and said that when he was young he found it difficult to choose between books and baseball. Both, he said, offered ways out of his small town, and he was a good baseball player, potentially he thought, a better second baseman than scholar. Then there was the Miltonist who once a semester would turn from Eden to Oklahoma and tell tales of his schooling, inevitably describing how friends in medical school circumcised each other and then suffered painful inconvenience when they got erections and their stitches popped loose. In the telling, Oklahoma seemed a richer garden than Milton's Eden, a place of broken stitches and bursting with hope, a place which one left, not solitary like Adam and Eve with "wandering steps and slow," but jauntily, apple in hand and stories on the tongue.

Perhaps behind vital education and religion lies not idea, a trumpet sounding before it, but modest, humanizing tale. Particularly appealing to me are creation stories. In one of my favorites the apple wasn't forbidden but was instead the loveliest tree in Eden, its branches moving in the breeze sweeter than harps. Drawn by the music on the wind and fragrance like beds of spices, Adam tried to pluck an apple from the tree. The stem of the apple was thick, however, and Adam had to slice through it using a sharp stone he found on the ground. After cutting off an apple, Adam wiped the stone on his thigh, in the process scratching himself and letting a drop of apple juice seep under his skin. Almost immediately the stone became a garnet, and Adam's thigh began to swell. Nine days later his thigh split open, giving birth to Eve, her breasts full, the ends red like apples and the nipples thick as stems.

In contrast to that of the serpent and Eve, this story is one of healthy appetite and love, not fear and temptation. The heaven it leads me to is not that of Revelation, a New Jerusalem surrounded by shining, bejeweled walls, smacking of exclusion and chilled affluence, a Palmer Square of the clouds in which kings of commerce tread narrow, golden paths. Not for me a Faberge heaven with gates of pearl, walls of jasper, and glassy domes spun from gold. My heaven is as large as breath and, like an affectionate bride awaiting her husband, is adorned with goodly weeds—literally weeds, plants of wayside and gully, abandoned pasture and hilly slope, the common, often overlooked plants of my New England: pigweed, scoke, bull rattle, sleepy catchfly, fleabane, steeplebush, wild carrot, cranes-bill, butter-and-eggs, Indian tobacco, and even beggar ticks and burdock. The heaven of my dream is a simple place, hospitable to plants and people of little cultivation. Absent is doctrine. The product of harrowing and plowing, fertilizing and pruning, doctrine disrupts peaceable kingdoms. Without roots in people and stories, it draws sustenance from abstraction and like a pale horse tramples the meek and the merciful. Fifteen years ago in Jordan, a Moslem fundamentalist told me that only a conflagration in which forty million people were killed could cleanse "the Arab nation." From its ashes, he said, Islam would rise, purified and glorious.

The mind is weak and doctrinal certainty enticing. In the hot embrace of doctrine, gentle people often become zealots, ready to level the towers of Cairo or fight over the Trinity, Predestination and Election, and Salvation by Faith or Works. In trying to become saints they forget humanity and become beasts. My fear of the seductive wiles of doctrine has driven me from formal faith and indeed from any kind of advocacy sustained by an abstraction. Partly as a consequence I am a conscious trifler. The man down to trifles is rarely up to no good, and passing days toying with matters of little concern, I let other people and the world spin peacefully along.

Most recently slogans on license plates have caught my attention, and I have written letters to governors about them. "Dear Mr. Casey," my letter to the governor of Pennsylvania begins, "*You've Got a Friend in Pennsylvania* made me feel wonderful when I first saw it. I was on my way back from having my piles chopped out at the hospital. Dr. Jurgen here in Willimantic did it. He chops out most of the piles in this part of Connecticut. He is old, and some folks say he ought to stick to sinuses and leave behinds alone. But he did a fine job on me and my bottom is just as rosy as a baby's cheek. Before, it was wrinkled up like a nest of tent caterpillars. Anyway, I have never been to Pennsylvania, and I didn't think anyone down there even knew me, much less was my friend, and all the way down the road I thought about the get-well card my friend must have sent and which would be waiting for me at home on the commode. That's where I keep all my cards because I just don't look at them once and then throw them away. No, I look at them again and again, each morning, don't you know, between eight and eight twenty-five, though I ought to say that since this operation I haven't kept so close to my schedule. I'm sure you can understand. Anyway governor, you can imagine my disappointment when I got home and there was no card from my friend. What sort of friend is that governor, that don't write when a person gets her butthole damn near tore off. I call that friend, governor, a shitass, and I'm writing to you to find me a new friend."

To Governor Hunt of Alabama I wrote a shorter letter. "Dear Mr. Hunt," it begins, "I'm Professor of Internal Medicine here in New

Haven at the Yale Medical School and, as you might guess am just a little bit interested in things anatomical. Recently I saw the Alabama license plate with *Heart of Dixie* written on it and that started me to thinking. Governor, why the heart of Dixie? Why not the liver or the spleen or maybe even the fundament? I talked to one of the big shots at the university around here and he said that as far as he was concerned Alabama was the 'Prick of Dixie.' He votes Republican and is a man whose opinion I respect. He is always dispassionate, and I ought to say right now that he can't be accused of prejudice. He wasn't, I am prepared to testify, born in Alabama, but Arkansas, Fort Smith, I believe."

Before mailing the letters I showed them to my friend Grahame. "Great God Almighty, Sam," he said, "you can't mail these. Write all you want about Beagon Hackett and religion. Nobody gives a hoot in hell about that sort of stuff. But if you mail these letters and somebody finds out you wrote them, you'll be fired. The governor of Alabama will call the governor of Connecticut and say you wrote him that the state was full of pricks. What would you do then?" "Well," I said, "I'd apologize and apologize publicly, saying I was wrong to insinuate that the fine citizens of Alabama were pricks. Recently, I'd say, I had met a splendid woman from Gasden who told me there wasn't a prick worth a damn in the whole state and that's why she moved to New England."

I haven't mailed the letters yet. It's not that I am frightened of losing my job, but that something important came up. Since birth my little girl Eliza has been sickly. She coughs terribly; her lungs get congested, and twice she has been in the hospital, once under an oxygen tent. Even when she looks well, her nose runs like a river. When she got sick again this past December, the doctor decided to run tests on her. Scheduled last, three weeks after the others, was the sweat test for cystic fibrosis. My love for Eliza knows no bounds, and as I thought about the possibility of her having a fatal illness, the world seemed to collapse like Jericho around me, my fine wordy constructs crashing silently into dusty nothingness. And so like many other fathers, frightened for a child and scared of life, I prayed. Living still in spite of all my ponderings, the old faith supported me. Then after three weeks Eliza took the test, and my heaviness turned joy. What a privilege it was, though, once again to carry everything to God in prayer.

Son and Father

"THE MORE I SEE OF OLD PEOPLE," my father said in the last letter he wrote me, "the greater my feeling is that the bulk of them should be destroyed."

"Not you," I thought when I read the letter, "at least not yet."

For years I imagined that I was different from, even better than, my father. Then one evening I walked into his room to ask about a book and found him asleep on his bed. Although I had seen him sleeping countless times, I was startled. His pajamas were inside out, as mine invariably are, and I noticed that we slept in the same position, left arm bent under the pillow, hand resting on the headboard; right leg pulled high toward the chest, and left thrust back and behind with the toes pointed, seemingly pushing us up and through the bed. Suddenly I realized Father and I were remarkably alike, the greatest difference being only the years that lay between us. At first I was upset. I had never consciously rejected family, but like the bottom of the bed against which I appeared to be pushing at night, my father and his life provided a firmness against which I could press and thrust myself off into something better.

As I looked at the old man lying on the bed, his thin ankles and knobby feet sticking out of his pajamas like fallen branches, I felt warm and comfortable. Instead of being parted by time and youth's false sense of superiority, we were bound together by patterns of living. His life could teach me about my future and my past, but, I thought, how little I knew about him. How well, I wondered, did any son know a father—particularly an only son, the recipient of so much love and attention that he worried about having a self and turned inward, often ignoring the parents about him and responding aggressively to concern with a petulant "Leave me alone."

In his letter Father said that he and Mother disagreed about the past. "I tell her," he wrote, "that her recollections are remarkable, albeit not necessarily accurate." My memories of Father are ordinary and consist of a few glimpses: such things, for example, as his running alongside and steadying me when I learned to ride a bicycle and his fondness for chocolate. Mother liked chocolate, too, and whenever Father was given a box of candy, he hid it in his closet where Mother could not reach it. The closet was dark, and as he grew older and his sight failed, he kept a flashlight in a shoebox. In a way, I suppose, past events resemble leaves on a tree. A multitude of little things make up life in full bloom, but as time passes, they fall and disappear without a trace. A few seeds blow into the garage, or memory, and get wedged behind spades, axes, and bits of lumber. If found or remembered, they are usually swept aside. Does it matter that Father rolled and chewed his tongue while telling a story or that after having drinks before dinner he would talk with his mouth full and embarrass me? Particular place is often necessary if the seeds lodged in memory are to sprout and grow green. Sadly, places vanish almost as quickly as leaves in October.

The Sulgrave Apartments, where I lived for eight years, and the long alley behind stretching through neighborhoods and drawing gangs of children to its treasures have vanished. When I was five I entered Ransom School. For the first months, Father walked all the way to school with me: along West End; across Fairfax, where Mr. Underwood the policeman waved at us; under the railway trestle and up Highland; past three small streets, Howell, Harding, and Sutherland. Slowly, as I grew surer, Father walked less of the distance with me; one morning he did not cross Sutherland; sometime later, he stopped at Harding, then Howell. Eventually he left me at the corner of Fairfax and I made my own way to Ransom under the watchful eye of Mr. Underwood. What I did when I was five, I can do no longer. The trestle and tracks with their caches of spikes, Highland, Harding, Howell, Sutherland, and Ransom itself, a scrapbook of small faces, have disappeared. All the associations that would freshen memory have been torn down for an interstate, going to Memphis or Birmingham, I am not sure which. Great washes of cars and trucks pour down ramps and rush through my old neighborhood. Traffic is so heavy that I rarely drive on West End, and when I must, the congestion makes me so nervous and the driving takes such concentration that I never think of Ransom, Mr. Underwood, or a little boy and a tall, thin man holding hands as they walked to school.

Father grew up in Carthage, Tennessee, a town of some two thousand people set high above the Cumberland River on red clay bluffs fifty-five miles east of Nashville. Since Carthage was the seat of Smith

County, sidewalks ran along Main Street, and Father and his brother Coleman used to roller skate from their house to Grandfather's insurance agency, downtown over the bank. Life in Carthage was slow and from my perspective appealingly unsophisticated. On the front page of the weekly newspaper alongside an ad for Tabler's Buckeye Pile Ointment were excerpts from the sermons of the Reverend Sam P. Jones, the local Methodist minister. "I wouldn't give whiskey to a man until he had been dead for three days," Jones said. "When an old red-nosed politician gets so he isn't fit for anything else," he declared "the Democrat Party send him to the Legislature." When a resident went away, a notice duly appeared on the front page. "D. B. Kittrell," the paper informed reader, "went to Nashville last week with about 40 fat hogs and has not yet returned."

Not much money was to be made in Carthage, and people lived comfortably. Every morning Grandpa Pickering walked downtown and had coffee with friends, after which he came home for breakfast. Only then did he go to his office. Grandfather's house was a white, clapboard, two-story Victorian with a bright tin roof. A porch ran around two sides; at one corner of the porch was a cupola; on top was a weathervane. Huge sugar maples stood in the front yard, and about the house were bushes of white hydrangeas; in spring they seemed like mountains of snow. In back of the house was the well, sheds, fields, a tobacco barn, and then a long slope down to the river. Bessie the maid cooked Grandfather's breakfast. She made wonderful shortcake, and whenever I was in Carthage, she gave me sweet coffee to drink. Bessie's first marriage had not been a success; James, her husband, was unfaithful, and one night when he returned from gallivanting, she shot him. Although James lost a leg, he did not die, and Grandfather got Bessie off with a suspended sentence. Later, after Grandfather's death, Bessie married a preacher and moved to Nashville. On Thanksgiving and Christmas she often came to our house and cooked. The last time she came she asked me if I was still catching bugs and snakes.

I don't remember any snakes in Carthage, and the only bugs I recall catching are tobacco worms. I took a bucket from the back porch and after walking down to the tobacco patch filled it with worms. Then I drew a big circle in the dust on the road and in the middle dumped the worms. The first worm to detach itself from the squirming green pile and to crawl out of the circle I returned to the bucket and carried back to the field. The others I crushed. Tobacco worms are big and fat, and if I lined up worm and sole just right and put my foot down quickly heel to toe, I could occasionally squirt a worm's innards two feet.

Grandfather died when I was young, and I have few memories of him. During the last months of his life, he was bedridden. Beside his bed was always a stack of flower magazines. All seemed to have been filled with pictures of zinnias, bright red and orange and occasionally purple zinnias, the only flower Father ever grew. Grandma Pickering outlived her husband, and I have clearer memories of her. She was strong-willed and opinionated, once confessing to me that she voted for Roosevelt the first time. In some ways Carthage may have been too small for her; she was interested in literature, and after her death I found scrapbooks filled with newspaper clippings, poems, reviews, and articles. Most of the poems were conventionally inspirational or religious and were typically entitled "Symbols of Victory" and "Earth Is Not Man's Abiding Place." Occasionally, though, I found other kinds of poetry, poems for the dreamer, not the moralist, poems which did not teach but which sketched moods. Pasted on the bottom of a page containing an article on "Shakespeare's Ideals of Womanhood" and a review of *For Whom the Bell Tolls* were two lines:

I've reached the land of Golden-rod,
Afar I see it wave and nod.

Much as it is hard to think of Father skating along the sidewalks of Carthage, so it is difficult to think of Grandma Pickering as a dreamer. Instead of bright, beckoning goldenrod, I associate her with a rusting red Studebaker. Almost until the day she died, she drove, and whenever she left Carthage for Nashville, the sheriff radioed ahead to the highway patrol, warning, "Mrs. Pickering's on the road." Along the way, patrolmen watched out for her, and when she reached Lebanon, one telephoned Father and then he and Mother and I drove out to a Stuckey's near the city limits and waited. After what seemed forever, she eventually appeared, inevitably with cars backed up behind her by the score, something that embarrassed me terribly.

Father told me little about his childhood in Carthage. I know only that he had an Airedale named Jerry; that on Rattlesnake Mountain, the hill just outside town, he once saw a huge snake; that he almost died after eating homemade strawberry ice cream at a birthday party; and that Lucy, the talented girl next door, died from trichinosis. Report cards provided most of what I know about Father's childhood, and in Grandmother's scrapbooks, I found several. Father entered first grade in 1915; Lena Douglas taught him reading, spelling, writing, arithmetic, and language; his average for the year in all subjects was ninety-nine and a half; for his first two years he was remarkably healthy and only missed three days of school. The Carthage schools proved too easy, and for a year in high school Father attended KMI, Kentucky Military Institute, a place about which he never spoke except to say, "Children should not be sent to military schools." After KMI Father returned to Carthage, skipped two grades, graduated from high school, and in 1925 entered Vanderbilt.

One of my undergraduate nicknames was "Machine," and once or twice when I walked into class intent on an A, people made whirring or clanking sounds. Father, it seems, rarely attended class; every semester at Vanderbilt his quality credits were reduced because of absences. In 1927 he skipped so many classes that the dean called him in for a conference. Story had it that if the dean got out of his chair and put his arm around a student's shoulders, the student was certain to be dismissed from school. Midway through the interview, the dean rose and approached Father. Swiftly Father got up and walked around the desk, and thus conversation proceeded in circular fashion, with the dean lecturing and pursuing and Father explaining and running. The result was probation, not expulsion. It was a wonder that Father had enough energy to elude the dean because he never attended gym class, a required course. Before graduation one of Father's physician friends wrote him a letter, urging the suspension of the requirement in Father's case, explaining, "Pickering has a lameness in his back." After reading the letter, the dean said, "No more lies, Pickering; out of my office." Father left silently and graduated.

Although Father majored in English during the great years of Vanderbilt's English department—the years of the Fugitives and the Agrarians—his college experiences were personal, not intellectual. From Carthage he brought with him the small-town world of particulars and familial relationships. For him, as for me, reality was apparent and truth clear, and he had little interest in hidden structures or highly wrought reasoning, making D's in psychology and philosophy. In later years he rarely talked about classroom matters unless there was a story attached.

When John Crowe Ransom assigned two poems to be written, Father exhausted his inspiration and interest on the first and got his roommate, who had a certain lyrical ability, to write the other. The week following the assignment, Professor Ransom read Father's two poems to the class, remarking, "It is inconceivable to me that the same person could have written these two poems."

"A matter of mood, Mr. Ransom," Father explained, and he was right. Whose mood seems beside the point, especially when the nonpoetic have to write verse. I inherited Father's poetic skills, and in sixth grade when I was assigned a poem, I turned to him and he turned out "The Zoo," a very effective piece for twelve-year-olds, featuring, among other animals, a polar bear with white hair, a chimp with a limp, an antelope on the end of a rope, and a turtle named Myrtle. Despite his lack of poetic talent, Father read a fair amount of poetry and was fond of quoting verse, particularly poems like Tennyson's "The Splendour Falls," the sounds of which rang cool and clear like bells. Father's favorite poet was Byron. The dying gladiator was a companion of my childhood, and the Coliseum seemed to stand not in faraway Rome but just around the corner of another day. College, however, probably had little to do with Father's enjoyment of Byron; the source was closer to home, Father's grandfather William Blackstone Pickering. On a shelf in our library I found *The Works of Lord Byron in Verse and Prose*, published in Hartford in 1840 by Silas Andrus and Son. The book was inscribed "Wm. B. Pickering from his father." Over the inscription a child wrote, "Sammie F. Pickering." Under that in a firm, youthful handwriting was written "Samuel Pickering, Beta House, Vanderbilt University, 1926."

Often holding three jobs at once, Father worked his way through Vanderbilt and simply did not have much time for classes. Yet he was always a reading man, and at times I suspected that there was nothing he had not read. Years later at his office, he kept books in the top drawer of his desk. When business was slow, he pulled the drawer out slightly, and after placing a pad and pencil in front of himself for appearances, he read. Despite the college jobs, such a reader should have done better than the B's, C's, and D's Father made in English. In part the small-town world of Carthage may have been responsible for his performance. Carthage was a world of particulars, not abstractions, a place in which Tabler's Buckeye Pile Ointment "Cures Nothing but Piles," a town in which Mrs. Polk, a neighbor, could burst into Grandfather's kitchen crying that her daughter Mary, who had gone to Nashville, was "ruined."

"Oh, Lord," Grandfather exclaimed, "was she taken advantage of?"

"Yes," Mrs. Polk answered, "she had her hair bobbed."

At Vanderbilt during the 1920s literary criticism was shifting from the personal and anecdotal to the intellectual and the abstract. Instead of explaining ordinary life, it began to create an extraordinary world of thought far from piles and bobbed hair. For Father such a shift led to boredom and the conviction that although literary criticism might entertain some people, it was ultimately insignificant. In the sixty years that have passed since Father entered Vanderbilt, criticism has become more rarefied, and the result is, as a friend and critic wrote me, "we write books that even our mothers won't read."

Carthage influenced more than Father's schoolwork; it determined the course of his career. Although Grandmother dreamed of the land of goldenrod, she stayed in Carthage and joined the Eastern Star. After graduating from Vanderbilt in 1929, Father went to work in the personnel department of the Travelers Insurance Company. Years later, he told me that he had made a mistake. "I did what my father did," he said; "I should have done something different, even run off to sea." An old man's thoughts often wander far from the path trod by the young man, and running away to sea is only accomplished in books and dreamed about when the house is quiet and the children asleep. For his insurance business, Grandfather traveled about Smith County in a buggy; occasionally he took the train to Nashville. Once when he was trying to settle a claim over a mule which had been struck by lightning (no mule ever died a natural death in Tennessee; mules were the lightning rods of the animal world), he stayed overnight at Chestnut Mound with Miss Fanny and Godkin Hayes. The next morning after breakfast, when he was climbing into his buggy, Miss Fanny asked Grandfather if he ever went to Difficult Creek, Tennessee, saying she had heard he was quite a traveler and had been to Nashville.

"Yes, ma'am," Grandfather answered. "I go there right much."

"Well, the next time you go," Miss Fanny said, "will you please say hello to Henry McCracken; he's my brother and I haven't seen him in over twenty years."

"What!" my grandfather exclaimed. "Difficult Creek is only twelve miles away, just on the other side of the Caney Fork River. Rome's Ferry will take you across in eight minutes." "Oh, Mr. Sam," Miss Fanny answered wistfully, "I do want to see my brother, but I just can't bring myself to cross the great Caney Fork River."

Father crossed the Caney Fork, but he didn't travel far. After working in Washington and Richmond, he was sent to Nashville in the late thirties. From that time on he refused to be transferred. Beyond Difficult Creek lay the little town of Defeated Creek, and for most of his life Father was content to meander through a small circle of miles and visit with the Miss Fannys he met. Personnel, however, may have been too easy for him. Reading books in the office, he became a character, albeit a competent one. "He was a bumblebee," a man told me; "he shouldn't have been able to fly, but he did. What's more he did things that couldn't be done." By the 1960s, though, the topography of Father's world changed. The wild growth of wealth changed the course of Defeated Creek, making it swing closer to home. People suddenly became not whom they knew or what they were but how much money they made. Strangers appeared, and instead of being identified by a rich string of anecdotes, they became bank accounts or corporations. It was almost impossible not to be swept up by the wash of money, and as Father's friends grew wealthy and began to possess the glittering goods of the world and to take trips beyond simple goldenrod to lands where orchids hung heavy from trees and butterflies bigger than fans waved in the sun, Father became envious. Although he occasionally criticized the affluence of certain groups—physicians, for example—he was not resentful. What troubled him most, I think, was how wealth changed conversation. Despite his wide reading, there was little room for him or Miss Fanny in talk about Bali or Borneo.

Disregard for possessions tempered Father's resentment of wealth. Although he liked shoes, both good and bad, and as a handsome man was vain on occasions like Christmas, when he wore a red vest, clothes, for example, mattered little to him. Outside the office he wore khaki trousers and checkered shirts that he bought at Sears. So long as the interior of the house was tasteful, something he knew Mother managed well, Father paid no attention to it. If a visitor admired something, Father was likely to offer it to him, especially, it seemed, if it was a family piece: an envelope of Confederate money or a Bible published in 1726 and listing forgotten generations of ancestors. As a child, I learned to hide things.

When I found a box of old letters in a storeroom at Aunt Lula's house, I hid them in the attic. When the day came, as I knew it would, when Father asked for them, saying he had a friend who would like to have them, I lied and said that I lost them. Of course saving everything was beyond me, and I often resented his forays through my things. Even today when I want a good tricycle for my children, I resent his giving away the English trike that Mother's father bought me in New York. Now, though, I understand Father's desire to rid himself of possessions. I behave similarly. I wear Sears trousers and shirts from J. C. Penney. I have turned down positions that would greatly increase my salary because I like the little out-of-the-way place where I live. I, too, alas, give away possessions. "You are the only teacher I have ever met," a graduate student told me recently, "who has two offices and not a single book." I don't have any books because I have given them away, out of, I think, the same compulsion that led Father to give away things and that kept him from becoming wealthy: the desire to keep life as clean and simple as possible.

Wealth clutters life, bringing not simply possessions but temptation. Money lures one from the straight and clear into darkly complex. The sidewalks in Carthage ran in narrow lines to the courthouse. Skating along them, a boy was always aware of where he was: in front of the Reed's house, then the Ligons', the Fishers', the McGinnises', and then by the drugstore, the five-and-ten, King's barbershop, and finally the bank or post office. Wealth bends lines and makes it difficult for even the most adept skater to roll through life without losing his way or falling into the dirt. Instead of enriching, wealth often lessens life. At least that's the way I think Father thought, for he spurned every chance to become wealthy. For some twenty years he managed the affairs of his Aunt Lula, Grandmother's widowed sister. Father being her nearest relative, Aunt Lula called upon him whenever anything went wrong. For three summers in a row, Aunt Lula fell ill during Father's two-week summer vacation, and we hurried back to Nashville from the beach to put her in a hospital. Aunt Lula owned a farm, 750 acres of land just outside Nashville in Williamson County. The farm had been in the family for generations, and when I came home from college at Christmas, I spent mornings roaming over it rabbit hunting.

Aunt Lula did not have a will, and when Father's closest friend, a lawyer, learned this, he urged Father to let him draw one up for her.

"For God's sakes, Sam," he said; "you have nursed her for years. She would want you to have the farm. I will make out the will tonight and you have her sign it tomorrow." Father demurred, and when Aunt Lula died, two relatives who had never met her shared the estate. Father put the land up for sale and received a bid of seventy-five thousand dollars.

"Borrow the money," Mother advised, "and buy the land yourself. Nashville is growing by leaps and bounds, and the farm is worth much more."

"That would not be right," Father answered, and the land was sold. Six years later it was resold for over a million dollars. Father kept the lines of his life straight and his temptations few, and I admire him for it; yet at night when I think about the teaching job I have taken this summer so the house can be painted and dead oaks felled in the yard, I sometimes wish he had not sold the farm. This is not to say that Father did not understand the power of money. He thought it important for other people and urged me to make the most of my chances, citing his younger brother Coleman as a warning. According to Father, Coleman was the talented Pickering and could have done practically anything; yet, Father recounted, he refused to grasp opportunities. Satisfied to live simply, Coleman was in truth Father's brother, a man wary of complexity, determined to remain independent and free from entangling responsibilities.

After forty most people I know realize that their actions and thoughts are inconsistent. Worried about gypsy moths, a child's stuttering, or slow-running drains, they have little time for principle and not simply neglect but recognize and are comfortable with the discrepancy between words and deeds. To some extent Father's attitude toward wealth reflected this state of mind. Behind his behavior, however, also lay the perennial conflict between the particular and the abstract or the general. From infancy through school people are taught the value of general truths or principles, the sanctity, for example, of honor and truth itself. As one grows older and attempts to apply principles to real human beings, one learns that rules are cruelly narrow and, instead of bettering life, often lead to unhappiness. The sense of principle or belief in general truth is so deeply ingrained, however, that one rarely repudiates it. Instead, one continues to pay lip service to it and actually believe in its value while never applying it to individuals. Thus during the turmoil over integration in Nashville during the 1950s and early 1960s, Father sounded harshly conservative. One day, though, while he and Mother and I were walking along Church Street, we came upon four toughs, or hoods as they were then called, harassing a black woman. "You there," Father bellowed, all 136 pounds of him swelling with his voice; "who do you think you are?" Then as Mother and I wilted into a doorway, he grabbed the biggest tough and, shaking him, said, "Apologize to this lady. This is Tennessee, and people behave here."

"Yes, sir, yes, sir," the man responded meekly and apologized.

Father then turned to the woman, and while the toughs scurried away, took off his hat and said, "Ma'am, I am sorry for what happened. You are probably walking to the bus stop; if you don't mind, my wife and I and our son would like to walk with you."

Although Father expounded political and moral generalities during the isolation of dinner, he never applied them to the hurly-burly of his friends' lives. He delighted in people too much to categorize and thus limit his enjoyment of them. Not long after the incident on Church Street, Father was invited to join the Klan. Around ten or eleven each morning, a man appeared outside the Travelers building, selling doughnuts and sweet rolls. As could be expected from a man who did not have to work too hard and who loved candy, Father always bought a doughnut and a cup of coffee and then chatted a bit. On this occasion, the man said, "Mr. Pickering, I have known you for some time, and you seem a right-thinking man. This Friday there is going to be a meeting of the Klan at Nolensville, and I'd like for you to attend and become a member."

"That's mighty nice of you to invite me," Father replied, "but I believe I will just continue to vote Republican."

As could be expected, Father was inconsistent toward me. Of things he thought comparatively unimportant—sports, for example—he rarely said much, except to moan about the Vanderbilt football team. When I was in high school, he picked me up after football practice, and unlike some boys' fathers, who filmed practices, had conferences with the coaches, and caused their sons untold misery, Father never got in the way. About social matters he behaved differently, urging me to do the things he never did—join service clubs, for example. "They will help your career," he explained. When he heard me taking a political stance that was not generally accepted and thereby safe, he intervened. Ten years ago I spent three months in the Soviet Union. On my return people often asked me questions; once during a discussion with businessmen Father overheard me say something "risky." "Pay no attention to my son," he interrupted; "he has been brainwashed." That ended the conversation.

Of Father's courtship of Mother, I know and want to know little. Toward the end of his life, he refused to tell me family stories, saying, "You will publish them." Quite right—I would publish almost anything except an account of his and Mother's love affair. Theirs was a good and typical marriage with much happiness and sadness during the early and middle years and with many operations at the end. They were very different, but they stumbled along in comparative harmony.

"When I first met him," Mother told me, "I thought him the damnedest little pissant."

"Your mother," Father often said, "does not appreciate my sense of humor." That was a loss, because laughing was important to Father, and for much of his life, he played practical jokes. Practical jokes are an almost implicit recognition of the foolishness of man's endeavors. Involving actual individuals rather than comparative abstractions like wordplay, for example, such humor flourishes in stable communities in which people's positions remain relatively constant and clearly defined. The popularity of practical jokes waned as the South grew wealthy. Money undermined community both by making people more mobile and by changing the terms by which position was defined. As people became financial accomplishments, not neighbors, cousins, sons, and daughters, they took themselves more seriously. When they, rather than a web of relationships over which they had comparatively little control, determined what they were, their actions grew increasingly significant. No more could the practical joker be seen as a friend; no more was his laughter benign, even fond. Instead, threatening the basis of identity by mocking, he undermined society. By the late 1960s Father had stopped playing practical jokes; before then, though, the going was good.

After selling some rocky, farmed-out land to a company that wanted to construct a shopping center, one of Father's acquaintances, Tuck Gobbett, built a twenty-room house outside Nashville. Known locally as the Taj Mahal, the house had everything: sauna bath, swimming pool, Japanese shoji screens around the garage, and even a pond with swans purchased from a New York dealer. In its garishness the house was marvelous, and Father enjoyed it, saying only, "The birds were a mistake. As soon as snapping turtles find the pond, it's good-bye swans." He was right; two years later the turtles came, and the swans disappeared. Father decided Gobbett went too far, however, when he got rid of the off-brand beagles he had always owned and bought an Afghan hound. The dog had a royal pedigree, and when Gobbett advertised in a kennel-club magazine that the dog was standing at stud, Father saw his chance. "Why is it," he asked me years later, "that mongrel people always want pure-bred dogs." Father then read about Afghans, learning quite a bit about blood lines. Able to disguise his voice, he telephoned Gobbett, explaining that he lived in Birmingham and was the owner of a champion bitch. He had, he said, seen the advertisement in the kennel-club magazine and wondered about the possibility of breeding the animals. Of course, he continued, he would first have to scrutinize the pedigree of Gobbett's dog. After Gobbett detailed his dog's ancestry, Father then supplied that of the bitch, which, not surprisingly, came from the best Afghan stock in the nation. Saying he would need time to investigate Gobbett's dog, Father hung up, promising to call within a week. During the week Father visited Gobbett. When asked about news, Gobbett excitedly described the telephone call, saying the bitch had "an absolutely first-class pedigree" and the puppies would be worth a thousand dollars apiece.

The next week Father telephoned, saying he looked into the dog and thought the pedigree would do. Although the owner of the bitch usually received all the puppies except for one from a breeding, Father said he did not want a single puppy. After this remark, he said he had pressing business and would call the following week to make arrangements for the mating. Gobbett was ebullient. "What fools there are in the world," he said. "There is money to be made in these dogs. The puppies will make me a man to be reckoned with in Afghan circles." As could be expected, completing the arrangements was not easy, but after a month and a half of conversations, the date and place were set. Then at the end of the final telephone call, almost as an afterthought, Father said, "There is just one thing though."

"What's that?" Gobbett asked.

"Oh, nothing important," Father said; "my dog has been spayed, but I don't suppose that will make a difference."

Father's humor was rarely bawdy, and the jokes he told were usually stories, gentle tales about foolishness. My favorite, one that I have often told, was called "Edgar the Cat." Two bachelor brothers, Herbert and

James, lived with their mother and James's cat Edgar in a little town not unlike Carthage. James was particularly attached to Edgar, and when he had to spend several days in Nashville having work done on his teeth, he left Herbert meticulous instructions about Edgar. At the end of his first day away from home, James telephoned Herbert. "Herbert," he said, "how is Edgar?"

"Edgar is dead," Herbert answered immediately.

There was a pause; then James said, "Herbert, you are terribly insensitive. You know how close I was to Edgar and you should have broken the news to me slowly."

"How?" Herbert said.

"Well," James said, "when I asked about Edgar tonight, you should have said, 'Edgar's on the roof, but I have called the fire department to get him down.'"

"Is that so?" said Herbert.

"Yes," James answered, "and tomorrow when I called you could have said the firemen were having trouble getting Edgar down but you were hopeful they would succeed. Then when I called the third time you could have told me that the firemen had done their best but unfortunately Edgar had fallen off the roof and was at the veterinarian's, where he was receiving fine treatment. Then when I called the last time you could have said that although everything humanly possible had been done for Edgar he had died. That's the way a sensitive man would have told me about Edgar. And, oh, before I forget," James added, "how is mother?"

"Uh," Herbert said, pausing for a moment, "she's on the roof." There was an innocence in Father's humor, perhaps a sign of softness, something that contributed to his not grabbing Aunt Lula's farm. In the eighteenth and early nineteenth centuries, Pickerings were Quakers and, so far as I can tell, gentle people who did not struggle or rage against life but who took things as they came, people who copied poems into family Bibles while recording the deaths of children. When seven-year-old Marthelia died in 1823, her father wrote:

When the Icy hand of death his saber drew!
To cut down the budding rose of morn!!
He held his favorite motto full in view—
The fairest Bud must the tomb adorn!!!

In general Pickerings lived quiet lives, cultivating their few acres and avoiding the larger world with its abstractions of honor, service, and patriotism. For them country meant the counties in which they lived, not the imperial nation. Years ago I knew John Kennedy had things backwards when he said, "Ask not what your country can do for you, but what you can do for your country." The great excuse for country, with its borders dividing brothers, was that it bettered the life of the individual.

With the exception of the Civil War, the struggles of the nation have not touched us. Coming of age between battles, few Pickerings have looked at the dark side of man's heart. Perhaps because of this, we are soft and, in our desires, subconscious or conscious, to remain free, have become evasive. Few things are simple, though, and this very evasiveness may be a sign of a shrewd or even tough vitality. Aware that those who respond to challenges and fight for a cause or success often are ground under, we have learned to live unobtrusively and blossom low to the ground and out of sight. Even when a Pickering does respond to a call, it's usually not for him. In 1942 the navy rejected Father's application for Officers' Training School because he was too thin. In 1944 Father was drafted; two days before he was slated to leave for training camp and after a series of farewell parties, he received a telegram instructing him not to report, explaining that he was too thin.

Not long ago my daughter Eliza McClarin Pickering was born. She was born, fittingly enough, in a hospital in a relatively small town. For four days she was the only baby in the maternity ward, and the nurses let me wander in and out at my convenience. With little to do, the nurses drank coffee, ate doughnuts, and talked. One night as I stood looking at Eliza in her crib, I overheard a conversation at the nurses' station around the corner. "I have worked at four hospitals," one nurse declared confidentially, "but this is the worst for poking I have ever seen. There's Shirley," she said, warming to the subject. "She runs out to the parking lot and gets poked every chance she gets. And Kate, there's not a bed on the third floor that she hasn't been poked in." Like Homer's account of those slain at the sack of Troy, the nurse's list of fallen was long and colorful. During the recital, the second nurse was silent. Finally, though, she spoke. "My word," she said in mild astonishment, "it's just a whirlwind of festivities."

Although few strong breezes blow through the lives of Pickerings, there are festivities, not shining affairs strung with bright lights but quiet events lit by words. After being married on my grandfather's farm in Hanover, Virginia, Father and Mother spent their first night together in the Jefferson Hotel in Richmond. Early the next morning they started for Nashville in Father's Ford coupe. On the outskirts of Richmond, they stopped for gas, and Mother bought a newspaper to look at the wedding pictures. She spread the paper out on the front seat and was looking at the pictures with Father when the man who was cleaning the windshield spoke up, saying, "It's a pity about that wedding. I feel so sorry for the girl."

"What do you mean," Father answered, jumping in before Mother could respond.

"Well," the man said, "she didn't marry the man she wanted to. She was in love with a poor insurance man but her father made her marry a rich fellow."

"Who told you that?" Father asked.

"Oh," the man answered, "a colored preacher that comes through here told me all about it. He preaches up in Hanover, and some of the members of his congregation work at her father's farm."

"Hmmm," Father said, "I hate to ruin your story, but look at the picture of the groom, and then look at me. This," he said gesturing toward Mother after the man had a good look, "is that unfortunate girl, and I am the poor insurance man. The preacher was wrong; sometimes in life poor folks carry off the prizes." And that's what Father did in a quiet way all his days. No prize of his was mentioned in an obituary; his name was not associated with any accomplishment; yet in the few acres he tilled and even beyond, at least as far as Carthage, he was known.

While at Vanderbilt, Father bought an old car. On a trip to Carthage it broke down, and, having to hurry back to Nashville to take an examination, one of the few times he attended class, Father left the car in Carthage and took the train. For a modest fee George Jackson, a black man, agreed to drive the car to Nashville once it was repaired. Father wrote out careful instructions and drew a map. Alas, George lost both, but this did not deter him. On arriving in Nashville, he stopped in a residential area, went up to a house, and asked where "young Mr. Samuel Pickering" lived. Amazingly, the people in the house knew Father.

They gave George clear directions, and he delivered the car. When Father learned that the map had gone astray and George had lost his way, he asked him how he knew whom to ask for instructions. "Mister Sam," George answered, "everybody knows you." The one time Father told this story, he laughed, then said, "What a world we have lost. Not a better world," he added, "but a different one. At times I miss it." Not, old man, so much as I miss you—not so much as I miss you.

Still Life

A STILL LIFE HAS ALWAYS HUNG over the sideboard in my parents' dining room. When I was small the painting frightened me, and I wouldn't look at it. The varnish over the oils had aged and turning dark hid the fruits in a pall of shadows. Like creatures from a troubling, half-remembered dream, forms hovered circular and indistinct on the edge of vision. In the painting fruits were piled on a table, covered with a white cloth. On the lower left side of the painting were pineapples, one cut open, its color pale and tubercular, like some entrail sliced in half, first wet and glistening then browning as it dried. Next to the pineapples were three pomegranates, one torn apart, seeds spilling across the table-cloth like drops of old blood, cracking and flaking. Behind and above the fruit was a greenish flagon, its spout hooked like the beak of a vulture and light preening from its sides like feathers iridescent in a broken shade. Along the lower right side of the painting were more pomegran-ates, translucent grapes, their leaves waxy in decay, and then a peach, broken open, the pit still in place and bulging like a tumor. In the shad-ows behind was a fluted bowl, rolling with what seemed to be apples, grapes, and peaches.

Until this year I wasn't sure what lurked in the background because I had never examined the painting closely. Then during a visit to Nashville in March, I took the painting from the wall and placing it in the sunlight looked at it carefully. Under the varnish brightness flowed like spring. Instead of white the pineapple was yellow, and the texture of the fruit was delicately, lovingly drawn. For their part the pomegranate seeds resembled red violets, not splintering, but glowing with promise and fertility. Instead of a vulture, craw swollen with carrion, the flagon smacked of newly turned earth and vines heavy with blossoms. Colors ran across the painting like a rainbow, down through the apples and across the grapes to the peach pit, pink and breathing, then over the pomegranates up through the pineapple to a stalk of firm, green leaves, tapering to sharp golden quills.

For a moment I was elated. If the painting were cleaned and hung over the mantel in our living room in Connecticut, it would glow throughout the year, I thought, like a warm welcoming fire, lifting expectations and pushing sadness out of sight into corners. That moment, though, passed quickly; something there was in me that preferred dark to light. Youth and the time of extravagant expectation were over, and instead of attracting, bright color, more often than not, repulses me. Rather than promising a future shining with lively possibility, colors remind me of joy left behind, all those things I once did and can never do again, all the things I imagined doing and now know I will never do. No longer did the painting frighten me, and as I hung it back above the sideboard, I realized I would not have it cleaned. Although part of me wanted light promise and bright hope to whistle through life, I could not help being drawn toward melancholy. There in the gloom about the fluted bowl and flagon lay my future, bleak reality, not now the easy intangible fluff of a child's dream.

Of course in contemplating the shadows of my still life, I occasionally see fruits clearly, apples red and orange, and peaches pink and fuzzy. Not only that, I am not always melancholy; in fact I frequently behave in ways more fruity than funereal. I have a bad back and three mornings a week I swim a half or two-thirds of a mile in the university pool. Swimming is boring; all one does is splash back and forth from one end of the pool to the other. Talking is impossible. The person who tries to talk is sure to swallow a mouthful of water, if not drown. After the swim the silence of the pool continues into the shower. Nakedness inhibits conversation and bathers turn their backs on words and each other, single-mindedly gripping soap and scrubbing. Like a grape unnoticed in the background of the still life, most mornings I pass unobtrusively through the shower, washing quickly and silently. Occasionally, however, words like fruit will ferment and last Wednesday when I walked into the shower and saw eight silent strangers, words burst out. "Well, girls," I said, ambling over to the wall, "this growing old sure isn't much fun. Damn it," I exclaimed to get people's attention while turning on the shower, "I've gotten so I can only eat one meal a day. No matter how many vitamins I take I can only manage a single meal and even then I can't eat dessert. Strangely enough," I went on, pausing to soap up my front side, "my sex life has also changed. Instead of four, I have to do it five, sometimes six, times a day. What a nuisance! Still," I said, vigorously rubbing the soap in, "that's not what's bothering me. It's this eating. I just don't know what to do. I'm too young to limit myself to one meal a day, so I have been thinking about taking monkey gland shots. You fellows have any suggestions?" I said, working the soap in and through a neglected cranny or two, before glancing about and adding, "You guys look pretty normal. One of you must have had this problem." The group, I am afraid, must all have been stalwart trenchermen with hardy three-meal-a-day appetites. No one spoke; the sound of lathering grew intense, and soon I had the shower room to myself.

Despite an occasional locker room outburst, however, my life is quiet and lean. Recently a student wrote a paper for me in which she described the rich sweets of German coffeehouses: strudel, apples dark with raisin or hazelnuts, all smothered with whipped cream; Sacher torte; Black Forest cake, cream and cherries, white and red, folded between layers of chocolate; pastry leaves bulging with mocha or hazelnut buttercream; and tarts, their fruits crisp and glazed atop mounds of vanilla cream, the whole sitting in scalloped shells, sparkling and resembling little, dumpy boats hung with jewels. The description freshened my appetite, bringing to mind younger, wandering days of morning coffee at Demel's in Vienna and afternoon tea at Louis's in Hampstead. Now I rarely travel, thinking the drive to Willimantic seven miles away a trip.

When I go to Willimantic, I usually take the children and stop at Frank's Bakery for milk and doughnuts. Frank's is sugary and functional, a lifetime away from my youth and dream sweets on silver carts. By the door is a cigarette machine; on one side is a yellow poster advertising the New England Tractor Trailer Training School. "Training People Today," the poster states, "for a Better Tomorrow." Along one wall is a series of shiny Ektachrome pictures depicting a man fishing, probably for rainbow trout, somewhere in the Canadian Rockies. In the distance above him jagged blue mountains reach toward the sky, while at his feet a stream runs through a long *S*, tumbling over rocks before pitching past a clump of green spruce trees. At one end of Frank's counter is a pile of plastic boxes from Benny's, the ninety-nine-cent price tags still glued on. In them are ornaments for cakes: a pink swan for thirty cents, a golf club and ball costing fifty cents, and again at thirty cents a silver heart with "Sweet 16" written in the middle. In boxes behind the counter are statues of brides and grooms for wedding cakes, the most expensive costing fifteen dollars and ninety-five cents and the cheapest eight dollars. On the counter itself are cakes, all covered with white icing and colored flowers, the favorite flower being a dark blue rose, surrounded by green leaves. In the icebox beside the cash register are cream pies costing five dollars: chocolate, banana, strawberry, and pineapple. The last time we went to Frank's Francis ate a "Yellow Bird's Nest," a doughnut-like pastry covered with sprinkles and filled with jelly and white icing. Edward ate a Cream Horn, a longish worm-like tube swollen with artificial cream. Both Horn and Nest cost sixty-five cents while Eliza's brownie cost forty-five cents. For my part I had not started the monkey gland regimen, so I sat quietly and didn't eat anything, although, to be honest, a chocolate doughnut covered with thick, brown icing and blue and yellow sprinkles tempted me.

For moments while the children ate, I drifted away on thought. My days are so calm that I spend much time thinking. Not surprisingly, I suppose, my thoughts reflect the stillness of my life. Almost never do I delve into the quick and the disturbing, and I generally ignore religious or political matters. When my friend Neil asked me whom I fancied for president, I answered that I didn't favor anyone, adding only that I wanted someone who had never been in the military. The best candidate, I explained, would be a coward, a person who connived his way out of the draft when young. A "track record" of avoiding conflicts was important, I said, lathering up the conversation, because such a person would probably do his best to keep himself, his family, the nation, and then what was more important, my family, at peace. The conversation with Neil was out of character. Rarely do I become so enthusiastic about matters governmental. Instead I ponder the immediate: carpenter ants in the attic and aging furniture in the living room. Recently I stored a Victorian chair in the basement. Manufactured during the rococo revival in the 1850s, the chair was designed by John Henry Belter and is the ornate wooden equivalent of a cluttered still life. Bunches of grapes, entwined not only with leaves and vines but with scrolls and what looks like roses, hang down the legs while vegetables, nuts, and flowers grow up the sides, eventually wrapping around a bowl of fruit at the top of the chair. With haunches rounder than eggplant, a putto crouches in the bowl, a conch shell at his ear. Instead of the busy roar of the sea and fruit spreading like kudzu, I wanted silence in my rooms, and I replaced the Belter chair with a smooth, finely finished Pembroke table. No matter how I try to push the quick and the lively into the basement and out of my living room, however, I am never completely successful. Something as small as exasperation with a dull swim or the legs of a table betrays me, and probably will always betray me. Instead of failing straight and tapering clean and narrow, the legs of my table are cabriole legs, bowed out and then sweeping back and around down to the floor and ball and claw feet.

Although age makes the still life easier to achieve, a still life is never completely natural and always requires forcing. In part, custom and its consort propriety impose quiet. Twelve or so years ago in more viny, rococo days, I attended much opera. As the melodies flowed, stopped, and then rushed ahead, stripping restraint from the emotions, much as cleaning removes varnish from a painting, I often pitched forward to the edge of decorum. The closest I ever came to tumbling into misbehavior occurred during the last scene of *La Bohème*. Shortly after a burst of passionately, mournful song, the heroine Mimi dies. Her lover Rodolfo is not immediately aware of her death, realizing it only after noticing the expressions on the faces of Bohemian friends. On first seeing the sadness in his friends' faces, Rodolfo is puzzled and strides about the stage, ignoring Mimi's body and asking what is wrong. At this point during a performance at Covent Garden, I almost rose out of my seat and yelled, "She's dead, you damn fool, she's dead—died of tuberculosis, don't you know." To keep from shouting, I balled my hands into fists and clamped my teeth down on my cheeks, cutting them, the blood pooling then oozing out at the corners of my mouth.

Silence comes easier now. I haven't chewed into my cheeks for years. Occasionally, though, I do have trouble being properly quiet. During my visit to Nashville in March, hearing aids came up in a conversation with a group of father's friends. Rapidly the men ran through the usual topics: expenses, batteries, and the difficulty of hearing in a crowd. Then, though, they discussed losing hearing aids. Everyone present had lost at least one, and most had no idea where they had lost them. "Well, I know what happened to mine," Mr. McGinnis said. "The dog ate it. I saw him do it. Ate it right off the top of a book." When the talk paused, I almost interrupted. "What kind of dog was it," I wanted to ask, "big dog or little dog; black dog, white dog, spotted dog, or old yellow dog; a dog with a long tail or short tail, or even a curly tail? And what kind of book was it the dog ate from? Hardback or paperback? Was it a cookbook or mystery?" Maybe, I suddenly thought, it was one of mine—

after all Mr. McGinnis was father's friend. Although my books weren't very good, I didn't want one to end up as a dog bowl. Eventually, I decided, the book wasn't likely to be mine. My sales were so low that only a handful of people in Nashville had read anything I wrote, and I was pretty sure I had talked to all of them already, and Mr. McGinnis wasn't among them. "Great God," I thought, "what a tale. I have to ask questions." Of course I didn't ask and, keeping silent before age, let the conversation drift away to another subject.

In saying that today I rarely travel farther from home than Willimantic, I overlooked trips to Nashville. In my mind real travel is associated with sidewalk cafés, dark chocolate, and mounds of whipped cream floating on rich, black coffee, not, I am afraid, with Delta Airlines, afternoon flights from Hartford to Cincinnati, then Cincinnati to Nashville, peanuts in little red or blue bags, and cans of Campbell's orange juice, made from concentrate extracted from fruit grown in Florida and Brazil. Because Mother and Father moved into a condominium last summer, this March Vicki and I and the children stayed in a Holiday Inn near Vanderbilt University. Since our room was near the roof of the hotel on the twelfth floor, Vicki refused to turn on the air conditioning, saying we might get legionnaire's disease. With one exception, nights at the Holiday Inn were still. One day, however, the empty rooms in the hotel were booked by delegates to a convention of Young Baptists. All through the evening our telephone rang and pranksters banged on doors and ran through the halls screaming. At half past eleven I finally called the desk and asked the hotel management to calm the children down. "We are trying," the clerk said, "but we aren't having much luck." "Didn't some preachers accompany the kids?" I asked. "Yes Sir," the clerk responded, "but we can't find any of them."

Every morning after breakfast I drove to Mother and Father's apartment. After leaving Vicki and the children with Mother, I took Father to Belle Meade Drugs. A group of young women had converted part of the drugstore into a bakery and sandwich shop called the Picnic. Ferns hung from the ceiling in baskets, and tables, chairs, and plates were blue and white, giving the Picnic the homey feeling of old delftware. Every morning Father and his friends met to talk about politics and hearing aids. The women who ran the Picnic were kindly affectionate, remembering birthdays and asking about ailing wives at home. Mornings at the Picnic were slow, but I didn't want them to end. Nevertheless, I knew that, like all picnics, the mornings had to end; knives, forks, plates, cups, and memories would be packed away. The old tablecloth, spotted and stained, would be rolled up; the trash gathered, the hillside left bare, and a day or two later no one would be able to tell that a picnic had occurred. "Daddy," Eliza, my three-year-old, said after we had been in Nashville for five days, "I love Ree-Ree and Baa-Baa, but I'm tired of going back and forth." Like Eliza I was tired of coming and going, but unlike her longings for a still life, I wanted to stem the inevitable falling away of friends and green hillsides, laughter and hampers bulging with fried chicken, potato salad, homemade rolls, and devil's-food cake.

At three or four every morning Eliza wakes to go to the potty chair. Almost always I hear her climb out of bed, then pad rapidly through the hall to Vicki's and my room. "Daddy," she says, and I get out of bed, turn the bathroom light on, hand her a cup of apple juice, and then sit with her. After she finishes, I go to her room with her, and as I cover her, she puts her arms around my neck and says, "I love you Daddy; you are the best Daddy in the whole world." When I return to my room, I often sit for a moment on the edge of the bed. Tears well up in my eyes and I long for permanence, a still life in which Eliza is forever small, telling me in the dark night that I am the best daddy in the world.

Although a still life cannot stop change, it can create the illusion of slowing time. In days uncluttered by bustle, hours sag loosely, and sometimes seem great bottomless bags. Duties and appointments rarely weigh me down, and I spend hours simply and quietly, just looking about. Last Saturday at noon I stretched out in the dell in my side yard. The daffodils which I planted last fall had begun to bloom, and I wanted to see what they looked like from the ground. Standing above them I was tempted to count blossoms. I wondered how many of the bulbs I planted came up and if I had gotten "good value." On the ground concerns about money and numbers disappeared. The daffodils seemed to stretch endlessly, lush pinks and reds, pale and bright yellows, golds and oranges, with stalks firm and green. Instead of passing unnoticed at my feet, colors were in my face, and the world seemed a patchwork of light. Behind me grew periwinkle, its blossoms, purple and starry, drawing bumblebees like eyes. Nearby were yellowish tufts of sweet William while all about were the dark green, almost metallic, leaves of gill-cover-the-ground. By summer the gill would not be so retiring, runners stretching in all directions and its leaves light green and alight with violet blossoms. As I lay on the ground I thought about ordering more daffodils, "to bring," as I told Francis my first grader, "more beauty into the lives of people passing on the street." In my mind I ordered Audubons, mostly white with pink about the cup; cherry spots, laundry clean petals and a shining orange cup; and Inca gold, a trumpet daffodil almost two feet tall and as yellow as an August sunset. I painted the bare ground with rainbows, mixing resplendents, yellow and red, lilac delights, coral ribbons, and Mount Hood, an old-fashioned white flower. Down the lip of the dell I scattered little waterperry, pinkish and fragrant, ten inches high; canarybird, slightly taller but still fragrant; and geranium, even taller but with a fragrance brighter than its white and orange blossoms. I don't know how long I lay in the dell. Clouds not minutes measured the day, and I started to leave only when the sun disappeared and a heavy mist began blowing across the yard. Even so, I didn't leave quickly, for while I lay on the ground a pileated woodpecker flew into the woods beyond the dell. Only once before, when I was a child in Tennessee, had I seen a pileated woodpecker, and I wanted to see as much of him as possible. His red head battering soft wood, he dropped from tree to log, flashing white and black. Only when he flew deeper into the woods and out of sight did I leave the dell.

Beside providing occasions to look at daffodils and woodpeckers, a still life frees one to write, not weighty books thick with the muscularity resulting from fast living, but soft books modest with easy observation. This spring I received a royalty check from the sales of a book published three years ago. "How much is it," Michael, an inquisitive friend in the English department, asked when I got my mail. "Sixty-eight sixty," I answered. "What," he exclaimed, "six thousand, eight hundred, and sixty dollars for a book which came out in 1985? Good Lord, what sales you must have had." "In three years," I said, putting the check into my wallet, "the book has sold 1,477 copies. The check is for sixty-eight dollars and sixty cents." The odd thing, and what I did not say to Michael, was that for just a handful of books a writer betrays: himself, others, and the private decencies of life. Actually it may not so much be the individual who betrays, but the still life itself, its quiet demanding to be broken, its emptiness filled. Much as the painting over the sideboard seemed blank, until looked at closely, so perhaps only the unexamined life seems empty and quiet. When open spaces trail across the canvas of a day, one, more often than not I suspect, hurries to brush in flagons, grapes, pineapples, daffodils, woodpeckers, whatever, alas, falls before hand or eye.

A month ago I made a second trip to Nashville. Father was ill, and so when Mother suddenly had to have an operation, I flew down. Days were long and barren, and so I filled them in. While Mother slept hard, I sketched her room in the hospital, brushing in the bed, its body like the chassis of a fork lift, dials along bulky sides, and at the foot a clipboard hanging, covered with cold, frightening numbers; the television suspended on an L, high on the wall and leaning forward, almost intruding into the bed, white letters underneath reading "Patient Educator Channel 6"; beside the bed a table shaped like a C, one side open so the top could extend over the patient; against the wall a small chest with three drawers and ball feet, this time with no claws. On the chest was a beige telephone, a clear plastic envelope inside of which was the schedule for the television, a beige cup with a bendable plastic straw leaning out of it, and a box of paper handkerchiefs, bouquets of roses on the sides. On the floor was a brown wastecan with a clear garbage bag inside; behind it and to the side, silver and sticklike, stood a "tree"; hanging from it were plastic containers, tubes curling toward the bed, liquid running through them like roots. In front of the window was a second chest; on top was a pot of yellow chrysanthemums wrapped in green paper and blue ribbon. Beyond were Venetian blinds and the windows of other rooms. In hard rigor three straight chairs sat against the wall while two sprinklers jutted down from the ceiling. Near the door was a round thermostat with numbers too small for old people to read. I painted the room, I suppose, because I didn't want to see Mother on the bed, old and weak and suddenly dying, her cheeks waxy and sunken, her left arm cradled around a stuffed Easter bunny—a bunny which Eliza has now named Noodlely and which she keeps in her bed next to Kitty.

Although Mother's room was a dreary blend of blue and beige, someone had painted a fishing scene on the doors of the elevator in the hall opposite. Unlike the pictures at Frank's Bakery, the scene was not exotic, smacking of Reelfoot Lake and the local. While ducks dropped toward the water feathering their wings, the sun set in yellow bars. On the horizon two men sat in a rowboat, fishing, not for trout, I found myself thinking and noting down, but for bass or crappie. Alert to details, I sketched in the canvas of hours, studying the halls and listening to the conversations of strangers. Much as the painter of Mother and

Father's still life meticulously sliced through pineapple and pomegranate with his brush, so I traced remarks with my pen. When I heard a woman in the hall describe a friend's trouble saying, "Her thyroid's done went out of berserk," I wrote it down. Late at night people often added details to my painting. During the long dying a nurse told me about her three miscarriages and Rosie talked about Mother. In November when Mother broke her hip and had the socket replaced, Rosie stayed in the hospital with her. Because she was taking a pain killer and on waking might have behaved irrationally, pulling at her hip, Mother's hands were restrained. On coming out from under the anesthesia, Mother raised her head, looked around, saw Rosie, then noticed her hands were tied to the railings of the bed. "Rosie," Mother said, "get a pair of scissors and cut these ropes. I'm going home." "Miss Katharine," Rosie answered, "I can't do that." "Well, then, you are fired," Mother exclaimed, letting her head fall back on the pillow before adding, "again."

The morning after Mother's death I drove to Carthage, my father's hometown, to arrange her burial in a family plot. Suddenly it was a redbud and dogwood spring in Tennessee, and amid the cedars along the road, pinks and whites stood out washed and wholesome. The grass was greener and the light deeper and yellower than in Connecticut, and I dreamed about returning to Tennessee, to the past, to sprigs of redbud in vases and magnolias in bowls like lilypads, and to Christmases of cedar not spruce trees, soft sweetbriar Christmases of sunny winter days. I wondered why I stopped academic writing, forsaking the comfortable, otherworld of leather-bound books and musty knowledge. Far happier would I have been if the details of the present had slipped off me like thin paint, leaving only a blurred track behind. Far happier I would have been blotting the moment into cloud. Happier still dropping searing experience at the library door and spending life roaming the cool, serene corridors of old learning. No longer, though, was I a scholar; I was now an essayist, a person to whom observation stuck, unaffected by conscious scrubbing and scrapping. Beside the road I noticed a sign for the Mourner's Bench Baptist Church. "Once Saved, Always Saved," the sign proclaimed. "Doubtful," said my cousin Katherine who with her daughter Ann accompanied me. "I wonder what funerals are like at Mourner's Bench," I said. "I don't know about that church," said Ann who works at a florist's shop, "but we make some of the damnedest palls imaginable for country burials. We just finished a humdinger. In the middle was a pink princess telephone made out of carnations. Written under it in big letters made out of white carnations was JESUS CALLS."

Although a still life makes one observant, it can also make life itself seem grotesque. Details slip out of context, and seem unnatural like wax fruit on a dining room table. Although the Nashville papers had already printed Mother's obituary, Mr. Dyer the Carthage undertaker asked several questions about Mother. "Why do you need this information?" I asked. "This is a small town," Mr. Dyer answered, "and every day, at ten in the morning, noon, and then again at four in the afternoon, the local radio station runs a program called 'Obituaries of the Air.' All obituaries as well as admissions and dismissals from the local hospital are read three times a day. It is the most popular program in Carthage." Later as we were leaving, I said, "Mr. Dyer, I do hope you got the right body." "Oh, yes sir, Mr. Pickering. Don't you worry," he answered; "I picked your mother up myself. The hospital ties a name tag to the big toe on the right foot, and I checked her toe twice." Most of the things I remember from my conversation with Mr. Dyer now strike me as funny: Mr. Dyer's calling coffins "the merchandise" and then later in the show-room as we examined the merchandise, his laying the green dress which I picked out for Mother's burial atop a modestly priced coffin and say-ing, "The dress just goes with this casket."

Many of the observations which cling to memory I would like to bury deep in forgetfulness, but as the pomegranate seeds in the still life dis-turbed my sleep as a child, so some of the details of Mother's burial break my waking hours, turning consciousness nightmarish. Worst are the expenses, not yet blackened by the hard varnish of time, the cold practicalities they reveal numbing and final: $200 for embalming; $75 for "other preparation of the body"; the same for "transfer of remains to funeral home"; "Immediate Burial," $580; the coffin, $1,065; then the vault, the plot markers, tent and grave equipment, the labor of digging and filling the grave, and finally the tax at $138.38, for a total of $3,208.38.

Although chilling detail clings perhaps with greater tenacity to the still than to the active life, there is compensation. A still life nurtures imagination. Not sapped by the fretful drip of days, the imagination gathers strength, flowing and shaping realities beyond small fact. It even overturns death, creating not simply illusions but a truth greater than mere detail: that despite the grave there is still life. Just this morning I left the baked earth and hot, dry plains of grief. Ranging through foothills and shards of color, I climbed toward ridges yellow in the sun. In the distance stood tall mountains, their peaks white, not with ice but with warm milk, dropped from the udders of God's flock as they grazed across the heavens. Far below me in another world lay the shaley slopes and dried rivers of death, brown seams now lost in sullen heat. I climbed until I reached a valley golden with daffodils and blooming with birds. There across a blue stream sat Mother, a floppy straw hat on her head, her dress spread about her like petals, and her arms full of wild mint. "Sammy," she said, smiling. "Mommy," I cried and ran to her, the sky above me a bowl, fluted and gathering my joy like peaches and pineapples and pomegranates.

Patterns

"JOHN," THE LETTER FROM THE DEAN BEGAN, "if you are going to jog during the day, two pm., 3/8/86, don't do it where you will be seen (Route 195). It presents a very negative view of university to the public." My friend John is a neat, orderly man. Although his running shirts usually have something like "Tony's Pizza" or "The Baker's Dozen" printed on the back, they are always clean, and his shorts are unrevealingly baggy and smack of 1958 and the country club. "The dean's right," I said when John showed me the note. "An old guy like you shouldn't be on the main road. Imagine what people think when the first thing they see at the university is your big behind. Only thin faculty under forty should even be allowed to walk near one ninety-five."

Although the dean's attempt to control jogging was silly, culture is based upon the general acceptance of patterns of behavior. Rarely are the patterns stated or consciously agreed upon, and often people are aware of them only when they are broken. Even those who imagine themselves outside society and thus untrammeled by convention are usually tightly bound to propriety. I am not one of the faithful, but even now I become upset when I remember what a banker said to me in Sunday school thirty-five years ago. On the day the banker visited the class, the subject of racial segregation arose. I was nine years old and lived in a world filled with black people. Although there were certain things, like attending school, that black and white people did not do together, I was unaware of subtleties and spent little thought on such matters. Black people were in all the places I liked best, out-of-doors in the dairy barn or in the house in the kitchen. They took care of me, picking me up when I fell down and cleaning my knees when I skinned them. I liked nothing better than watching Mealy churn milk or "helping" Bessie or Lizzie make a chocolate pie. And so when the banker said that black people were inferior and should not be allowed to eat in restaurants with whites, I was puzzled. What the man said did not seem right, and raising my hand like a good little boy who had studied his Sunday school lesson, I said, "Sir, you must be wrong because the Bible says, 'All men are created equal.'" The man glared at me, obviously angry, and I wondered what I had done. "Do you think," he finally said, "that some nigger in north Nashville is equal to you?"

Most violations of propriety involve manners. Although they do not sear like the banker's words, strangely enough they cling to memory with a tenacity far exceeding their significance. Eight years ago I attended a performance of Noel Coward's *Blithe Spirit* at the National Theater in London. At the time I was writing a book, and life was drab. Except for buying food, I rarely left my room, and two weeks often passed without my speaking to anyone but grocers. A light comedy like *Blithe Spirit,* I decided, was just the thing to pick me up, and on arriving at the theater I settled happily into my seat, gleefully anticipating magical pastels and seltzer bottles. Until the first intermission everything fizzed along frivolously; immediately in front of me, however, sat two young women. During the break between acts they removed brushes and fingernail files from their purses and spent the intermission brushing each other's hair, then cleaning their fingernails. Tweezers appeared at the second intermission, and the girls plucked each other's eyebrows, paying close attention to hairs growing above the bridge of the nose. A curly hair over one girl's nose proved particularly pesky, and I was about to suggest her friend hire a backhoe for the job when suddenly the hair tore loose, bringing with it a long taproot and a ball of skin.

Instead of chuckling over Coward's comedy of manners, I left the theater fuming. Later I realized I should not have been upset. Like the girls' behavior, manners themselves are arbitrary and, if not comic, are often absurd if examined closely. Why, for example, should a man stand when a woman enters a room or give up his seat on a bus? Once upon a time when women were forever pregnant and died by the droves in childbirth, relinquishing a seat was reasonable. The stronger vessel should have sheltered the weaker. Nowadays women are not always enceinte; indeed, my wife Vicki was the first woman on our street to have a baby in ten years. Moreover, other things are different now too. Men are weaker than women. Women live longer and are less likely to commit suicide, become alcoholics, or have nervous breakdowns. If manners were raised upon reason, men would not stand when women entered a room. Women would stand, open doors, and pull out chairs for men.

Manners, of course, are not reasonable. Whenever a woman enters a room and I notice a man remaining seated, I condemn him much as I condemned the girls in the theater. Still, if manners for me are part of a civilizing pattern of behavior and something not to be thought about rationally or tampered with, they frequently strike youth as silly or repressive. Youth is right; patterns of behavior do control and repress. For the most part, however, people don't notice their influence. Indeed, what passes for spontaneity is frequently a manifestation of manners or "upbringing." And in truth, ordinary life would be exhausting if a person had to analyze all his prospective actions. What should be thought about, though, is another's advice, particularly when it suggests behavior that does not seem right. From the twenty or so years I have been teaching, I have few regrets. Only one cloud really darkens memory. One day early in May I walked across the green at Dartmouth College. Spring had come and the lawn was crowded with people. Blue jeans had melted away, and young girls blossomed like crocus, yellow and purple, aglow with smiles and hope. No one seemed in a hurry, and people milled about absorbing the promise of the season. Then suddenly the mood was broken. A student came out of a building and seeing someone he knew yelled, "Fuck you." The cry bounced back and forth off walls, and by the time the echo died, spring had faded. Before realizing it, I crossed the green and stopped the boy. I was too angry to say anything sensible so I told him to be in my office the next morning at eight o'clock.

Walking back to the English department, I wondered what I would say the next morning. By then a lecture on manners would strike the student, and me, as pompous. At a loss, I went to an older, distinguished, and supposedly shrewd colleague for advice. "This is easily taken care of," he said and then explained what he had once done. Something about what he did jarred, but since he was more experienced and I could think of nothing else to do, I suppressed doubt and followed his suggestions. The next morning when the student appeared in my office, I told him to sit down. Then I turned away and began grading papers. I heard my watch ticking and time passed slowly, each second seeming an age. Finally the student burst out, "Aren't you going to say anything?" I turned around slowly, looked at him, and then said, "Get out." "What?" he said, "Get out," I repeated, "you aren't worth talking to." He got up, started to speak, but then slumped out silently. For a moment I felt exhilarated. The feeling, though, like spring on the green soon passed, and ever since I have felt small and guilty. Never again have I followed a colleague's advice without mulling it over, and over. What I did was cruel. I stripped the boy of dignity and self-respect and, if he resembles me, gave him a recollection which will always make him cringe.

In rebelling against one pattern youth usually falls into another pattern and behaves uninterestingly. Young people play head games. A few dye their hair black and comb it upward into spikes. Some let it grow long and wear it in ponytails, while others shave their heads. Beyond this and like things, revolt rarely goes. Rebellion quickly drains energy and ceases to be fun. As one grows older what brings ever-increasing pleasure is the attempt to fit things into place. Without linen closets, dressers, secretaries, highboys, desks, and tool-chests, life in an acquisitive society would be practically impossible. Much as one generation unconsciously absorbs the manners of the previous generation, so people inherit sideboards, corner cupboards, and sugar chests, pushing in their possessions alongside those of their ancestors. Instead, though, of inhibiting and crowding, the past often excites and invigorates. Digging through inheritance, material or cultural, unearths mysteries. In a small box in a great-aunt's house, I found keys to compartments on the Louisville and Nashville Railroad. The keys were numbered; one was stamped 3516 while the other was D64283. What, I wondered, was their significance? Had an ancestor traveled from Nashville to Louisville on a honeymoon and kept the keys as a memento? Although this at first seemed plausible, I rejected it. On a wedding trip the husband would have the keys. Not only was it unlikely that he would take the railroad's property for sentimental reasons, but it was improbable that a blushing Victorian bride would ask for the keys as remembrance of the journey. Although I was unable to fit them into the experience of people locked in the past, the keys opened my imagination. Soon I was rolling along the rails from Nashville to Louisville, spinning through a starry night, silver with gentle love.

Inherent in the exploration of patterns is also pleasure in discovering variation. In my family is a set of Rose Medallion china, supposedly the first set shipped from China to the United States. Whatever the set's history, though, the workmanship is wondrous. The plates resemble pages torn from rich, imaginary leather-bound novels. On one a dancing master twists daintily about in little green slippers; on another a flower seller holds orange blossoms up to pale, smiling ladies. On a third a deferential teacher reads to a group of girls; behind them a small bird with yellow wings sits with his blue, iridescent head cocked and a black eye fixed on the teacher's scroll. Like gardens the plates burst with life: bushes of pink roses, piles of orange and pink melons, bunches of daisies with yellow centers and blue petals, and mounds of red and black berries. Although each plate is unique, the set is clearly of a pattern. Within the pattern, though, there is variation. On the stem of a flower clings a grasshopper or a beetle with an orange head and a black ring around its neck. Discovering variations pleased me almost as much, I think, as it pleased the craftsmen to make them.

Patterns form boundaries and provide foundations. Without a pattern to work both with and against, creation or individuality may be impossible. Outside patterns things seem to vanish into a black unknown. Whatever the case, high creativity is beyond my grasp; play, however, comes easily to hand. Always my play depends upon commonly recognized patterns, usually verbal ones. I like to tinker with aphorisms and twist their meanings, writing, for instance, about a man "whose bite is much worse than his bark." Of late, descriptions of wine have caught my eye. Since an extraordinary number of wines seem, according to dinner party goers, to be full-bodied, I serve vintages more interesting to the palate. The wines on my table are "spindle-shanked," "big-breasted," or, as Vicki said the other day, of a Médoc, "gloriously well-hung."

My life does not come from a storybook or a travel brochure. In my house father knows worst. When we go to the beach, somebody steps on a piece of glass, and the car gets stuck in the sand. When I ask Edward to put his bristle blocks up after cleaning behind him and Francis and Eliza all day, he doesn't smile, kiss my hand, and say, "I will do it right now, Daddy, because you do so much for us." No indeed—Edward squares about, sticks out his chin, and shouts, "I hate you." Instead of upsetting me, such exchanges delight. Like insects on the Rose Medallion, they awaken and intrigue because they are unexpected. Since life never spins along in an ideal storybook pattern, the unexpected is often the usual and possibilities of disappointment and unhappiness are forever present. The best antidote against disillusioning disappointment or, what may be more likely, boredom is awareness of and delight in pattern. For fifteen years I have been at home and in bed by ten o'clock on

New Year's Eve. Although accounts of high hilarity fill magazines, and acquaintances regale me with stories of ripe, juicy foolishness, I have never been dissatisfied. Each New Year's Eve Vicki and I toy with the holiday pattern. This past year we celebrated conventionally enough with champagne, albeit at five-thirty at dinner in the kitchen with the children, feasting on Gorton's all-natural fish sticks, Hellmann's tartar sauce, lima beans, and fudge cake.

Akin to the pleasure of variation is enjoyment of the unfinished. Perhaps because they seem imposed rather than natural, the polished and the highly finished ring false. Suspecting that nothing can ultimately be finished, people often find the highly polished deceptive and superficial. In contrast, the unfinished invites completion by the imagination and thereby lures one into labeling it genuine. Of course, the unfinished may not be genuine but only dirty. When Vicki and I lived in Syria, we went out of our way to eat hummus in a combination café and barbershop deep in the Hamadeus Souk in Damascus. The café had only one table downstairs, and people who ate there shared it with the barber. Upstairs was more room, but part of the ceiling had fallen and pigeons nested in the rafters. Consequently the floor was covered with feathers and droppings splattered the tables. Yet, unaccountably, the filth did not offend us and, invariably, we ate upstairs and enjoyed it.

Being part of a pattern, on the other hand, not only gives scope for creativity but provides continuity, from which come assurance and meaning. Each year a battered, one-legged Santa Claus hangs at the top of our Christmas tree. Santa's beard is now gray with age, and his jacket has faded, becoming more orange than red. Although we add shiny new ornaments to the tree each year, Santa will not lose his place at the top. He has been there for over forty years; when I was nine and he was four, Winkie the cat tore off his leg. As people think about holidays past and the fallings from life, the long groaning board of friends and family whom they will not see again, Christmas can be melancholy. Somehow old Santa at the top of the tree veils time's passing and softens the hard awareness of mortality.

Along with comforting continuity, patterns can increase the significance of life. A pattern implies structure and meaning. As a result people work hard to discover patterns and thereby escape the terrible feeling that life is meaningless. Universities depend upon the hankering for pattern for their existence, and long classroom hours are spent searching for and explaining patterns. Usually explanations are weighed heavily in favor of the complex and against the simple and the random. The significance for society is great; perhaps the inordinate complexity of the legal system, for example, results from lawyers' having spent seven years in the university. At the same time, however, that belief in pattern creates deceptive complexity, it can also reduce things to false simplicity. After any event, academics are always ready to impose pattern and discover cause and effect. To cure the ills of society, theorists propose methods of instruction. What a theorist predicts will result from a method, however, is not always what occurs. This past fall on *Wonderworks*, a television show for children, my son Francis watched "Booker," an account of Booker T. Washington's struggle to read. Meant to be inspirational, the show attempted to teach black pride and drive home the lesson that work and diligence brought rewards. Francis's classmates in nursery school come from a globe of countries and in a prism of colors. Yet during his two years at school Francis has seemingly been oblivious to color. At the end of "Booker," however, he turned to me and, instead of saying something about persistence, he said simply, "I am glad I'm not dark."

A person had better enjoy variation because breaking out of a pattern is almost impossible. Events are bound to repeat themselves throughout life. Like a refrain, following a cluster of deceivingly different stanzas, the same things recur. I first sang "Heartbreak Hotel" in the old gymnasium at Montgomery Bell Academy in Nashville, Tennessee, in 1956. I was a sophomore in high school and stood on splintery bleachers. The moment sticks in memory, in great part because I have sung "Heartbreak Hotel" many times since, despite my now being older than fifteen and the song's being always out of date and place. In spring 1976 at a dinner with businessmen in the Rossiya Hotel in Moscow, I drank too much vodka and joined a small band in the hotel, entertaining people with parts of "Hound Dog," "Don't Be Cruel," and "Heartbreak Hotel." Ten years have passed since I was in Russia, and almost that long has passed since I tasted vodka. Today I rarely go near drink, and my colleagues think me solid, even dull.

Alas, breaking out of a pattern is as hard for a human as it is for a songbird. Occasionally I find myself humming "Heartbreak Hotel," and last month I gave another public performance. A visiting literary luminary was on campus, and I was supposed to have dinner with him. My friend John held a cocktail party in his honor. A committee meeting ran overtime, and I arrived late. Having swallowed a gallon or two of fuel, the luminary was well lit and argumentative. I fancy myself a minor light and, not wanting to be outshone, I quickly forced down some high octane and was soon ablaze. After the pumps ran dry at John's house, those among us who were glowing went to dinner at the Mansfield Depot, a train station now converted into a restaurant. Two hours later John and I stepped outside. The food had been good, and the conversation loud. The stars were shining, the snow was melting, and so, like the whippoorwill at dusk, I burst into song. John joined me and the rails rang with "Dim, Dim the Lights," "Hearts Made of Stone," "Roll with Me, Henry," and of course "Heartbreak Hotel." After "Heartbreak Hotel," John and I finished our business and went back inside for coffee. About six minutes later the night freight rolled past. "Good God," the luminary said, "if you fellows had remembered Bo Diddley or Howling Wolf, all the ambulance men would have found of you would have been two hands with dicks in them." "They would have reckoned you were going fishing," a man at the next table said. "That's right," the fellow across from him added, "but just for minnows." Word of the fishing trip spread quickly, and when I showed up in the English department the next afternoon, the first person to see me said, "Well, if it isn't old Izaak Walton."

I don't understand money matters, and while friends have made bundles on insurance and fried chicken, hospitals and self-rising flour, I have sputtered along, taking the standard deduction, and saying, "Pickerings weren't made to make money." This past fall, though, when a collection of my essays appeared, I forgot the family pattern and got greedy. When patrons of a local library invited me to read from my book, I suddenly saw the way to gold. The book sold for $14.95, but I could purchase copies wholesale. If I bought ten copies wholesale and sold them at the reading retail, I would make a nice profit. Including postage my ten copies cost $91.68. By the time I arrived at the reading, I had already sold the books—in my mind at least. Unfortunately, as I parked the car, I noticed the librarian carrying an armful of my books into the library. There was nothing I could do but leave my copies in the car. The patrons had invited Vicki to the reading; she came, and we left the children and twelve dollars at home with a baby-sitter. Because the reading did not start until fairly late in the afternoon, Vicki did not think she would be able to get back to the kitchen and slap dinner together before the children fell asleep, so before we left home, we ordered a large pizza, one half bare and the other covered with mushrooms and sausage. Along with two Greek salads, the pizza cost $11.42. Thinking the reading would be over at 4:45, we ordered pizza for five o'clock. The reading ended at 4:15, and so Vicki and I drove around to kill time. Unleaded gas was $1.04 a gallon, and we probably used a gallon and a half at a cost of $1.56. When all was added together—books, baby-sitter, pizza, and gas—the reading cost $116.66. At the reading I autographed, appropriately enough, ten books; for that number my royalty is about $9.00. Thus my loss on the day was $107.66. If my book ever became popular and I was asked to give many readings, I would soon be bankrupt.

Not even shock can fracture a pattern. "I wish your wife to breed in safely," a friend wrote last year from Syria, "I congratulate you in anticipation by son." Vicki and I had two boys, and, like my friend in Syria, I assumed the third baby would be male and had already named him Samuel Innis. I knew nothing about little girls and did not know what to say when the doctor told me we had a nine-pound eight-ounce girl. By the end of an hour, though, I had settled into a pattern comfortable for fathers of daughters. I began to worry about her meeting and marrying the right sort of man, and that night when I called John to tell him about Eliza, I said, "You and Cathy can come by to see the baby, but don't bring those nasty little boys of yours."

Preaching platitudes about discovery, self-realization, inhibition, and freedom, people who lead conventional lives often urge others to break out of patterns. During the first year we were married Vicki and I spent six weeks in the Dodecanese Islands. Because it could almost be stuffed in a thimble, Vicki carried a tank suit with her on the trip. As we wandered through the islands and discovered nude beaches, I urged her to leave the suit in her suitcase and "frolic unhampered by prudery." On Rhodes, Kos, Patmos, and Mykonos, Vicki wore her bathing suit. One day, though, while we were traveling to a small island off Paros, I noticed she did not have her suit. "You are not going to have much fun," I said. "You forgot your suit." "I haven't forgotten my suit," she answered, "and I am going to have a helluva time." "Oh," I said.

When we got to the island, Vicki went straight to the beach. A few people were there, most wearing suits. Vicki dropped her towel right in the middle of the people. Then without saying a word, she took her clothes off, shook her hair, stretched her arms toward the sun, and, after what seemed an age to me, ran splashing into the water. "Come on," she shouted, "the water is great." I hesitated; despite what I urged upon Vicki, swimming naked really wasn't my sort of thing. Still, after all I had said, I didn't have a choice; I sat down, undressed, and made my way to the water as unobtrusively as possible. Once in, I squatted down and, paddling about like a floating toadstool, kept the water safely up to my chin. Not Vicki—she dove and splashed about in the shallows. For moments she would stay out of sight; then suddenly she would burst into the sunlight, white and pink and blowing mouthfuls of water at me. "What's wrong with you, old hide-under-the-surface?" she shouted, her breasts shaking and drops like rainbows all about her. Never again did I accuse Vicki of prudery. On Santorini, the next island, I even praised her suit, saying it offered good protection against sunburn and sharp rocks. Now, safe years later in landlocked Storrs, when the children are quietly abed and I am weary with writing, I sometimes think about Paros and see Vicki leaping into the sun, blue water falling from her in clean, bright streams.

"Everybody in the world needs watching," Josh Billings wrote, "but none more than ourselves." Studying the self can become a habit. Compared to most habits, though, examining the patterns of life is harmless. Love and laughter often lie at the heart of patterns, laughter at foolishness and love growing from appreciation of the world. Many years ago Beth, one of my first loves, visited me at my grandmother's house in Virginia. My step-grandfather plowed his garden for vegetables—corn, butter beans, snaps, and tomatoes; my grandmother baked a yellow chocolate layer cake, and Peggy the maid cooked a country ham. The food was wonderfully satisfying; during those years, though, I had a big appetite, and not long after a meal I was usually ready for a snack. What I wanted to nibble on most was Beth; unfortunately, the house was full of people. To have some time to ourselves, we drove to Williamsburg. Scores of visitors were there, and as we strolled hand in hand along the streets it seemed we would never be alone. Then I remembered the maze behind the governor's mansion. Under its high hedges and along its twisting paths we could lose ourselves, and others. Happily the garden was practically empty, and warm with affection Beth and I plunged into the maze. For several minutes we searched for the solitary heart of the maze. When we reached it and Beth turned to me, her eyes big and brown, I put my arms around her and kissed her heartily. What I had forgotten was that the maze was sunken and that people walking nearby could see into it. As I got ready to kiss Beth again, cheering and clapping broke out. We pulled apart, looked around, then up, and saw a bus load of tourists waving at us. For a moment we were embarrassed, but then we laughed and, waving at the people, kissed again for their pleasure before we left.

Not long ago when I told Vicki about something I was thinking about writing, she said, "That's ordinary. Why write about it?" The question was good, and I guess I think and write about ordinary things like a boy kissing a girl in a maze because such is the stuff of patterns, not simply the love and laughter of my life, but the love and laughter of the lives of strangers. I have not seen Beth in over twenty years, but I heard that she like me has three children. If we were to meet in the maze tomorrow, we would sit in the quiet center and talk about our children. Maybe we would kiss, just once for old time's sake, because that, too, is part of a pattern.

Pictures

I LIKED THE PICTURE on our Christmas card this year. Vicki took it one October morning after I had been raking leaves. She brought a kitchen table into the yard, and while Francis, Edward, and I sat in a big pile of leaves, she put the camera on the table and, after setting it on automatic, ran over and dropped down beside us. "How did you like the card," I said while visiting my parents in Nashville during the holidays. "Well," Mother answered, "at least you can't see the garbage cans." Last year Vicki took the picture in the side yard near the garage. Although she didn't notice them at the time, our garbage cans were in the background. When the picture came back from the developer, Vicki saw the cans and asked me if we should use it on the card. I said yes, arguing that the cans were "us." Instead of being plastic tubs that hardly made a sound when trundled out to the road, they were metal and behaved like real garbage cans. Whenever a wind overturned them, their tops blew into neighbors' yards and their bottoms clattered down the driveway and crashed into the woodpile. I usually heard them tumbling about and, feeling comfortable, invariably said, "Listen to that wind; there's going to be a storm."

My idea that the cans somehow revealed a real us did not impress Mother. "If it is honesty you are looking for," she said, "take the next picture in the bathtub." Mother had a point, and this year we made sure that there were no cans in the background. Of course putting a family picture on a Christmas card is hokey. Not many people we know do it. The literary folk among our acquaintance send cards depicting nativity scenes taken from medieval psalters, while businessmen and doctors send cards with illustrations of spare Scandinavian Christmas trees or Santa Claus hurrying about in a Mercedes loaded with smoked salmon and Johnnie Walker. Still, I thought Mother would like this year's card, and when she did not, I examined all the cards she received. She kept them in a silver, shell-shaped nut dish in the living room. Our card wasn't among them, and it wasn't there, I decided, because it was too informal for the room. In the few cards with family photographs, people wore their best clothes. Mothers and fathers dressed in grays and dark blues with touches of red and green here and there. Little girls wore pink dresses and white leather shoes, while little boys wore short pants suits and shirts with Peter Pan collars. Deep in the leaves the overalls our boys wore were not noticeable, and Vicki, wearing an orange and yellow sweater, looked like autumn itself. The trouble with the card was me. I wore a blue and white T-shirt. On the front was a profile of an Indian with three feathers in his hair; above his head was printed "Tarzan Brown Mystic River Run."

What a good race it had been, I recalled as I thought about the card, a sunny day along a road near the tall ships at Mystic, and I had run well. For my parents the shirt evoked no memories, and, seeing only unseasonable and indecorous dress, they longed for the formality traditionally associated with holidays. That formality, however, is often as posed as holiday snapshots. Life is frayed around the collar, wears T-shirts, and rakes leaves. By bringing things into ordered perspective, photographs distort living. Not long ago Vicki and I received a packet of pictures from a relative with whom we spent Thanksgiving. The scenes in the pictures were arranged. On the dining room table were a linen tablecloth and napkins, ornate nineteenth-century candelabra, silver goblets, and plates with blue and gold bands running around the edges. Wild rice, turkey, beans with mushrooms, sweet potatoes, and a score of cut-glass dishes containing brightly colored condiments rested on the sideboard. Beside it stood our hostess, knife and fork in hand, ready to serve the meal. The people sitting around the table were smiling and seemed happy and relaxed. The smiles, however, were just clothes put on for the occasion; beneath them was tension. Our hostess was an alcoholic; barely able to stand for the picture, she collapsed and had to be carried to bed halfway through the meal. Most people had left when she reappeared four hours later, explaining, "That was the worst sinus attack I have ever had."

As clear photographs blur truth, so correspondingly, and perhaps fittingly, an individual's perspective distorts clarity. When looked at through the long lens of living, no event is ever what it first seems. In one of the simplest photographs we received, our little boys and their cousin sat on a couch. In his hand each child held a toy pilgrim or turkey. The photograph was balanced; the three children were evenly spaced out; on each side of the couch was an end table; on top of each was an arrangement of yellow and white chrysanthemums. On the back of the photograph, our hostess drew a smiling face and wrote, "HOW CUTE!" Cute the children may have been, but when I first looked at the photograph I did not see them. Instead I noticed a small green and gold china pelican on one of the tables. It was Herend china; for some time I had given Herend figurines to close relatives for Christmas. "It was funny how that began," I thought as I held the picture. Years ago in London I had gone to Asprey to buy a leather satchel to hang over my shoulder. Many men in London wore them, and I thought one would make a good carrying case. Asprey is an expensive store; a footman in top hat and tails opens the door for customers, and the saleswomen look like rich aunts from the right part of the country. I was ill at ease, and when a woman asked if she could help me, I found it difficult to describe what I wanted.

"I'm looking for a pocketbook to throw over my shoulder," I said. When the woman did not respond immediately, I hurried forward, adding, "You know, the kind homosexuals carry."

"They are not," the woman answered after a pause, "all homosexual. Some are French."

"Oh," I said, feeling and probably sounding like a punctured balloon. "I guess I don't want one." Then glancing quickly around in hopes of finding something else to talk about so I would seem less foolish, I asked, "I need to buy my mother a present. Do you have any suggestions?"

"Ah," the woman answered, "we have just received a shipment of Herend china; the figurines make most attractive gifts."

After putting my parents' Christmas cards back on the dish, I stood up and, glancing around, noticed that there were no photographs in the room. On the walls were paintings and portraits and an occasional print; photographs were in the back, private part of the house, on chests and night tables in bedrooms and on shelves in dressing rooms. Unlike the portraits, which seemed permanent and had hung in the same places as far back as I could remember, photographs appeared ephemeral. Whenever Mother received new pictures of Edward and Francis, she forced them into frames in front of old pictures. When the frames became filled and started to bow, she took the old pictures out and stuffed them carelessly into a box at the top of her closet. Throughout the house were boxes like this, out of sight and cluttered with photographs and remnants of time past.

In my old bedroom was a sugar chest filled with scrapbooks. The first part of each scrapbook was organized with pictures and papers arranged neatly. Like life, though, the scrapbooks soon got out of hand, and at the end of each book pictures were pushed in haphazardly; the bindings of the books split, and, like stones eroded from the face of a cliff by wind and water, negatives had slipped loose and rolled through layers of memories to litter the bottom of the chest. My scrapbooks were on top, and I wanted to hurry through them. Pictures of myself usually make me uneasy. When Vicki brings a group back from the developer, I look at them once, then consign them to the attic. Returning to them months and even years later embarrasses me and makes me feel guilty. As I age and my world constricts, I do not want to confront my past and be compelled to judge it and then regret life missed. This time, however, I went slowly through the scrapbooks and looked at each picture. I am not really sure why. Because I had examined the photographs on my parents' Christmas cards almost dispassionately, maybe I started out interested in the photographs simply as photographs. Whatever my motivation, however, I soon left the world of the abstract and entered that of the personal.

In scrapbooks, pictures are not isolated; letters, newspapers, cards, written materials of all kinds frame them. In one book, I found a letter addressed to "3rd Lt. Sammy." Mailed to me from El Paso in October 1945, it was from Jack Spore, who lived with his relatives in an apartment on the same landing as ours. Jack was about to be discharged from the army, and he wrote, "Tell Tigue and Kaka I may be home sooner than they expect—and to have plenty of coffee on hand so you and I can drink our coffee together." I have always been a poor athlete, but in school, I tried hard and played just about everything, in the process suffering untold anxiety. As I read Jack's letter and looked at pictures of me holding football helmets, tennis rackets, and baseball bats, I remembered a football game my junior year in high school. The game was important, and since I was a rarely used substitute, I did not expect to play. At the end of the third quarter, we led by two points, but the other team made a first down on our eight-yard line and appeared certain to score. The evening was cool, and despite the excitement I was dreaming blissfully and safely in the middle of the bench when I heard, "Pickering, get in there at left tackle." The coach had made a mistake, and when the other team came out of its huddle, I prayed they would run the ball the other way. Just before the ball was snapped, though, the referee blew his whistle and approached me. It was Jack Spore. I had not seen him for eight years; at the end of the third grade, my parents and I moved into a house in the suburbs. "Sammy," Jack said loudly, "if you hurt any of these boys, I am going to tell your Mommy and Daddy." Then blowing his whistle again, he shouted, "Play ball."

Although scrapbooks are filled with tokens of success, looking through one brings failure sharply to mind. "He has achieved what I predicted for him when he came here," a dean of my college wrote to my parents twenty-five years ago; "he's our finest type, and we are grooming him for a Rhodes Scholar Candidate—I hope you'll encourage him in this." My parents followed the dean's suggestion, but as this year's Christmas card illustrated, grooming has never done much for me. On the same page as the letter was a photograph of a friend and me going rabbit hunting in 1960. I still have the jacket I wore in the picture. Although it has more tears than buttons, I wear it everywhere in the fall. "Did you make that coat?" a university administrator asked me when I walked into his office. "No," I answered. "Well, you sure fooled me," he said, "because it looks like you made it—in the garage with a hammer and nails."

I fell in love for the first time in nursery school, but love didn't become a nuisance until the sixth grade. That year Santa Claus brought me a book entitled *For BOYS Only*. In it a Dr. Richardson lectured schoolboys on proper behavior with girls. "There are lots of ways of having good times with girls. Let's not choose the wrong ones," he urged. In the sixth grade following the good doctor's advice was easy. Sadly, that happy state of simplicity lasted only a few years. In the scrapbooks were pictures of Irene, Alice, Becky, Pam, Rita, and a classroom of others. Times always seemed to start out "good," but inevitably they ended wrong; smiles turned into frowns, and bright interest became boredom. Among my old loves was a picture of Vicki. Her hair hung over her shoulders, and she wore jeans, a green cashmere sweater, and a double string of pearls. Her right hand rested jauntily on her hip, her eyes were laughing, and her mind was on love. Now Vicki's hair is short like a boy's. She wears support hose to shore up veins broken down by three quick pregnancies, and when she travels, it is not with love on her mind but earaches, antibiotics, and cough syrup.

People sentimentalize while looking through scrapbooks and often imagine meeting old loves and friends. Characters in photographs are not real and can be controlled, buried deep for years then dug up and molded to suit a whim. Actual people do not behave so conveniently, and if faced with the choice of renewing a long-interrupted friendship or looking at a picture and creating a past and a future, I suspect most people would choose the photograph. As a boy I spent summers on my grandfather's dairy farm in Virginia; during those years my closest friends were the Cutter boys, five country children with whom I lived days of building, catching, and exploring. In the scrapbooks were several photographs of us together. Looking at the boys, I wondered where they were and imagined our meeting. What a lot we had to talk about. Would they remember the sliding hill, the bamboo woods, and the mud turtles we fished out of a swamp near the Tappahanock and turned loose in the spring? Would they know what finally happened to the crazy man who broke into the dairy, telephoned the house, and threatened to cut my throat? For two days he roamed through the woods eluding the sheriff and a posse of searchers. Even as I drifted along in the comfortable shade of memory, I knew I was only indulging myself. My life had diverged sharply from those of the Cutters, and I had become part of a safe formality. Although my clothes are tattered and formless, at the core I am acutely sensitive to propriety and knew I did not want to entertain the Cutters. Two of them had been in prison, and I realized little good would come from our meeting. Two years ago James Cutter called Mother in Nashville and asked for my address, saying he wanted to visit me. Mother told him I was out of the country and would not be back for at least four years. When Mother told me what she had done, I wanted to cry, "Oh, Mother, how could you? We were best friends." Instead I said, "Thank you, you did the right thing."

Outside Nashville on the road to Chattanooga, there used to be a modest white clapboard church. In front of the church was a sign reading "Founded on Calvary in 33 A.D." Nashville has grown, and the Chattanooga highway has become an interstate, too busy and expensive for little churches and bordered instead by shopping centers, condominiums, motels, and restaurants. Like my memory of the Chattanooga road, scrapbooks always contain pictures of places long gone. With stalls for horses and cars, the garage of Grandfather Ratcliffe's house outside Richmond was larger than the house in which I now live. After the house burned, Grandfather bought Cabin Hill, a farm deep in Hanover County. Redoing the house was a labor of love, and near its completion, when I was four and a half, Grandfather wrote me. "This beautiful picture on the back of your letter," he said, "I will hang up in my new house that I am having fixed, and I do not want any little boys to pull any of the paper off of the wall, and if they do, it is no telling what will happen to them. I am fixing everything as nice as I know how," he continued. "I am working my finger nails to the bone to get food for you and your Mother when you get here." With magnolias throughout the grounds, long rows of pink and white dogwood along the drive, and a forest of boxwood about the house, Cabin Hill bloomed like spring in an album of pictures. The reality now resembles autumn. The farm has been divided, and the gardens plowed under for a housing development. Even worse was the fate of Grandfather Pickering's home in Carthage, Tennessee. In one picture my father and his brother Coleman, aged six and four, stood in front of a two-story Victorian house. A porch wrapped around two sides of the house; on it were a swing, rocking chairs, and a child's hobbyhorse. Behind the house long gray fields sloped down toward the Cumberland River. The house isn't there now; four years ago it was moved to make room for a grocery. Since my memories of Cabin Hill and Carthage are clear, the photographs frightened me. Instead of eliciting sweet reveries, they made me aware of the evanescence of things and my mortality, built not upon stone and wood but upon soft flesh and brittle bone.

In the sugar chest were many items from my parents' pasts. Two of my father's baby teeth were in an envelope labeled "Samuel's First Teeth Shed, June 1915, Age 6 Years, 11 Months." In another envelope supplied by "The City Barber Shop. Sam King, Proprietor. North Side Public Square. Carthage, Tennessee Box 201" was a lock of Father's hair. The color was a kind of fawn blond, just the same as Edward's, and I showed it to Vicki and Mother and Father. Although the childhood mementos of people whose lives were quickly gathering toward an end are endowed with pathos, finding the envelopes pleased me. The similarity between Father's and Edward's hair linked generations and seemed a sign of continuation. Although I looked at the mementos of my parents' childhoods, I hurried through the photographs and keep-sakes of their adolescence and young, unmarried years. In a jewelry case in the attic, I found the love letters Father wrote Mother before they were married. When I saw the handwriting and read the postmark on the first envelope, I knew what the letters were, and I quickly closed the jewelry box. My children and their children could read them, not I. The only photographs I paused over that showed my parents as young adults were those in which I appeared. After my birth, their worlds were mine. Before I was born, their lives seemed private. Mother was lovely, and when I found pictures of her at dances at Princeton and Washington and Lee, showing dalmatians at the Orange Lawn Tennis Club, and shoot-ing trap on Long Island, I felt like a voyeur. Pictures of distant relatives did not affect me the same way. A photograph of a great-grandmother with lace billowing up to a button-like gold earring in one ear and then rolling in rich curves over her shoulders reminded me of Annie, an old love rounded and warm as the damp summer earth.

Not all the pictures of Mother as a young woman bothered me. Occa-sionally something on the edge of a photograph caught my attention. On the way to the Maryland Cup Race, Mother, her date, and another couple stopped for a picnic. In the background of the picture was their car, a wonderfully boxy Rolls-Royce, a car I now associate with the pampered rich but one in which I would like to travel once. I want to feel special. A single ride, though, would be enough; more might corrupt me and make me think I was superior. Mother's date for the race was Ernest. Although Ernest had been her best beau for a time, I did not mind look-ing at him. His expression was bland and had none of the seductive power of the bold, appraising glance that marked photographs of Father in the 1930s. Ernest was certain to be disappointed in love, and I traced his courtship up to the telegram he sent on the eve of Mother's wedding, apologizing for not attending. TERRIBLY DISAPPOINTED, it read; BUSI-NESS ENGAGEMENTS PREVENT BEING THERE STOP MY SINCEREST BEST WISHES ERNEST.

In the library were several family albums. Bound in leather, they resembled books from the back; across the front ornate metal buckles clasped them shut. Inside were pictures taken from the 1860s through the 1880s. Unlike the people in the scrapbooks, few of these people were immediately identifiable. There were women with heavy stovepipe curls, in dark dresses bound at the neck by brooches, or with roses in their hair; little girls in high-topped button boots and bloomers; boys wearing new hats and checkered vests out of which hung watch chains; and soldiers—three young men in Confederate uniforms, then a Union captain with his hair slicked down, who signed his picture "Yours Truly Tom Waters." Exchanging pictures was fashionable in the last part of the nineteenth century, and every town had a photographic studio. On the back of pictures were the photographers' names and addresses: B. W. Rose, Corner, Main & Broadway, Paris, Kentucky; J. H. Van Stavoren's Metropolitan Gallery, 53 College Street, Nashville, Tennessee; A. D. Lytle, Main Street, Baton Rouge, Louisiana. My great-grandfather came from Ohio, and the albums contained photographs taken in Athens, Cincinnati, Portsmouth, and Springfield. Unlike this year's Christmas card, which turned my thoughts inward to Mystic and memory, the photographs thrust me outward as I tried to identify people in the pictures.

I started leafing through old books in the library. The going was slow, and soon what I searched for was less important than what I found. In a family Bible was a copy of the *Athens Messenger* for January 12, 1899. My great-great-grandfather's obituary was on the front page. "During the last week," the article recounted, "he grew gradually more infirm, and early Sunday morning, after he had journeyed long and journeyed far, there came for him the twilight and the dusk, the mist gathered over the mirror of memory, the pulse throbbed faint and low, and finally ceased to beat on earth forever." Like catacombs into which individuals disappear to become part of great heaps of bones, the yellow, spotted pages of the Bibles reeked of death and families gone from memory. Unlike the death that stalks through my days, making me tremble at the names of diseases, death in the Bibles was not terrifying. The saddest losses were often adorned with poetry. When two young sisters, Elizabeth and Mary Perkins, died on September 12, 1829, their father wrote, "They were lovely and pleasant in their lives, and in their death were not divided. Departed ones," he continued, quoting verse,

I do not wish you here,
But though ye are in a lovelier land,
Among a sacred and a holy band,
For you is yet shed many a bitter tear.

Unlike the accounts one hears of friends who are dying, the comments and remembrances in the Bibles were reassuring. My grandfather Pickering died when I was small, and although I have often heard he was a gentle, kindly man, I remember little about him except that he grew marvelous strawberries. He sold insurance, and his office was above the bank. Eight years after his death, a note appeared on the editorial page of the *Carthage Courier*. I found the note in a Bible, and it made me happy, not bringing cold and disorder to mind, but long neat rows of red strawberries. "An unprepossessing, probably little noticed metal sign, its enamel chipped with age," the note said,

is fastened to the stairway entrance of a business building here, proclaiming to his friends in life, the destiny of a man in eternity. The sign reads:

SAM PICKERING
UPSTAIRS

Rummaging through the old books enabled me to identify some people. A little girl about eight years old and dressed completely in white from high-buttoned shoes and stockings to the ribbon in her hair was Alice Garthright, my great-grandmother. During the Battle of Cold Harbor, her home was turned into a Union hospital. The blood, so the family story goes, dripped from floor to floor and gathered in pools in the basement. Stories about the Civil War abound in my family, and I found much that touched on the conflict. When fighting broke out, my great-grandfather joined the Ohio Volunteer Infantry and fought in Kentucky and Tennessee. An older brother, Levi, was killed at Perryville, and an obituary of a younger brother, Joseph, recalled that "a memory of war days was his capture by General Stonewall Jackson at Harper's Ferry, when Jackson was storming through the Shenandoah Valley." Great-grandfather became adjutant of the Fifth Tennessee Cavalry. At the end of the war, he was stationed at Carthage, where he married and settled. After the war people collected photographs of generals, much as children collect baseball cards today. Many of the albums must have come from the Pickerings. Although one contained pictures of Robert E. Lee and Jefferson Davis, in most a headquarters of Union generals appeared: Grant, Sherman, Thomas, O. M. Mitchell, Hooker, Rosecrans, McPherson, Butler, and Crook, all taken from negatives in Brady's National Portrait Gallery and published by E. & H. T. Anthony, 501 Broadway, New York.

I did not linger over the generals. Even pictures of great-grandfather in uniform and what must have been members of his troop did not attract my attention so much as photographs of unknown Confederates. Not only does success gradually fade into the ordinary and thus become uninteresting, but the elation of triumph so overwhelms other feelings that celebratory photographs rarely appeal to the imagination. Instead of reflecting a tapestry of emotions, such photographs only capture the simple brightness of success. Rarely do they hint at the dark complexity of life and provoke wonder. In wonder is the stuff, perhaps not of thought but of sentiment—sentiment that smoothes the edges of time and turns loss into gain, making the defeated more human and more appealing than the victorious. As deaths, not births, in family Bibles attracted me, so the losers drew me, and I searched for glimpses of their lives. Little things turned up: from a desk in the attic first a bit with "7TH VA CAV CSA" stamped on it and then a single letter dated "February 16th 1864." "My Dearest Maggie," Mollie began,

> I have intended replying to your welcome affectionate letter ever since its reception but have company staying with me all the time & parties &c engrossing all time. I had rather have had a quiet time all my own in which I could have written long letters to loved friends, yet we owe certain duties to society & when there is any gayety we generally are constantly occupied. We have had a great many parties dinners &c . . . I am becoming I very much fear too dissipated. We have 8 or 10 companies of Cavalry in the county. The Regiment to which my Brother is attached is now at home, & he is with us. I was at a large dancing party, given by the Signal Corps, which is stationed a short distance from us. My Brother, a Capt. friend from one of the R———D [Richmond] Howitzers & my sister accompanied me. I danced until 4–1/2 o'clock & got home just before day.

The dancing would not last. In less than a month Grant would take command of the Union forces. Leading the Army of the Potomac through the Wilderness, Spotsylvania Court House, Cold Harbor, and Petersburg, he drove Lee to Appomattox and surrender in April 1865. In February 1864, though, the Army of the Potomac had not crossed the Rapidan, and the dancers played. "The Capt.," Mollie wrote,

staid with us ten days & we had many invitations out. Then I had a young lady staying here. One Saturday we went up to see a Tournament. There were eleven Knights, dressed in pretty & very becoming costumes. The cavalry had a dinner & dance on the same day & all passed pleasingly. I was invited to another party a few days since & two nice beaux came to take me but I declined. Thursday I am invited to a "grand Military Ball," given by the soldiers, several hundred invitations issued. I expect to go. Most of the girls will dress in silks. They expect a fine time. A Cousin of mine will dress in black velvet & pearls. She is a beauty & will look superbly. I will accompany her. I see some of Col. Robbins Command some times. They are stationed about 20 miles from us & have amusing dances some times. Mr. Tornkins looks so well. The Sargt has not yet returned & when asked by Mr. T—when he would do so, his reply was by singing "When the Spring time comes gentle Annie."

Major Robinson, Mollie wrote, "is the general heart-breaker of this community. I hope I will pass unscathed." There were breaks between dances and after songs and tournaments, and Mollie was not unmarked. "Maggie dear," she concluded, "is there any appearance of peace in R———d? Do they express any hopes as to the termination of this most evil & unnatural struggle? Oh! When will we be at peace. It seems so long to look forward to—perhaps years—long weary years may escape & those most cherished will find a soldiers grave. Oh! Maggie what an awful thought! & is such a time a season for gayety—I feel condemned."

The life my great-grandfather lived in Carthage, a small town on the edge of the Cumberland Plateau, was far different from that of northern Virginia. The wife he married there was the daughter of a blacksmith, James McClarin, who after emigrating from Ireland had made his way south from Pennsylvania and who, as someone wrote beside his name in a family Bible, was known as Pittsburgh Jim. His daughter Eliza Jane was not beautiful. Because she wore a brooch containing a photograph of Great-grandfather, I identified her. Her lips were narrow, and her mouth cut straight across her face. Her cheeks were thin; and her hair, twisted in small curls, was plastered down over her forehead. Her nose, too big for her mouth and cheeks, was masculine and domineering. There were no pearls or velvet, just the brooch, a white collar, and a plain checked dress. Named William Blackstone after the legal scholar, perhaps my great-grandfather wasn't interested in gaiety. When the music stopped in 1865, he was on the winning, and the right, side. Among the old books in the library was the "Memorial Record" of his funeral in 1919. The Good Samaritans–Colored Society sent flowers. "These flowers," the accompanying card stated, "are sent in grateful remembrance by the descendants of Slaves you helped to free. They will ever remember that through all the intervening years you have been their faithful guide and friend. May thy slumbers be peaceful and thy awakening pleasant in the arms of a liberty loving God."

The scrapbooks contained many photographs of the descendants of slaves: Bessie, Wilna, Mealy, Lizzie, Marie, and John Derrycote bigger than a barn and carrying me on his shoulders. Writing about these photographs is difficult, and I would like to turn from them as I did Father's love letters. Would that I could always see the springtime of my life through a haze. Age and its consort, knowledge, have, however, burned off the mist, and although I want to remember the hours spent with servants as forever golden, I have learned better and feel sick at heart when I think of seventy-year-old men calling a six-year-old boy "Mister Sammy." Among family papers was the will of Philip Claud, a distant cousin. Claud's will was made out in Williamson County, Tennessee, in April 1845. Claud seems to have owned quite a bit of property. To his daughter Matilda he bequeathed "the following negroes, to wit Wiley and Evaline"; to his son Eldridge he left Amy; to William, another son, "a negro boy named Joe"; and to Frances, a daughter, "a negro boy Anthony and a negro girl Phillis." Caroline, William, Mary, Clarissa, Sandra, Sarah, Martha, and Felise were left to other members of the family. "It is also my will and desire," Claud added, "that any increase of the above named slaves may have hereafter shall be considered and taken as bequeathed with their mothers."

In 1885 a relative in Kentucky discussed the Civil War in a letter. "It may be that Providence," he wrote, "was working out a great problem, the freedom of the negro race—which no doubt in the End, will be the best thing for us, both as a People & as a Nation!" When I was a child, the end was not in sight. Even now when I read about velvet and pearls, hear stories about my grandmother's grandmother playing the piano while field hands stood outside the parlor window singing hymns, when I recall plucking chickens in a tub of steaming hot water with Mealy, walking with Lizzie to her home in Frogtown, and driving with Grandfather to the Voodoo Man to get a hex removed from the dairy—when such things come to me, liberty and right are far out of mind. In a family Bible published in 1726, just the book of Luke was marked. A thin black line ran down the margin alongside selected verses, but only verse 20 from chapter 15, recounting the history of the Prodigal Son, was underlined.

For someone the verse was important because two thick lines underscored it. "But when he was a great way off," Luke recounted, "his father saw him, and had compassion, and ran, and fell on his neck, and kissed him." My memory is prodigal, reveling in recollections of childhood spent with the descendants of the people for whom Great-grandfather fought but who still needed, if not a guide, at least a hand toward greater freedom. Unlike the Prodigal Son, who turned his back on faraway places and returned home to lead a good life of right deeds, I left home. Memories that should have made me struggle for decency, if not justice, became artifacts, stripped of meaning and posed like holiday photographs.

Like prints sliced from an ancient folio, then framed in gold leaf and hung in an airy reception room above green plants and an Empire table, servants have appeared in my writings as parts of a decorous and soothingly smooth whole. Maybe I am too hard on myself. Like photographs, memories are packed away in sugar chests and brought out, for the most part, when it is convenient. Memories that make people uncomfortable or threaten propriety are discarded or buried deep in an attic of the mind. Days filled with uncomfortable memories become unlivable; people struggle to order and dignify their lives. Perhaps they are wise to banish indecorous Christmas cards, indeed, indecorous and disturbing thoughts. After the war William Blackstone became clerk of the county court, chief clerk of the Tennessee legislature, and then postmaster. "He filled all these positions," his obituary noted, "with unusual accuracy, care, and neatness, and wrote a splendid hand." For me, feeling vulnerable and thinking more about death and its effect upon my young children, neatness occasionally seems all important.

Tucked in among the Bibles was *Familiar Scenes; or, The Scientific Explanation of Common Things*. "I began this book in Mr. Morris School," my grandfather wrote and on the back binding listed nine students attending the school in 1885: himself, Ada Salter, Josie Myers, Charles McClarin, three Sanders children, and Ernest and Julia Fisher. At the top of page 5 he wrote,

> If how to be rich
> you wish to find
> look on page 109

Immediately I turned to page 109 and read, *"Mind your business."* The advice was good, but no Pickering, so far as I know, has ever followed it closely. At least none have been wealthy. Maybe one of my boys will, but I doubt it. If they resemble me, they will spend too much time rummaging through the past and other people's lives to mind any business. I have brought all the old family photographs, letters, books, and bibles to Connecticut. Those that are not framed or on my bookshelves are packed in trunks in the attic. On top of the material in one trunk is an envelope that slipped out of a scrapbook and fell to the bottom of the sugar chest. Stamped on it is the return address of Grandfather's business: "Pickering & Highers Insurance, Carthage, Tennessee." Inside are copies of the Christmas cards Vicki and I have sent. To please Mother I have decided to pose in a coat and tie next year. In the future some member of the family will look at the cards. I wonder if he will notice differences in dress. I hope so, because I am going to wear the coat and tie more for him than for Mother.

After the Daffodils

NOT LONG AFTER SAMP GRIGGS MOVED to Carthage and opened an accountant's office beside Read's drugstore, he got a sty on his eye and went to Dr. Sollows. "Now Sollows," he said after the sty had been lanced, "what sort of people live in this burg?" "You've just come here from Lebanon," Dr. Sollows answered. "What were folks there like?" "Scoundrels to a man, even the children," Griggs said shaking his head, "mean, narrow, suspicious, you name it." "Oh," Dr. Sollows said, "I am afraid that you are going to find the same people here." Later that afternoon Jeb Buchanan visited Dr. Sollows to have a sore throat swabbed. Like Griggs, Buchanan was new to Carthage, recently having started a small soap and candle manufacturing business on Spring Street. "Dr. Sollows," he said, "you have lived in Carthage for almost fifty years. What are people hereabouts like?" "Well," Dr. Sollows answered, "you have come from Crossville. What did you think of people there?" "Goodness me, I hated to leave them," Buchanan answered, "they were the best folks in the world—always friendly and kind—real neighbors." "Don't worry," Dr. Sollows said smiling, "don't worry, you will find the same folks here."

A person's town is often what he makes it. For twelve years I have lived in Connecticut. Although my children were born in Willimantic and I have been wondrously happy here, I did not really think Storrs home until Father died in April. His death broke my last strong tie to childhood and Tennessee. Often during the past decade I thought about returning to the South. Such thoughts lessened my enjoyment of Storrs. Dreaming of the beauty of other places, I neglected the small hills rolling green outside my window. At Father's death, though, the elsewheres drifted away like a low mist. In the sun I suddenly saw bobolinks pitching white, black, and orange down the side of Horsebarn Hill. In the wet meadow below, redwinged blackbirds called, their cries unwinding like brittle twisted springs. Near the chicken houses on Bean Hill kingbirds gathered on the fence, while above the trees buzzards rode the wind, the long feathers at the tips of their wings sweeping upward, dark against the silver light and blue sky. Storrs was home, and suddenly I wanted to know its good places better. Often in the past, in the shank of spring, that time after daffodils and before peonies, I visited Father and Mother in Tennessee, returning to Connecticut only to pack the car for Nova Scotia and our farm in Beaver River. And so in the middle of May I began taking long walks. Although I wandered throughout Storrs, I spent much time on the university farm, roaming the meadows and woods bounded on the south, north, and east by the Gurleyville Road, Old Turnpike, and Fenton River respectively, and then on the west by Route 195, curving over the hills like a flattened ashcan.

Father's death severed a taproot, one that had not, perhaps, sustained me for a long time but one that I, nevertheless, wanted to believe nourishing. Now in the green damp of late May I thrust myself outdoors, hoping the land would pull fibrous roots from me, binding me to dirt and enabling me to absorb place. At first I walked almost aimlessly, my only purpose being to stroll through hours. Observations would inevitably come, I believed, thinking that if I noticed five or so interesting things after walking four hours, I might see six or seven after eight. Often I began walking at dawn and stopped at eleven o'clock. Afterward I went to the Cup of Sun for coffee and an apple bran muffin. I carried much gear and wore rough clothes: jeans, rubber boots, a long-sleeved green shirt given to runners who completed a ten-mile race in Norwich six years ago, a sweatshirt with a friendly white husky dog on the front, and then a floppy Tilley sailor hat that I could tie under my chin. In order to drink coffee I took off my backpack. Red and black, the backpack had four separate compartments. In them I stuffed pencils, a ruler, guidebooks, small round plastic containers for insects, rubber bands, and samples of plants—on this particular morning cuttings of white campion and cypress spurge and then twiggy shoots of shadbush and white willow. Atop the pack I set my binoculars, and then, so I could sit comfortably, I spread the contents of my pockets over the table: a four-by-five-inch yellow and blue spiral notebook, a number-two pencil, a hand lens, my wallet, change, house keys, eyeglass case, and a small pocketknife given Father as an advertisement over forty years ago. Under a rectangular window on the side of the knife was the inscription TO MY FRIEND. When the blade was opened, the inscription slipped out of sight, and FROM GEORGE HEARN appeared.

I looked bedraggled, and with my gear spread about me like skirmishers few people approached. On this morning as I examined shadbush with the hand lens, a member of the English department walked over. "Sam," he said looking down at the table, "what have you been doing?" "Research," I said, whereupon he laughed and turned away. For a moment I was angry, ready to damn the study of literature as trivial, having little to do with life, but then I, too, saw the paraphernalia around myself. The very things that taught me about the natural world also separated me from it. In roaming through woods, pencil and pad in hand, I resembled the English teacher who spent days in the library. While I tried to identify trees and flowers, looking at bark and leaves, he examined sheaves of paper, searching for quirks of penmanship and personality. Even worse, I was not able to put the landscape together like a book, binding and words complementing each other and forming a green whole. For me the natural was broken into a series of discrete entities, not articles or even chapters. My vision was narrow, and rarely could I broaden a walk to include, for example, both birds and flowers. Although I made sketches and took samples of plants home, I could manage only one guidebook at a time. After many hours, of course, bits of things stuck together, but they were only bits, the beaver in the Ogushwitz meadow to alders and willows, the wood thrush to shaded, damp deciduous woods, catbirds to low perches and weathered mossy rocks, and rose-breasted grosbeaks to the tops of trees and bundles of new leaves golden in the high light.

On walks I saw many birds; most were common birds in common places: pigeons and sparrows around barns, finches near houses, warblers in alders, and starlings bustling in waves across fields cropped by sheep and cattle. Occasionally I saw birds that I never noticed before: a rufous-sided towhee in an oak near the Fenton River, and an indigo bunting iridescent in the south pasture on Horsebarn Hill. Often I spent long silent minutes watching birds. At the edge of the woods under Bean Hill a brown-headed cowbird showed off for females, singing, puffing up, and then toppling forward, making me think of a dark, lumpy marshmallow falling slowly off a stick into a fire. Behind the dairy barn swallows gathered mud for their nests in the red barn on Bean Hill. Sliding and dipping through the air, their tail feathers streaming behind them, they dropped to the ground near a cattle trough and after plucking strands of grass picked up lumps of mud before spinning off blue and orange across the pasture to the barn. Birds did not provoke deep thought, although I came to think the mockingbird the writer's bird, imitating the calls of neighbors but still having a distinct style. In truth the more I walked the more artificial profundity seemed. Even ideas raised upon close observation seemed false, constructs of people not satisfied with the simple truths of sight and sound. Sometimes I stopped observing and tried to imagine myself part of the landscape, a flicker bobbing for ants or just a wing turning through a tree or time. Of course I could not slip into the land. Not only did the gear I carried set me apart, but I was forever nervous about deer ticks and Lyme disease. In the dairy barn was a Holstein with an arthritic knee swollen larger than a soccer ball, and every day before leaving the house I sprayed my trousers with Permanone Tick Repellent and then cinched rubber bands around the legs just above my ankles.

Although deer trails curved through the woods like interchanges on a superhighway, I rarely saw deer. When two suddenly rushed away from me along a slope, I thought their white tails the undersides of the wings of great birds, turning sideways to get through brush before gathering themselves for flight. Other animals were about. At the edges of fields were rabbits and squirrels, some of these last red but most gray. In the fields were groundhogs. Indeed groundhogs seemed everywhere. Bill, who spent last summer in a burrow under a brushpile in the back yard reappeared, and one evening Eliza and I watched him eat the stems of dandelions. The next day Eliza collected a basketful of stems and put them on a rock outside his burrow. Beavers built a dam in a corner of the Ogushwitz meadow. Beavers are wary, and although I brought home a pack full of wood chips for the children, I saw only the beavers' handi-work, not the animals themselves. Below the beaver pond a family of muskrats lived under a low bank along the Fenton River. Often I watched them swimming, their tails curving after them like thin, shiny gray snakes.

Although I can recognize the calls of some birds—robin, mocking-bird, oriole, catbird, yellow warbler—birdsong seemed always to run clear but mysterious through the woods. Rarely did I locate birds high in the trees. In exasperation I began paying more attention to the ground and open spaces than to the woods. Down the side of Horsebarn Hill dandelions bloomed like bushy tablespoons of butter. Along the south-ern slope of Bean Hill winter cress blossomed in yellow bunches. Below the Kessel memorial the field was white with pennycress, shepherd's purse, and star chickweed. Pushing through the grass in the Ogushwitz meadow were clumps of bluets, buttercups, sedges ragged and tawny, hawkweed, cinquefoil, robin's plantain, and blue-eyed grass. In the woods at the edge of the meadow barberry bloomed, bumblebees clasping the small orange blossoms beneath the arching stems. Willows had gone to fluff, but on the road over Horsebarn Hill chokecherry bloomed, its flowers forming small cones of white and yellow. Along the stone wall bordering the cemetery and beside Unnamed Pond autumn olive throbbed with bees. Bunched in thick clusters, its blossoms resembled small horns, blowing sweetness, creamy and fresh, down the hillside.

Toward the end of May, butterflies bloomed like the flowers: whites, bright yellow sulphurs with a band of black bunting around their wings, mourning cloaks, ringlets orange and gray with a black eyespot at the tip of their forewings, and then suddenly swimming through the alders and willows at Unnamed Pond a wave of red admirals. Triangles of yellow and black, dotted with blue and red, swallowtails hung like sugar on cherry trees. I had trouble distinguishing one cherry from another, forever confusing the black with the chokecherry. In truth I have always had difficulty identifying trees. Some trees, of course, stood out: the white pines tall on the hill below the piggery, hemlocks along the Fenton River, and the great white ashes near the sheep barn. Other trees I recognized because I liked them: the hornbeam, for example, its twisted gray trunk rolling smooth and hard like a worn granite ridge. My favorite tree was the beech. Just above Kessel Pond was a grove of beech. No matter the weather nor the time of day the beech gleamed. Their leaves papered the ground white and almost lacy while their smooth trunks flowed upward in columns, not lifting a heavy roof but reaching open-armed for dappled, fluted light, one moment yellow, the next green, the next pale blue.

Among the trees I longed to be a painter. Only with a brush, I thought, could I capture the chill damp rippling under a hill early in the morning or the sunny wind shaking through a locust, turning new leaves into bunches of yellow grapes. Words were too broad for the melancholy and then the joy behind the light—the lonely sense that everything, including the self, ended, followed by the realization that one was, despite the binoculars and guidebooks, a part of everything:

After the Daffodils → *317*

the red lip of a pig-ear mushroom and the white band at the tip of a king-bird's tail, part of biological processes running far beyond the moment. Still, I wanted to capture the textures of my days. I envied the impressionists at Cos Cob and Old Lyme, those painters whose small brush-strokes turned spring's broken colors into lyrics of light and shadow. As I stood among the beeches I knew that such efforts, maybe even truth, lay beyond my skill, and so I turned to metaphor. Instead of describing an object as it really is, metaphor describes it obliquely in relation to something else. As a result metaphoric descriptions are always slightly askew and artificial.

Just south of the beeches Kessel Creek turned through a sharp fold between ridges and fell quickly down to the Fenton River. As I stood on a ledge above the creek, I thought how its course resembled courtship. Much as uncertainty lured the lover, so the broken rocky slope along the creek challenged the walker and seemed almost an invitation to excitement and discovery. Pitching, twisting, then splaying wide for a moment before gathering and tumbling narrowly between two great rocks splattered with lichens, the creek at first seemed to offer an infinite variety of woodland delights, its course a rich green band of false hellebore, skunk cabbage, Solomon's seal, and cinnamon ferns. In places where the light fell through the trees in shutters violets and wild geraniums bloomed purple and pink. Near the top of the ridge was rough purple trillium; farther down gay wings blossomed low and shy, the change from one flower to the other almost an emblem of the transforming power of love. The course of an eastern creek, though, does not run smooth. Despite spicebushes, cool and dry on the air, the way down the ridge was tangled and salty, more tiresome than stimulating. Halfway down I came upon a black racer sunning himself. Too weary to be excited I sat down near him on a rock. For ten or so minutes while I rested, he tolerated me. When I stood to continue downstream, he turned and slowly poured himself through a crack.

I didn't follow the creek all the way to the river. Near the end the going got tough. Sharp shrubs pinched in low over the creek, and then the watercourse itself suddenly flattened out into a small delta of loose black mud. As I turned aside to a path cutting steadily across a hill, I thought of the river as marriage. As the creek finally did not lead me to the river, so I thought, courtship often did not lead to marriage. For two miles from the Gurleyville Road to the Old Turnpike the Nipmuck

Trail ran along the river. In pursuit of metaphor I walked the trail. The way was broad and gentle and, unlike the creek-bed, seemed to invite one to pause, even to rest. Along the trail hemlocks draped over the water, soft and almost as domestic, I thought, as sofas fat with pillows. On the higher banks near the Old Turnpike lady's slippers bloomed in open spaces under laurel. Beside the trail the river flowed solidly. At first glance its bed appeared a joyless reach of drab brown. Much as the vitality of a good marriage, however, is unobtrusive, lying private beneath the surface of home, so the riverbed was muted. For anyone willing to pause and look, the river flowed with color, blue tipping over from the sky, whites and greens falling from trees, silvers and reds hanging from rocks, and browns running off in the light to rust and gold.

As man forever creates unity, be it metaphoric or not, so he analyzes. In doing so, he often destroys, not simply impression or truth but life itself. Like the observations of my walks actual experiences are often random and bundled together only by contrivance. A mydas fly sunning itself on a gray stalk of last fall's goldenrod and comfrey, its creamy pistils pinching the purple flowers inward to form waists, making them resemble small, formal dresses, have little in common—other than the mind of the person observing them. Random impressions, however, make life seem arbitrary, if not meaningless, something people don't like to face. To avoid confronting such a realization people have become addicted to meaning. The longer I walked the less satisfying I found simple observation. I wanted to see complexity and understand links between things. I wanted to explore the unknown and in it perhaps find knowledge or scientific fact.

To this vague end, I borrowed a blacklight trap from the agricultural school. Used for surveying crop parasites, the trap was just over five feet tall. Roughly resembling a weather station it stood on three legs. Made from iron pipe, the legs formed an equilateral triangle on the ground, the distance being a yard from one leg to another. Suspended between the legs was a galvanized tank resembling a shiny bucket in which one put a small pad of poison. Above the bucket a funnel rose up to the base of the bulb; the bulb itself was sixteen inches tall; four metal fins twenty-three inches long and six and a half wide jutted out from the bulb, quartering the space above the funnel and resembling a small paddle wheel stood on end. Despite the name blacklight trap, the bulb glowed blue when turned on. At night insects flew into the bulb and fins and, momentarily losing their ways, tumbled down through the funnel into the bucket where they died. I set the trap up in the front yard but used it only one night. Not all insects died immediately. When I opened the trap the next morning, many were still alive, if only barely. Small dark bubbles oozed from the mouths of beetles, while the antennae of moths quivered like minute ferns in a breeze. In wanting to know my place, I destroyed. I felt guilty and remembered the child who once entombed inchworms in clay coffins and then stuck pins through the clay. One careless experimental night, I thought to myself, erased years of gentle living, years in which the only insects I killed were carpenter ants. When Eliza saw the insects, she cried and asked me not to use the trap again. Edward's reaction was worse. He thought the trap "great" and said I should use it until I had boxes full of bugs. What I had was almost astonishing. A dusting of minute gnats, a quarter of an inch thick, covered the bottom of the bucket. Half-buried among them were a bumblebee, small scarabs the size of kernels of corn, two minute tree fungus beetles, ichneumon wasps, and assorted flies: crane, caddis, and may. Appearing toasted brown and almost edible were twenty-three maybeetles. Like small light chips of newsprint, moths crumpled together in mounds. Many were the dull gray color of litter, beer cans tossed into a wood fire, burned, and left to age through a season. I identified some moths: the arched hook-tip, its orange wings curving out and to the side like the arms of a swimmer using the breaststroke; the pink-legged tiger; the white-dotted prominent; and the black-letter dart, a bar on the front edge of its forewing resembling a block of charred wood, the middle bitten out by fire but the ash gray and unfallen.

I spent a morning examining the insects. Before lunch, however, I dumped them out in the yard. Curiosity and remorse, even walking, occupied only part of my days. The little business of living filled most of my hours. After dismantling the trap, I wrote and mailed a check to the Internal Revenue Service. Instead of applying Father's overpayment to next year's tax as instructed, they mailed it to me, forcing quarterly payments upon me. Unlike comfrey and the mydas fly, death and matters monetary seemed naturally linked. Since Father's death in April, I had filled out enough forms to set up as an accountant and put Samp Griggs out of business. Even at Father's burial money was a concern. "Sammy," an older woman asked, referring to my being the source of a character in *Dead Poets Society*, "Sammy, how much money did you make on that movie?" "Two and a half million, and I'm still celebrating. This funeral has hardly dampened my spirits," I said, fibbing so the woman would have a story to tell her friends. Father himself enjoyed tales about death and money and would not have thought the question out of place. When Slubey Garts was dying, so Father told me, his wife called Turlow Gutheridge to the house so Turlow could make a list of people who owed Slubey money. "Slubey," Turlow said, "state your affairs briefly." "Ennion Proctor owes me forty-eight dollars," Slubey answered. "Praise God," Sarey Garts, the widow-to be, interrupted; "sensible even at the end." "Kilty Bryden," Slubey continued, "owes me sixteen dollars and twenty-four cents." "Glory, glory," Sarey interrupted again, "rational to the last." "To Ben Meadows," Slubey went on, "I owe three hundred dollars." For a moment the room was silent, then Sarey cried out, "The poor soul, listen to him rave."

Our car is six years old, and two days after paying Father's taxes I drove it to Capitol Garage in Willimantic to be tuned up for the trip to Nova Scotia. While the car was being worked on, I walked to Windham Town Hall and watched swifts flying about the old chimneys. Repairs to the car cost $162.56. The expense was worthwhile. For the trip we load the car, even strapping suitcases and my pond net on the roof. On our return to Storrs we are more heavily laden. The children bring home rocks and shells, and Vicki always has two boxes of children's clothes. In Yarmouth, Frenchy's sells factory rejects and secondhand clothing. For thirty cents Vicki can buy a shirt that would cost twelve dollars in Connecticut. My mother disapproved of our buying used clothes. "My God," she exclaimed when I told her, "the children will get AIDS." "Mother, we wash the clothes, and besides," I said, "You can't get AIDS from clothes." "Well," she said before she hung up the telephone, "if anybody would know about such things you would—after all you have done!" As the first week in June swung to an end and peonies started swelling, I thought about Nova Scotia. I wondered what Bertha Shifney and Otis Blankinchip, characters from my essays, had been doing. Bertha, I heard, had a hard case of shingles. "The hope of dying," she said later, "was the only thing that kept me alive." For his part Otis erected a sign on Goudey Road just before it dipped and ran through Crosby Creek. In spring the creek often overflowed and washed the road out. "WARNING," Otis wrote, "When this board is out of sight the creek is dangerous."

In May a collection of my essays was published. The first reviews were good, and in hopes of sales growing luxuriant before the leaf miners and twig pruners set to work, I agreed to appear on a local television program called *Profiles*. The show was filmed in the living room, and I wore a green sport coat that had belonged to Father. Two days later a reporter from the *New Haven Register* interviewed me. A photographer accompanied her to Storrs, and he took pictures of me standing on a stump reading my book aloud to grass and scraggly remnants of daffodils. When he finished, I asked where he was going next. "To Old Lyme," he said, "to take pictures of a woman who has a nut museum." "Oh," I answered, my vision of fame running all to stalk and gray seed. Family matters also filled days. At six o'clock twice a week Vicki and I took the boys to Sunny Acres Park for rag ball. While the boys played, I pushed Eliza and her friend Lindsey on the swings. On Saturday, Francis had a piano recital; that Sunday, Eliza was a pink lollipop in a community dance. The previous Sunday I was a marshal for the university graduation and wore a big, floppy hat that made me resemble a blue mushroom or a giant hunk of spiderwort. Some days I could not walk because I gave talks. After messages had been read from the governor of Connecticut and then the Pope, I spoke to participants in a "Peace Games Festival." I suggested that the starling would be a better symbol for our country than the bald eagle. If the starling were the symbol, maybe, I said, we would not see ourselves as majestic, lonely, and powerful. Maybe we could come to think of "our nation as just one good country among many good countries." Although I didn't mention it, the starling was more numerous than any other bird in Connecticut, something my walks confirmed. The day after the festival I spoke to a group of school superintendents in Farmington. The following afternoon was the Northwest School picnic. Vicki made tuna-fish sandwiches and chocolate chip cookies and carried a bowl of "veggies": sliced tomatoes, celery, and carrot sticks. For a dollar one could buy a huge chocolate sundae. Instead I ate four cookies, after which I went to the soccer field with the first grade and did the bunny hop, the hokeypokey, and the chicken, or at least a dance in which one pretended to be a chicken, making clucking sounds and flapping his arms. Walking had perked me up, and at the Peace Festival I wiggled through several African dances with middle-school students. Four days after the picnic I delivered the commencement talk at Quinebaug Valley Community College in Danielson. The next night I was speaker at the senior citizens' spring dinner in Mansfield.

When I was not roaming hills, playing with children, or saying in twenty minutes things which, if challenged, I could not have explained in twenty years, I read the mail. A woman who heard me speak thanked me for "sharing your very essence." A man sent a batch of questions ranging from "Have you siblings?" to "How does one expand on truth without causing confusion or moving into untruth?" A girl I dated in college ran across one of my books in Iowa. After reading it she wrote, "You were the only popular boy I ever knew who didn't try to be like everybody else. Remember the weekend at Sewanee," she continued, "when I had my first purple passion and I started crying? You were a great comfort to me." Any popularity I may have enjoyed had long since slipped from mind. A bomb of grape juice and grain alcohol, purple passion still fermented in recollection, however, fumes rising from the past to turn my stomach even today. Comforting I suppose I was. Indeed until just before I graduated from college, I was always comforting, though I labored, and labored hard and unsuccessfully, to be a great deal less.

Letters led me on walks through the past, and coming home from a long morning of wandering fields and woods, I looked forward to the mail. One day early in June, I received an article written about me by a classmate of Tom Schulman, author of *Dead Poets Society*. The writer, Greenfield Pitts, was a banker, though when I taught him twenty-six years ago he was Wade Pitts, a reddish, freckled, pudgy fifteen-year-old. Of course all fifteen-year-old boys are either pudgy or skinny, as, for that matter, all fifty-year-old English teachers are paunchy, unless they jog, in which case they are gaunt and bearded. Writing that I had had an "extraordinary effect" upon him and his classmates, Greenfield described the extent to which I was the "inspiration" for John Keating. The me I read about was different from the man who roamed Storrs identifying birds and smelling wildflowers. Did I really stand atop my desk "declaiming 'Alas, poor Yorick'" to the globe? Did I hop about in trash cans and run out of the classroom and talk through the window? As I read, I wanted to say, "You bet your sweet ass I did," but alas, poor me, I couldn't remember. One day, Greenfield recalled, when the boys showed up for class, the door was shut. When they knocked, a voice said, "Come in, gentlemen." They entered, but I was not in sight. Only when I said, "Take your seats," did they discover I was under the desk. For the next fifty minutes I read Thoreau with "great gusto." "I will never forget his admonition taken from his day of reading Thoreau from under the desk," Greenfield ended his article: "Do not find when you come to die that you have not lived."

An article like Greenfield's is dangerous, even for a respectable middle-aged woody Republican. Because I was walking and forgot an organizational meeting, I had recently been "elected" chairman of the committee that recommended promotions within the English department. After putting Greenfield's article down, I wrote a memo to the committee. "So far," I began, "no one has applied to our committee for promotion. It has, however, been suggested to me by a member of the administration, indeed by a member of the inner circle, that our department is so top-heavy with full professors that we are violating the spirit of diversity. To bring us in line with university guidelines this influential maker and shaker has suggested that we consider demotion as well as promotion. 'As promotion is an appropriate reward for some people so,' this person states, 'demotion is an appropriate reward for others.' This unnamed person is not, I rush to add, implying that certain members of our department are layabouts, only that they are undeserving and that we have not apportioned rewards well. To this end I invite you to consider the subject of demotion. For my part I don't believe that people should be demoted through the ranks at one rewarding swoop. No, I believe demotion should be accomplished gracefully in a step-by-step fashion. Thus, for example, the professor would be demoted to associate professor, the associate professor to assistant professor. As for assistant professors, they could be kicked out on their behinds. I look forward to hearing from you on this important and pressing matter. Be prepared to be criticized for even considering this subject. But all our right-thinking colleagues, no matter their new ranks, must applaud our energy and deep, abiding concern for academic integrity."

The next morning the sun was warm and bright. The first of my peonies burst into bloom, red petals wrinkling around yellow centers. I returned the blacklight trap to the agricultural school, on the way dropping the memo off at the English department. That afternoon I took my last walk, strolling along the Fenton River and then pushing up through the woods under Horsebarn Hill. I saw three American toads and two garter snakes. Mayweed and wild madder had suddenly flowered. In a low, open spot blue flag blossomed. Black-winged damselflies perched on spicebushes and fluttered in the sun along Kessel Creek. This time, though, I was not walking for observation but for trash. For four and a half hours I collected trash: plastic cups, a frying pan without a handle, a used disposable diaper, an empty pint of butterscotch schnapps, the sharp pieces of a broken bottle of Richards Wild Iris Rose wine, and then cases of beer cans—Budweiser, Keystone, Rolling Rock, Busch, Old Milwaukee, Schaeffer, and Lausthaler. Afterward I felt good walking up Bean Hill, almost as if I atoned for those insects. Waiting for me at home was a letter written by a boy living in Chicago. He wanted to be a teacher; not only that, he said, he collected "autographs of famous people" and "would appreciate it if you could send me an autographed picture of yourself." I was glad he wanted to be a teacher, I answered, adding that I always had fun teaching. Unfortunately I didn't have a photograph of myself, at least not one that wouldn't give a child nightmares, so I drew a picture. Despite admiration for the Connecticut Impressionists, I am not an artist, and I appeared in the drawing as a three-and-a-half-inch thermos bottle with bread-loaf feet, short arms, ears like windmills, and a nose like a lopsided croquet mallet. At the end of the letter I said that I wasn't famous. "I was ordinary," I explained, "a daddy with three small children, a person who spent free hours wandering the hills and fields of his hometown, looking at birds, wondering about the names of trees and flowers, and then sometimes picking up trash."

The Traveled World

THE LAST SATURDAY IN MAY Francis drove me to Hanover, New Hampshire, and we looked at Dartmouth College. Thirty years ago I taught at Dartmouth. Not much had changed. In the middle of the green, men and women in Bermuda shorts practiced fly-fishing. Students were blond, and if not six feet two or three inches tall, looked like quick, muscular soccer players, "cookie-cutter kids," Francis said, "baked by prep schools." To vary the day I took Francis to the basement of Baker Library to show him the famous, and hideous, Orozco murals. As we strode into the room, a middle-aged woman leapt up from a table and ran over. "Sam," she said. "Wendy," I said. The last time I saw Wendy was twenty-four years ago. She was headed for San Francisco in a Volkswagen bus, not flowers in her hair, but big yellow sunflowers with purple centers painted on the doors of the bus and a white spitz named Miranda on the front seat beside her. "Sam," she said, reaching out to a blond boy standing beside her, "this is my son Bill. He is seventeen." "This is my son Francis," I said gesturing to the red-headed boy on my left. "He is seventeen, too." While our sons stood holding their chins in their palms, wondering what to make of their parents, Wendy took my hands and asked, "Has life been good?" "Yes," I said, "it's been great." "For me, too," she said. "It's been great. What a gift. What a glorious gift."

Wendy and I did not chat long. She was helping her son write a history paper, and Francis and I were roped to a schedule that included Williams and Amherst. Still, as we stood in the dank basement, the air dried and sweetened, the grapy fragrance of the locusts blooming along the interstate suddenly billowing honeyed and delicate through the room. "Who was that lady?" Francis asked as we stepped out of the library and started back across the green toward our car. "A girl I know," I said. "She's not a girl. Daddy," Francis said. "She is your age." I almost told Francis that the Wendy I knew would always be young.

But instead I talked about writing, explaining that for an essayist life was fresh and people blooming, no matter their ages.

The Monday after the trip was Memorial Day. The parade started at nine o'clock at Bassetts Bridge Road. Marchers strolled along Route 195 for three hundred yards then turned right into the cemetery in Mansfield Center. Each year marchers are the same: bands from the high and middle schools, both playing patriotic music, "Anchors Aweigh," "The Star-Spangled Banner," and "America, the Beautiful"; a pound of dogs, small dogs on leashes, the others, Labs, panting and drooling; volunteers from the South Eagleville Fire Department; antique cars crammed with children tossing hard candy and unshelled peanuts to onlookers; the high school Latin club shaking banners and spears and pulling a small two-wheeled chariot; and then a crowd of Cub and Brownie Scouts and recreational base and softball teams, the players ranging in age from six to twelve. Charles arrived at the parade late, and his little boy Jimmy stood on the shoulder of the road, kicking his right shoe through gravel until his team, "Mansfield Supply," appeared. Jimmy then darted onto the pavement, and sandwiching himself between two outfielders, skipped down the road. This year Eliza played French horn in the middle-school band, and she marched next to her friend David, wearing khaki trousers and a light blue shirt with "Mansfield Middle School" stitched above the left pocket in dark blue.

The parade ended under a sugar maple in the cemetery. The master of ceremonies was the mayor. Each year he says the same thing, "When the Brownie Scouts start to nod, the speakers cut the words off." This May no one talked long. The town's representative in the state legislature read a message from the governor. The mayor mentioned "sacrifice" and "love of country." A Congregational minister said three prayers, and townsfolk recited the Pledge of Allegiance. Near the end of the ceremony a six-man honor guard fired a ragged three-round salute. Vicki and a simple boy collected the brass shell casings, Vicki, three, one for each of the French horn players in the middle-school band, the boy, the rest. The casings were two and a half inches tall and half an inch in diameter. Stamped on the bottom was "LC 75," the letters, Eliza guessed, standing for light carbine. People milled about after the parade, nibbling doughnuts and discussing schools and sick friends. Roger ambled over, leading Marty, his six-year-old daughter, by the hand and told a story. Euple Brainard, he recounted, was the laziest man in Ashford. Because Euple had borrowed harvesting tools for years but had rarely returned them, neighbors decided to bury him alive. They tossed him into the back of a pickup and were on their way to the graveyard when they met Toby Crocker, mayor of Ashford. Toby asked where they were taking Euple. When the men told him, he was shocked. "Look," he said, "I'm willing to give Euple some peas. They will keep him alive for a while, and he won't have to borrow from you." "Are the peas shelled?" Euple asked, half-raising himself on his left elbow. "No," Toby said. "You'll have to shell them yourself." "Well, then, boys, drive on," Euple commanded, slumping back in the truck. "This parade is the high point of the year," my friend Peter said later, his youngest son sitting on his shoulders, hands wrapped around Peter's head like blinders. "Yes, it is," I answered. "Nothing can match it."

The parade made place appealing. That afternoon I wandered the university farm. A knobby colt bounced across a pasture and nuzzled me when I leaned against the fence. Swallows looped around the beaver pond, not only barn and bank but northern rough swallows, too. Rain fell in mid-afternoon, and a female scarlet tanager foraged under brush at the edge of the pond. Along the Fenton River alternate-leaf dogwood bloomed, the flat white clusters ragged with blossoms and buds, these last minute mallets, green staining their tops. A great crested flycatcher called from a dead tree, each cry spinning like a bicycle bell, all the tin melted out of the sound. "Did you have a good walk?" Eliza asked when I returned home. "Yes," I said, "I saw a great crested flycatcher in the Ogushwitz meadow, the first I've seen there in twenty years."

The Wednesday after Memorial Day I flew to Nashville to give the commencement address at Montgomery Bell Academy, a country day school I attended in the 1950s. Edward, my fifteen-year-old son, accompanied me. Nashville and graduation being more formal than Storrs and school days, I bought Edward a blazer at the Salvation Army store across from East Brook Mall. Originally sold by the English Shop in West Hartford, the blazer cost four dollars and fit Edward perfectly. On the flight from Providence to Nashville, I read some of *The Night Crew*, an airport best-seller written by John Sandford. After ninety-six pages, I laid the book aside and studied the wrapper on a package of Cheetos, six sandwich crackers filled with "Golden Toast Cheese." On the front of the wrapper appeared an orange leopard with a black nose shaped like a heart. The leopard wore sunglasses and raised the pad on his left front paw, making the thumbs-up sign. Baked by Frito-Lay, the crackers contained 140 calories, 130 of which were fat calories. If a gourmet had "Questions or Comments," the wrapper instructed him to call 1–800–352–4477, on weekdays between 9:00 and 4:30 Central Time.

Edward and I stayed in Belle Meade with Bill Weaver, my oldest friend. Recently a brood of thirteen-year cicadas hatched. When I walked near trees, cicadas exploded outward in gusts. At first the gusts were dark, but as the insects separated from each other, veins on their wings seined sunlight out of the air, creating halos. "I can hardly go outdoors," a woman told me at the airport. "I imagine the bugs getting in my hair, and I go cold all over." Measuring one and a quarter inches, the cicadas had bulbous red eyes, and their wings seemed lacquered, the veins a bright but aged orange, the spaces between stained glass. When I was a boy, I spent summers in Virginia on Grandfather Ratcliffe's farm. Each summer I caught scores of cicadas. In Nashville I did the same. Edward caught them, too, calling them "flying fiddles" and handling them gently.

The first night we were in Nashville Bill took Edward and me to dinner at the Belle Meade Country Club. I ordered a brace of braised quail, "almost boneless" and gamy with liver, wild rice, and mushrooms. Alas, by meal's end the bones had molted, transforming the soft meat into hard humerus and sternum, making my stomach dance the giblets. I longed for a wishbone that would lift me from the table and deposit me far from coffee and dessert. On returning to Bill's house, I fluttered into the side yard and like a cowbird shoveled the quail out of the nest. The quail cost twenty-two dollars, and later Edward asked, "Didn't you feel bad throwing up such an expensive dinner?" The next morning Edward and I went to Vandyland, where I drank a pick-me-up, not a feather of the bird that pecked me, but a double-chocolate soda. For fifty years I have drunk sodas at Vandyland and its predecessor, Candyland. Whenever I visit Nashville, I have a soda. After the soda I drove around Belle Meade. Many new houses were huge, "hide-and-seek houses," Edward labeled them, "places in which people could vanish and not be found by a pack of bloodhounds."

The man who wrote the movie *Dead Poets Society* attended MBA. Early that afternoon a statue commemorating the film was unveiled. The statue was sentimental. A student sat in a captain's chair, staring into space, an open book on his lap, inspiration glazing his eyes. To the student's left stood a teacher, slim and fresh with intellectual vigor, his right hand resting lightly on the boy's left shoulder. "Thank God, the two are clothed, and the teacher is only tickling the boy's shoulder," a man standing beside me said. "I feared the statue might smack of the intimate glory that was the Greek educational way. What a relief!" "Yes, what a relief," I echoed wanly, having just noticed the plaque beneath the statue. Engraved on the plaque were lines from Tennyson's poem "Ulysses":

> I am a part of all that I have met;
> Yet all experience is an arch wherethro'
> Gleams that untravell'd world, whose margin fades
> For ever and for ever when I move.

Yipes, I thought reading the plaque. In four hours I delivered the graduation address. In great part the talk I had prepared was a pastiche of instructive maxims, urging students, for example, to broaden themselves in college so that in after-years hours would rest lightly upon their shoulders. "If you ponder becoming a lawyer," I advised, "take courses in ecology and evolutionary biology. If you know you are going to be a chemist, study music and theater. Participate in life so you will have a rich life." Unfortunately I wandered beyond the platitudinous. Because motivational speakers inevitably urge students to set high goals so they "can achieve great things and make a difference," I reminded the graduating class that their real accomplishments would probably be domestic and immediate, not distant. To buttress my argument I also quoted "Ulysses." Instead of praising Ulysses, however, I celebrated his son Telemachus. "In Tennyson's poem 'Ulysses,'" I said, "the hero Ulysses tires of governing Ithaca in his old age. He remembers the great battles at Troy and his twenty years wandering the Mediterranean. And so turning the kingdom over to his son Telemachus, Ulysses leaves Ithaca. 'Come my friends,' he says to his old comrades, ''Tis not too late to seek a newer world. / Push off, and sitting well in order smite / The sounding furrows; for my purpose holds / To sail beyond the sunset, and the baths / Of all the western stars, until I die.'"

"When I was young and first taught poetry," I continued, "I thought

Ulysses heroic, the type of person, who, as he put it, found it dull to pause, to make an end, not to shine in exciting use. Well, I have changed. I now think Ulysses a man who drowned, not seeking, as he phrased it, the Happy Isles, but who drowned in irresponsible selfishness. My hero is now Telemachus, remaining at home to govern, to mow grass, to take out garbage, to lend his strong arm to the weak— to a mother when she totters into old age, to a child weeping because of night terrors."

For children capable of imagining Happy Isles, roving Ulysses is admirable. I, though, have aged into being responsible Telemachus, and as I looked at the plaque, I knew I was too tired to draft another speech. "Edward," I said, "start the car when I stand. If you see me leap from the platform and come running, open the door." In my talk, of course, I said other things, most of which, however, revolved around appreciating the immediate. "The lessons you learn in college will sometimes come from class," I said,

> but most will not be what your teachers or parents expected. Oddly, I think the most valuable lesson I learned here at MBA was on the athletic field. I was the school's worst athlete. I could not catch or throw a ball. I could barely run. I struck out seven straight times when I played baseball. My senior year the coach did not award me a letter. The captain of the team talked to him after the letter assembly, and I got my letter in physics class. From sports I learned that I was never going to be wonderful in anything. I learned to be satisfied with small matters, getting, for example, into a football game for three plays. I learned that real success and pleasure lay in appreciating ordinary doings. No one in this courtyard will change the world. You can, however, change your back yard and maybe your neighborhood.

The talk was personal, like my essays. "What the world calls achievement does not often produce genuine pleasure. In vain moments," I said, "I look at the books I have written, and I marvel. Looking at them is not pure enjoyment, however. Dissatisfaction nags at me, and I wonder why I have not written more and better. I wonder why Oprah has touted the books of my friends Wally Lamb and Kaye Gibbons and ignored my writing. The answer is that Wally and Kaye are better writers than I am. Someone will always be better than you. Realize this and learn to enjoy the everyday so you don't squander the bright ordinary hours."

In the talk I urged graduates to support their school. "In the years ahead," I said, "you won't remember MBA very well, but you will, at least once or twice, come back. You will walk around buildings and run your hands over bricks in hopes of awakening association and recalling the boys with whom you played and studied. A scrubbed young student will approach and ask if he can help you. But he won't be able to imagine what you are looking for. As I glance around this courtyard, I see men whom I have not seen for years, but whose memories are dear to me and whom I love. Many of you will become benefactors of this school. In public you will say that you are benefactors because you believe in education. In private you will remember Jeffrey and Garth, Richard and MBA, and you will smile."

After the talk Edward and I ate dinner at Sportsman's Grill on Harding Road. Later I drove through Belle Meade one last time so Edward could see "lights shining from the big houses." Seeking a new anything at middle age is too dislocating to be attractive. Edward and I spent the night at the Shoney's Inn in Lebanon. Six years ago Vicki and I stayed in the same motel while driving from Houston to Storrs. The next morning Edward and I drove to Carthage. I told friends in Nashville that I was going to visit graveyards and talk to dead Pickerings. Three generations of Pickerings are buried in Carthage, and after placing a pot of chrysanthemums at the head of the family plot and sending Edward off to search for snakes, I talked to Mother and Father. I described the children's appearances, and I told them how fine the children were and how much I loved them. "They are almost as nice as you were," I said. I recounted Edward's success in school and in right field on the junior varsity baseball team this spring. I warned them that he had decided to go out for football next fall. The second week in June, I said, Eliza was going to History Day in Maryland. "She also took a test," I said, and won a medal as "Best Introductory Latin" student in Connecticut. Similarly Francis did well on the college entrance examinations and at the end of school was spending three weeks riding a mountain bike in Colorado and Utah. I broke the bank account to send him on the trip because crew had been disastrous. Last year Francis rowed in the first boat, and the coach told him he had the smoothest stroke in the eight.

Unfortunately a new coach appeared this year, and Francis did not row a single race. In practice he rarely got to row, and if he rowed, he rowed in the girls' boat. "One afternoon," I said, "I came home early and found him in his room crying, the only time I have ever seen him cry." "So," I continued, "I'm sending him out west to sweat crew out of his hide in hopes he'll come home feeling good about himself." Although I missed Mommy and Daddy terribly, I did not talk long to them. They did not respond to my chatter. Moreover, I became teary. If Edward saw my tears, I knew he would be upset, and for him I wanted the trip to be an arch through which gleamed happy, light experiences.

Before leaving Carthage, I stopped at Sanderson Funeral Home. Mr. Sanderson was a childhood friend of my uncle Coleman. Coleman died in the previous August, and I asked the director of the home to tell Mr. Sanderson about Coleman's death. Before I left the director gave me two cloth tote bags. Printed in a claret band across the middle of one side of the bag was SANDERSON FUNERAL HOMES INC. Arranged in neat lines above and below the band like rows of tombstones were sixty-eight claret medallions an inch and a quarter in diameter, a white S and the date 1904 in the middle of each medallion. Curving like a halo over the top of each medallion was the phrase COMMITTED TO EXCELLENCE. "The very slogan," my friend Josh said after I showed him the bags when I returned to Connecticut, "the university uses as a motto." "Since the funeral home was founded in 1904," Josh continued, "an educational grave robber must have stolen the phrase."

On a trip to the south six years ago Vicki and I spent a night in Red Boiling Springs, an old resort town, twenty-three miles north of Carthage near the Kentucky border. Edward and I repeated the stay. The road from Carthage wound through small valleys, hills rising above them like cupcakes bristly with trees. On damp slopes shining sumac bloomed, and nodding thistles bent over fences like congregations dozing in church. Tobacco barns huddled against hills, their tin roofs rusty and their sides warped gray and weather-beaten. In panlike fields corn stood knee high. Tractors pulled carts across bottom land. Usually two people sat in a cart, one person to the right, the other to the left, both pushing small tobacco plants into the soil.

Edward and I stayed at the Thomas House, a restored hotel. The Thomas House perched on a knob above Salt Lick Creek. This spring Edward said he wanted to be either an entomologist or a herpetologist, and before dinner we explored the banks of the creek. Four northern water snakes lay ropy on a ledge, red saddles broad across their backs and yellow gleaming like bits under their lower jaws. Atop a rock a yellow-bellied water snake curled almost invisible on a cushion of dried grass. While robins foraged under maples, a phoebe bobbed on a telephone wire, and a kingfisher swooped and circled the creek. At dusk lightning bugs rolled over the knob. Small bats wagged overhead, and perfume from tangles of honeysuckle suddenly blew luscious along the slope. Under a board lurked a pedunculate ground beetle. When Edward held the beetle, it swiveled and hissed. On a trip people ponder meals more than they do at home. For dinner at the Thomas House, Edward and I ate country ham, biscuits, mashed potatoes, creamed corn, and beans and bacon. For dessert we had strawberry pudding. On the bedside table in our room lay a book containing comments from previous guests. Salt in the ham made my heart drum. In hopes of muffling the beat I read the comments. "My wife and I thank you for allowing us to grace your home," a man from Selma, Alabama, wrote. "The stay has given us the opportunity to grow even closer together in the Lord." "After thirty years as husband and wife," a Californian declared, "we're still learning that the best things in life aren't things." "Everything was great until about twelve o'clock," a woman from Knoxville wrote, "then something in the wall began fluttering and chirping." The something was swallows. They made such a ruckus that I got up at five and walked the grounds, looking at trees.

While tulips and oaks surrounded the Thomas House, down the east side of the knob grew pignut hickories, shaggy silver maples, and two persimmons, the bark on these last thick square blocks, gray across the tops of the blocks, but black in furrows. During the trip Edward and I visited the Hermitage, the home of Andrew Jackson east of Nashville, then the battlefield at Chickamauga in north Georgia. In April tornadoes bounced through middle Tennessee, toppling scores of trees. As I walked across the lawn at the Hermitage, I heard chain saws whining and smelled the smoky sawdust of red cedar. The day was so bright that historical fact bleached into mirage, and Edward and I spent more time wandering the scrub behind the spring house than we did in the mansion itself. Privet bloomed, and magnolia blossoms unfolded, the white on petals so pure it seemed distilled. In shade, nuts on beeches were orange; in the sun they appeared green. Dirt daubers pasted nests to the sides of wooden buildings, the pipes looking like clusters of chopped roots. Snout butterflies whisked a path, and cicadas flurried through the day, their wings chattering.

Although hearts had been pounded into powder at Chickamauga, again the day was so bright that I didn't glimpse a shadow of the past. Near the spot where Polk attacked Thomas's corps on the last day of battle, I caught a fence lizard, the first I'd caught in fifty years. Catching lizards was easy when I was a boy. Age has slowed me, however, and for a moment I thought the lizard would elude me as it dodged around and up the trunk of a small tree. Edward had never held a spiny lizard. "They are beautiful, aren't they, Daddy," he said before placing it on a nest of leaves. "Yes, they are lovely," I said, memories of my Virginia, the acrid taste of boxwood and the thunder billowing dark along the Pamunkey River in late afternoon, pushing Chickamauga out of mind. One day, according to an old tale, two acquaintances walked along a dirt road. Suddenly they chanced upon a horse standing by a fence eating grass. "I could steal that horse and cut your throat," the first man said, "and no one would find out." "God would be my witness and avenge my death," the second man said. "We'll see what your God can do," the first man said, pulling a knife from his boot and stabbing his companion in the heart. Next spring a grapevine grew on the spot where the man died and wound around a fence post. A single bunch of gray and white grapes clung to the vine. Bees swarmed around the fence, preventing passersby from plucking fruit from the vine. One humid fall morning the grapes burst, and a flock of mockingbirds broke from them, all the birds singing, naming the murderer. The truth of story is rarely that of history, and although Edward and I studied two score monuments at Chickamauga, the inscriptions did not rattle like musketry through emotion. We walked across Dyer Field up the south slope of Snodgrass Hill to the South Carolina monument. Like mica flickering in the bed of a shallow green river, black-eyed Susans, purple clover, ox-eyed daisies, and Queen Anne's lace sparkled amid the grass. On the base of the monument a weary infantryman held a rifle and an artilleryman grasped a plunger ready to swab the barrel of a Napoleon. For a moment I glanced down the hill and imagined lines of gray and blue wavering in the heat. But then I stepped behind the obelisk. In the shade a middle-aged couple kissed. The man had a handlebar mustache. His belly swung over his trousers like roe, and he wore a creamy yellow shirt. The woman wore a bright pink blouse and khaki shorts, and varicose veins coiled down the side of the calf on her right leg.

Edward and I also spent two days roaming the Cumberland Plateau at Sewanee. Edward wanted to hear "the eloquence of the canebrake rattler" and see copperheads curled like pies on ledges. Alas, we saw only two snakes, a red-bellied snake half a shoelace in length and a black racer which slipped across our path, vanishing like a draft when a window is shut. Still, we saw scores of millipedes, all wedges and rammers. Brown and two inches long, the rammers seemed chains of metal rings. The insects' legs extended from the trunks of their bodies, resembling the legs of Victorian tables, curving like *S*'s turned sideways. The wedges were dark brown with orange or yellow lines separating the segments of their bodies like washers. Instead of walking, wedges rolled forward as if surfing the crests of three waves. Early in the morning wood thrushes called from damp woods below Morgan's Steep. In the afternoon hawks shrieked and rode thermals above Proctor's Hall, a box-shaped stone tunnel. Most spring flowers had swollen to seed. But at the sunny beginnings of trails American ipecac bloomed, and along humid paths spiderwort stamens hovered loose and yellow above purple webs of petals. Fire pinks twisted from cracks under sandstone overhangs and sprawled lazily along the ground, their stamens flaring like matches. While leaves of leafcup sliced hillsides jagged, pools of May apples filled dells, yellow rectangles splotching the umbrellas of leaves, the green fruits floating above the ground, bobbing in shallows. Greenbriar tangled tops of slopes while poison ivy and Virginia creeper knotted trees and boulders together. Redbud, sassafras, and tulip tree saplings sprouted in hedges. Above them fanned witch hazel and spice bush. For the first time I saw mountain hydrangea, the sterile outer flowers on clusters, three petaled, broken fans.

Above the undergrowth towered sycamores, buckeyes, and white oaks. During the rambles I noticed bark: jerky strings of black locust; gray trails melting down northern red oak; the red cork of large chestnut oaks; and the light gray bark of small tulip trees, blue strips drifting then spreading, dammed behind green mounds. When I rested, I noticed small things, circles of maidenhair ferns then fragile ferns spilling out of crevices. Under a ledge gray-and-white orb weavers hung webs, and a green salamander pressed itself against stone, gold patches glittering like nuggets along its back. Days were hot. No matter what we saw and how we rested, walking exhausted us. Late the second afternoon we swam at Lake Cheston on the Sewanee campus. Afterward I drove to the Dairy Queen in Monteagle, seven miles away. I bought us each a medium-sized cone dipped in chocolate and costing $1.25. We ate the cones outside, sitting in plastic chairs at a green plastic table. Vanilla seeped in rivulets through the chocolate and, running over our hands, dripped onto the table. We watched the Monteagle policeman cruise back and forth waiting for speeders hurrying off the interstate. Above us stood a sign advertising the Dairy Queen. "Family Owned and Operated. Established in 1962, By Don and Phoebe Underhill," the sign said. "This is a glorious life," I said, biting off a hunk of chocolate. "You bet it is," Edward said. "What fun."